Migrant Labour in
South Africa's Mining Economy

This book is a study of the origins of migratory labour and racial discrimination in South Africa's premier industry, the gold mines of the Witwatersrand. Based upon government records and private business archives, it examines the highly competitive world of mine labour recruiting at the turn of the century and concludes that this regimented labour system was the product not only of the mining companies but also of political pressures and economic needs in South African society. The system was remarkable for the hardship it imposed, for the size of the labour force recruited – more than 200,000 low-wage black labourers were delivered annually to the industry's grim, barrack-like compounds – and for the fact that most of the workers were African pastoralists without previous industrial experience. Forced to work in appalling conditions amid much squalor and disease, more than 50,000 miners died on the Witwatersrand in a single decade.

In tracing the development of the recruiting system, Alan Jeeves shows how a large proportion of the labour supply came to be controlled by private labour companies and recruiting agents, who aimed both to exploit the workers and to extract heavy fees from the employing companies. The gold industry struggled for years against the internal divisions which created the competition for labour, until at last the Chamber of Mines, with the support of the state, succeeded in driving out the private recruiters and centralizing the system under its control. This study of the interests involved in the struggle for control of the black labour supply reveals much about the forces which created and now entrench racial domination in South Africa's industrial economy.

ALAN H. JEEVES teaches history at Queen's University.

i

Migrant Labour
in South Africa's
Mining Economy

The Struggle
for the Gold Mines'
Labour Supply
1890–1920

ALAN H. JEEVES

McGill-Queen's University Press
Kingston and Montreal

©McGill-Queen's University Press 1985
ISBN 0-7735-0420-6
Legal Deposit 1st quarter 1985
Bibliothèque nationale du Québec

South African Edition
ISBN 0 85494 847 3
Witwatersrand University Press
1 Jan Smuts Avenue
2001 Johannesburg, South Africa

This book has been published with the help of a grant from
the Social Science Federation of Canada, using funds provided by the Social Sciences and Humanities Research
Council of Canada.

Graphic Design: Peter Dorn
Typesetting: Typesetting Systems Inc., Kingston, Canada

Canadian Cataloguing in Publication Data

Jeeves, Alan, 1940-
  Migrant labour in South Africa's mining economy

Bibliography: p
Includes index.
ISBN 0-7735-0420-6

1. Migrant labour – South Africa. 2. Gold miners – South
Africa – Supply and demand. 3. Recruiting of em-
ployees – South Africa. 4. Blacks – Employment – South
Africa. I. Title.

HD8039.M732S65 1985   331.7'6223422   C85-098108-5

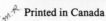

Printed in Canada

This edition is not for sale in the Republic of South
Africa, Swaziland, Lesotho, Botswana, and South West
Africa/Namibia.

Contents

Illustrations

Tables

Preface

This book examines the development of the migrant labour system in South Africa's premier industry, the gold mines of the Witwatersrand. Based largely on mining company archives and surviving government records, it focuses on the contending interests which created the system and became its main beneficiaries. As a result of a number of local studies recently completed or now in progress, the real complexity of the mining industry's labour system and the extent of regional variations within it are beginning to become apparent; but many more such projects will be required before a comprehensive history of mine labour can be written. Rather than attempting another local study, I have tried to complement the emerging literature on the socio-economic basis of migrancy with a project focused on the centralized institutions created by the mine owners to recruit this labour and control it effectively. This approach grew out of my earlier work on the business history of one of the principal mining houses and its political role at the turn of the century.

Although concerned with regional variations in the mobilization of migrant labour, the book's emphasis is on gold-mining policy and recruiting practice, as these developed at the centre of the subcontinent's economic power. I am also interested in the politics of migrant labour and the way in which various collaborating groups – white and black – fought first to entrench themselves in the labour system and then to protect their position and profits when they came under attack from the industry's central recruiting organizations, struggling to assert monopoly control. The persistence of migrant labour on the mines is bound up with the entrenchment of the industrial colour bar, and I found myself drawn into the extensive historiographical debate on the nature of the relationship between these two distinguishing characteristics of the mines' peculiar labour system.

An emphasis on the development of institutions, while narrow in one sense, did enable me to look broadly at the recruiting system throughout the region, not only in South Africa itself, but also as it developed in southern Mozambique and the low-wage recruiting zones far to the north. While the development of labour policy by successive governments and the Chamber of Mines are important concerns, I also wanted to understand the role of less powerful groups. Black headmen, "runners," and other collaborators were vital in labour mobilization, as were the rapacious white recruiters and contractors who battened onto the gold industry as indispensable suppliers of recruited labour almost from the beginning. Black mineworkers themselves significantly affected by their actions, as individuals and collectively, the methods and mechanisms of labour mobilization. The boardrooms are important, but I have also tried to show the system at work, on the mines, in the streets of Johannesburg, and in the countryside.

The sources for an institutional study of labour mobilization in southern Africa are very rich. For the pre-Union period, I drew principally on the surviving records of the Transvaal colony, 1902–10, particularly the important Secretary of Native Affairs Archive, the parallel records which survive from the Cape Native Affairs Department, and supplemented these with various printed sources and newspapers. Perhaps the single most important official archive, which relates to the periods both before and after Union in 1910, is the Native Labour Bureau collection in the central archives group of the Transvaal Archives Depot in Pretoria. The bureau was set up at the end of 1907, and its extensive records are an excellent source for all aspects of gold-mining labour policy and much else. From the beginning, the bureau worked very closely with the Chamber of Mines and an extended correspondence internal to the mining industry can be found in its files. There is unfortunately as yet no inventory for the collection, but the researcher is well rewarded for the volume-by-volume search which is required to use this archive effectively. To supplement the bureau's files, I made use of the Union Native Affairs Department records and the archive of the secretary for mines, both in the central archives group.

Concerning the mining industry itself, the records of H. Eckstein and Company in the Barlow Rand Archive, Sandton, give a unique inside view of the development of policy on all the key labour and industrial issues. As the Johannesburg representatives of Wernher, Beit and Company in London, which dominated the industry at that time, the Eckstein partners carried on a continuous correspondence with their principals. These letters, extending from about 1890 to the time of Union, massively document this company's central role in the formulation of labour policy for the industry as a whole. Since the partners frequently served as presidents of the Chamber of Mines, the H. Eckstein collection contains much material copied from chamber files. As one of the editors of the Lionel Phillips papers, I was permitted by Barlow Rand to consult parts of the Wernher, Beit collection and of its successor firm, the Central Mining and Investment

Corporation. Pending completion of inventories, these collections are not open to scholars. The Chamber of Mines has not adopted a consistent policy on access to its valuable records. A few scholars seem to have had unrestricted access to the records up to about 1922; most have been entirely excluded. I was given permission to consult a very limited number of files but no opportunity to see inventories or even to know the scope of the collection.

An attempt to trace the private papers of the labour agents and contractors, who controlled an important part of the mine labour supply in the early years of the century, yielded little result. The private papers of J.S. Marwick, the Zululand and Swaziland contractor, are housed in the Killie Campbell Africana Library in Durban but contain virtually no material pertinent to this study. Fortunately a number of the contractors testified before the various government commissions investigating labour policy. Thus the minutes of evidence of the select committee on the native labour regulation bill (1911) and of the Native Grievances Inquiry (1913-14) are particularly valuable and illuminating on the role of the private contracting companies in the intense competition for migrant labour which prevailed before about 1919. I was able to identify no survivors from the early days of the recruiting industry whom I could interview.

Outside South Africa itself, the records of the British South Africa Company in the Zimbabwe National Archives, Harare, are an important source for the struggle to control the migrant labour flow from beyond the Union's Limpopo border. I had planned to consult the records of the Portuguese colonial administration in Maputo, but from my base in South Africa, this could not be done during either of my research trips. Fortunately the official collections from the South African side and the H. Eckstein records, although no substitute for the Portuguese documents themselves, contain very extensive material on the policies and outlook of Portuguese officialdom in Mozambique at the turn of the century. These records have been supplemented by the correspondence of British consular officers in Lourenço Marques, who were generally very well informed of developments in the colony. Pertinent British Colonial Office collections were consulted, using the extensive microfilm runs and photocopies of original correspondence and confidential print on deposit in the Transvaal Archives Depot. Since there is considerable duplication between the British and the South African collections, I cited the South African source wherever possible.

A number of individuals and institutions assisted me in the completion of this work, and I wish to record my gratitude to all of them. During the early stages of the project, I was able to spend a summer in the library of the Royal Commonwealth Society in London and am indebted to the librarian, Mr D.H. Simpson, and his staff for their assistance. I would like to thank the librarian of Rhodes House, Oxford, for permission to consult the Charter Consolidated collection and the Keeper of the Public Records Office for permission to use the confidential print. Barlow Rand kindly allowed me to use the company's invaluable archive; Mrs M. Fraser, the archivist at Barlow Rand, gave advice on the use of the collections. At the University of the Witwatersrand, Johannesburg, I received assistance in the acquisition of microfilm from the university archivist, Miss J. Biddles. At the University of Natal, Andrew Duminy, Paul Maylam, and Philip Warhurst drew my attention to pertinent research material from their respective fields, as did Philip Bonner at the University of the Witwatersrand and Dunbar Moodie at Hobart and William Smith colleges. The staff at the Transvaal Archives Depot and the State Library both in Pretoria gave helpful advice concerning their respective collections, as did the staff of the Cape repository in Cape Town.

My colleagues, Arthur Keppel-Jones at Queen's and Jeffrey Horton, now retired from the University of Natal in Durban, have given me much advice and assistance on this and other projects over many years. The following scholars read and commented on the manuscript at an earlier stage: Jonathan Crush, Paul Maylam, Dunbar Moodie, and David Yudelman. William Beinart shared research material with me and gave me the benefit of his extensive knowledge of recruiting in the eastern Cape. At the University of the Witwatersrand, where I often found myself during frequent trips to South Africa, I benefited from many discussions with the regular members of the African studies seminar and the Department of History, including particularly Noel Garson, Phyllis Lewsen, and Bruce Murray. I would also like to thank Rodney Davenport at Rhodes University and Robert Kubicek of the University of British Columbia.

In the preparation of the work for publication, Connie Munro at the University of Natal typed early drafts of several chapters. Shirallee Reed at Queen's did an excellent job with the final manuscript. During the summer of 1982, Ruth Parry worked with me as a research assistant, verifying the notes and bibliography with speed and precision. I am indebted to the Canada Council and its successor organization, the Social Sciences and Humanities Research Council, for a sabbatical leave fellowship and later a research grant and to the Advisory Research Committee of Queen's University for several grants, particularly for conference travel, which enabled me to share my preliminary findings with other scholars.

Abbreviations

AA	*African Affairs*
BRA	Barlow Rand Archives, Sandton
BSA CO.	British South Africa Company
CAD	Cape Archives Depot, Cape Town
CMAR	Chamber of Mines, *Annual Report*
CML	Chamber of Mines, Johannesburg, Archives and Library
CNA	Cape Native Affairs Department
CO 879	Colonial Office, Confidential Print, Series: African, South
CS	Archive of the Transvaal Colonial Secretary, TAD
DNL	Director of Native Labour
ERPM	East Rand Proprietary Mines
GMC	Gold Mining Company
GNLB	Union Government Native Labour Bureau Archive, TAD
GOV	Governor of the Transvaal Archive, TAD
HC	Archive of the South African High Commission, TAD
HE	H. Eckstein and Company Archive
ICI	*Evidence and Report of the Industrial Commission of Inquiry, 1897*
ICS	University of London, Institute of Commonwealth Studies, *Collected Seminar Papers on the Societies of Southern Africa in the 19th and 20th Centuries*
JAH	*Journal of African History*

JCI	Johannesburg Consolidated Investment Company
JPFP	J.P. FitzPatrick Papers
JPL	Johannesburg Public Library
JSAS	*Journal of Southern African Studies*
JUS	Union Government, Secretary for Justice Archive, TAD
MIC	*Report of the Mining Industry Commission, 1908*
MNW	Union Government, Secretary for Mines Archive, TAD
NGI	*Report of the Native Grievances Inquiry, 1914 (Buckle Commission)*
NGI, CA	Native Grievances Inquiry, Commission Archive, TAD
NRC	Native Recruiting Corporation, Ltd.
NTS	Union Government, Native Affairs Department Archive, TAD
PM	Prime Minister of the Transvaal Archive, TAD
RM	Resident Magistrate
SANAC	South African Native Affairs Commission, 1903–5 (Lagden Commission)
SNAA	Secretary of Native Affairs Archive, Transvaal Colony, TAD
SNA	Secretary of Native Affairs
TAD	Transvaal Archives Depot, Pretoria
TLC	*Report of the Transvaal Labour Commission, 1904*
TMLC	Transvaal Mines Labour Company
UG	Union Government
WNLA	*Witwatersrand Native Labour Association*
ZA	Zimbabwe Archives, Harare: British South Africa Company Collection

Migrant Labour in
South Africa's Mining Economy

Introduction

For almost a century gold mining has dominated the South African economy. Even today, after many years of rapid economic growth and diversification, the gold mines remain the principal source of foreign exchange and a major contributor of state revenue through taxation. They continue to be one of the country's largest employers of both white and black labour. In the early years of this century, the industry's dominance was, if anything, even greater than in the 1980s. Secondary manufacturing was only beginning to develop. Farming although extremely important was still struggling and had yet to receive the massive state subsidies which converted the inefficient pastoral estates of the nineteenth century into the agri-businesses of modern white South Africa. Altogether farming probably employed more people than gold mining but did so in more varied, less visible and influential ways. The dominating size of the gold industry, the importance of its contribution to export earnings, its superior organization and capacity to influence governments all meant that its labour and other policies have had an enormous demonstration effect in other economic sectors.

By 1910, only twenty-four years after the first discoveries on the Witwatersrand, the mines had created a labour system which delivered more than 200,000 unskilled black workers annually to the Witwatersrand. There was no precedent for labour mobilization on this scale anywhere in Africa. Since all but a few thousand of these workers were migrants who remained on the mines on average for less than a year, a much larger pool of potential labour was required than represented by those actually at work at any one time. Most were completely without previous industrial experience. Recruited from throughout southern Africa, they left their pastoral and agricultural pursuits to work on unfamiliar tasks in a regimented, totally alien, and dangerous industrial environment. The emergence of this remarkable system of labour mobilization is perhaps the single most im-

3

portant feature of the early industrialization of South Africa. Although relying on African migrant workers from the beginning, the mining companies required many years to perfect the institutions needed to recruit this labour and to control it effectively. The skilled labour force could be drawn from the ranks of experienced white miners imported from overseas, but a variety of circumstances ensured that the industry would seek the bulk of its labour from the indigenous black population.

While the Kimberley diamond mines were able to meet their modest need for unskilled labour almost entirely from "voluntary," unrecruited workers, the gold mines' much larger requirements and minimal wage rates forced them to set up an elaborate recruiting network and to extend its operations throughout the subcontinent. Mine labour recruiting soon became a major employer in its own right of white and black labour agents and subordinate "runners." Throughout southern Africa, colonial governments came to the support of the industry, hoping to secure for their territories a share of the gold bonanza by delivering contract labour to the mines. The companies sought allies too in African chiefs and local notables without whose active support they could never have hoped to draw labour in the required numbers from the main recruiting districts.

An examination of the particular way mine labour recruiting actually developed reveals the diversity of interests which profited from it and therefore worked to entrench the system. While the mine owners certainly played a key role, they frequently found their control of recruiting challenged by regional governments bent on extracting higher levels of taxation, by mercantile and recruiting associations searching for higher fees, by independent labour contracting companies seeking to control the supply, and by key black collaborators in the countryside. In doing much to promote labour migration to the mines from Basutoland and Bechuanaland from the turn of the century, the British administrations there worked not primarily to promote the interests of the mining industry but rather to serve their own desperate need for revenue.[1] Similar policies implemented by the Cape government were prompted by the same motives. At a time of severe depression, the requirements of the budget took precedence over the fear and hostility of the mining industry which Prime Minister Merriman and several colleagues undoubtedly felt. To pressing fiscal need was added strong political pressure, as eastern Cape commercial and recruiting interests demanded and got policies which quickly made the Cape a recruiting centre for the mines second only to Mozambique. These compelling political and economic difficulties rather than any subordination to "hegemonic" mining capital explain the labour policies of the Cape and other regional governments.

In Pondoland, as William Beinart has shown, chiefs and headmen saw labour migration under the cattle advance system as a means of accommodating the demands of the regional economy, while maximizing the benefit to themselves and minimizing social disruption.[2] Cattle advances helped to ensure that benefits of the migration would accrue to the families rather than to the migrants themselves. Through the advance system, furthermore, the return of the younger men from the mines was assured and the authority of the older generation maintained. Far from immediately undermining the peasant economy in Pondoland, migrancy helped to preserve it, at least in the short run. It did this by providing needed capital for agricultural improvement, and by providing an outlet for surplus labour released by technological change (the use of ploughs and draft animals) in the agricultural economy. Although the mine owners knew that cattle advances cost huge sums and led to much abuse by defaulting mineworkers, they found themselves compelled to tolerate the system for some years, so great was their need for labour. Very often it was regional governments, African chiefs, and local recruiting interests rather than the Chamber of Mines which determined the way black labour was mobilized and used on the Rand.

This formidable recruiting system and the associated racial division of labour quickly became the industry's most notorious feature. From the outset, the mines provided patterns of labour mobilization and exploitation which were soon copied throughout the economy. Oscillating labour migration and the industrial colour bar which continue to disfigure South African society are everywhere regarded as the grotesque legacy of the mining industry. On the left, historians have emphasized the role of profit-maximizing Randlords, while other explanations focus on the role of the racialist white trade unionists and politicians. Yet the development of the central element in the mines' labour system, the institutions created to recruit and control black migrant labour, has not been seriously examined. For example, in Francis Wilson's major study of labour on the gold mines, fewer than three pages in a two hundred-page book are devoted to the emergence of the Chamber of Mines recruiting organizations. Simon Katzenellenbogen's recent work on Mozambique-South African relations, although centrally concerned as it had to be with labour, dealt only cursorily with the evolution of WNLA structures in the Portuguese colony. Even Sheila van der Horst's earlier, more detailed discussion gives scant indication of the formidable barriers which stood in the way of monopsonistic recruiting, of the creation of an employers' monopoly.[3]

From the radical standpoint, neither F.A. Johnstone nor Rob Davies in their full-length studies of the mining industry's labour history gave much attention to the actual methods and institutions which the industry developed to supply its insatiable demands for black labour. More recently, both Marian Lacey and Norman Levy have also ignored the critical role of the private recruiting companies in the making of the unskilled labour force and the entrenchment of migrant labour.[4] In fact both liberals and radicals have shared the view that cooperative recruiting was easily achieved in the industry and that it was somehow the natural result of the domination of a very few large mining groups. Monopoly capitalism held sway, and the Chamber of Mines controlled everything. Thus the Witwatersrand Native Labour Association (WNLA) and the Native Recruiting Corporation (NRC) developed smoothly, almost inevitably as the instruments of the industry's control of black labour. Monopsonistic recruiting emerged easily as the big corporations moved to the full-scale exploitation of the huge deposits of low-grade ore. Since the mines dominated the economy, they had little to fear from the rivalry of outside employers, at least in the first twenty-five years or so. These generalizations seem to command widespread acceptance in the current literature. In much of this work, the mining industry and its labour systems are simply taken to be largely undifferentiated and for the most part free of internal dissension.

Of course there is much truth in the received view in either its liberal or radical version. A few, tightly interlocked, multinational financial groups obviously did dominate the industry. The pressures of rising costs and falling yields in the low-grade ore certainly drove them relentlessly to the economies which large-scale migrant labour alone looked like supplying.[5] The bleak labour system which resulted did provide an all too attractive model which was soon widely copied in the economy. Despite all this, however, the mines achieved centralized control of recruiting only with great difficulty and prolonged effort. An examination of this central dimension of gold mining suggests the weakness of mining capital rather than its strength during the whole period before 1919. In these years, the maintenance of a regular supply of cheap black labour was frequently threatened by internal conflict between the mining groups. Far from exercising monopsonistic control, the Chamber of Mines often had to defer to private recruiters and labour contractors, representing much less economically powerful but politically well-connected interests.

The Witwatersrand ore formations contain gold deposits which in extent and uniformity are unparalleled in the world. In its early years, the mining industry did not face the kind of uncertainties which had characterized all previous gold mining. It confronted problems of another sort, however, which were almost as serious.[6] To refer to the uniformity of the Rand ore formations is to make a relative statement. In relation to alluvial deposits, the gold content on the Rand was regular and dependable. It varied substantially from place to place along the reef, however, and sharp local fluctuations upset planning even within individual mines.[7] Certain requirements of mining development aggravated the difficulty, particularly the need at the very outset to determine which of the ore bodies in a particular mine could be profitably extracted and which had so low a grade as not to warrant development. This was the crucial decision. Once a company had developed its mine, sunk its shafts and located its drives, the design might be prohibitively expensive to change. It was much cheaper to sink a large shaft to begin with than to enlarge a small one later on.

Since the price of gold was fixed throughout this period, the payability or not of a particular ore body depended, first, upon the yield in gold per ton of ore and, second, on the critical matter of working costs. These factors determined the "pay limit."[8] Geological exploration could give the mine owner some indication of the quality and extent of the ore in his mine. Working costs, however, resulted from social and economic forces which lay only marginally under his control. A conservative company, which developed only its richer and clearly payable ore, might find itself, assuming a subsequent fall in working costs, with vast tonnages of now payable but inaccessible ore. Conversely, a gambling mine management, developing its low-grade ore bodies on the basis of an optimistic view of the future, might find itself faced with substantial capital losses if costs failed to fall. Richer mines suffered from these considerations to a lesser degree than poorer ones, but most of the mining houses had one or more mines where cost problems were critical.

These requirements of mining development – the need to invest and develop at the outset for the whole life of the mine – tended to make gamblers of the Randlords. So also did the very nature of the mineral question. The behaviour of generations of miners, speculators, and hoarders testifies to the peculiar fascination of gold, to which the flint-eyed captains of Rand finance were far from immune. The same individuals who might cheerfully have left tons of, say, uneconomic copper in a mine dedicated themselves on the Rand to the single-minded pursuit of the last possible pennyweight of gold. Thus was the propensity to gamble intensified. Nevertheless, the mine owners sought to hedge their bets and so to protect themselves from the various uncertainties to which they were vulnerable. The group system of control was one device for accomplishing this. Through provision of centralized managerial, secretarial and engineering services for several mines, central control could rationalize mining administration and reduce management costs as well as enable the owners in effect to subsidize the poorer mines from the profits of the richer ones during periods of adversity.

As another device to control working costs, the industry made a determined effort to equate its problems and needs with those of the white society at large. Through the Chamber of Mines and through the press which the mines controlled, the owners stressed from the beginning that the welfare of white South Africa itself depended upon the health of the gold industry.

More subtle was their effort to make the demands of the industry as a whole coincide with the needs of its weakest producers. The Randlords enjoyed considerable success in promoting the notion that the profitability or not of the low-grade mines should be the index of the health of the entire industry.[9] Whenever the low-grade producers experienced trouble, mining spokesmen would declare the whole industry in crisis and warn that without corrective action, the prosperity and even stability of Transvaal society would be threatened. Galloping unemployment, social instability in the white community, and falling government revenues were recurring spectres in industry propaganda. Simple ruin would await the country if it failed to rescue the low-grade mines. Such arguments had another often unnoticed but very important effect. They identified the welfare of the industry and of the whole society with a particular development strategy, one which aimed to maximize output. Steady expansion usually involved mining ores of lower grade, and this in turn required lower costs. From this simple premise, a whole host of demands on government followed, for the labour, tax, and other policies which would guarantee profitability in conditions of great uncertainty and risk.

The degree of success which the Chamber of Mines enjoyed in its efforts to identify the survival of the low-grade producers with the welfare of the entire society is revealed in the reports of the plethora of mining commissions and inquiries which from 1897 had been established by successive governments. Invariably the special problems of the low-grade mines figured prominently in these investigations.[10] Not until 1907 when the Botha government established the Mining Industry Commission did the state finally make a (not very impressive) effort to look critically at the arguments advanced by the mines to justify favourable treatment. Earlier, the chamber had dominated both the Industrial Commission of Inquiry (1897) and the Transvaal Labour Commission (1903), just as it afterwards strongly influenced the Low Grade Mines Commission (1919). Because of its near monopoly of the information needed to assess the highly technical problems of Rand mining, the chamber found its presentations rarely challenged. Commissions of inquiry had little choice but to rely upon chamber data and even chamber expertise in conducting their investigations. Even the Mining Industry Commission of 1907–8, though inclined to be very critical of group mining and financial practices, failed to make an effective case because it too had ultimately to rely upon industry data. In South Africa, the state did not develop for many years the capacity required to look critically and independently at the problems of the mining industry.[11]

These general considerations help to explain why the Randlords committed themselves so early and so thoroughly to high-cost, (relatively) low-profit exploitation of the low-grade ores. But there was nothing inevitable about it. In the medium term good profits could have been made by concentrating upon the richer ores on the basis of a not much reduced scale of operations. During various periods of adversity, the mining groups did just this but reluctantly, for they were loath to leave any but the most marginal ore bodies unworked. Before the Anglo-Boer War the mines operated such a policy, concentrating, as Peter Richardson has shown, on the relatively high-grade South Reef and leaving much of the lower-grade ore.[12] In many cases these marginal ore bodies had been developed in the mine but were left unextracted in the hope of a subsequent fall in working costs. When production resumed in 1902, a determination to recover these lower-grade deposits made the mine owners even more anxious to bring costs down. After World War I, when sharp inflationary pressures in the economy again threatened profitability, the chamber proposed to close down several low-grade properties temporarily. A government subsidy to maintain pumping was requested. The chamber took the view that production could be maintained by higher output in the better mines. Throughout the period, these low-grade mines were risky ventures, highly vulnerable to small increases in costs. The failures and difficulties of numbers of such mines are one reason (though not the most important) to explain the wastage of large capital sums and the rather low return to the industry upon gross capital investment, as calculated by Frankel.[13]

In fact other developments than these explain fully the initial commitment to low-grade mining. The basic investment decisions came during the mid-1890s at a time of unparalleled optimism about the future of speculative Johannesburg mining issues. As a result, most of the groups committed themselves to the development of ore bodies which would become marginal producers in all but the most buoyant economic circumstances. The consequences of these policies could not easily be evaded after the Anglo-Boer War when chronic slump replaced boom and mining costs failed to fall fast enough to compensate for windfall profits achieved hitherto in the stock market. Labour costs in particular proved stubbornly resistant to the attentions of government and industry alike.

After the war, the industry confronted the consequences of its own earlier optimism and a host of new problems besides. The investment of large capital sums in mining development before 1899 led to huge losses of dividends and interest when operations had to be suspended almost entirely for the duration of hostilities. Deep-level mining required, in any case, the bulk of the investment for shaft sinking, equipment, and ore reduction works years before production and therefore earnings could begin. Two and a half years of bitter war added another long, unproductive period. Johannesburg mining magnates therefore wanted urgently to resume operations at the earliest moment so as to recover the millions lost in interest and foregone dividends. Additional pressure came also, of course, from Milner's Reconstruction administration, equally anxious to see production restarted

9   Introduction

on the Rand. As South Africa's one substantial, taxable asset, the mines were essential to the achievement of the high commissioner's political objectives.

Although spokesmen for the mines have always tried to portray their impressive achievements as a triumph of free enterprise capitalism,[14] the leaders of the industry themselves have assiduously courted state assistance from the beginning of gold mining in the South African Republic in the 1870s to the present.[15] There is a close parallel with the great transportation companies which built the lines of rail across western North America in the latter part of the nineteenth century, engulfing vast tracts of the public domain and huge government subsidies in the process. American and Canadian governments came to the support of the railways for some of the same reasons which brought South African governments into partnership with the mining houses. Politicians saw railways in the one case and gold in the other as the basic instruments of nation-building. Clearly the main instruments of national expansion could not be left entirely to private enterprise. Furthermore, governments soon learned that private companies either could not or would not do the job unaided by government. The North American railway companies took their assistance in the form of direct cash subsidies and in land. Although the mining industry did not require cash subsidies until the 1960s (when certain low-grade mines were subsidized), it did require throughout its history an enormous legislative and administrative effort to organize the black labour supply – a crucial element in mining costs.[16]

In the eventual establishment of a powerful, centralized recruiting system, the state played a central but for many years ambivalent and contradictory role. It is true that the industry simply could not have established its system, which took forty years to perfect, without the massive and persistent intervention of governments. Through pass laws and other coercive statutes, the state regulated the movement of Africans and brought them under a harsh industrial discipline. Although blacks resisted recruiting abuses, low wages, and deplorable working conditions continuously, their attempts to do so invariably provoked massive police repression on the side of the mining employers. In this situation, the advantages to the owners of a rightless, easily controlled black proletariat offset the inefficiencies inherent in the system of migrancy itself. The industry's demand for coercive labour legislation had ample precedent in the earlier collaboration between white farmers and the state to force blacks into the wage markets through master and servant acts, making breach of labour contracts by workers a criminal offence; antisquatting laws, designed to prevent Africans from securing tenancy rights on white-owned land; and other restrictions on African rights to own and occupy land.[17]

In the actual conduct of recruiting operations, however, governments played a more equivocal part. State mediation was essential in the interminable conflicts within the industry over black labour problems, and ultimately only the state could bring under control the rapacious, independent recruiting companies which constituted the most formidable barrier to the completion of the mines' cooperative system. Throughout most of the period, governments intervened in these matters reluctantly and hesitantly. As noted above, the state had other needs and other interests than simply those of the mining industry to consider. Moreover, politicians required many years before they could accept a large permanent role for government in the actual recruitment of migrant labour. Both before and after Union, they shrank from the prospect of direct control of the mines' recruiting effort, fearing that it would soon involve them in complete responsibility for the industry's labour needs. However, when the Chamber of Mines demonstrated over a quarter of a century its absolute inability to do the job alone, governments found themselves gradually but inexorably drawn in.

Several reasons explain why the mines required state support in this area. First, most South African blacks persistently rejected mine employment, especially underground, where any alternatives were open to them. Africans knew well enough about conditions on the Rand, which mines were to be preferred to others, about wage levels, and about the availability or not of alternative employment.[18] Even before the South African war, officials were actively involved in efforts to overcome this resistance. During the Crown Colony period, 1900–6, the administration made still greater efforts in the same direction. Considerations of mining economics also led the companies into a close dependence upon government. The peculiar nature of the Witwatersrand ore formations (and the uncertainties which this produced in a highly cost-sensitive industry) made the companies vulnerable to any upward movement in the wage bill. Conflict and rivalry between the various mining houses exacerbated labour shortages and made it harder for individual mines to get and keep black labour. Unable through their own institutions to control competition among themselves, the owners looked increasingly to government to impose the necessary discipline.

These same considerations drove the mining industry into alliance with neighbouring jurisdictions to mobilize the labour of the entire region.[19] It is often argued that cost constraints forced the mines to get as much of their labour as they could where it was cheapest, on the northern periphery of the subcontinent.[20] In fact, recruits from Nyasaland, northern Mozambique, and adjacent territories actually cost more than labour recruited in South Africa itself.[21] The former received comparable wages, but the cost of recruitment and transport was higher. In addition, the mines had to pay special fees to the Nyasaland government and to the Portuguese chartered companies which supplied most of this labour until the Union government banned employment of tropical Africans on the mines in 1913. The attraction of the labour of the periphery lay in the lack of competition from other employers either resident in those regions or outside them and in the prospect of developing a regular and dependable source of labour completely under the control of the Chamber of Mines recruiting organizations. Wage scales on the Rand mines far exceeded what the farms and mines of Southern Rhodesia–the main competition–could pay. Local Nyasa planters with average wages one-twentieth the rate on the Rand were even less of a threat in the labour market of Nyasaland and adjacent territories. To protect themselves, these employers agitated to exclude the gold mines' recruiters. If the Chamber of Mines could neutralize the political opposition of these competing employers, it could hope to control the supply from the hinterland. Competitors in these regions from South Africa itself could be ignored since no other industry could mobilize the capital or create the organization required to recruit and transport labour on a large scale over the hundreds of miles which lay between Zambesia and the main South African labour centres.

For over a full decade from 1902, the mining industry put unrelenting pressure on the Transvaal government, its Union successor, the imperial government, and the colonial administrations of Nyasaland and Mozambique in its efforts to control the emigrant labour from these sources.[22] Like the miners from southern Mozambique and the Chinese, the tropical migrants accepted long-term contracts. They added another stable element to a labour force subject to violent fluctuations because of the reluctance of South African blacks to take mine employment except as a last resort, and their refusal when they did come to accept work for periods exceeding six or nine months at the most. Moreover, large numbers of South African miner-peasants would regularly depart from the mines in the spring and early summer in order to plant their crops for the following season. The industry relied on recruits from Mozambique and the north to offset this.

These and other uncertainties which caused unpredictable fluctuations in the labour supply tended to aggravate competition among the mining groups and even between mines within a group. For the Chamber of Mines, the record of the first twenty-five years pointed irresistibly toward the need for centralized control of labour recruitment. Although the chamber represented virtually all of the mines on the Witwatersrand, it was dominated by representatives of the most powerful mining groups. The largest of these, the H. Eckstein/Rand Mines complex and the Gold Fields group, consistently favoured noncompetitive recruiting. Despite this, the chamber repeatedly failed both to eliminate competition within the industry and to secure effective control over the independent labour recruiters and contractors who exploited endemic divisions and rivalries among the mining groups to entrench themselves in the labour market. These labour agents were the real beneficiaries of competition and the major barrier to its elimination. From the earliest days of the industry through to the 1920s, mine labour recruiting remained an unstable, expensive, conflict-ridden enterprise. Even a cursory examination of the history of labour recruiting makes a joke of the idea that mining capitalism was all-powerful in this period. These supposedly hegemonic Randlords – the "Imperial" capitalists – could not even drive from their own backyard the illicit recruiters and labour touts who routinely plundered the mines of their labour supply. The touts provided facilities for dissatisfied, underpaid black miners who deserted in droves from the Rand. Throughout this period, the Rand remained a happy hunting-ground for the black and white labour thieves who defied the WNLA and the NRC. Away from Johannesburg, the same type of recruiter carried on his activities with even less risk. The struggle to control the mine labour market involved not only elimination of intra-industry competition for labour, but also successfully bringing to heel the independent recruiters and labour contractors.[23]

Chamber of Mines personnel had promoted these objectives almost from the start, and the industry's own efforts to organize a common labour system date from about 1890. The first cooperative recruiting company, the Rand Native Labour Association (1897), forerunner of the WNLA (1900), emerged seven years later. However, neither these organizations nor the later Native Recruiting Corporation (1912) achieved complete control of the demand for labour. Important groups and individual mines remained outside the monopsony throughout the first two decades of the twentieth century. More significantly, independent recruiters and recruiting companies, some of them very powerful and well connected, remained active in the field. Unable to deal with these dissident elements themselves, mining leaders quite naturally sought the support of government. The dissenting mining groups and the independent recruiters replied in kind. As a result of this sort of conflict, the South African state found itself pressed toward intervention in the mines' labour system. Acting at first as referee between the contending factions, governments found themselves pushed toward support of a centralized non-competitive system. A single system under Chamber of Mines control promised to bring a modicum of order to recruiting, to help solve the political difficulty posed by the conflict of competing interests, and above all to serve as an alternative to a state-run recruiting system.[24]

On more than one occasion, the Chamber of Mines suggested that the government itself assume complete control of the mines' labour supply, and this remained the preferred solution for many years.[25] They pressed Milner for a state system at the time the WNLA was formed, and remained hopeful that he or some bold successor would take the whole vexed issue out of their hands. Although in these years no issue of economic policy received more attention from government than the maintenance of gold mining profitability (state revenues after all were at stake), the politicians never seriously considered actually running the recruiting system as a state enterprise. The grounds of their reluctance are not clearly expressed in the surviving records, but some of their concerns and fears are easy to establish. Even Milner did not want the open, public identification with the mining industry that direct management of its labour supply would involve. As modern radical literature puts it, the state was concerned to maintain its "relative autonomy" as against rival classes and interest groups. Given the contemporary hostility toward and fear of mining capitalists, the "Hoggenheimers" of the cartoonists in the popular press, so widely expressed throughout white South Africa, the reason for this is clear. Winning elections and staying in power depended on it. During this entire period, moreover, mine labour recruiting had been riddled by scandal, corruption, and practices which could not be openly acknowledged. This was another reason to devise a labour system which kept state officials at arm's length from the recruiters.

More importantly, the whole direction of labour policy was very much a subject of continuous, often heated public debate in these years. In the press before Union and in the first Union Parliament, F.H.P. Creswell, the radical politician and white labour theorist, and his supporters used every opportunity to denounce the migrant labour system as fundamentally aimed at destroying the white working class. During a period of substantial labour militancy, the politicians had to be sensitive to the propaganda of these tireless critics who had achieved some remarkable successes in their efforts to mobilize white workers for politics. Spokesmen for the commercial farming lobby and their parliamentary representatives were also quick to see and to denounce any attempt to meet the mines' black labour needs at their expense.[26] These various critics had done much to expose recruiting scandals and grotesque abuses connected with the treatment of black workers and conditions on the Rand. The state already found itself blamed for tolerating many of these evils and the resulting dreadful mortality. To assume control of recruiting would likely involve complete responsibility for their remedy and much greater political embarrassment.

Within these parameters, South African governments manoeuvred to support the mines' recruiting efforts, while attempting to avoid complete identification with them. Historians are coming to accept that even a government as basically wary of the Randlords as Kruger's had initiated pass laws and similar measures.[27] Well before the turn of the century, the Cape enacted antisquatting, tax, and other measures quite obviously aimed at mobilizing labour for mining and other employers.[28] The important contribution of the Reconstruction government to labour mobilization in the Transvaal is well known.[29] Before Union, no government did more for the mines than Louis Botha's Het Volk administration in the Transvaal, 1907-9.

Although Het Volk had loudly condemned the Randlords in the election campaign which brought the party to power in 1907,[30] its leaders began working privately to establish a cooperative relationship with the industry even before the voting began.[31] Within a few weeks of their victory, Botha's deputy, Jan Smuts, launched a mediating effort which composed apparently irreconcilable differences within the Chamber of Mines on labour issues and undoubtedly prevented the collapse of the WNLA.[32] Without his efforts disastrous consequences for the mining groups could not have been avoided. Later, in 1909, Het Volk negotiated a revision of the *Modus Vivendi* with Portuguese Mozambique upon terms which gave priority to ensuring the mines' East African labour supply. In return, the Portuguese demanded and got concessions on railway and customs policy which caused serious embarrassment to Botha's government in its relations with the Cape and Natal at precisely the time when good intercolonial relations seemed essential to the success of the drive toward South African unification. Few policy steps are more revealing of this government's real priorities than its handling of the complex negotiations involved in the Transvaal-Mozambique Convention of 1909.[33] Similarly, the first Union government played a key role in negotiations between the Portuguese and the Chamber of Mines, notably during 1912–13 when a deferred pay scheme was set up. Once this began to work properly it augmented substantially the pay-off in gold to the Mozambique colonial administration from the migrant labour system. The South African government accepted this despite the wrath of the Johannesburg shopkeepers and their trading associations which feared a severe loss of business if the mines augmented the flow of repatriated earnings to Mozambique.

While political considerations of this kind did not prevent substantial assistance to the mining industry, they did suggest caution as governments responded to its various demands. Apart from this, there were other, important limitations on the ability of colonial authorities throughout the subcontinent to meet the requirements of the mines.[34] In the early years of this century, the South African state lacked both the information and the administrative expertise to formulate policies which could effectively direct the labour and other economic priorities of the country. Measures aimed at mobilizing labour for the gold mines or other employers frequently did not work. In these years, government and industry alike recognized usefulness of hut and poll taxes in making Africans aware of the "dignity of labour." Mine owners called for higher taxes to force blacks out of their kraals so that they might take up the task of "helping their neighbours," as one Randlord put it.[35] Before Union, all colonial governments raised taxes levied on Africans in response to the demands of mine owners and other employers as well as for revenue. However, they found ordinary taxes to be a rather blunt instrument for labour mobilization. The more successful peasants could and did find money for the sale of crops and beasts and so avoided the need to leave the land, although it is true, as Colin Bundy has demonstrated, that the number who could do this diminished steadily in the late nineteenth and early twentieth centuries.[36] In any case, the simple imposition of a tax could do nothing to direct the labour which might be thus mobilized to the employers who needed it most.

When these still rudimentary bureaucracies tried to refine their instruments of labour mobilization, difficulty quickly developed. Take the labour tax written into the Cape's Glen Grey Act, for example. Under the act, Africans who had not accepted employment outside the district during a specified interval became liable to pay a special tax. Passed by the Rhodes ministry in 1894, this statute stands as the epitome of capitalist-induced, labour-mobilizing legislation. After all Rhodes himself had a hand in drafting the bill and what better evidence could be sought for probable motives? Yet the labour tax was never effectively enforced even in Glen Grey. When the government extended other features of the act across the Kei in the years which followed, it did not include the labour tax which had been strongly opposed not only by Africans but also by Native Affairs Department officials. Within a few years the tax was dropped altogether.[37] In the end, the view of officials, not those of labour-hungry Randlords or even Rhodes himself, determined the way the government implemented and administered the act. The intention of successive Cape governments during the 1880s and 1890s to mobilize labour for various employers, including the gold mines, can easily be demonstrated, but their methods were crude and their success partial at best. It took severe depression in the early twentieth century and much more thorough-going measures by a more efficient administration to turn the Transkei and adjacent territories into a labour pool on a scale exceeded only by Mozambique. Until "market forces" and the effect of successive agricultural calamities in the African territories had added their effect to the efforts of these pre-Union governments, relatively little labour went to the gold mines from the Cape. Even then a massive recruiting effort, involving huge expenditures, was required to make the eastern Cape districts large-scale suppliers of mine labour.

The gold mines' recruiting system emerged as the hard-won product of thirty years of intense competition and bitter struggle between contending interests inside and outside the mining industry. Interminable conflict between rival mining houses continually frustrated the efforts of the Chamber of Mines to eliminate competition for labour. Equally important in perpetuating competition were the machinations of the squadrons of independent labour agents, trader/recruiters and contractors who swarmed on the fringes of the industry. These men played a central role in labour mobilization throughout South Africa, as the mine

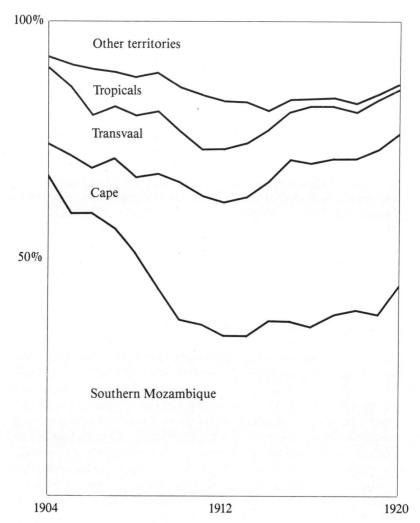

100%

Other territories

Tropicals

Transvaal

Cape

50%

Southern Mozambique

1904   1912   1920

FIGURE I
Principal Sources of Mine Labour, 1904–20
SOURCES: WNLA *Annual Reports*; Native Labour Bureau estimates; data are approximate.

owners recognized. Competition served the interest of the independent recruiters because it tended to bid up the fees for their services. Mine labour recruiting provided easy, sometimes lucrative employment for thousands of blacks and whites. For the black recruiters and "runners," working for the labour companies was definitely preferable to working on the mines. For unemployed miners and other whites "down on their luck" the recruiting industry served as an employer of last resort. As one industry spokesman explained, few mine managers could resist anyone who came along claiming he could "get boys."[38] As a result huge numbers of whites moved into and out of the recruiting system. While many did not last, hundreds had established themselves as successful labour agents by the early twentieth century. They managed to corner a large part of the labour supply and fought hard to maintain their position when the Chamber of Mines began to organize its monopsony. An industry-wide cooperative system threatened them not only because it would permit agreement among the employers to lower recruiting fees, but also because it would involve rationalization and employment for many fewer white recruiters.

Three full decades elapsed before the mining industry became sufficiently unified and sufficiently confident of its own labour organizations to begin openly to oppose the independent recruiters. Even then the chamber had frequently to defer to the wishes of the more successful among them. The independent recruiters enjoyed structural advantages in the system which explain their remarkable ability to frustrate the intentions of much more powerful economic interests. During the early years of unregulated recruiting, the successful labour agents had entrenched themselves in most of the main recruiting centres. They were local people, well known to the inhabitants and sometimes trusted by them. Frequently they were traders upon whom the black population had been driven to depend for credit by government policy and adverse economic circumstances alike. The resident trader/recruiters usually had the contacts with chiefs, headmen, and other notables without which successful recruiting could not be carried on. In some areas, most strikingly in the eastern Cape, the independent labour agents became politically powerful. They formed associations, allied themselves with chambers of commerce in the larger centres and put pressure on their regional members of Parliament for policies which would maximize the benefit from recruitment for the Rand to the areas which supplied the labour. Such policies usually involved additional expense for the mines. On certain kinds of issues, the labour agents showed themselves to be more adept lobbyists than Randlords, who had vastly more money to spend and usually far easier access to officials and politicians.

Even a cursory examination of government labour policies reveals the complexity and difficulty of the political issues which confronted the politicians. In developing their policies in this crucial area, governments had to manoeuvre carefully among a number of competing interest groups. Frequently serious differences developed among the mining houses on the proper policies which the state should pursue. The recruiters and labour contracting firms had interests which put them into conflict with the mine owners. The labour needs of other employers, especially the farmers, had always to be considered.[39]One example will illustrate a general problem. A few years after the Anglo-Boer War, the Cape government developed an assisted voluntary labour system, designed to help Africans reach the gold mines without the intervention of a recruiter. Resident magistrates and later a new class of official, the labour registrars, would provide information and assist with the necessary arrangements. Most of the mining companies backed the scheme which promised labour without the need to pay recruiting fees; they could easily pay the rail fare of the volunteer and still save money. Mine managers naturally preferred voluntary to recruited mineworkers because the former tended to be better, more contented workers. The migrants themselves stood to benefit from the scheme which offered a means of escape from the recruiter and usually free rail fare. Ordinarily the recruiters paid the fare and recovered the cost from wages. On this particular issue, the state and the mines had a community of interest with the blacks against the labour agents. When the recruiters and the allied local chambers of commerce mobilized themselves for politics, however, the Cape government felt compelled to move cautiously and to deny any intention of undermining the position of the recruiters. Equally, the mine owners declined to risk the anger of these powerful interests. Privately they continued to assure government of their support of the voluntary system; quietly they did what they could to encourage volunteer blacks to come to the mines, but they dared not risk a frontal assault on the recruiters.

The decade following the Anglo-Boer War saw the independent recruiters at the height of their power. They dominated the business and used their commanding position to extract lucrative terms from the mine employers. The independents virtually drove the WNLA from the South African colonies (it survived in Mozambique, at first precariously) and brought to a standstill the Chamber of Mines' first sustained bid to create an employers' monopoly. They could not have achieved this without the support of dissident mining groups which stood out from the chamber, hoping to benefit in conditions of labour shortage by refusing cooperation with the other houses. Nevertheless the victory against the WNLA was impressive testimony to the strength of the independent labour agents themselves and the associated contracting firms. By 1907 all of the mining groups, including those which had relied on the WNLA, had been forced either to establish their own native labour departments or to accept contracts from one or more of the independent companies.

Although the struggle to bring all of the mining groups into line behind the WNLA and then to eliminate or incorporate the independent agents failed at this time, it did have important effects on the character of the recruiting system. During the 1890s much of the mine labour came from very small scale operators, often from itinerant touts who roamed the countryside catching labour where they could and delivering the recruits personally to the mine. Their activities were either completely unregulated by government or nearly so and extortion and force were their common methods. Even better established trader/recruiters worked on a very small scale and often quite alone. After the war steadily increasing demand began to outrun the capacity of this ill-organized, anarchical system. Moreover, the frequent resort of the touts to fraud and coercion could easily disrupt the labour supply from particular districts. The WNLA represented a too-ambitious attempt to replace a host of small operators with a single organization run by the chamber. The WNLA's rivals saw too, however, that larger, more efficient labour companies were needed. In the struggle to control the labour supply, the independents began to come together in self-defence. As a result, a number of labour contracting firms had emerged by 1906–8, each with its network of labour agents in one or more of the main South African recruiting centres. The new companies tried to break into Mozambique as well but were prevented by the Portuguese government's determination to remain true to its arrangement with the WNLA. These companies varied in size, but some of them were large and could supply several thousand black miners annually to the Rand.

The process of partial consolidation was pushed forward as a result of government intervention. Both the Transvaal and the Cape administrations wanted to bring the recruiters under more effective control. Officials saw that their unregulated activities frequently caused disturbances in the African areas and could easily jeopardize the flow of labour. They preferred to deal with recruiters employed by a mining group or under definite contract to them. These men could be held to account for their methods, while the free-lance touts operated under no such restraints. The Cape had a Labour Agents Act on the books from 1899 and the Transvaal Reconstruction administration also began to license agents. As the competition for labour intensified in the postwar period, abuses multiplied and both governments began to extend their regulations and to enforce them more vigorously. In this effort they also tried to cooperate more effectively than had been possible previously. Native Affairs Department officials in both governments met frequently on recruiting matters. When the Transvaal government established a Native Labour Bureau in 1907, the Cape agreed that its control over certain aspects of mine labour recruiting should be extended to its densely populated black territories, the Ciskei and Transkei. Perceiving the need to establish greater accountability in the recruiting industry, the colonial governments tended to favour the larger companies, the activities of which could be more easily monitored. But there were limits on their ability to do this. Neither government dared openly to support a complete chamber monopsony (from an administrative standpoint the preferred solution) because they feared the political power of the independent labour contractors who had led the fight against the WNLA.

The emergence of larger-scale recruiting organizations in the decade after 1902 definitely marked an important step toward the formation of the

Native Recruiting Corporation in 1912 and the later completion of an industry-wide cooperative system by 1919. In the short run, however, it did nothing to reduce competition, to lower recruiting costs or to curb abuses. In some respects, the struggle for labour became fiercer and more unrestrained. The labour-contracting firms and the native labour departments, which some mining houses continued to use, had greater resources with which to pursue their rivalries. Some of them were controlled by men with good political connections, and in practice state regulation of the industry was weak until well after Union. Moreover, few of the mining houses remained loyal even to their own contractors. An individual mine manager, hard pressed to find labour to maintain production targets or to permit expansion, rarely turned down an offer of labour from any source, whatever his group administration might have told him about exclusive contracts, taking labour only from recruiting companies under contract to the group, and so on. Three circumstances led finally to the completion of the chamber's victory over the independents. By 1919, all of the mining houses at last agreed that there was more to lose than could possibly be gained by competition. Second, by stages after Union, the state gradually found the means to police the recruiting system more efficiently and in effect to ensure that the mines and their recruiters kept to their agreements. Third, increasing numbers of miners began to evade the recruiters and make their own way to the mines as volunteers. This phenomenon, which is discussed in chapter 5, contributed significantly to the eventual demise of the independent labour contractor. Nevertheless recruiters in the field, the vital link in the whole system, retained a quasi-independence for many years. Even when it secured entire control of all recruited labour from South African sources, the chamber's Native Recruiting Corporation had to deal carefully with its recruiters.

The workers who were drawn into mining employment in this way entered a working environment which was dangerous, brutal, and onerous. An analysis of the recruiting system requires a brief discussion of the conditions in which these workers lived and worked. This account describes the situation as it was in about 1910. While important improvements, particularly concerning health and disease, were implemented over the following decade, conditions remained bad throughout the period covered by this study. On arrival in Johannesburg, the recruit was taken to a central depot to await assignment to his particular mine. At the depot, he received a cursory medical examination by being paraded with all of the other recent arrivals past a medical officer who rejected few of the recruits that he saw. The grossly unfit, the seriously undernourished, and those obviously under-age were singled out for closer examination and possible repatriation or assignment to nonmining employment. A labour bureau inspector interviewed the recruits to explain again the terms of the mine contract which had been negotiated at the time of recruitment. This was a new provision introduced by the authorities because of widespread misrepresentation on contracts which resulted directly from intense competition for labour. While far from perfect, it did provide some protection.

After a short period at the government compound in Driehoek or Germiston, the recruit would be picked up by a black official, an "induna" or "police boy," of the mine to which he was contracted, and taken to the compound. Depending on the size of the mine, this could be a rough collection of huts, housing a small group of workers, or a complex of barracks accommodating several thousand. The worker would be assigned to a room housing typically from twenty to fifty of his fellows and given one of the tiered concrete bunks which would be "home" for the contract period. While off shift, the miners could leave the compound – they were not "closed" in the sense of the Kimberley compounds to which the workers were confined during the entire contract period – but movement in and out was carefully monitored by the compound police. Since 1905, government regulations had laid down standards for compound construction, air space, and food. Despite this, many of the older compounds remained dark, unsanitary, and overcrowded. With their concrete bunks and floors, the newer compounds could be kept clean enough but were bleak and cold in winter. Large ventilators at either end of the compound, installed at government insistence as a health measure, contributed to this. The 1905 ordinance had required the mines to improve the food supplied as part of the contract, and the staple mealie meal (maize) porridge was now augmented with fresh vegetables and meat. But these regulations were loosely enforced at best.[40] A 1908 report on the compounds of the Robinson group at Randfontein condemned several of them as "unfit for human habitation." The food at all of the Robinson compounds was inadequate even by the minimum standards of the ordinance and frequently withheld as a punishment.[41] Ten years later these compounds still received criticism from the bureau. Only the Robinson mines were known to punish the work-force in this way, but inspectors' reports of the period indicate that conditions were far from adequate in many of the compounds.[42] As a result the incidence of illness, particularly from pneumonia and dietary deficiency diseases, remained high.

Most of the workers on the mines were recruited for underground mining which in comparison with surface work was onerous, dangerous, and therefore very unpopular. Surface workers could be found in sufficient numbers from volunteers presenting themselves at the mine. At this time, the principal underground task was hand-drilling in the stopes to prepare the ore bodies to be charged with dynamite and blasted. The day's work began at four or five A.M. when the compound police rousted the workers out of their bunks and began moving them to the shaft head for the trip below ground.[43] At some mines there would be an issue of mealie meal porridge or bread and perhaps tea before work began, but at others no food at all was given in the morning. On arrival at the shaft the workers found themselves packed into cages for the descent via the winding apparatus to the working levels of the mines. The cages were usually extremely overcrowded and there were many accidents.[44] Occasionally, it seems, the mines used the ore trucks, the skips, to transport the miners. Once underground, the miners faced a wait of two or three hours before work could begin. Safety regulations required that a white ganger check the stopes before start of the new shift, and the whites did not begin to go underground until perhaps 7 o'clock, hours after the blacks had been herded from their compounds.[45] These rules were among the important of the colour bar provisions protecting the gangers from black competition. It was recognized by just about everybody that the "boss boys" were perfectly capable of checking the stopes for misfired charges. In many cases they were actually doing it but only after the ganger had arrived underground.

The "hammer boys," who did the drilling, worked in teams under a "boss boy" and a ganger. On most mines at this time, the first task of the team when it finally arrived in the stope was to clear the rock broken during the previous shift into the ore boxes and trucks ready to be trammed by other workers to the shaft and hauled to the surface. Until this was done, of course, they could not get to the ore body at the stope face and begin drilling. Few of the mines recognized this onerous period of "lashing" (shovelling) as part of the day's work, and on most no portion of the wages for the shift was attributable to the lashing.[46] Payment was based instead on completion of the required hole for the dynamite charge. Specifications on the different mines varied but usually called for a hole, hand-drilled into the ore body to a minimum depth of thirty inches but more usually thirty-six, forty-two, or even occasionally forty-eight inches (reduced after 1910 to a standard thirty-inch minimum). Workers who could exceed the minimum, and many did, received a small bonus for each additional inch. On the other hand, in the frequent case that the task was not completed, the workers usually received no payment at all even if the hole was only an inch or two short of the requirement. In that event, a "loafer's ticket" was issued and the shift did not count toward the completion of the contract. All of the evidence indicates that the loafer's ticket system was rife on the mines and a well-recognized way of cutting labour costs. Since much of the underground mining was handled on a contract system in which the white ganger was debited for the cost of supplies and labour and paid according to results, there was a direct incentive to cheat blacks of their wages in this way.[47] Eventually the state legislated to require the mines to make partial payment for holes which were short of the required minimum and to provide a probationary period for the new miner before a loafer's ticket would be issued. Owing to the high proportion of cancelled shifts, the typical six-month contract, actually requiring 180 completed shifts, could take nine months or even longer to complete.

To perform their daily task, the "hammer boys" used a sharpened piece of drill steel and a hammer. They worked in a crowded, narrow stope which offered, if they were lucky, perhaps three or four feet of head room. Ventilation was rudimentary, the stope dusty from the broken ore and usually very hot. In all but the best mines, sanitary arrangements were practically nonexistent, and the men relieved themselves in the drives and stopes. They worked in the dark with only a few candles providing dim illumination. If the worker was unfortunate, out of favour with his ganger, or simply very efficient (such a worker was more likely to complete a difficult task), he might be assigned a hole in an inaccessible part of the stope, perhaps directly overhead, requiring him to hammer at an awkward and painful angle and making the task doubly difficult to complete. Despite these obstacles many of the "hammer boys" became sufficiently expert and sufficiently strong to finish their drilling before noon, even after the long wait at the shaft and an hour or more of lashing. In that case, he was free to leave the stope, but usually faced another long wait at the underground station before the cages were reattached to the winding apparatus to take the men to the surface. During most of the shift, the shafts were not available to transport men, since they were hauling skips loaded with ore. Most of the workers would not get back to the surface, therefore, earlier than the late afternoon. For others, the day's work did not end until well into the evening, twelve or fourteen hours after they had left the compound in the morning.[48]

After work, the miners faced the long walk back to the compound. Before 1912 or 1913 when major improvements were undertaken, few of the mines had change houses at the shaft head. Consequently, the overheated workers returned to the compound dressed in ragged shorts which is all that most of them wore underground. In winter, this contributed to the very high incidence of pneumonia which carried off huge numbers particularly of the so-called "tropical migrants" from the regions north of 22° SL. The main meal, usually a shovel of mealie meal with perhaps a scattering of vegetables and some rough meat or offal on Saturday, came after work. The workers were then free for whatever remained of the day, but they had to be ready to go underground again before dawn the following morning.[49] This was the pattern six days a week. Under the caption, "the Life of the Mine Native," the *Rand Daily Mail* succinctly described the plight of the work-force:

The contract Kaffir on a mine demands so little. He puts up with so much. In every phase of mine life one sees this. Whether it is a matter of waiting about in wet clothing for a skip, or shivering on the surface in the early morning air of winter, or doing a couple of hours lashing without being paid for it, or receiving indifferent hospital treatment, or getting a loafer's ticket for not being able to drill 30 inches under almost impossible conditions, or any one of a dozen other matters, the Kaffir is cheap. It only costs 10 [pounds] to kill him and 30 to fifty [pounds] to deprive him permanently of all earning powers.[50]

At this time, the industry provided practically nothing in the way of recreation for the work-force. At mines close to Johannesburg or other Rand towns, the workers could leave the compounds for whatever comforts or entertainment might be available in a nearby black "location." Mines which had such locations in their vicinity always had much less trouble recruiting a work force than those which did not. At the locations, the off-duty "bachelor" migrants might hope to find women and usually liquor which was banned by law but readily available. Liquor and home-brewed beer were in fact routinely found in the mining compounds themselves, despite endless police raids and searches by the compound staff. Since the availability of liquor was another well-recognized recruiting device, government officials who were attempting to enforce prohibition knew that compound officials and labour contractors were often involved in the illegal traffic. As part of the food ration, most of the mines served a low-alcohol version of traditional African beer which had been approved by the state. This was justified on dietary grounds, since the brew was thought to have antiscorbutic properties. Not surprisingly, given the conditions under which they lived and worked, many of the workers were after stronger drink. During the 1890s, rampant drunkenness, particularly on weekends, was the pattern on many mines, and a large percentage of the work-force would be incapacitated when work resumed on Monday morning. Closer government supervision after the Anglo-Boer War produced some improvement, but the problem remained serious throughout the period covered by this study.[51]

The harsh working conditions, poor food, excessive liquor and beer consumption, and unhealthy compound environment contributed to very high rates of illness, accident, and death. Closer government regulation and grudging investment by the industry in improved facilities produced slow, halting improvement in the two decades after 1902, but first-time recruits and others in certain high-risk categories remained very vulnerable throughout the period. Recruiting from north of 22° SL was finally banned when the industry failed to reduce mortality rates in excess of 100 per thousand per annum on many of the mines. These deaths resulted mainly from pneumonia, but would have been many fewer had the mines provided proper hospital and nursing care. Public exposure of this industrial health scandal finally forced systematic action after about 1912. Many thousands of workers died, however, before the causes of high rates of illness and accident were properly addressed. Official death rates actually underestimated the real extent of the mortality, since many workers were repatriated when they fell ill and died after leaving the mine.[52] Most of these deaths were never recorded.

Throughout the period covered by this study, the hospitals and dressing stations provided by the mines constituted part of the problem rather than the means of alleviating it. As late as 1921, a Union medical inspector described the underground dressing stations, manned often by ill-trained African attendants, as "death traps." Injured workers received essential first aid there, and many hours might elapse before they would be moved to hospital. The aid stations were actually major sources of infection which was ever-present in the hot, unsanitary underground passages of the mine. Even a slight wound could result in catastrophic, uncontrollable infection and a slow, grisly death. Workers who found themselves in a mine hospital whether as a result of illness or accident stood a very good chance of not leaving it alive. The director of native labour repeatedly condemned the standard of hospital care on the mines. In 1913 after prolonged efforts to secure improvements, he still complained that the care given by most mine medical officers was "shockingly inadequate."[53] Very few companies employed full-time doctors in their black hospitals. The mine medical officer typically combined his duties there with an extensive private practice. He might attend the hospital for perhaps an hour a day when he could be faced with a large number of acute cases, many more than could be properly examined in the time available. He would be unavailable at night and usually during an emergency. In these circumstances he could not properly supervise the poorly trained white staff and black orderlies.

The Native Labour Bureau was convinced that many of the pneumonia deaths were attributable to the neglect and poor standard of nursing of the mine doctors and staff.[54] At a time when sulfa drugs and penicillin were unavailable, intensive supervision and nursing care were considered essential to recovery from serious pneumonia. Very high death rates among pneumonia patients in the mine hospitals followed from the failure to provide this. During 1911, the Union's first minister of native affairs, Henry Burton, was shocked at what he saw on a tour of several mine hospitals.[55] His visit came nearly a decade after the government first began to press the mines to improve their hospital services. To the minister, the persistence uncorrected of this grave health situation was a measure of the cynical unconcern with which most mining companies responded to the medical needs of their workers. Adequate standards of hospital care emerged only in the decade after about 1912 when, at the insistence of the government, the Chamber of Mines began to underwrite the cost of medical research and to provide high-quality centralized hospital services. Before that, the mines' medical services were condemned by virtually every disinterested observer who saw them.[56]

For the vast majority of black mineworkers, therefore, their period of employment in the industry was cheerless, onerous, and very dangerous. It was also closely controlled. The mines had already evolved the essential elements of the quasi-military organization which still characterizes the system today. Simple logistical considerations, involving the movement of thousands of miners daily from their compounds to their workplaces far underground, required strict regimentation. Much of this supervision was provided by black collaborators–"boss boys" underground, compound police on the surface. In these years many of the mines used Zulu collaborators in these supervisory jobs, particularly in the police. Since the Zulu were underrepresented as an ethnic group among the mineworkers, this represented an obvious effort to use ethnic differences and rivalries for control purposes. Policies to segregate the workers by ethnic group in the compounds were similarly designed to prevent combination against management and facilitate control.[57]

While the workers were closely disciplined and controlled, their supervisors were not. Both on the surface and especially underground, Africans faced a high risk of assault from the white staff and the black police. Gangers found guilty of assault faced dismissal from their positions, heavy fines, and even jail terms. Prosecutions were very difficult to bring, however, despite the efforts of the inspectorate of the Native Labour Bureau. Moreover, a white miner who was caught and dismissed would find it quite easy to find a position on another mine. It appears that most cases never came to trial. Fearing reprisals, black miners were understandably reluctant to bring charges. Inspectors found it difficult to prosecute. They would usually only hear of a case several days after the event. The courts were reluctant to convict on the uncorroborated testimony of black complainants. The white gangers usually stuck together, and the suspected assailant might be protected also by the underground officials of the mine, the mine captain and the underground manager.

Against these and other evils, the black miners were far from helpless. In the chapters which follow, many examples are given to show how recruiting for the mines was affected by black perceptions of conditions there. A mine which had a reputation for brutality or where the death rate from disease was high could find itself effectively boycotted. Each mine had its distinctive African name, a name which was often descriptive of conditions which obtained on it. The presence, for example, of an unsympathetic compound manager on a given mine could quickly become widely known, with disastrous effects on recruiting which might take years to overcome. The constant flow of labour to and from the mines ensured that the supplying districts were well informed of changes in conditions there. The recruiters and their "runners" were also important sources of information. It is true that these agents of the mines had an interest to represent conditions as favourably as possible. Misrepresentation was dangerous, however. Workers would boycott a recruiter whom they felt had cheated them. In fact the recruiter was more likely to join in workers' complaints, since his livelihood depended on the willingness of the miners to go to the companies for which he was recruiting. By 1906, the Chamber of Mines' recruiting arm, the Witwatersrand Native Labour Association, was completely discredited in the eyes of the recruits from the South African territories. It was known throughout the country as "Mzilikazi," the name of the first Ndebele king who had led his people on a successful campaign of conquest through the western Transvaal and Bechuanaland before settling in what is now southwestern Zimbabwe. The workers who so identified the WNLA meant the term as an epithet, a synonym for tyranny and oppression. The WNLA got this reputation not least because its rules required agents to recruit for general distribution in the industry without regard to bad conditions on particular mines or worker preferences.[58] Worker distrust of the WNLA was apparently inflential in the collapse of its South African operations, and the chamber never was able to reestablish its presence there. When the mines began to resume noncompetitive recruiting in the South African territories, they were forced to establish an entirely new organization for the purpose. This was the origin of the Native Recruiting Corporation which emerged in 1912. The general superintendent of the NRC, H.M. Taberer, frequently brought workers' complaints concerning conditions on particular mines to the attention of the authorities. He knew that the success of the NRC depended partly on its willingness to support its recruits in this way. Taberer's intervention was instrumental, for example, in the labour bureau's decision to convene the important Crown mines investigation which took place in 1913, and which found much to condemn in the labour practices of one of the industry's largest employers.[59]

Workers' resistance to oppressive or dangerous conditions was not confined to these indirect methods. Particularly brutal white gangers could find themselves waylaid in a dark, deserted part of the mine. Despite the risk to themselves, many miners did bring complaints to the labour bureau inspectors and the not-insignificant number of successful prosecutions for assault may have acted as something of a deterrent.[60] Of course, many workers did not remain on an unsatisfactory mine to make a protest. Faced with a bad situation, whatever the cause, thousands of them simply defaulted. This was particularly the case in the period from 1906 to 1911 when competition for labour was most intense, the size of the labour force was expanding rapidly, and the workers found themselves in a sellers' market. Desertion was facilitated also by inadequate police and administrative systems for the apprehension of defaulters. Heavy penalties for desertion had long been on the books, but by later standards many escaping miners easily evaded prosecution. By 1911, the government in cooperation with the industry had done much to tighten its network of control which produced a sharp decline in the number of successful desertions.[61]

As a further means of protest, the black miners conducted an impressive number of strikes, work stoppages, riots, and go-slows during this period. This was especially the case between about 1913 and the outbreak of the major black strike in 1920. To all of their longstanding grievances was added the sharp fall in the already very low level of real wages as a result of severe wartime inflation. While most of the work stoppages were short-lived, relatively small-scale affairs, a number of them did show Africans organizing their protest among several compounds of the same mine and even between compounds of neighbouring mines. This kind of activity was of course particularly marked during the 1920 strike. It appears that the workers were beginning to perceive their common interest in opposition to the mines. This was despite attempts of the companies to segregate them on an ethnic basis, to isolate the compounds from each other and to intimidate the workers with the massive use of official violence. The number of protests and the defiance shown by the workers of both mine and governmental authority is impressive given the intensity of the reprisals which such stoppages invariably provoked. Official records of the period show the South African Police acting routinely and with great severity in support of the mine officials. The black compound police on most of the mines were notorious for their brutal and officious handling of the workers. The white compound staff usually went about armed, and very many of these protests ended with shooting and much bloodshed. Since the 1913–14 strikes by the white miners, which had resulted in serious violence, the mine officials and the government lived in fear that the black workers would follow the example of the whites. The Buckle Commission had been established in 1913, partly to investigate black miners' grievances in order to prevent outbreaks, but also to suggest control measures and quasi-military methods of dealing with them.[62] Consequently the slightest protest among the workers at this time met with very severe retaliation. Yet the work stoppages continued and even intensified throughout the period of the war.

Impressive as these strikes undoubtedly were, they must not be allowed to mask the reality of a closely controlled, tightly regimented working environment which provided few opportunities for worker protest. Although high rates of desertion are an important indicator of the miners' ability to evade unpopular employers, most endured without overt complaint conditions which even by contemporary standards were frequently appalling. This is true even after full allowance is made for covert forms of protest which have been skilfully identified by Charles van Onselen.[63] Most strikes were quickly suppressed with great brutality and violence. By about 1912, the state had become much more efficient in the apprehension of deserters. The always limited capacity of workers to challenge the system declined steadily after 1920.

An equally controversial dimension of the relations of the mining industry and the state concerns the development of the colour bar and the relationship between the racial division of labour on the mines and the origins and persistence of the migratory labour system. That the two are closely connected is generally agreed. Historians are divided over the nature of the relationship. The origins of the statutory colour bar can be traced to blasting regulations introduced in Kruger's government in the 1890s. Milner's Reconstruction administration wrote into the Labour Importation Ordinance (1904) a much more elaborate and thorough-going racial division of labour. By stipulating that the Chinese labourers introduced under the ordinance would be banned from a long list of skilled and semiskilled mining tasks, the government hoped to overcome the strenuous political opposition which had developed to importation from the Afrikaner political association, Het Volk, and from elements of white labour on the Rand. An anti-Chinese coalition emerged led by Louis Botha and Jan Smuts for Het Volk and by the militant former mine manager, F.H.P. Creswell. Eventually these various discriminatory provisions were consolidated and entrenched in regulations under the Mines and Works Act, 1911.

The few historians who have looked at the origins of the colour bar have approached the problem in a rather reductionist way. So-called liberals and radicals have offered opposed but equally one-dimensional interpretations. Sheila van der Horst presented the classic liberal analysis in her pioneering *History of Native Labour in South Africa*. She did not doubt that the entrenchment of the colour bar could be explained by pressure on government from racialist white trade unionists and allied politicians. This in turn removed from the mine owners any incentive to move away from the migrant labour system as a means of making more efficient use of their black workers:

The social policy which has resulted in the continued use of migratory labour and the compound system has had further consequences in influencing the organization of Native labour on the mines. Employers in the mining industries are prevented from making full use of the capacities of Natives. Consequently they employ Native labour as a relatively undifferentiated mass, and ... they have turned their attention rather to preventing competition from driving up the rates of pay and the cost of recruiting than to devising widespread incentives to Natives to increase their efficiency.[64]

Arguing the radical thesis in direct opposition to this analysis, Rob Davies stood the liberal interpretation on its head: "the racial division of labour, its entrenchment in law, and indeed the imposition of segregation within the work process itself, were a direct product of the pursuit of profit by mining capital."[65] In the same article, he stressed that the "crucial determinant" in the development of racial stratification on the mines was the "subjection of Africans to the 'exploitation colour bars'," that is, to all of the various administrative and legislative measures which served to promote and to entrench the migrant labour system. He argued that the entrenchment of migrancy on the mines by the capitalists forced the white trade unionists to espouse the colour bar as their only defence against cheap black labour. As G. Fredrickson has suggested in his recent study, each of these analyses catches one important dimension of the labour situation on the gold mines in the early twentieth century.[66] Neither interpretation, however, offers anything like a complete explanation of the origins of the mines' peculiar labour system.

The colour bar cannot be seen either as the exclusive product of racial prejudice in the white labour unions or as a necessary result of the pursuit of profit by mining capital. During the late nineteenth and early twentieth centuries, the pattern of labour mobilization and race relations on the mines was still in flux. The colour bar operated much less rigidly, and the migrant labour system itself had not been perfected. The colour bar and the migrant labour system evolved together. While they interacted, the relationship between them cannot simply be seen in terms of cause and effect. Before the 1920s, the Chamber of Mines had not completed the monopsony nor achieved complete control over the recruiters and labour agents required to reduce costs and to wring maximum financial benefit from the cheap labour system. Moreover, the mine managers themselves and their compound managers expressed a good deal of uncertainty about the desirable direction of labour policy. It is true that most viewed cheap migrant labour as essential to a mining strategy based on maximum exploitation of low-grade ore. They believed that the industry could not afford the higher wages needed to tempt the black workers into permanent employment and train them to displace the whites in skilled work and supervision. Almost from the start, however, a minority wanted to stabilize the black work-force, pay it better, provide family housing, and get the resulting benefits in greater productivity. A number of important experiments with this approach can be cited.[67]

In rejecting this strategy, the Chamber of Mines did not simply succumb to the racialism of the white trade unionists and their political allies, as van der Horst argued; nor was its standpoint dictated soley by mining profitability, as Davies suggested. By 1906-7, the militancy of the white workers had become a major factor in industrial relations on the Rand. Several key mining controllers saw that they could replace some of these recalcitrant and expensive whites with their increasingly skilled black workers. This would have involved a move away from migrancy, the development of locations for a large-scale permanent force of married blacks with their families on the Rand, and a willingness to introduce greater pay differentials between unskilled and semiskilled black workers. The Chamber of Mines actively considered but then rejected this option at the time of the 1907 strike. The owners knew that labour stabilization would involve a drastic change of system and much expense. As racialists, several of the key leaders could not believe that a sufficient number of blacks would be capable of the more skilled jobs (even though in a large number of cases they were already doing the work). Some felt a duty to the white community and wanted to maintain a stratified, racially hierarchical society with the whites clearly on top. Although willing, even eager, to confront the white unionists whose strike they broke in 1907, the Randlords were more reluctant to oppose the new Botha-Smuts government in the Transvaal. This government had shown its power over mining capital by ordering the repatriation of over 50,000 Chinese workers, a step which most mine owners believed would lead to disaster. Moreover, Smuts particularly had shown sympathy with English-speaking labour on the Rand, flirted with Creswell's theories of an all-white Rand, and expressed a desire to increase employment for whites on the mines, especially indigent Afrikaners. For the mines to embark on migrant labour stabilization, with its corollaries of massive black urbanization and a frontal assault on the industrial colour bar, would directly counter what the government had been trying to achieve, risk further damaging confrontation, and possibly lead to a full-scale alliance between the government and the white miners' union.

Finally, another constituency had to be considered. In the Native Affairs Department, senior officials had opposed the growth of large-scale permanent black settlements on the mines for several years. They argued that such settlements would be hard to control and would become centres of prostitution and crime. They also pointed to probable adverse social consequences in the development of racially mixed slums in the vicinity of the mines.[68] In deciding against a labour strategy likely to promote permanent black urbanization, the mining leaders had in mind all of these factors. Knowing they faced a dangerous set of choices they opted for a decision which minimized risks, involved minor modifications in the existing sytem, and avoided a direct confrontation with the government and the civil service. In the short run, the problem of white labour militancy was handled by the employment of unskilled, mainly Afrikaans-speaking whites as supervisors at low wages.

In fact, among all of the various interests which were concerned about the direction of labour policy on the gold mines, there was a growing awareness of the choices which lay before industry and government on labour matters. In each sector – chamber, the white miners' unions, and government – leaders could be found with fundamentally opposed conceptions of the future of labour policy in South Africa. From the beginning of the conflict over Chinese labour in 1902–3 until the strike of 1922, labour matters stood at the centre of political debate. During this long period, politicians, leaders of the Chamber of Mines, and white trade unionists had to make choices between real alternatives. The direction of labour policy emerged from the balance of these contending forces. Crude racialism sometimes determined policies in the Chamber of Mines just as the pursuit of profit and self-interest powerfully affected the standpoint of the white operator groups.

An examination of recent historiography on the early period of South African industrialization reveals a welcome emphasis on hitherto neglected aspects of the economic history of this racially divided society. The work of Johnstone, Davies, Lacey, and others has done much to expose the role of mining capital in the emergence of the migrant labour system.[69] Yet the preoccupation of these authors with current political concerns led them to some questionable judgments. Like many historians before them, they have tried to identify the historical actors who can be held responsible for today's iniquitous system. An earlier generation of "liberal" historians found much to condemn in the role of the imperial government. By its misguided interventionist strategies at the turn of the century, according to this interpretation, the imperial state provoked a militant Afrikaner reaction leading utlimately to the triumph of apartheid after 1948. Writing over twenty years ago, Leonard Thompson summed up that view: "there can be little doubt that Lord Milner and the Unionist Government wrought harm in South Africa. Encouraging unattainable aspirations among British South Africans, increasing anglophobia among Afrikaners, and doing little to improve the prospects of the non-whites, they made it immeasurably more difficult for the peoples of South Africa to establish for themselves a stable and humane society."[70]

Scorning political analyses of this type, recent writers on the Left have maintained a concern to trace the origins of contemporary evils and suggested that these cannot be attributed either to the legacy of British imperialism or exclusively to Afrikaner nationalism. Instead they find its beginnings in the political economy of national and international capitalism. Marian Lacey, for instance, ended her recent study with the programmatic judgment that modern apartheid has its origins in the emergence early in this century of a "national economic strategy" designed to "ensure that the prime interests of mining capital were secured."[71] Although this approach raised a host of significant questions and lines of inquiry when first suggested by J.A. Hobson, F.H.P. Creswell, and other contemporary radicals, it has ended paradoxically in the Lacey book by obscuring the underlying dynamic which entrenched oscillating labour migration and, more generally, by drastically simplifying the origins of existing economic inequality.[72] A closer examination of the processes of labour mobilization suggests that, far from being the alien imposition of a small group of international capitalists, the mining industry's labour system emerged from the interaction of a variety of conflicting interests within the white community and among black collaborating groups. It was the product of political pressures and economic needs widely diffused in southern Africa's racial and ethnic communities. The very persistence of this system through nearly a century suggests how various and deeply entrenched were the interests which it sustained.

PART ONE

Foundations, 1890 – 1910

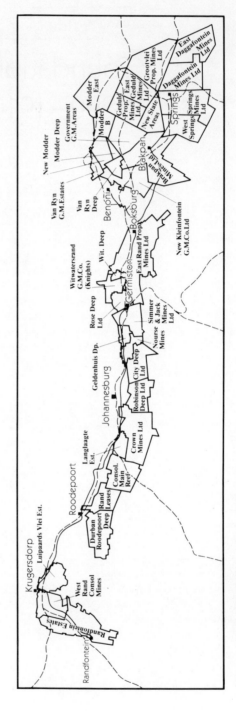

Map 1 Johannesburg and the Witwatersrand

CHAPTER ONE

Mining Capital
and the State under
Kruger and Milner

The decade of the 1890s saw an enormous expansion in gold mining on the Witwatersrand. The industry developed the first of the deep-level mines at this time, which required very large capital investment. Expansion resulted from two main factors. The boom conditions in the share market in 1894-5 and to a lesser degree in early 1899 offered an advantageous time to seek new capital. Companies emerged which never would have been launched in ordinary circumstances.[1] Moreover, the financial houses on the Rand were enabled, through their market operations, to take profits which probably exceeded – at least for some of the groups – the profits from actual mining.[2] After 1895 the possibility of securing windfall profits in this way largely disappeared; henceforward profit depended to a greater extent upon the performance of the mines themselves, including the marginal companies floated during the boom. The second factor which encouraged expansion was the confident belief that working costs would come down through reform in government policies and through technological innovation.[3] Here were further inducements to investment in the development or ore bodies which could not be profitably worked under the then prevailing conditions. That this type of gambling investment was being made may be illustrated from the experience of Rand Mines, a well-managed and highly profitable company controlled by the industry leader, Wernher, Beit/Eckstein. The Rand Mines chairman, L. Reyersbach, later noted that the mines of his group had several million tons of low-grade ore developed in the 1890s and ready for extraction whenever cost reductions made this possible. He regarded the speedy exploitation of these deposits as a matter of priority, and estimated the average yield of this low-grade ore at 16s per ton, compared with an average yield for operating mines of 40s per ton in 1897 and 34s. 6d. in 1906.[4] Here is evidence of an optimism verging upon recklessness.

Within a very short time after the first discoveries, then, the owners became aware that they were dealing with an ore body which presented both unprecedented opportunities and extraordinary difficulties. Ore of this low grade, present in such vast quantities, could only be worked on the basis of sophisticated industrial organization, requiring not only capital on an unprecedented scale for gold mining, but also application of the latest technology in ore reduction works and metallurgical processes. The days of the small company and the individual digger had passed even before the end of the 1880s. The Rand industry did share one characteristic with most previous strikes, however. In the eyes of most investors, the Johannesburg mines remained speculative investments, requiring a high rate of return. When planning for the future, those mining capitalists, who took the long view and were interested in more than windfall profits in the stock market, had to keep these elements of risk always in view. Totally unexpected developments could completely disarrange their capital markets with dramatic suddenness. The whole industry had faced extinction in the early 1890s when the mines encountered at depth resistant ores which defied reduction by any known metallurgical process. Only the fortuitous development of the Macarthur-Forrest cyanide process saved the industry on that occasion. Moreover, the availability of development capital depended not only on factors internal to the industry but also, obviously, on the state of capital markets in London and Europe over which the Randlords could exercise very little influence.

Another important element of uncertainty was contributed by the recurrent political crises of the period, the increasing tension in Anglo-Transvaal relations, and the growing reluctance of the Transvaal government to undertake the reform of its industrial and labour policies which the industry as a whole was coming to regard as essential. At the very time when the mines began to look to the government for greater support, relations were poisoned by the Jameson Raid. The failure of this abortive plot against the republic led to the exposure of several leading magnates who had been involved in what amounted to an attempted revolution. Their motives varied but figuring prominently among them was a determination to secure a government more sympathetic to the mines than Kruger's Boer-dominated state could afford to be. A lurid political trial followed; the courts sentenced the ringleaders to death; they were then dramatically reprieved by the state president, and some of them were deported to England. After the failure of another major reform effort in 1897–8, the largest finance houses gave up entirely on the Kruger regime and eventually threw in their lot with the imperial government. This hastened the crisis which led to war in 1899.

The collapse of the stock market boom late in 1895 and the uncertainties created by the Jameson Raid at the end of the year, brought cost problems to the fore and exposed the precarious position of the low-grade producers. When the stock market collapse was followed immediately by the political crisis, investors fled from Rand shares and remained wary until the short-lived partial recovery in the first half of 1899. Even firms closely involved with Kruger's government and not involved in the attempted revolution suffered serious losses at this time. The most important of these were the Johannesburg Consolidated Investment Company, representing the Rand interests of the flamboyant Barney Barnato and his nephews, the Joel brothers, and the J.B. Robinson company, Randfontein Estates. Both firms were heavily committed to low-grade mining, and experienced serious difficulty after 1896. Testifying before the Industrial Commission of Inquiry in 1897, the JCI consulting engineer, W.L. Hamilton, estimated that his group had £2 million tied up in idle plant and equipment.[5] E. Brochon of Randfontein Estates noted in his evidence that, while the reform demands of the industry would produce only an 8 per cent reduction in working costs, this was a matter of "life and death" for many companies.[6] Even the dominant company, Wernher, Beit/Eckstein, briefly considered closing a number of its poorer mines in 1897.[7] Though hard evidence is lacking, it appears that the operating mines were also working the richer ores in the prewar period and leaving as much of the low-grade ore in the mines as possible. It was not then a requirement, as it is today, that a company work to the average grade of the ore in the mine.[8] Both because of rising costs and because of the difficulty of raising development capital in a stock market for Rand mining issues which remained depressed and uncertain, the three years preceding the outbreak of the Anglo-Boer War constituted the most serious crisis for the mines since the temporary collapse of 1890–1 when technical problems had threatened its survival. A solution to the crisis of 1896–9 had to be sought in the political sphere.

As the sources of easy profits began to disappear, the deficiencies of the Kruger government and the high cost of labour became of more serious concern: "it is generally recognised that the gold industry on the Rand is now entering upon a period of transition ... There can be no doubt that the Transvaal mining industry is as yet but in its infancy. There are millions of tons of reefs in the country all containing gold in small quantities. The great question is how to extract gold at a sufficiently low cost to show a profit ... The most acute of the difficulties under which the mining industry struggles may be set down to unskilled government and unskilled labour."[9] For the period immediately after the Jameson Raid, there is considerable evidence that economic pressures of this sort had begun to force a response from the controllers of the industry.[10] Not surprisingly, the executives of the weakest, financially very vulnerable firms responded most quickly and directly. Two of the Randlords previously friendly to the Kruger government had suffered seriously from the share market collapse. By 1896 both Barney Barnato of Johannesburg Consolidated Investment and J.B. Robinson began openly to demand reform from the government. Within a year,

Robinson seemed to abandon his alliance with Kruger altogether and gave financial support to the state president's opponents in the presidential election campaign of 1897–8.[11] As these and other groups began to look more critically at the policies of the government and at some of the costs of chronic political and personality differences within the industry, a more united Chamber of Mines began to emerge. The industry now displayed a greater willingness to come together in an effort to reduce costs than ever before.

The group controllers did not find it easy, even in their new, straitened circumstances either to achieve or to maintain unity. To all of the old rivalries between them, they had added after the Jameson Raid a formal split in the industry. Those companies which had not been involved in the conspiracy left the Chamber of Mines to form their own association.[12] Historians have stressed the purely political motives of these dissidents.[13] They were Germans who hoped that the raid would discredit the "British" firms and lead to a German ascendancy in the Transvaal. Or they hated Rhodes and wished now to take advantage of the fall of the Colossus and his friends. As a result of Jameson's invasion of the Transvaal, Rhodes had been forced to resign as prime minister of the Cape Colony, and he also lost control of the management of the Gold Fields company. His business rivals now hoped to exploit these developments in order to overtake the companies which he and several key associates had controlled. Support for this judgment can be found of course in the surviving statements of the members of the new Association of Mines. J.B. Robinson, George Albu, and others of this group all condemned the raid. Some went further to suggest – correctly as we now know – that the imperial government had itself conspired against Kruger's republic.[14] Behind this strident rhetoric lurked other, more mundane motives, however. With the two largest and financially most powerful mining houses, the Gold Fields and Wernher, Beit/Eckstein, discredited by the Raid, their rivals had economic motives to put as much distance between themselves and the guilty companies as they could. Amandus Brakhan, Johannesburg manager of A. Goerz and Company and one of the leaders of the association, made just this point to Georges Rouliot, a senior Eckstein partner in Johannesburg. The members of the association counted on favourable treatment from Kruger's government and hoped in this way to escape the financial crisis confronting the entire industry.[15] Even the press saw material motives behind their anti-British, pro-republican rhetoric: "in our mind there is little doubt that the Association thought it could 'better itself' by abstaining from the Chamber's meetings."[16] Untainted by involvement in the abortive coup and protesting their loyalty to the old regime, the dissident members of the association expected substantial material rewards for their loyalty.

By late 1896, the members of the Association of Mines had come to doubt that their hopes would be realized. Before long the loyalists in the chamber began to find their former colleagues more willing to cooperate on a range of common issues. For instance, the two groups worked jointly during 1897 to put pressure on the Industrial Commission of Inquiry which the republic had finally appointed to investigate the grievances of the industry. All agreed that the mines must be united if there was to be any chance of significant concessions from the state on railway rates, the high cost of dynamite charged by the monopolists, labour policy, and related matters. The association and chamber executives met frequently together to plan their strategy at the forthcoming hearings of the commission.[17] Through the first half of 1897, suspicion between the two groups remained great, however. There was active personal dislike between individuals in the two camps; and the members of the association continued to hope that their political loyalty would receive its material reward from the republic. Yet the countervailing pressures making for unity continued to grow stronger. When Kruger's advisers failed to implement most of the major concessions to the industry recommended when the Industrial Commission issued its report late in 1897, the effect was to push the mining houses toward reunification.[18] In November, a reconstituted Chamber of Mines once more took over representation of virtually the entire industry.

Even before this was achieved, the establishment of better relations within the industry made possible some very important initiatives on labour policy. Not only did the groups agree to reduce wages and establish an industry-wide standard, but they also cooperated in the formation of the Rand Native Labour Association, forerunner to the WNLA. To make these measures effective, they combined to pressure government for more efficient administration and control of the migrant labour force. As early as 1890, the Chamber of Mines wrote candidly to the government that "Private enterprise has repeatedly failed in attempting to organize and maintain an adequate supply of Kaffirs. The task must be undertaken by the public authorities, and the Chamber trusts that the Government will lend it their indispensable assistance."[19] Specifically, the industry requested a more vigorous enforcement of the pass law, measures to stop the "molestation" of Africans en route to the mines, and the creation of depots along the main routes to shelter migrant workers. In addition the chamber wanted direct encouragement of mine labour by government officials in the rural areas.[20] Failure of the government to act effectively in these matters[21] led the industry in 1893 to establish a Native Labour Department of the Chamber of Mines in an effort to coordinate policy and to reduce competition for labour among the groups.[22] William Grant became the chamber's native labour commissioner and inaugurated the close relations which existed from then on between the Chamber of Mines and the industry's various recruiting organizations. Inadequately staffed, starved of resources, and without the means of enforcing a common policy on the industry, this department was at first no more successful in handling the problem than the chamber itself had been before 1893.

In 1895 the Chamber of Mines, after several years of agitation, induced the Volksraad to enact a special pass law applicable in "labour districts" (defined under the act to coincide with mining districts). The act had been drawn up for the industry by the native labour committee of the chamber using Natal models. The new pass law provided for a rudimentary form of influx control, restricting access to the towns; and it required Africans to wear a metal arm badge (amended later to a requirement that an official pass be carried), numbered as a means of identification. The act prescribed penalties for various offences, particularly desertion from employment.[23] The republic also had a general pass law applicable outside mining districts and likewise designed to control the flow of labour.[24] Moreover, the Master and Servants Act (a legacy of the first British administration of the Transvaal) provided criminal penalties for breach of labour contracts. The requirement of a special pass law for the Rand followed directly from the industry's inability to restrain competition for labour among its own members.

The promise of greater government action to control labour and recruiting practices enabled the groups to initiate their plans to reduce wages and to establish a cooperative recruiting system. Most members of both the chamber and the association signed the wage agreements cutting rates by 30 per cent in two stages, one in late 1896, the second a few months later. The participants adhered to the new schedule despite a widespread though short-lived work stoppage by the black miners and the subsequent departure of a number of them. (These efforts by black mineworkers to organize combined opposition to the wage reductions were short-lived. Rinderpest and other problems in the African rural areas forced a large number of peasants to seek employment on the mines in the first part of 1897 and more than offset the departure of the protesters.) The same firms participated in the Rand Native Labour Association which also emerged from this round of negotiations. All of the members of the Association of Mines except the Robinson group joined the new labour organization.[25] They hoped that eventually the RNLA would succeed in driving out the independent recruiters and labour "touts" who had come to control the labour supply as a result of endemic suspicion and rivalry between the mining groups themselves.

The new labour supply company failed to justify fully the hopes of the men who had set it up. The mines continued to compete aggressively for labour; the independent labour touts and thieves were not driven from the business. But the new arrangements constituted a significant advance over the purely voluntary coordination which the Chamber of Mines had tried to organize through its Native Labour Department established in 1893. The

1896–7 agreements stipulated that the labour records of the participating firms would be subject to audit as a means of enforcing compliance. Moreover, the member companies set up a joint committee of the association and the Chamber of Mines to work toward even closer cooperation in labour matters. Early in 1897, as a result of the temporary influx of black workers to the Rand owing to the rinderpest epidemic spreading rapidly through southern Africa, the committee was able to implement the second stage of the proposed 30 per cent wage reduction for unskilled workers. Despite continuing problems of enforcement, these measures did produce some significant savings in labour costs.[26]

During the 1890s, the cheapest and easiest recruiting took place on the Rand itself. Mine managers regularly "recruited" their labour from each other. Labour touts and African runners in the pay of one mine management would procure desertions from the compounds of neighbouring mines through promises of better pay or conditions.[27] Some of these touts were freelancers, paid by the head; others seem to have been salaried employees of the various mines. As long as no ready means existed of identifying deserters, it proved impossible to control this activity. The new pass law was designed specifically to eliminate "thefts" of labour from one mine by another. Very significantly, the implementation of the new pass law in 1896 coincided with the wage reduction agreements of late 1896 and early 1897[28] and with the formation of the Rand Native Labour Association. Since the group controllers could not restrain the fierce labour competition of their own managers, the effectiveness of the wage agreement and the new recruiting organization depended on the republican administration.[29] In effect they wanted the state to act as referee, and through the pass law to lay down rules which would curb destructive competition for labour. J.P. FitzPatrick wrote: "it seems to be a fact that practically all the Compound Managers ignore the provisions of the Pass Law and they re-employ deserters freely. We are helpless to prevent this in the face of the Government's inaction and the gross maladministration of the law ... Although we censure these men as much as we like, we are not prepared to proceed to the extreme of sacrificing a manager for breaches of this kind ... Notwithstanding all the fulminations of Directors, no Manager would dismiss or prosecute a Compound Manager who had been of value to him."[30]

With the managers and the recruiting staff raiding each other shamelessly for labour and employing any available labour tout and thief for the purpose, prospects of genuine cooperation in recruiting were not good. Quite unfairly, the Kruger government received the blame for the situation and found itself condemned for "maladministration" of the pass law even though the main offenders, as FitzPatrick acknowledged, were senior mine employees themselves. Unsurprisingly, the "theft" of labour remained a problem (though now on a reduced scale) up to the outbreak of war.[31]

Despite continuing difficulties which frustrated repeatedly efforts to eliminate competition for labour among the mining houses, the agreements of 1897 concerning wages and joint recruiting constituted a major advance over anything achieved previously. They were accompanied by efforts to reorganize the recruiting system in Mozambique, already the main supplier of black labour for the mines. At the request of the industry, Kruger's government negotiated with the Portuguese to regularize access to the colony for licensed mine labour recruiters and to adjust the heavy fees which the Mozambique administration levied on emigrating black workers (or at least on those whom they could catch). The Transvaal-Mozambique agreement of 1897 offered major concessions to the Portuguese administration which already supplied over half of the gold mines' black labour supply. The new agreement confirmed customs concessions negotiated in 1875 by the government of T.F. Burgers, under which Mozambique received most-favoured-nation status. Concerning imported goods arriving in the Transvaal via Lourenço Marques, transit duties were not to exceed those levied by the British coastal colonies. The railway clauses of the agreement stipulated that rates would be adjusted to protect the Delagoa Bay line's one-third share of the traffic in the event that the Cape and Natal embarked on another rate war as the Cape had done in 1895. In a not very successful effort to exclude the rapacious independent labour touts, the governments agreed that only recruiters employed by or under formal contract to employers should be licensed. By early 1897, the new Rand Native Labour Association and other mine labour companies had expanded their efforts in various parts of the Portuguese East African colony.[32] The agreement of 1897 was the forerunner of the better known *Modus Vivendi* which the Milner regime negotiated with Mozambique at the end of 1901. The latter confirmed and extended the concessions which Kruger's government had earlier negotiated.

At the request of the chamber the republican government also acted against the illicit liquor dealers who swarmed on the Rand, and in 1897 it finally legislated the total prohibition of sale to Africans. The mining law of the republic, furthermore, was notoriously favourable to the big interests. Though much of this legislation was badly administered, it does reveal very well the extent to which Kruger's government, despite its post-raid suspicions of the industry, was drawn into a close alliance with it. After the war, the Master and Servants Act and the liquor law, like the pass laws, were taken over by the Reconstruction government with only changes in detail.

In pursuit of favourable legislation, the industry soon found itself working closely with government officials. Both as members of official chamber deputations and on an individual basis, mining leaders had easy access to the republican executive, including the state president himself.[33] J.B. Robinson used his good knowledge of Afrikaans and his initially friendly relations with Kruger to the distinct advantage of his various Randfontein enterprises.[34] Some companies maintained an office in Pretoria. The Wernher, Beit/Eckstein group deputed one of the partners to handle the "Pretoria work," much of which involved acting as a kind of lobbyist. These activities cost money. Christian Joubert, the "chief" of mines, and other government officials received presents, shares on favourable terms, and other inducements. The chamber tried to "improve" the Volksraad by bankrolling members thought favourable to the industry, a fruitless but costly business. The mine owners also tried to buy support in the presidential elections of 1893 and 1898 and met with similar lack of success.[35] During the 1898 campaign, J.B. Robinson in cooperation with Wernher, Beit/Eckstein channelled funds to the support of Schalk Burger and P.J. Joubert against Kruger, with Robinson himself playing the improbable role of clandestine campaign manager and bagman.[36]

In the rural areas, particularly of the northern Transvaal, the touts put a number of the native commissioners on the payroll.[37] In return these men either bribed or more likely coerced African chiefs and headmen to turn out levies for the mines.[38] They achieved considerable success, and by 1899, the northern Transvaal was a significant source of African labour for the mines. Moreover, it appears that the mines had begun to price the republic's farmers out of the labour market. In an apparent attempt to offset this, the Volksraad enacted a measure in 1896 providing for the payment of chiefs in return for agricultural labour. Those who provided over fifty labourers in a year were to receive five shillings a head. Lesser bounties were prescribed for smaller numbers.[39]

Relations between the government and the industry deteriorated steadily after 1896 and were brought to a crisis by the growing diplomatic conflict between Great Britain and the South African Republic. As part of a militant campaign against republican independence, imperial officials took up the grievances of the Chamber of Mines, and several of the leading companies found themselves drawn into the struggle. When various efforts by neighbouring colonial governments to mediate failed, war broke out in late 1899 and produced two and a half years of bitter struggle and devastation. The disruption caused, the deterioration of plant and equipment, and the loss of interest upon invested capital owing to the suspension of operations exacerbated cost problems for the mines. In the aftermath of war, the mining houses had to deal with the consequences of their expansionist policies in the 1890s. On the basis of prewar investment decisions, they had already committed themselves to low-grade mining and thus to the cost constraints which this involved. With the return of peace, they naturally wanted to restore profitable operations in the shortest possible time. Their anxiety to get control over mining costs sometimes led them into actions which were simply short-sighted. For instance, the black wage rate of thirty shillings (minimum per month of thirty shifts) established just after the war was absurdly low and counterproductive. Since Africans were already extremely reluctant to return to the mines, any reduction of wages could be expected only to aggravate the shortage. The industry itself recognized this and at the end of 1902, returned to the (still low) fifty-shilling average established in 1897.[40]

Even before the formal end of hostilities in the Peace of Vereeniging in May 1902, the mining industry and the government began the formidable task of rebuilding the African labour force on the Rand. By mid-1899, the mines had over 100,000 blacks in employment, and of these only a few thousand remained in early 1902. Although a popular contemporary view was that the black population had done well out of the war and no longer needed to accept such unattractive employment as mine work underground, there is little evidence for this inherently improbable notion. What is clear is that in 1902 and 1903, the military and civilian administrations continued to use a huge number of workers for railway and harbour work and for the repair of war damage. These employers simply paid better than the chamber's reduced rate which applied during most of 1902, and they offered much more congenial working conditions than the mines with their disease-ridden compounds and dangerous underground conditions. Disrupted communications in many districts also inhibited the flow of labour to the Rand.

Despite the successful renegotiation of the *Modus Vivendi* at the end of 1901, Chamber of Mines recruiters were not able to resume operations in Mozambique until well into the following year, and they required much longer than that to establish the elaborate network of camps needed before any large-scale recruiting could begin. In the eastern Cape, African peasants remained reluctant to accept mine employment until more serious distress throughout the Transkei and Ciskei coupled with a massive recruiting effort subsequently mounted by the industry left them little choice in the years after 1905. Before the war, the mines had recruited substantial numbers from the northern Transvaal, relying on the coercive methods of local native commissioners whom they bribed for the purpose. The Milner administration was slow to reestablish control over these districts after the war and its officials risked dismissal if they accepted favours from the industry. Although eager to assist the mines in recruiting and pressed to do so by Godfrey Lagden, the Transvaal commissioner of native affairs, magistrates and native commissioners had to be circumspect in their methods. As a result, levels of African employment on the mines remained well below those of 1899 for several years.

Since both the industry and the Reconstruction government badly needed not merely restoration but a substantial enlargement of the supply, the continuing shortfall led irresistibly to the demand for labour importation.

The case for the introduction of foreign indentured workers was made in the majority report of the Transvaal Labour Commission (1903) which Milner had established for the purpose, and the first Chinese workers arrived on the Rand at the end of 1904. The decision to opt for labour importation did not in the least diminish the pressure on the government from the mine owners for a range of administrative measures which would enhance the local supply of unskilled workers, although it did lead the WNLA to reduce its recruiting efforts in some of the less promising South African recruiting districts.[41]

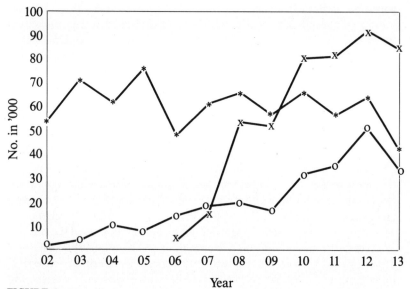

FIGURE 2

Mineworkers Received, All Sources, 1902–13

SOURCES: Chamber of Mines and WNLA *Annual Reports;* Native Labour Bureau estimates.
* WNLA recruits.
o Voluntaries, including new arrivals only, not transfers from the mines or other employment.
x Contractors' and non-WNLA recruits, including NRC for 1913 only.

Under the Reconstruction administration a much closer working alliance developed between mining leaders and the government than had been possible during the Kruger years. At last the mine owners had, as they thought, a regime committed to the maximum exploitation of the Rand and equipped to be both honest and efficient. Even those magnates who had been closest to Kruger's government now expected immediate and far-reaching reforms. The Chamber of Mines lost no time in making its wants known.[42] As early as 1900, the chamber suggested that the government take over entire responsibility for mine labour recruiting. In a rare display of good judgment, the government refused this request, one indication that Milner had no intention of serving the industry at the expense of his broader sociopolitical objectives. In fact the Crown Colony government always had to balance the demands of the mines with the other claims upon it. The priority given to rural development (the so-called colonization schemes), for example, led frequently to conflict with industrial policy. Since the charge of capitalist domination was already current, both in Britain and in South Africa, Milner had strong political reasons to avoid identifying the government too closely with the mining industry.[43]

Shortly after civilian rule was reestablished in the Transvaal in 1902, the government raised direct taxes on mining revenues substantially. Authorities resurrected the republic's moribund profits tax (legislated in 1898) and raised the rate of tax from 5 to 10 per cent. The extension of the municipal boundaries of Johannesburg rendered residential property of many mines liable to local rates.[44] There was some compensation in a considerable reduction in the price of dynamite. Milner told FitzPatrick, the president of the chamber in 1902, that the mines would have to look for their savings not to the area of direct taxation but rather to improved administration.[45] What this meant in terms of labour policy soon became clear. Although declining to establish a state-run recruiting system, officials provided fundamental administrative support for Chamber of Mines' efforts to reduce competition for unskilled labour. They reorganized the pass department, appointed inspectors, and set up a "finger impression" branch to facilitate positive identification of deserters.[46] New labour agents' regulations (proclamation 38 to 1901) prohibited recruiting in labour districts.[47] In spite of the expanded system, the mines continued to complain of a high rate of desertion.[48] Desertion did not solely arise from cutthroat competition between rival mine managers. Horrific conditions in the compounds and underground gave Africans ample reason to desert without being incited to it by avaricious labour touts and labour-starved mine managers. Competition among the mines for labour provoked higher levels of desertion, however, and aggravated an already serious problem.

In the first year or so of the new government, several of the magnates became involved in various official administrative jobs. In particular, the partners of Rand's leading house, Wernher, Beit/Eckstein, accepted a number of key posts. Later this close identification with the Milner regime became a serious embarrassment to them.[49] At the lower end of the bureaucratic echelon men with mining company experience were also frequently appointed, notably in the inspectorate established as part of the Native Affairs Department to police conditions on the mines, to check violations of the pass law, and to act as the "protectors" of Africans. At least in the early years this amounted to setting the wolf to guard the flock. That a flow of personnel also took place from the government to the industry

48   Mining Capital and the State

tended to cement the alliance between them. When the Witwatersrand Native Labour Association was established in 1900 to replace the derelict RNLA, its first general manager, Major G.A. Goodwin, had been an official in the Transvaal military government. Before long T.J.M. McFarlane and T.M.C. Nourse succeeded him as joint general managers. The latter had served as officer-in-charge of native affairs before the inauguration of civilian rule. Early in 1902 Frederick Perry, who had earlier served in the Colonial Office, left his post as Milner's imperial secretary to replace Harold Strange as chairman of the WNLA. These men had moved easily in high government circles and now brought their contacts to the service of the mining industry. Indeed, the line dividing industry from government tended at times to blur. Certainly Perry often acted at the head of the WNLA as if he was running a government department rather than a private corporation. On occasion the commissioner of native affairs, Godfrey Lagden, who was himself notably sympathetic to the needs of the mines, felt obliged to criticize Perry for this.

Using the correspondence files of the Native Affairs Department it would be easy to make a case that Lagden and his officials answered rather to the chamber and the WNLA than to their superiors in government. They exchanged an extensive and partly private correspondence on a regular basis. Lagden received the monthly reports of the executive of the chamber as a matter of course. The WNLA also forwarded to him the bimonthly reports of the general managers to the board of management which often contained highly confidential information implying the use of recruiting methods at variance with government policy.[50] Lagden and his secretary of native affairs, W. Windham, met frequently with leading officials of both the chamber and the recruiting association. They treated the chamber with extreme deference. Whenever Lagden had occasion to criticize some industrial deficiency, he preferred to write a private note to the senior official of the company concerned or to speak informally to the president of the chamber. As a result, many complaints did not even come officially to the attention of the government. Mining leaders for their part frequently briefed Lagden and sought his approval in advance of major and even minor policy changes. Frequent informal exchanges and often close personal relations must have reduced the independence of the Native Affairs Department, and the chamber may have intended this. Having been consulted privately by the industry during the planning of policy, Lagden must have found it more difficult to voice official criticism at a later stage.

This close relationship between the mines and Native Affairs Department officials developed at every level of the administrative hierarchy. The department inspectors rarely criticized their opposite numbers, the compound managers. A departmental report on the competence of the latter was notably generous in its assessments, especially in view of the scandalous condition of most of the compounds at this time.[51] The statistics of the department unwittingly gave evidence of just how the inspectors conceived their role. During 1902 and early 1903, these men, who also held the title of "protectors" of Africans on the mines, investigated thirteen cases of assault upon black mine workers by their white overseers and twenty-eight complaints concerning wage irregularities. In the same period well over 3,000 Africans were disciplined for breach of contract and for other statutory offences against their employers. When the Native Affairs Department published these figures, they caused sufficient stir to provoke a question in the British House of Commons and a subsequent inquiry by the secretary of state.[52] Scattered through the files of the department are several references to work stoppages caused by short-lived strikes of black mineworkers. On such occasions, the mine management would invariably contact the nearest inspector. In each case, the inspector ordered the Africans back to work, threatening those who refused with immediate arrest for breach of contract. Officials made every effort to identify the leaders of the strikes and to bring them to trial.[53] Far from being in any meaningful sense the "protectors" of Africans, the inspectors acted primarily in the interest of the owners to enforce a harsh industrial discipline.

However, there is another dimension to the relations between the Native Affairs Department and the mining industry. In the area of health and compound conditions the department did act with vigour and (after a long struggle against complacency and neglect in the industry) eventual effectiveness. Without exception, all of those connected with these matters testified to the bad situation which had prevailed before the war. Throughout southern Africa, a regular traffic existed in black labour for the mines. Once en route to the Rand, an African would typically pass through the hands of two or three labour touts (in effect having been sold from one to the next) before reaching his destination. Those who arrived safely at the mines after running a gauntlet of avaricious labour agents, government officials, predatory farmers, and actual thieves, met a new set of horrors. Among the witnesses before the Transvaal Labour Commission in 1903 were several men with direct experience of compound conditions in the immediate prewar period. A former compound manager at the Crown Reef mine spoke of the "drink-sodden condition, want of discipline and general moral decay" of the Africans on the mine.[54] The Rev. E. Croux described the "fearful corruption and contamination" and the constant illness in the compounds which he had been allowed to visit.[55] Perhaps the most graphic description was given somewhat later in a private letter to Lagden:

No man, with any claim to manhood, could have gone thru those [prewar] experiences and not have realized the indescribable horror of it. To say that at weekend

I carried my life in my hands is putting it mildly; it was a constant case of having to quell riots among natives frenzied with drink, and I fear that in the process I had over and over again to adopt methods which ... would ordinarily have qualified me for gaol. I have never used a revolver tho I always carried one, but I have been thru riots with a heavy sjambok and with that quelled the disturbances but almost at the cost of some natives lives. The horror of it I shall never forget.[56]

Mortality statistics are not available for this period, but the death rate could not have been less than eighty to one hundred per thousand per annum. On some mines and during the winter months these grim figures would be exceeded by a substantial margin.

Very quickly after the return to civilian rule in the Transvaal, the Native Affairs Department began to press for reform.[57] Compound managers were brought under a degree of control and like the labour agents required to hold government licences. Native Affairs Department inspectors began to report on compound conditions and to gather mortality statistics. The reports and the statistics revealed a shocking situation, little if at all improved since the war.[58] Armed with incontrovertible evidence of endemic disease and high mortality on the mines, Lagden approached the chamber to insist upon reform. Lagden's paternalism was outraged by the situation revealed in the inspectors' reports. To effect a transformation became something of an obsession with him. The intention of publishing mortality statistics gave him a lever with which to act on senior mining company officials.[59] Before long improvements began to take place in the compounds.[60] Moreover, the Chamber of Mines itself and the WNLA eventually responded, although at a very leisurely pace, by underwriting inquiries and research into the causes of disease among the black labour force.[61] Even here, however, in an area where Lagden himself expressed concern and took a personal interest, the department treated the mines with great leniency. They received considerable time to carry out the improvements and in the interval protection from adverse publicity. Low-grade mines or mines nearing the end of their productive lives received exemptions from improvements involving the expenditure of large capital sums.

That Lagden was able to persuade the industry to initiate reform had partly to do with its fear of censure by the home government.[62] His department also responded to the mounting evidence that adverse compound conditions seriously interfered with recruiting. WNLA agents in the field, Transvaal native commissioners, and officials of the Cape and Basutoland pointed this out repeatedly.[63] Lagden also used their evidence in his efforts to secure reform. Yet the leaders of the industry responded very slowly to the evidence that their own self-interest would be served by a reduction in mining mortality.[64] Lagden had to resort to threats in order to force improvements. For years he fought with J.W.S. Langerman to get the

Robinson group to provide decent conditions in its compounds. On one occasion, Lagden virtually ordered Langerman to accompany him on a tour of the Robinson compounds. Even this did not work. Only when the commissioner threatened to withdraw the passes from the group's labour force did it begin to act.[65] Even then conditions on the Randfontein mines and in the compounds remained grossly unsanitary and over-crowded for several more years. Eventually, the reluctance of the owners to accept minimum standards voluntarily prompted legislation. The Coloured Labourers' Health Ordinance, 1905, prescribed minimum standards for compounds and food supplied and gave the Native Affairs Department power to enforce compliance.[66] In some respects the ordinance aggravated the health problem in the compounds by establishing minimum standards of air space and ventilation and by requiring concrete bunks and flooring which could be easily sluiced out. As a result the bleak, overcrowded compounds now became windswept and bitterly cold in the high veld winter. This undoubtedly contributed to the incidence of pneumonia and other diseases which carried off enormous numbers of workers, most especially those from the tropical north, in these years. Despite well-intentioned legislation and extended efforts of the Native Affairs Department to make the mines adhere to it, the death rate among blacks on the mines, mainly resulting from disease rather than accident, remained disastrously high for another full decade.

Even the minimal degree of friction generated by efforts to extend some protection over the black work-force tended to be an exception in the generally cordial relations between the Transvaal authorities and the mine owners. The government gave indispensable assistance to the WNLA in its efforts to widen the catchment area of its recruiting operations. The negotiation of the *Modus Vivendi* with Portuguese Mozambique upon terms markedly favourable to that government reflected the priority given to increasing the labour supply. Milner had to resist vehement demands from the Cape and Natal governments for reduction, even elimination of the preferential railway and customs arrangements which the Kruger government had negotiated in 1897. In order to avoid any possibility of antagonizing the Portuguese and jeopardizing the labour supply, rightly judged vital to the rapid restart of mining operations, Milner's Reconstruction government conceded virtually nothing to the coastal colonies and instead confirmed the terms of the 1897 agreement with Mozambique virtually unchanged. These terms must have been highly embarrassing to the high commissioner himself, since they involved trade and other privileges for a foreign state which were denied to the Cape and Natal, constituent parts of the empire. The arrangement violated the cherished principles of imperial unity on which Milner had built his career and could only retard the goal of South African unification, the professed aim of his whole South African policy. Increasing friction between the Transvaal and the coastal colonies on the railway and customs issues remained a major problem for imperial policy-makers right up to the achievement of South African Union. The *Modus Vivendi* was accompanied by a secret agreement (negotiated with the knowledge and consent of the Transvaal government) between the WNLA and the Mozambique authorities. The private arrangement gave the WNLA a near monopoly of recruiting in the territory. Non-WNLA agents simply found their applications for licences declined. The crown colony administration also put effective pressure on London to sanction an experimental recruiting scheme in the British Central African Protectorate (Nyasaland) and made a determined though ultimately unsuccessful bid for access to the labour of the East African territories.[67]

In the Transvaal recruiting areas themselves, government officials also gave priority to ensuring the black labour supply for the mines. Godfrey Lagden made certain that his own native commissioners never forgot their duty to "encourage" mine labour in their districts. Just how far these native commissioners should go to promote the objects of the WNLA was a delicate matter. Early in the Reconstruction period, Chamberlain warned and Milner agreed that there must be no suspicion of forced labour as under the republic.[68] Though the Native Affairs Department respected this instruction, the line between force and persuasion tended to be a fine one. On one occasion, the native commissioner of the northern division wrote in alarm to Lagden that a recent court case had turned up "matter suggestive of forced labour" for the mines. A riot had broken out during the recruiting operations in the area. The native commissioner explained that "the matter resolves itself into the carrying out only of the intricate internal management of a somewhat powerful native tribe." A facility with euphemism in the preparation of official reports evidently helped those working in the Native Affairs Department at that time.[69] Lagden tolerated such incidents so long as they did not draw unfavourable publicity. Indeed the emphasis he gave to the promotion of mine labour almost certainly encouraged his officials to employ methods which could not be officially condoned.[70] Undoubtedly he knew of the methods being employed by the WNLA. Toward the end of the crown colony period, he wrote to Selborne that the WNLA regularly provided "presents and bribes" to Portuguese officials and to native chiefs and headmen: "No doubt, it has been necessary for private [labour] associations to have large amounts of secret service money at their disposal to be expended without question or doubt" – "not corruptly," he added in the margin, "but as a pure matter of business." He asked that this memorandum not be passed on to the new Botha government, which was about to take power in the Transvaal, as it might be "misunderstood."[71]

During these years, the mines certainly, and the government arguably, gave priority to the maintenance of a regular and dependable supply of black labour on the Rand. The Randlords themselves demonstrated repeatedly their inability both to anticipate their own labour requirements for any distance into the future and to predict the supply situation. The problem was, however, complex. In any given month, several thousand migrants would arrive at the WNLA central depot in Johannesburg. These were the Africans recruited by WNLA agents from a catchment area which embraced the subcontinent. In addition a significant number would arrive at particular mines, having made their own way to the Rand as volunteers. Still others were offered at particular mines by the independent touts and labour thieves who continued to swarm on the Rand despite the best efforts of the WNLA to exclude them. The most successful of the touts had networks of contacts among traders and African notables who fed them a steady stream of migrants. In that same month there would be an outflow of several thousand Africans whose contracts had expired, who were repatriated (or simply kicked out of the compounds) because of illness, who had deserted or died.[72] Both the inflow and the outflow fluctuated, sometimes violently, and made planning difficult.

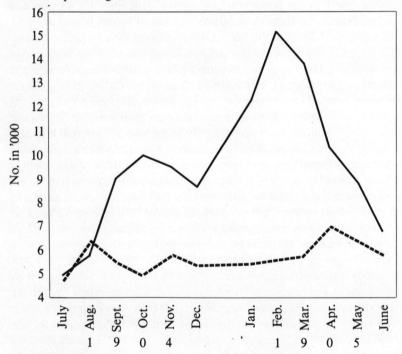

FIGURE 3
Recruiting Levels, Mines and Industrial Works, 1904–5
SOURCE: CS 1085/3142/05

—— influx   ▬▬▬ exodus

In part, these changes in recruiting levels could be anticipated. The rate of recruiting in South African districts invariably fell during the spring and early summer. Black peasants tried either to remain at home during these months or to return from the mines in order to undertake planting. On the other hand, as winter approached in April or May, the mines knew that they could expect a surge in the local supply. More generally, South African blacks would normally accept only short-term labour contracts which added volatility to the supply situation. The importance of Mozambique labour lay partly in the use that could be made of it to offset these uncertainties. Long contracts meant continuity of employment and greater efficiency, both of which offset the high cost of transportation. Mineworkers from Mozambique and the so-called tropical territories had to sign at least one-year contracts, and most stayed for eighteen months or even longer. For the same reason, the mines fought hard to retain access to Chinese labour. Given sufficient warning, the WNLA could adjust its recruiting levels in Mozambique to compensate for the inevitable shifts in the South African supply. Nevertheless, the overall size of the unskilled labour force remained prone to large, unpredictable short-term fluctuations. An increase in recruitment levels in one month would inevitably produce an accelerated outflow six to twelve months later as the contracts of these workers expired. Any sudden change in recruiting levels – either up or down – could catch the industry unawares. A sudden increase in the supply during the first months of 1905, for example, resulted in the mines actually turning away labour. Since the Randlords had been shouting only two years before about the labour shortage, this caused severe embarrassment not only to them but also to the government. An equally sharp downturn in the supply later that same year (like the earlier increase, sudden and unanticipated) produced a panicky reaction in both the chamber and the WNLA.

The WNLA represented an effort to control demand, to prevent wage competition, and to allocate the available labour on the basis of the crushing capacity of member companies (as established by a standing committee of mining engineers). In periods of sufficient supply the system worked fairly well. In periods of falling recruitment levels, trouble invariably followed. Under pressure to maintain production targets, mine managers would start to cheat. They engaged in clandestine recruiting; they offered under the table bonuses, or they attempted to secure a higher rating from the WNLA by exaggerating their crushing capacity and thus claiming a higher proportion of the available supply. The evidence suggests that breaches of the monopsony were endemic both in the last years of Kruger's republic and at intervals during the Reconstruction period. J.B. Robinson, for example, though a member of the WNLA until late 1906, almost certainly maintained his own agents in the Cape who supplied him with "volunteers" outside the WNLA system.[73] Labour agents' regulations in the Transvaal and the other colonies imposed constraints upon the recruiting methods of licensed agents. Moreover, at Lagden's insistence, the WNLA had bound itself to the medical examination of its recruits. Though only loosely enforced, these regulations materially increased recruiting difficulties for agents trying to operate within the law. Clandestine recruiting was, of course, affected by none of these constraints. During periods of adversity, few mine managers could resist the temptation to cheat even though they knew that their advantage would persist only so long as most of the WNLA members bound themselves to its rules.

Shortfalls in the supply inevitably produced acrimony within the association as to just what those rules should be. At such times the question of wage levels became the divisive issue. In public discussion, most industry spokesmen held – as indeed many of them continue to hold – to the target worker argument. On the premise that the black worker had limited needs and would work only until he satisfied them, they drew the unwarranted conclusion that wage increases would actually reduce the labour supply because each worker could achieve his "target" over a shorter contract period. This standpoint ignored massive evidence that the mineworkers were extremely well informed about prevailing rates and that the overall rate of supply was highly sensitive to fluctuations in wage levels. Reflecting these considerations, the mine owners' private views revealed a rather more sophisticated understanding of the relationship of wage rates to the labour supply. During 1902, when available labour fell far short of stated needs, an acrimonious public dispute erupted within the WNLA and the Chamber of Mines on the wage issue. With the resumption of production earlier in 1902, the industry had implemented a minimum rate of wages which at thirty shillings (thirty shifts) was substantially lower than the rate agreed in 1897.[74] As the labour shortage continued during 1902, one group within the industry argued for a return to the 1897 rate, while others, cleaving to the target worker argument, fought for the maintenance of the thirty-shilling minimum. Despite efforts to present a united front on the occasion of the visit of the secretary of state (early in 1903), the chamber could do no more than register the two basic viewpoints on the wage issue.[75] In the end the proponents of the increase had their way. They secured acceptance of a complicated wage scale based on the 1897 agreement, prescribing a "maximum average" wage of fifty shillings per thirty shifts and allowing for limited incentives through piece-work rates.[76]

A much more serious labour crisis in 1906 badly damaged and partly destroyed the monopsony. Trouble followed from the coincidence of recruiting difficulties and a threatened withdrawal of official support from the WNLA as a result of political changes in Britain. The fall of the Unionist ministry at the end of 1905 brought to power Sir Henry Campbell-Bannerman's Liberal party, which was hostile to the Randlords and determined to deny them further supplies of Chinese labour or any other form of official support. The timing of this political misfortune for the Johannesburg mining industry could not have been worse, for they now needed government backing more than ever, particularly on labour matters.

The first few months of 1905 saw a sharp increase in African employment on the Rand, reaching a peak in April when 107,756 black workers were employed in the mines. An equally sharp downturn followed, beginning in September and increasing in intensity for over six months. The low point arrived in July 1906 when only 90,420 Africans were employed. Thereafter a gradual recovery took place, but the April 1905 figure was not exceeded until February 1907.[77] In the event, increasing numbers of Chinese (imported under licences issued before the Unionists left office in December 1905) compensated for the fall-off in African employment, and the total nonwhite labour force remained relatively constant. What alarmed the owners, however, was the almost simultaneous fall of the Unionists and the formation of a Liberal government in Britain committed to ending Chinese labour. They saw the foreign supply endangered at the very time the African labour force was also declining in numbers. The shortfall in the supply of migrant labour together with the major political changes under way from late 1905 both combined with problems of an internal nature between the rival mining houses to put at risk the cooperative recruiting system built up laboriously since 1897.

The crisis over the future of the WNLA had several dimensions. It resulted partly from long-standing rivalries within the industry, not only those which pitted J.B. Robinson's Randfontein group against most of the other houses. Despite agreements to conduct recruiting operations according to WNLA rules, individual mine managers in all of the groups routinely engaged in competitive recruiting whenever this seemed to offer even a temporary advantage. By the end of the Reconstruction period, the industry had begun to take its rivalries into the political sphere, as had frequently happened under Kruger's regime, and to seek from the emerging Transvaal political parties policies favourable to the divergent interests of the different controlling groups. Because the mining industry could not maintain a united front on critical labour issues, the constituent groups became separately vulnerable to outside interests, anxious to break into the lucrative business of mine labour recruiting. From the early days of the mines, independent recruiters and labour contractors had worked the fringes of the business. After 1902, the Chamber of Mines hoped that the WNLA would gradually assimilate or absorb the independents. Since the member mines never gave their loyalty to the recruiting association, however, it did not become powerful enough to achieve this. Political crisis and sharp factional conflict within the industry during 1906 and 1907 gave the independents their chance to turn the tables on the WNLA. By the end of 1906, WNLA recruiters had been largely driven out of their main recruiting centres in the South African colonies. The association stood in very real danger also of losing its hold on Mozambique, as the more successful independent recruiting companies, operating in alliance with the Randfontein group, turned their attention covetously to the largest single source of mine labour. The struggle to control the migrant labour supply would continue intermittently for more than twelve years.

CHAPTER TWO

Toward a Racial Division of Labour on the Witwatersrand

The political upheavals which accompanied the shift from "Milnerism" to self-government in the Transvaal brought serious new complications to the Johannesburg gold industry, as it struggled to restore prewar levels of profitability. Most of these involved, directly or indirectly, the labour supply situation. In Britain, the election of 1906 confirmed in power a hostile Liberal party, avowedly suspicious of Randlords and determined to deny them further supplies of Chinese labour. Even before its election victory, the Campbell-Bannerman government announced major constitutional initiatives designed to devolve responsible government on to elected assemblies in the Transvaal and Orange River colonies within a short interval. Both these proposals seemed to jeopardize mining interests because they threatened to throw power to local political groups hostile to the mines. Leaders of the Chamber of Mines soon became involved in open factional warfare aimed at preventing an anti-Randlord coalition, perhaps in alliance with the Liberals, from taking power in the colony. During the difficult years of postwar recovery after 1902, the industry had received powerful support from the Milner regime in the Transvaal and from the British Unionists. Now, in 1906 and 1907, the threatened withdrawal of state support, both in Britain and South Africa, was menacing in the extreme.

Political turbulence compounded difficult economic circumstances. The gold mines were suffering from chronic shortages of development capital.[1] The industry was also threatened by a serious cost squeeze, and it faced no fewer than four labour crises. In addition to the Chinese labour issue, there was the threatened collapse of the WNLA. Third, an eruption of white worker militancy in the first industry-wide strike disrupted production for several weeks in mid-1907. Underlying the migrant labour problem and the white miners' strike was the fourth issue, the basic question of the racial division of labour on the Rand which defined the scope of employment open to the competing white and black labour forces. Although already entrenched in legislation and fortified by customary operating procedure on the mines, the colour bar now began to display signs of inherent instability. The black mineworkers' improving level of skill and the mine owners' desire to make more productive use of their cheap labour posed a dual threat to the position of the white miners. Any one of these problems by itself would have been serious; together they called into question the future profitability of the gold mines.

From the industry's standpoint, the conjunction of political uncertainty and labour trouble was particularly unfortunate because several of the larger mining groups were on the eve of a major period of reorganization designed to facilitate renewed expansion. Still not fully recovered from the effects of the Anglo-Boer War, they now aimed to make larger output and various economies of scale compensate for declining gold yields and falling profit ratios: "Increased scale of working, wherever practicable, must be our motto. Economy, efficiency, and the advantage to the country of a gradual decrease in working costs are the salient points to bring home to the people."[2] This was the view of Lionel Phillips, senior partner in Wernher, Beit and Company, who had returned to South Africa to resume control of the firm's Johannesburg house in 1906. Like many of his colleagues, Phillips was counting on technological innovation to help bring the mines out of their slump. In 1905 and 1906 the industry had begun to introduce tube mills. This much improved method of crushing ore promised to expand output and to raise gold recovery levels.[3] There was the prospect, too, of large labour savings through the development of a small, hand-held rock drill. Holes for blasting could then be drilled more rapidly with less labour and in narrower stopes so that there would be less waste rock to put through the gold reduction works. Though the perfecting of this tool required the work of many years, the more cumbersome and inefficient machine drill became extensively used on the mines at this time.

Technological innovation would complement financial reconstruction and facilitate the development of much expanded units of production. In these ways, the mine controllers hoped to restore profit ratios and to tempt the wary European investor back to Rand mining stocks. None of this could work, however, without political stability and a solution to the industry's labour problems. Speaking at the annual meeting of the Gold Fields group in London late in 1907, the chairman, Lord Harris, stressed the importance of sympathetic government: "He laid emphasis on the enormous amount of capital and work entailed in connection with the deep levels. Consequently investors needed special sympathy and encouragement [from the state] otherwise capital would be frightened away with results disastrous to South Africa."[4]

Serious concern about working costs lay behind both the emphasis on the need for political peace and the push toward the large-scale financial reorganization then planned or under way in the industry. In 1906, for example, the Wernher, Beit group's Johannesburg house reported on the prospects of three deep-level mines which seemed to be symptomatic. At the Geldenhuis Deep, the Rose Deep, and the Durban Deep there had been a decline in the average grade of ore extracted of 2s.5d., 2s.6¾d., and 4s. per ton respectively. At the same time, costs per ton had increased; the figures were 3s.6½d., 2s.9¾d., and 1s.8d. The firm attributed part of the added cost to the introduction of Chinese labour, and as the Chinese became more efficient, some improvement was expected. But Johannesburg argued that a long-term solution required bringing these and other mines together in enlarged production units.[5] A more broadly based study prepared by a smaller mining house, Consolidated Mines Selection, derived much the same conclusion from a different mix of evidence. Comparing data of 1906 with those of 1902 when production was only just resuming after the war, this study showed sharp increases in production, to 13,302,880 tons milled (from 3,439,927) and working profits, to £5,530,000 (from £2,150 ,000 in 1902); working costs had dropped an encouraging 3 s. per ton. The problem in all these apparently favourable statistics was that profits on a tonnage basis had fallen badly; working profits were off 4s. per ton and net profits 4s.6d.[6] Projecting these figures produced an ominous picture and reinforced the view that remedial action was urgently required.

As a result of studies such as these, a number of very large mining concerns were then in prospect. Some were the product of amalgamation plans; others of anticipated expansion into new mining areas. On the central Rand, south of the city, Wernher, Beit/Eckstein led with the formation of Crown Mines, perhaps the single most important of the new amalgamations. It was completed by 1909. Further east, George Farrar and his associates in the Anglo-French group (Wernher, Beit/Eckstein had a large interest) were negotiating to enlarge substantially the East Rand Proprietary Mines (ERPM). On the other side of Johannesburg at Randfontein near Krugersdorp, J.B. Robinson had plans to expand some existing mines and to resurrect several hitherto moribund companies which he had floated in earlier, more optimistic days. Finally, on the far east Rand, exploration was under way and plans well advanced to open some giant, new mining concerns which would dwarf most of the original mines in the older areas.[7] The successful implementation of these and other ambitious projects depended, as the industry viewed the situation, on establishing political stability, reassuring the investors, and solving recurring labour difficulties: "In the Wernher, Beit-Eckstein group of mines we are merely waiting for the return of confidence – which means the ability to raise fresh capital or the justification for investing capital in hand – in order to start a campaign of expansion on a large scale."[8] These aims were obviously interrelated, but in 1906 and 1907 the immediate problem was political. Without a political solution favourable to the industry, the other difficulties could not be effectively addressed.

This blunt message was at the core of Sir Julius Wernher's speech to the shareholders at the annual meeting of the Central Mining and Investment Corporation in mid-1906.[9] One of the industry's shrewdest and most respected financiers, Wernher had established Central Mining only one year before, partly in order to take advantage of an expected resurgence of interest in Rand mining stocks. That boom had never materialized and now Central Mining's balance sheet was "not a thing to be proud of." Central Mining was an investment company only; it operated no mines and existed only to channel investment funds to established and prospective mining concerns. At the moment, Sir Julius was not a buyer. Worn out by overwork and depressed by the recent death of his partner, Alfred Beit (they had pioneered with Rhodes at Kimberley in the seventies), Wernher bleakly canvassed the prospects of reducing or even selling out the interests of the partnerships in South Africa. This was impossible in 1906 unless he had been willing, as he was not, to sell up at firesale prices. Hence he waited, but he was not sanguine. To the shareholders, he explained that "although prices have lately been exceedingly tempting, we have hesitated, in consideration of the political outlook, to put more money into South Africa until we could see the position more clearly." Wernher complained of recurrent investor panic induced by apparently irresolvable political crisis and added that the gold mines had become "the sport" of the parties. Thousands had been ruined, and there was little prospect of improvement in the future.

Pessimism prevailed at mid-year; by December, Wernher and most of his associates were gloomier still. Senior executives in the Chamber of Mines were correctly predicting an election victory in the Transvaal for the openly hostile Het Volk Nationalist coalition led by Louis Botha and J.C. Smuts for Het Volk and Richard Solomon and H.C. Hull for the English-speaking Nationalists. Much of the cement for this unlikely coalition of former republican generals, Cape lawyers and professionals, Johannesburg politicos and renegade mining men came from a shared hostility to the Chamber of Mines. Their victory would necessarily mean the eclipse of the chamber-backed Progressive Association, a contingency bad enough in itself. Worse seemed likely to follow since the Het Volk people were already known to be in close touch with the British Liberals, many of whom were avowed enemies of the mining industry on Chinese labour and other issues.[10] There was evidence, too, that members of the coalition were flirting with leaders of the now militant forces of white labour. Most unpleasantly of all, these same men had managed to detach the eccentric Randlord, J.B. Robinson, from the Chamber of Mines. Robinson and his henchman, J.W.S. Langerman, openly backed Het Volk. In Britain,

Robinson urged on the Liberals in their opposition to Chinese labour, getting in return their support for his campaign to smash the chamber-sponsored recruiting organization, the WNLA (he was convinced, as usual, that he could do better on his own). To the mining companies grouped around Wernher, Beit/Eckstein and loosely allied in the Chamber of Mines, little but trouble could be expected from the probable political victory of these hostile interests. How would an industry still not recovered from wartime disruption and struggling to attract overseas capital fare at the hands of these dangerous governments in Britain and South Africa? In the worst case, how could it withstand the simultaneous loss of its Chinese labour, the threat to the main source of black labour in Mozambique, and a militant campaign by white labour, backed by the new Transvaal government?

These alarming prospects exercised the mining leaders in the year before the 1907 election. Not surprisingly, chamber politicians, led by FitzPatrick and George Farrar who had been closely identified with the Reconstruction regime and who remained stalwarts of the Progressive party, were the most vocal of the radical pessimists. They gave widespread publicity to the disastrous effects of withdrawing Chinese labour should Het Volk win the election. They estimated that over six thousand Europeans on the mines would lose their jobs; gold output would decline by 40 per cent; and local mining expenditure worth £6.5 million a year would be lost to the city.[11] This was for public consumption, but private correspondence reveals that concern within the industry was genuine and serious. Lionel Phillips wrote to London a few months before the Transvaal election: "to sum up the political and industrial situation, I may tell you in the nearest simile I can find, that Fitz and I both feel held fast in the jaws of a vice, and in a state of the most horrible uncertainty as to which way the screw is going to be turned, a sensation which I know is fully shared by all of you at home."[12] In these circumstances, there could be no question of additional investment; capital expenditure, he noted, "must of course be curtailed in every possible way." He would only sanction projects essential to the group, "which come what may regarding [Chinese] labour, will continue working."[13] Reporting on an interview with the high commissioner, Lord Selborne, in January, Phillips explained that he had issued a stern warning: "capitalists will not put further money into this country so long as they run the risk of hostility and consequent loss through the action of the Legislature."[14]

The Het Volk election victory in February, though expected, increased despondency. FitzPatrick's colleague, Sam Evans, wrote grimly to London: "It is melancholy to reflect that after all our sacrifices the industry should come again under the government of the Boers with a severer burden than it had before the war ... The papers speak of the Progressive members of the new Assembly as likely to form a compact and strong opposition. Can the representative of the mining industry afford to be strong when the new

Government has the industry completely at its mercy as regards the labour question and a host of other questions? The Boers can do us enormous harm by simply remaining passive and letting the existing laws take their course."[15] The absurd note of self-pity masked an element of real concern. These mine owners were alarmed not only by the fear that the new government would act against them in a number of ways, but also by its lack of experience in administration. The South African policies of the British Liberals on labour and the Transvaal constitution had been formulated, they believed, in ignorance of local conditions. Few doubted that Het Volk would be equally inept. That Botha's cabinet included a number of able men was conceded, but the best of them were written off as "theorists" rather than as practical "men of affairs." Thus even if the industry was not actually plundered, it might still be wrecked through accident and misgovernment. There was the uneasy feeling, too, that Botha and his friends might begin to use their new power to pay off some old scores. Because several of the leading Randlords had committed themselves openly against Het Volk and the Nationalists, their fears of retaliation were intensified. None were more vulnerable than the partners of Wernher, Beit/Eckstein, and Phillips wrote to London just after the election, only half in jest, that "you may have yet to consider the advisability of forming a Dutch Company to take over our interests in this country!" He soon recanted these extreme views, but the statement suggests the climate of incipient panic in which these men were then working.[16] Despite the real and open hostility which characterized industry–Het Volk relations in 1906–7, negotiations had been undertaken at an early stage with the intention of finding a basis of accommodation. To explain this it is necessary to return to the political situation as it was on the eve of the Liberal election victory in Britain at the beginning of 1906.

Shortly after arriving in London for talks with the new government in January 1906, J.C. Smuts and other Boer leaders held important but little-known meetings with Sir Julius Wernher and Alfred Beit, the two most influential leaders of the mining industry. Their firm dominated the industry; and through their financial connections in the City of London and on the continent they could influence decisively the flow of capital to the Rand. Although the initiative for the meetings with the Boer leaders came from Smuts, the correspondence of Wernher shows that the desire for accommodation was strong on both sides: "whatever the strictly legal position [with respect to Chinese repatriation] Govt. has always the whip hand as there are so many ways of enforcing their will ... Whilst all the electioneering is going on [in Britain], one cannot get hold of influential people of whom we know many and with whom one can have [an] exchange of views."[17] The interview with Smuts convinced the London partners that an accommodation was possible.[18] Although wary and distrustful of Smuts, they did not disregard his insistence that a basis for agreement could be worked out. The same line was put forward by Dr F. V. Engelenburg, the editor of *De Volkstem*, when he saw Wernher late in February: "The conversation ran pretty well on the lines with Smuts and he expressed as keen an anxiety to come to an understanding with the mine-owners, hinting very strongly what support they could give on labour and Chinese, but he made it quite clear that it was a question of bargaining and, if possible, before the elections."[19] Evidently Smuts and Engelenburg attempted to trade the promise of concessions on mining industry matters for political support (or at least neutrality) in the forthcoming constitutional discussions which were to prepare the way for full responsible government in the Transvaal. Wernher declined any such bargain, saying that "we would always endeavour to get a British majority, as the past history did not warrant us to *expect anything from a Boer majority*,"[20] but he must have been heartened by the evidence of their flexibility on the economic issues. As a result of these conversations, the London partners began to urge their Johannesburg colleagues to detach themselves from too open identification with the policies of the previous (Milner) regime and to suggest that criticism of Het Volk and the Liberals in Britain should now be muted. Wernher particularly expressed the hope that compromises with the ascendant political forces would be possible. With the more vehement of the Johannesburg people, particularly FitzPatrick, who had so closely identified himself with Milner and who was one of the most prominent Progressive politicians, these cautionary letters had little effect.[21] Knowing FitzPatrick's views, Wernher was measurably less forthright in urging restraint on him than he was with the senior Johannesburg partner, Lionel Phillips.[22] Even Phillips took considerable persuading. Commenting on the conversations with Smuts, the latter wrote in March 1906: "it is quite evident that he [Smuts] adopted the old tactics of Boers: 'Why do you oppose us? Why don't you throw your lot in with us, and we will look after your material interests? Why do you meddle in politics and such things, when you only want to make money?' There might be a great deal under existing conditions to justify all persons who are responsible for, or interested in, the mining industry to take Smuts' advice, *if he could give you a guarantee as to the way you would be treated afterwards*."[23] Clearly a good deal of suspicion and distrust existed on both sides. For his part, Smuts had been stronger in giving vague assurances and making soothing noises than in providing definite pledges. On the capitalists' side, so long as Wernher and Phillips could reasonably hope for a Progressive victory, they would not do more than listen to what the Het Volk people had to say. To go further would be to offend gratuitously the politicians among them, especially FitzPatrick and Farrar, with no guarantee of good treatment from Het Volk if it did win the election.[24] Any such crude attempt to change sides at the last moment would not have been believed in any case.

Most industry leaders probably shared Phillips' general pessimism that a Het Volk victory would be an ominous event. The situation seemed especially bleak not only because of the commitment of the new government to Chinese repatriation but also because a definite alliance seemed to be emerging between the leaders of Het Volk and certain prominent labour men. For some years F.H.P. Creswell had been promoting experiments designed to prove that the mines could be worked almost exclusively with white labour, both skilled and unskilled. Even before the election, the Het Volk leadership had begun to show interest in his ideas. Smuts in particular was watching Creswell's experiments closely.[25] The white labour scheme fitted nicely with Het Volk's policy on Chinese labour. Their policy was "repatriation and replacement," and according to Creswell, the Chinese could readily be replaced by unskilled whites. The Johannesburg *Star*, indeed, thought the Chinese factor to be Creswell's overriding motive.[26]

In evaluating Creswell's theories, the new cabinet was probably also influenced by the looming menace of white unemployment which already threatened the stability of the Afrikaner rural community. As early as September 1905, Het Volk had approached the Chamber of Mines for assistance in placing one thousand "poor burghers" on the mines at five shillings a day. Once in office, Botha wrote again to the chamber stressing the seriousness of the situation and urging cooperation.[27] Of course white unemployment was also a serious problem in Johannesburg, and the government was receiving deputations demanding action.[28] A modest scheme of state-financed relief works began at this time, and a number of indigent Australian families were "repatriated" by arrangement with the Australian government.[29] Mounting indigency provides the context explaining official interest in a scheme predicated upon the economic viability of replacing blacks on the mines with unskilled whites.

Creswell drew his inspiration not so much from the trade union movement on the Rand as from a tradition of racialist Uitlander populism which had emerged in Johannesburg in the early days of the mining industry. This urban radicalism is an important but little studied phenomenon in the Transvaal British community. Even before the Anglo-Boer War, it offered a point of contact between Afrikaner leaders and many Uitlanders who had come to share resentment of the mining industry and the big interests which dominated it. The pro-Kruger newspaper, the *Standard and Diggers' News*, expressed in the 1890s some of the same views which Creswell was later to develop in more systematic form.[30] At bottom, their simple idea was to run the mines in the interest of the white community at large rather than of a few Randlords. In the cry of "the people versus the interests" there was potential, both before and after the war, for a cross-cultural Anglo-Afrikaner political alliance linking city and countryside and bringing together the dispossessed and threatened classes in both language groups.

State power was the instrument by which this could be achieved. In developing his dream of an all-white Rand, Creswell was looking far beyond the mundane matter of white employment on the mines. He wanted to preserve the Transvaal as a "white man's country" in which the independent European of small means would be protected from the threat of black competition, simultaneously freed from capitalist domination, and given an honoured and respected place. In Creswell's thinking lurked much of the manager/clerk's resentment of the big interests which so visibly dominated Johannesburg's mercantile and industrial scene. "Hoggenheimer" was a spectre for men of this class just as much as or more than it was for sections of the Afrikaner elite.

Creswell's radical notions had obviously revolutionary implications for the Transvaal gold mines.[31] The corollary to his demand for the employment of whites throughout the range of mine labour occupations was his attack on the whole system of migrancy. This vital aspect of the Creswell analysis has not been given much attention by historians, perhaps because he anticipated almost completely the current radical view of migrant labour. Basic to his thinking was the view that migrant labour constituted unfair competition for whites, that it was a highly artificial system of labour mobilization and one which could not be sustained without the support of the state. Only the legislative and administrative backing of the government, he insisted, made the employment of migrant labour on such a vast scale feasible and attractive for capitalists: "We have seen that the attractiveness of coloured labour to the mines is due to special legislation and special administrative aid and support: that it is to that extent an artificial thing, and not a natural attribute of the labour itself."[32] He meant, of course, the pass laws, the hut and other taxes, the antisquatting laws and the host of administrative measures which forced blacks out of the reserves. Together they constituted the response of southern African governments to the insatiable demands of white employers, most especially the mine owners. For the time being he was willing to tolerate the continued presence of local blacks on the mines, but thought that a quota should be established for foreign Africans. The quota should be reduced annually, he argued, with a view to excluding the mines eventually from their principal sources of supply outside South Africa. Through the quota and more importantly by tearing down the artificial legislative supports of the system, he hoped that the "natural superiority" of the white worker would assert itself and large numbers of them would come into the employment which was legitimately theirs.

Creswell stressed that his objective extended far beyond a mere increase in the number of whites on the mines. In the words of the Mining Industry Commission Report, that would be "comparatively useless."[33] The essential objective was to revolutionize the labour system on the mines and by this means to alter the ratio of white to black labour decisively in favour of the former. To achieve this the colour bar, as entrenched in the Labour Importation Ordinance, could at best be a partial measure. The main point was to strike at migrancy by denying the legislative measures which, in his view, alone sustained it. Deprived of the support of the state, migrant labour would wither and die.[34] This was the hope of the white community for which the Creswellites argued with missionary zeal.

The leaders of Het Volk had flirted with the Creswell program during 1906; they briefly drew closer to him in 1907 as the appointment of the Mining Industry Commission showed. Yet support of his theories was never more than partial. Smuts described the issue of unskilled white labour as "difficult" and argued that the government needed more information.[35]He and his colleagues decided to let the capitalists and the Creswellites fight out their differences in testimony before the commission. The approach to Creswell may also have been intended as a warning to the mining magnates of what might befall the industry should it attempt to thwart the ascendant political forces in the colony. By 1908, the Mining Industry Commission had served the purposes which had led to its creation. After a short parliamentary debate which elicited only equivocal comments from the government, the cabinet shelved Creswell's report with little ceremony.

Protecting the position of white labour on the mines was, of course, not merely a theoretical issue in these years. The debate over Chinese importation and the ensuing regulations governing their employment had already extended the operation of the colour bar. The issue came to the fore again during the miners' strike of 1907. Trouble began in May as the industry attempted to reorganize underground work in pursuit of greater efficiency. The management at Knight's Deep, a property controlled by the Gold Fields Group, had raised from two to three the number of machine drills which a white ganger was expected to supervise. Not only did the change threaten the ratio of white to black on the mine but it also directly involved wage rates. By late in the month miners had struck all of the central Rand Mines, except those of the J.B. Robinson group. The leaders declared a general strike on 22 May, and in response to the threat of violence the Botha government secured the intervention of imperial troops by the 25th.[36] Support for the strikers was never more than partial, and although some miners remained out for several weeks, production scarcely declined. Nevertheless, important issues emerged in the 1907 upheaval, including most of those which figured in the 1922 Rand Revolution.

Government and industry united to condemn the threat to the social order allegedly posed by the strikers. In fact, the importance of the strike lies partly in the opportunity provided for a rapprochement between the new Het Volk government in the Transvaal and leading elements in the Chamber of Mines. During the disturbances, the mining companies resorted to the employment of large numbers of inexperienced Afrikaners as strike-breakers. The government put their number at 2,000 in early June, while Louis Reyersbach, then president of the chamber, thought that 2,500 to 3,000 might have been involved.[37] Untrained in mining work, these men were capable of little beyond some general supervision of blacks. Even in this they depended on the backing and expertise of the shift bosses, mine captains, and underground managers. Almost certainly much of the actual knowledge required to maintain operations (according to the chamber, production hardly declined during the strike) must have been supplied by the well-trained black and Chinese work-force. After the strike ended, many of these ill-trained white miners kept their positions, and indeed their numbers were augmented substantially in the years which followed. In 1907 when this important development was only beginning, government and industry had complementary reasons to welcome and encourage it. Both hoped (though they were very wrong in this) that the new Afrikaner mineworkers would be immune from the militancy which had infected the Miners' Union. The capitalists expected the recruits to be satisfied with their substantially lower wages, while the government, sharing this view, hoped that the mines would be encouraged by the savings to employ more Afrikaners.[38] Naturally they saw in this development a partial solution to the already very serious problem of Afrikaner indigency – one consistent with good relations with the mining industry but not involving acceptance of the extremist views of the Creswellites.

In a different way to the labour strategy proposed by Creswell, the employment of these Afrikaner indigents had equally revolutionary implications for the Transvaal gold mines. These whites were not and had little incentive to become skilled miners of anything like equivalent expertise to the immigrant mineworkers whom they now displaced. Neither were they to be employed in any numbers in unskilled tasks as competitors of the blacks. They became "gangers," supervisors of blacks, who as a group now performed a much wider range of semiskilled and even skilled positions underground than they had ever done before. The job colour bar, customary and statutory, prevented the blacks from actually holding – still less being paid for – these more skilled positions, but there is little doubt that in an ever-growing range of tasks, much of the actual mining expertise came increasingly from the blacks. This reality made possible the strike-breaking tactics of the Chamber of Mines during 1907. The decision to hire unskilled Afrikaners which introduced an important new element in the mine labour force involved much more than a short-run response to the militancy of the Miners' Union, however. It was also a product of the mining industry's concern about Creswell.

Believing that it was practically impossible and anyway undesirable to work the mines on an all-white basis, the more prescient owners saw the need to counter the appeal of the Creswell doctrine to the Het Volk government which was deeply concerned about white employment particularly in the Afrikaner community. Employment of this new group also appealed, of course, as a means of undercutting the militancy of the established, mainly immigrant miners, at least in the short run.[39] The long-run effects of this new policy were far-reaching and probably unanticipated. As F.A. Johnstone and Rob Davies have acutely noted, it began a process of "deskilling" which eventually made these new miner-supervisors highly vulnerable to displacement by more expert and much cheaper blacks.[40] Just because they were so vulnerable, the Afrikaner mineworkers became some of the most militant opponents of later efforts to extend the scope of black employment on the mines. In an entirely predictable way, they became dependent on the legal and customary colour bar in proportion as their position on the mines became "structurally" weaker.

In the immediate aftermath of the strike, however, the mine owners were slow to exploit opportunities to alter the labour balance decisively in favour of the blacks. To do so might involve dismissal of some of the Afrikaners they had just hired and jeopardize their new friendship with Het Volk. Moreover, these men were products of their society and shared prevailing racialist views about the limited capacity of Africans–"mere muscular machines" in the jargon of the day. Simple prejudice prevented full perception of the capacity of the black miner. Also cost constraints, while always serious in the postwar period, were not nearly the problem they later became. After World War I, for instance, fundamental questions of profitability forced mine owners and managers, whatever their racialist views, to make better use of the cheapest element of their labour force. Yet leading members of the Chamber of Mines did not hold their racialism blindly or unconditionally even in 1907. Mining industry correspondence indicates that most of the owners preferred a racially based society with the whites clearly on top. Some of them recognized a kind of social obligation to subsidize (in effect) the whites on the mines in order to preserve this kind of a society, but not if it would put at risk the long-term profitability of the mines. Even before the strike of 1907, one of the mining groups had concluded that the industry might have soon to consider a radical change in its labour system: "I think it is worth having one more try to continue running the country upon the old lines of the white man in the superior position and the black man kept in his place. There is no doubt that for the ultimate good of the country this is the right policy, and not until it is clear that the Chinamen are to be sent away would it be wise to think of a change of system."[41] Lionel Phillips was writing to his principals on the eve of the 1907 election which did bring Het Volk to power and confirmed the policy of eventual repatriation of the Chinese labour force. The "change of system" referred to was exactly the policy which the Chamber of Mines began to implement in a major way only after World War I and which did much to precipitate the revolutionary upheaval in 1922. It involved a thorough-going attack on the colour bar by moving blacks into a wide category of semi-skilled jobs and an attempt to alter the ratio of black to white underground decisively toward the blacks. Surviving mining industry records reveal that the industry was definitely considering development of such a system at a time when they faced probable loss of the Chinese. The 1907 strike did even more to cast doubt on the "old" policy of "the black man kept in his place." The chairman of the General Mining Corporation, George Albu, explained that he had had his eyes opened during the strike. As a result of the upheaval, he had learned that the mines had been "grossly over-staffed" with "so-called skilled [i.e., white] labour."[42] The industry could do with fifteen to twenty per cent fewer whites and with a corresponding saving in working costs. He now argued that the mines should put aside "sentimental" considerations and do away with the "unnecessary surplus."

The Het Volk government's decision to phase out Chinese labour followed quickly by the 1907 strike precipitated a major debate in the Chamber of Mines on labour policy. This involved the owners in a fundamental reassessment of the place of whites on the mines, and the extent to which blacks could be moved into supervisory and semiskilled jobs. In this debate the future of the colour bar was necessarily very much at issue. Despite their racialism, many of the owners were beginning to recognize, like Albu, that much more productive use could be made of black labour with substantial cost savings. Two major reasons explain the decision of the chamber not to move decisively in this direction at that time. One was the social argument that the owners had an obligation to run the industry in a way which would not undermine the dominant position of the whites. As one of the Randlords put it, "it is not a practical policy to go on heedless of the facts as they are and try to reduce working costs exclusively by throwing out expensive white men and adding them to the unemployed."[43] By 1907, however, the view of George Albu, quoted above, was coming to the fore, that the owners should now put aside "sentimental" considerations of this sort and develop a black labour system. The more important reason why this was not implemented until the industry ran up against far more serious cost constraints after World War I had essentially to do with political considerations. In the first year or two of the Het Volk government, a political deal was struck between the state and the chamber which had very important consequences for labour policy in the industry.

On the eve of the 1907 election, Lionel Phillips thought that an arrangement could be made with Het Volk.[44] If the mines agreed to maintain the "old system" of white supremacy in employment, he hoped that the government might be induced not to repatriate the Chinese. He saw complementary interests which might promote accommodation. Supposing they came to power, the Het Volk people, like any other governing party, would want a prosperous mining industry. They would especially need the white employment which an expanding industry could provide if they were not to be speedily overwhelmed by the twin menace of white unemployment in the cities and mounting Afrikaner indigency in the countryside. This was correct, and as Phillips hoped, a deal eventually emerged but not just the one which he had first envisaged. Phillips and his colleagues in the chamber worked out the basis of accommodation with the politicians in the two or three years following the election. The bargain can be baldly summarized. Het Volk insisted on eventual repatriation of the Chinese, and they got from the mines an employment strategy which pretty much maintained the existing ratio of white to black underground, while substituting some cheaper Afrikaner labour for the more expensive immigrant whites displaced in the strike. The effect of this was further to entrench the job colour bar, and the mines temporarily dropped any idea of radical alteration of the existing racial division of labour on the mines. In return, the chamber got assistance from the government in suppressing the labour militants, important help in mobilizing and organizing the black labour supply, and phased withdrawal of the Chinese. Smuts and his colleagues also speedily dropped Creswellian notions of an all-white Rand. Finally in 1909 they renegotiated the *Modus Vivendi* with Mozambique on terms which gave priority to securing the mines' southeast African labour supply.

The decision of Het Volk in 1908 to dump Creswell and to cement a working relationship with the Chamber of Mines can be simply explained. After the election of 1907 had revealed the shape of Transvaal politics and given Het Volk a legislative majority against all comers (labour elected only three members), its leaders must have realized that they had little to gain from embracing a divided labour movement and much to lose by permanent estrangement from the capitalists. Creswell's extremist rhetoric and the sheer volatility of white labour disturbed, mystified, and ultimately frightened the leaders of a conservative, largely agrarian party. The decision to bury the Mining Industry Commission Report followed from their disenchantment with Creswell; while the use of British troops during the 1907 strike was striking evidence of their fear of the labour movement. Since white labour remained weak politically, the cost of these drastic steps was small at first. Once Afrikaners had flocked into the mines and when the Labour and Nationalist parties had mobilized them for politics, the situation was dramatically transformed. This development lay fifteen years in the future, however. In 1907 Afrikaners were the antidote to labour militancy not the cause of it.

In taking note of Het Volk's swing toward the mining industry, Rob Davies argued that the emerging alliance represented the policy "of the more backward agricultural and manufacturing fractions [which] were to a large extent dependent upon the market created by the mining industry, and ... did not therefore wish to impair future inflows of capital."[45] Since Davies fails both to identify these interests and to demonstrate that they had influence on the party, the question of their role must remain open.

On the mining industry side, the prospects of accommodation were enormously strengthened by the essential pragmatism of key industry leaders. Both Phillips and Wernher thought from an early date that the political wind was blowing in the direction of Het Volk. They feared that their firm would be made to suffer for its previous identification with "Milnerism" and that a Het Volk government, if it was not actively malevolent toward the gold industry, would at best be incompetent. Still, if their fears were realized and the election went against them, that government would have to be dealt with – mutual economic dependence bound industry and government tightly together – and they would in the end have little choice but to accept whatever terms the government offered. By August 1906, Phillips had followed the lead of his London principals and himself made direct contact with the Boer leaders. He continued to hope for a Progressive victory until the end of the year, but he was already hedging his bets: "Our policy must from now [on] be one of *real* conciliation. I do not mean that we should not let Fitz fight for all he is worth *politically*, but, behind the scenes, we must try to get on terms with the Boers (if we can!) regarding *industrial matters*. The salvation of the country lies in pushing the mines and husbandry as much as possible."[46]

Immediately after the Het Volk election success, Phillips proposed to his partners that their firm take the next step. For years they had retained FitzPatrick as their political expert, supporting and assisting him to become the colony's most colourful and influential English-speaking politician. He had just won a major victory against Richard Solomon in a Pretoria constituency. But the Progressive party had gone down to defeat and in the new dispensation, Phillips saw that FitzPatrick was a distinct liability. Writing to London only five days after the Het Volk triumph, Phillips wasted no ink on sentiment or loyalty to their old partner:

One thing seems to me clear beyond a doubt, namely that some satisfactory means should be found of retiring FitzPatrick from the firm. We shall be far better off without a partner directly in politics, and his position would be immeasurably strengthened. It is of course absurd, holding in view the enormous interests we represent, that we should not take an active part in politics in a country where the one industry with which we are associated must be so tremendously influenced by legislation; but there is no doubt active interference by us in the political arena gives great opportunities for the cry that we wish not only to rule the mining industry but the country too.[47]

This was done later that year and FitzPatrick helped to a retirement from the firm which left him with the means to carry on his political career independently. Phillips added in this letter that he agreed with his London colleagues, Wernher and Eckstein, that "other people must be left to fight the Imperial battle now, assuming that it has to be fought at all." And he concluded on a note which mixed guarded optimism with the overriding pessimism which dominated his view at that stage: "if Boer intentions are to foster the mining industry, there is no need for us to be in politics, because we shall certainly be consulted behind the scenes; and if on the other hand, they intend to restrict it, we are powerless and must then take care of ourselves and of the interests we represent as best we can."[48] For the next several years, he worked single-mindedly to ensure that it was the first of the options which he sketched that came to pass.

On the government side a similar desire to build on the contacts of 1906 soon manifested itself. After their electoral victory, they moved swiftly to reassure the Randlords. The prime minister, General Botha, himself met a deputation of magnates in London during May 1907.[49] Those present had asked that the Chinese might be gradually phased out so that disruption of mining production could be minimized. Botha was sympathetic and assured them that the policy of his administration was "repatriation and replacement." This was taken to mean that the Chinese might stay until adequate local supplies of labour were secured, and that the government accepted a responsibility to assist the mines to replace the labour they would lose. Just at this time a partly fortuitous and quite remarkable improvement in the supply of African labour became evident and this also helped to allay the anxieties of the mine owners.[50]

In South Africa itself, members of Botha's cabinet were quick to reinforce the prime minister's repeated assurances that while the Chinese had to go, this implied no overriding hostility to the mining industry. Lionel Phillips reported to his principals on the results of one such interview between a colleague in another mining group and the new Transvaal treasurer, H.C. Hull: "Hull also told King [that] they intend to make the niggers work and see the wages brought down. This does not of course tally with their declared intention of letting the Chinese go, because the reduction of numbers would result in greater competition for the available labour, and does not square with the reduction of pay. Hull also said 'we are going to flood them with labour', but did not say how or where from."[51] Phillips believed that the government might negotiate with the Portuguese colonial authorities to increase the supply available from Mozambique under the *Modus Vivendi*. Negotiations in fact had been under way for some time concerning this agreement which since 1901 had guaranteed the gold mines access to their most important local sources of supply in return for customs and railway concessions to the Portuguese. A new agreement, the Transvaal-

Mozambique convention, was not actually concluded until 1909, however. Phillips also knew that the government intended to approach the imperial authorities to secure renewed access to the labour of the Nyasaland protectorate.[52] Because of the extraordinarily high levels of mortality, recruiting from Nyasaland (though not the movement of unrecruited volunteers which was judged impossible to prevent) had been suspended since January 1906. In any case, Phillips doubted that either of these sources would provide a long-term solution.[53] He and his colleague, Wernher, feared that government would act precipitately on the basis of its facile optimism concerning the availability of black labour. They would get rid of the Chinese and only then find that their high hopes concerning alternative labour supplies were groundless.[54] In the end it was the pessimism of the Randlords which proved to be groundless. The government got them their labour, though this was due as much to circumstances as to state initiatives.

Whatever their doubts and fears about the new government, many mining industrialists must have supported a conciliatory policy simply out of an awareness of the capacity of that government to inflict irreparable harm. Again, Phillips wrote pessimistically about the new cabinet: "Botha, although he may have capacity, has no practical experience whatever; Smuts, though brilliant, is entirely theoretical; Japie de Villiers, a young barrister with no previous experience; Hull, an enigma; E.P. Solomon, a brainless old woman; and Rissik, a man though very sound and shrewd, much more versed in science than in business."[55] Nevertheless, he was well aware that these men and their Liberal allies in Britain held most of the cards: "war is all very well as a last resort," Phillips wryly remarked, "but even if in the end by starting an active campaign against the Liberals at home and against the Boers here, a Conservative Government did get back into power [in Britain] with a mandate to put things right ... the mining industry would have been pretty well ground into powder before all this could happen."[56]

Of course, the situation was not nearly as one-sided as Phillips's melodramatic statement tried to suggest. The mines had means to protect themselves. In the same letter, he referred to a cable sent to Lord Rothschild, asking him to use his influence with General Botha. The Transvaal government would doubtless wish to raise a loan, and the view of Lord Rothschild ought, therefore, to carry weight, as Phillips coyly put it. In another letter of the same date to Friedrich Eckstein, Phillips wondered whether the mining houses should support the share market in the event of a precipitous government decision to repatriate the Chinese all at once. He answered his own query in the negative, pointing out that forced selling would have an "appalling" effect upon the share prices and, therefore, he believed a "sobering" effect upon the government. In these and similar devices the industry had means to prevent the state from taking radical measures against it. The mines could make the cost of such measures unacceptably high. As Phillips remarked, failure to maintain investment levels or a decision not to support the share market could have immediate and serious general economic effects.

Before long, the Botha government moved from assurance to definite action on the labour issue. By the time the Transvaal legislature met again in June, the prime minister was able to announce a series of concrete steps which his government had already taken to reorganize the migrant labour supply within southern Africa. In a major policy statement, the prime minister reported that his government had already established a Native Labour Bureau, "in connection with the Native Affairs Department," which was to "regulate the supply of labour to the mines," to "supervise the recruiting of native labour in South Africa," and to ensure that migrant labour was "better controlled and more systematically conducted." Botha's remarks included a good deal of scarcely veiled criticism of the mining industry's own recruiting organization which had ignominiously collapsed through internal dissension the year before. The Native Affairs Department also had evidence that growing numbers of Transvaal Africans were seeking work independently and avoiding the labour agencies.[57] Through the Government Native Labour Bureau (GNLB), the government meant to encourage this development which could lower recruiting costs and reduce wasteful competition for labour. In his policy statement to the legislature, Botha added that the GNLB was already organizing its work in the Cape where it would "in future supplement the efforts of private recruiters with vigorous and independent action." Unlike its counterpart, the Rhodesian Native Labour Bureau, the Transvaal bureau did not itself solicit recruits.[58] It was, furthermore, exclusively a government-managed affair in contrast to the RNLB, the board of management of which was dominated by mining industry representatives.[59] On the Rand itself, the GNLB was to "safeguard the interests of the natives in the labour districts, thereby inspiring them with increasing confidence in their employers." Government hoped that better treatment would encourage the mine labour supply. However, improvement in this respect was halting at best, not least because the GNLB had to be simultaneously the "protectors" of Africans and the enforcer of a severe industrial discipline. Nearly a year after the establishment of the bureau, Cape Africans still complained that they needed a representative of their own government to attend to complaints.[60] Nevertheless the GNLB's authority slowly developed and from the beginning it supervised both the recruitment and the treatment of mine labour.[61] Later in 1907, the Bureau was separated entirely from the Native Affairs Department.[62]

The decision of the Transvaal government to become more closely involved in the recruitment and supervision of mine labour was not simply a product of its desire to compensate the industry for the imminent loss of the Chinese. The government also responded to the demonstrated inability of the Chamber of Mines to maintain an agreed recruiting system for the industry. During 1906 the operations of the Witwatersrand Native Labour Association had fallen into disarray within the South African colonies. At the same time its hold on Mozambique was threatened. The WNLA operation had never worked very well in South Africa itself, and the association was finally forced by widespread evasion of its rules by member companies to release them from their agreement to undertake independent recruiting: "the disintegrating tendencies ... are so strong that certain modifications will have to be faced. The groups could not agree to renew cooperation and many mine managers believed that more labour would be secured if they were able to use independent recruiters."[63] This judgment derived from the reports prepared by the WNLA general manager, T.J.M. Macfarlane, on the operation of the intergroup recruiting monopsony. On the mines where the books were complete enough to check (defaulting managers sought, not unnaturally, to cover their tracks) investigation disclosed numerous irregularities. J.B. Robinson's mines were certainly not the only violators, but they had been among the most successful. General Mining and JCI also received condemnation for "gross irregularities."[64] The WNLA recruiters operated at a major disadvantage vis-à-vis the independents since the former had to recruit for general distribution in the industry, that is for unpopular as well as popular mines. Knowing this, many Africans preferred to deal with independent recruiters so that they could be sure of getting to the mine of their choice. Anarchy in the labour market was bad enough in itself. What made it worse was the resulting danger of a new round of wage increases. While the risk was real it should not be exaggerated, as by 1906 there were other constraints on wage competition within the industry: "The chances are, however, that these fears as to a material increase in Kaffir wages [if the WNLA should break up] are exaggerated. Judging by our pre-war experiences, it is hardly likely that this will happen to any extent. Notwithstanding the serious shortage and free recruiting, the rate of wages paid to natives in 1899 was lower than it is to-day. Besides, the groups which are most inclined to act independently control mines which can least afford to increase the pay of their kaffir labourers."[65] This statement tried to minimize the likely consequences of what was generally recognized to be a grave situation, but it is true that the declining grade of ore and higher nonlabour costs would encourage the groups to restrain wages. As the statement noted, groups with predominantly low-grade mines in their portfolios would be hardest hit by wage competition. It was estimated that four of the six mines in the Goerz group, for example, would have become unpayable if African wages rose above two shillings a shift.[66] The WNLA tried unsuccessfully to bind member companies, which it now agreed could recruit competitively, to an agreed scale of wages. Competitive recruiting with a common wage scale tended of course to be inherently unstable and probably impossible to police. Because the poorer mines were the most vigorous competitors, however, wage rates did not in practice rise very much. Competition appeared in other ways.[67]

The establishment of the GNLB followed directly from the inability of the mining groups to restrain labour competition in their own umbrella organization. Industry spokesmen did their best to disguise this unpalatable reality. In a long memorandum reviewing the history of labour recruiting on the gold mines, Frederick Perry, chairman of the WNLA, argued that there could be no industrial expansion on the Witwatersrand until the labour supply was secure: "the provision of a certain and adequate labour supply must come before anything else."[68] More unskilled labour had to be obtained at prevailing rates of pay: "For an increase of [labour] costs will at once throw not only future, but a number of mines now working outside the payable limit." Since the government had cut the industry off from "practically an unlimited quantity of labour" in northern China, it was responsible, Perry tried to argue, for replacing them.[69]

Support for direct government involvement in mine labour recruiting came also from another quarter within the industry. J.B. Robinson used his relationship with Het Volk to appeal to General Botha, urging the authorities to act. Of course this renegade wanted support for his own clandestine efforts to sabotage the WNLA and establish free recruiting. He argued in a way that was bound to appeal to the new government, claiming that with state support the mines could attract more than enough labour to replace the Chinese. Paradoxically J.B. Robinson, as the principal low-grade mines owner, would necessarily lose heavily if competitive recruiting provoked a new round of wage increases.

At about the same time as these interests within the industry made their approach to the government, a minute arrived from authorities at the Cape expressing renewed concern at the failure of Transkeian Africans to seek mine employment in sufficient numbers. This question had exercised officials in both governments for at least two years. The Cape government blamed conditions on the mines and argued that with better treatment and assured redress of grievances, Transkeian Africans would accept mine employment in greater numbers. At the end of 1905, Jameson's government had proposed the appointment of a Cape agent at Johannesburg to represent the interests of local Africans and to promote the labour supply.[70] The Transvaal authorities agreed to the appointment of an inquiry commission, but when the commission reported against the proposal for an agency, the Cape allowed the matter to drop. During these negotiations, the Transvaal government complained that Cape mineworkers were about the worst on the Rand. Godfrey Lagden, the Transvaal commissioner of native affairs, replied to the Cape government that these Transkeians had caused "incessant trouble," that they were "conspicuous for their insubordination" and "a disturbing element in the mine economy."[71] Beyond appointing the commission and exchanging recriminations, the two governments did not act on the problem for another fourteen months. Then, in 1907, the Cape raised the matter again, noting their own eastern territories had ample labour available and there was a pronounced shortage on the Rand. The well-known aversion of Cape Africans to mine labour was diplomatically attributed to unexplained "prejudice" and to a dislike of underground work; the minute also cited misrepresentation by labour agents and runners. In private, Cape officials did not disguise their criticism of conditions on the mines.[72] The 1907 minute also included an outline of the scheme later agreed between governments to establish a mechanism to facilitate the movement of Cape "voluntaries" to the mines.[73] These anxieties of the Cape government were of course related directly to their perception of the needs of whites across the Kei. The prosperity of the trading community, ministers pointed out, "largely depends" on the "state of the labour market."

Cape ministers became still more concerned when they received evidence that recruiting for the Rand in the colony's eastern districts had come almost to a complete standstill: "[ministers] have received representations from independent sources, officially and otherwise, which indicate that recruitment of native labour in the Transkeian Territories for the Rand Mines has practically been stopped."[74] The prime minister asked the Cape governor to request a report from the new Transvaal administration. Jameson stressed that labour was readily available in the Transkei and that the cessation of recruiting was "very injurious to trade." The concern of the government reflected a stream of protest from the eastern Cape where magistrates, labour agents, traders, and other commercial interests anxiously voiced their alarm.[75] Although the Botha administration assured the Cape that the cessation of recruiting operations was temporary, the incident lent urgency to talks already under way between the two governments on the development of a common labour policy.[76] Cape ministers had sent Sir Walter Stanford north in March/April and he saw representatives of the industry and the Transvaal government. Stanford urged his ministry to maintain the pressure on both the Chamber of Mines and the Het Volk administration for closer coordination of labour policy.[77]

After the visit of Sir Walter Stanford, negotiations followed at a ministerial level, and in June 1907 a provisional memorandum of agreement was signed by the new head of the Transvaal Native Labour Bureau, H.M. Taberer, and the acting secretary of native affairs at the Cape, Edward Dower.[78] The central purpose of the agreement was to facilitate the movement of the so-called "voluntaries" (unrecruited Africans) to the mines. Africans travelling in "batches" of ten or more were to be provided with railway passage and food en route "free of charge." Funds advanced by the governments for this purpose would be recovered from the prospective employers. This was not a recruiting scheme and it did not involve the allocation of labour to particular mines. The government system was set up in a way which tried to avoid some of the pitfalls which had caused the collapse of the WNLA.

The Chamber of Mines monopsony had broken down partly because of the inability to devise an equitable way of distributing the recruits among the member companies, especially in times of shortage. A standing committee of mining engineers established complements for each mine. The individual companies then received from the WNLA that percentage of their complement which the available supply bore to the total of all of the complements. The committee had been unable to prevent the mines from submitting false data to inflate their complements and so corner a higher percentage of the available supply. The worst offenders were, as always, JCI and Randfontein Estates.[79] The situation was further complicated by the need to pay attention to mineworker preferences, and some mines were vastly more popular than others.

This new Cape-Transvaal scheme evaded the problem by declining all responsibility for the distribution. Africans arriving at the bureau's depot in Johannesburg were to make their own deal with employers who then reimbursed the bureau for railway fares and advances for food. The employer in turn could recover these costs by deductions from the workers' salary (this was what was meant in the memorandum of agreement specifying that railway fares and food were to be provided to recruits "free of charge"). Africans recruited by private agencies – the so-called contractors, which typically recruited, transported, and sometimes even housed, fed, and delivered mineworkers to particular mines in return for a flat fee per shift worked – also had to report to the bureau's labour depot but only for the purpose of medical examination and vaccination. Africans seeking non-mining employment on the Rand were entitled to make use of bureau facilities but could not receive the "free" railway fares and rations provided under the Cape-Transvaal agreement.

The establishment of the GNLB in 1907 and the immediate extension of its operation into the Cape marked a major new involvement for government in the regulation, recruitment, and control of mine labour. The decision to extend the role of the state in this way was the result of several considerations. When it decided to go through with the repatriation of the Chinese, the Het Volk administration felt an obligation to make good on its claim that adequate labour was available from within South Africa. Direct government action was imperative because the industry's own recruiting agency was visibly in disarray. Finally, the new scheme was a response to the request from the Cape for assistance against the effects of recession in its eastern districts. Higher levels of the mine labour employment would bring much needed cash into the economy of the Transkei and the Ciskei. The agreement signed by Taberer and Dower brought the Cape and the Transvaal into very close collaboration on labour matters. The extension of the labour bureau's operations into the neighbouring colony marked another of those tendencies toward South Africa-wide integration of policy, characteristic of the decade before Union. In these arrangements and in the parallel steps which were taken with Natal, can be seen the outlines of a labour strategy for South Africa as a whole. Thus the Native Labour Regulation Act of 1911 did not so much create a policy for the new Union of South Africa as affirm and consolidate measures already agreed between governments before Union.

By mid-1908, government efforts to promote the labour supply for the mines, together with its cooperative standpoint on the 1907 strike and other issues, had transformed its relations with the mining industry. Even the gloomy Wernher could now express satisfaction with an administration about which he had been extremely pessimistic only one year before. In July he wrote to Phillips about his recent address to the shareholders at the annual meeting of the Central Mining and Investment Corporation:

You will notice in my speech at the meeting to-day that I expressed general satisfaction with the Government. I did this especially in order to give you a good backing in the task which you have before you and in which you have been so successful. We all know that mistakes are made, but, taking a general and broad view, everybody seems agreed that the men are trying to do their best. Even Perry [the WNLA chairman] had to admit this, and he added that it would be difficult to find more capable men in South Africa at the head of affairs than the present [Transvaal] Government. I hope I have not been too flattering, but I think it was better to say what I meant then to indulge in a kind of half praise. My remarks in this connection may not quite please some of our progressive friends, but that cannot be helped. I tried to smooth things out as well as possible by saying that if the Opposition ever came into power they could be assured of our most loyal support.[80]

From Wernher, high praise indeed.

Even before the implementation of these reforms which Wernher and other Randlords praised, the flow of labour to the Rand had begun to improve dramatically.[81] In Johannesburg, industry leaders attributed this to the prevailing depression and to declining employment levels in other sectors of the economy. Thus the government initiatives acted to reinforce a trend toward higher levels of black employment on the mines. But the architects of the Native Labour Bureau and of Transvaal-Cape cooperation aimed not only to enhance the supply of labour but also to control the private recruiters and supervise conditions on the mines. Unsurprisingly, they gave priority to the first objective, and in the areas of control and supervision, the bureau failed to produce much improvement during the first years of operation.

Developing a unified labour policy for the Cape and the Transvaal turned out to be fairly straightforward; establishing the machinery to administer it effectively required the work of many years. The measures agreed in 1907 marked only the timid and hesitant beginning of a prolonged and costly administrative effort. Since officials and politicians gave priority to increasing the labour supply, they had necessarily to defer reforms which might conceivably hurt recruiting levels. The assisted voluntary scheme, for example, which despite official protestations to the contrary, aimed to undercut the private recruiter, was not fully worked out until 1909–10, when registry offices under the control of the GNLB took responsibility for labour matters from the Cape resident magistrates. The labour registrars received orders to encourage voluntary enlistment for the mines.[82] They had little success. Reviewing the operation of the program in 1914 as part of the Native Grievances Inquiry, Commissioner H.O. Buckle, chief magistrate of Johannesburg, called it "an undoubted failure," and he placed the blame squarely on "the competition of the private recruiters."[83] Only after Buckle reported did the government begin to act vigorously to reduce the number of recruiters and to control the often cutthroat competition of those who remained. These steps, coupled with the partial restoration of the recruiting monopsony in the formation of the Native Recruiting Corporation in 1912, did at last curb the anarchy which had long plagued the labour market.

Negotiations with Natal in pursuit of an agreed recruiting policy proved to be more difficult and protracted than in the case of the Cape. Under its Touts Act, the garden colony had tried to ban recruiters for outside employers altogether. During his travels around South Africa, the director of the GNLB, H.M. Taberer, held talks with the Natal prime minister, F.R. Moor, in July 1907. According to the Transvaal government minute which summarized their discussion, Moor stated that Natal was eager to cooperate.[84] Nevertheless, there were difficulties. Moor did not want Natal Africans to be in contact with other blacks at the labour bureau's Germiston compound. Taberer replied that Africans remained in the compound only for twenty-four hours, that it had separate rooms and that, therefore, there was no question of the different ethnic groups being "mixed up" together. Moor was not satisfied with these explanations and went to extraordinary lengths to insist on his government's objections. Separate facilities would have to be provided, and – a remarkable concession for this tightfisted administration – his government was prepared to pay for them. Just at this time white Natal was engaged in savage repression of a "native rebellion," which was widely, though erroneously, attributed to the baneful influence of Kolwa (Christian) and other "modern" Africans.[85] Perhaps the paternalist Moor feared that his Africans would be "spoiled" by contact with presumably sophisticated and corrupt "mine boys" from elsewhere.

Natal had other objections to the proposed cooperative recruiting scheme. Moor refused to permit a system of cash or cattle wage advances as inducements to promote the labour supply. Evidently he knew of the chaos which wage advances had produced in the recruiting industry in parts of the eastern Cape, especially Pondoland. As an alternative, Moor wanted a deposit and remittance agency reestablished so that part of the pay of the black miners could be withheld and issued to them on their return.[86] The buoyant effect of repatriated wages on colonial economies had always been a major incentive for neighbouring jurisdictions to permit the mines to compete for labour against local employers. Finally Moor insisted that the Transvaal government agree to guarantee his government against loss arising from the issue of travel warrants to Africans bound for the mines. As in the Cape these advances were recoverable from the mineworkers' wages. Losses would arise through deaths and desertions.

Generally, the Natal government argued that Taberer had underestimated the administrative burden which a cooperative labour agreement would place on the colony's native affairs department. Behind all of their reservations, other motives can be detected. Moor's hedging probably resulted from the hope that the Transvaal would provide some sweetener, some financial inducement to secure his agreement. For several years, Natal had been trying to get better terms of access to Rand markets and lower railway rates in order to increase the colony's shrinking share of the traffic. These negotiations were continuing simultaneously with the discussions on labour matters. The conclusion is irresistible that Natal ministers saw labour as a bargaining chip in the contest for preferential access to Rand markets. Perhaps also Natal's cautious approach reflected the old fear that competition from the mines would create a labour shortage and drive up the colony's chronically low black wages. For years they had prohibited recruiting for outside employment altogether.

By November 1907, however, Natal was coming into line. Ministers informed governor Matthew Nathan that they were now prepared to render "every assistance" to the Transvaal GNLB and that they had appointed the undersecretary of native affairs, S.O. Samuelson, to coordinate policy with Taberer. An amendment to the Natal Touts Act gave the mining industry access to the labour supply in the colony and in Zululand early in 1908.[87] While the Transvaal gave no definite *quid pro quo* on railway matters, Natal ministers could still hope that cooperation on the labour supply would help their case on the other issues as discussions continued. Moor did secure agreement to one of his demands. The Botha government agreed to the establishment of a Natal labour agency in Johannesburg outside the control of the GNLB.[88] In any case recruiting levels for the mines in Natal remained disappointing. In 1908 and 1909, the mining groups recruited barely a quarter of the labour in Natal that they secured from the Cape.[89]

These initiatives of the Botha government in enlisting the cooperation of neighbouring colonies on labour matters contributed markedly to a striking improvement in the supply situation. In the three years before Union, recruiting levels shot up and the number of additional recruits more than made up for the loss of the repatriated Chinese labourers. The Cape emerged as a major supplier of mine labour, second only to Mozambique. Nevertheless serious problems remained. An all-out effort to promote labour recruiting meant little emphasis on the supervision of labour agents and of conditions on the mines. Competitive recruiting and the abuses resulting therefrom grew worse in these years.[90] Conditions in the compounds and underground on many of the mines remained deplorable.

The conclusion is inescapable that the efficient, economical organization of the black labour supply proved to be beyond the capacity of the mining industry itself and of these pre-Union governments. Not until the Union brought national government, some unity of purpose, and the resources to fund a national bureaucracy did the recruiting industry begin slowly to yield to effective organization. The creation of the Union of South Africa cannot, of course, be regarded as a direct response to industrial needs or capitalist pressure. Indeed the leading architects of Union, Botha, Smuts, and Merriman, saw their grand design partly as a device to check the baneful influence of Randlords. Only a united South Africa on their argument would be strong enough to stand out against the machinations of international capital. Certainly also the mining capitalists had little direct influence on the design of the new constitution. Lionel Phillips was consulted by Smuts to some extent. His former colleague, FitzPatrick, and the ERPM chief, George Farrar, attended the convention as representatives of the Transvaal Progressive Party. The terms of Union had largely been worked out beforehand, however.[91].

Yet the mining industry needed Union, and many of its leaders knew it.[92] Led by the gold mines, the South African economy had outrun the management capacities of the often feuding colonial governments. In railway and customs policy, for example, their increasingly bitter conflicts handicapped the Transvaal in its negotiations with the Mozambique government concerning the *Modus Vivendi* on black labour, railway, and trade issues. Consequently negotiations were prolonged and efforts to secure amendments to the agreements which regulated WNLA recruiting in Mozambique were compromised. The price was paid by the mining industry. Despite some successes, the various South African colonies had also demonstrated by 1909 their inability to manage the intractable problems created by the migrant labour system in what was now visibly a single, subcontinental economy. It took the much stronger and more cohesive Union administration a full ten years to bring these problems under control.

PART TWO

The System at Work

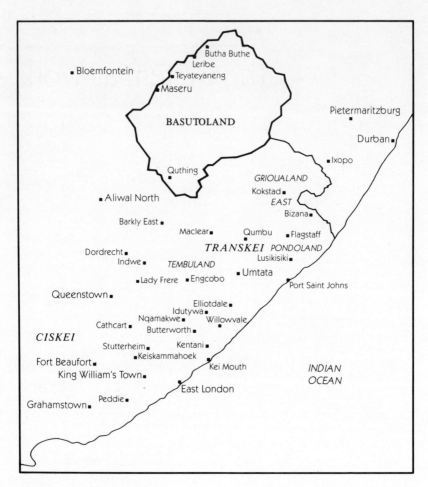

Map 2   The Eastern Cape

CHAPTER THREE

The Making of a Labour Pool: Recruiting in the Eastern Cape

Despite the important efforts which were made to extend more effective government control over mine labour recruiting in the period 1907–9, growing competition for labour produced near anarchical conditions in many districts.[1] As the Chinese labourers were repatriated, labour demands on the mines increased and the collapse of the WNLA in South Africa (though not in Mozambique) at the end of 1906 removed the industry's own controls on destructive competition for labour. The establishment of the Transvaal's GNLB and the resulting development of interstate cooperation on labour matters did little at first to curb abuses. In most colonies, labour agents and their runners had long been required to hold licences and to provide security deposits, but in practice the checks were few and did little to impede their work. "Con men" abounded in the business. Although officials inspected labour contracts before the workers' departure for the Rand and checked them again at the bureau's Johannesburg compound, misrepresentation of contracts and terms of service reached endemic proportions. Magistrates and bureau officials did what they could to investigate complaints, but they were too few and already overburdened with work. In any case, given the volume of contracts, control could only have been nominal.[2]

As the different mining groups rushed to establish or to enlarge their separate recruiting organizations and freelance labour contractors sought to exploit the opportunities created by intense intra-industry competition for labour, the number of recruiters and runners jumped alarmingly. Even more than before, mine labour recruiting now became a major employer in its own right with hundreds of agents and thousands of runners. The recruiting system operated partly independently of and sometimes even in competition with the industry which it had been created to serve. In some districts, apparently, the sheer number of runners employed came to threaten the labour supply for the mines.[3] Since labour recruiting was potentially far more lucrative for blacks than mine labour employment, more and more Africans sought employment as runners. According to one industry spokesman, in some northern Transvaal districts virtually "all the boys" had become runners, creating an extraordinary situation where the recruiting system itself became the major competition for the mines' black workers: "owing to the high price paid to runners, [a runner] is able to earn by bringing in very few boys enought to keep him for some weeks, and ... therefore he just busies himself bringing in those one or two boys and then does nothing else."[4] It was certainly no intention of the white recruiters to create a class of indolent black collaborators, exploiting the system in this way. In the Cape, the secretary of native affairs, Edward Dower, wrote in mid-1908 that the colony was "overrun with 'Runners' who have recourse to all manner of tricks and wiles to filch one another's recruits."[5]

Apart from the trader/recruiters and other white residents of the principal recruiting districts, many other whites entered the business at this time. For the urban unemployed, mine labour recruiting sometimes seemed an easy way to recoup one's fortunes. Take for instance the activities of the Straw family, father and sons. Straw senior, an unemployed coal miner in 1910, approached a former employer, W.T. Hallimond, then manager of the Rose Deep gold mine, with an offer to "supply boys." If Hallimond could give him a job, he would recruit a large number of blacks with whom he had formerly worked on the coal mines. Like most labour-short managers, Hallimond could not resist, and as a result Straw's sons briefly joined the throng of touts and runners competing for labour in the Transkei. Less fortunate than most, they were soon picked up by the authorities on suspicion of illegal recruiting. It was no isolated case. Most observers agreed that a significant percentage of black labour came to the mines in this way.[6] Mine managers also routinely used black mine police as unlicensed recruiters, sending them back to their home districts on leave with orders to escort small gangs of workers back to the mines.[7] All of this aggravated competition led to rampant dishonesty and greatly increased recruiting costs. Clearly the situation had gone badly wrong when the mining industry's own recruiting system was endangering the labour supply which it had been created to promote. As the number of runners and agents grew beyond all reason, not only in the northern Transvaal and the Transkei but also throughout southern Africa, competition intensified, and the temptation to indulge in fraudulent practice became irresistible.[8] Despite this, the industry could not and governments did not act decisively to curb abuses for many years.

The case of the eastern Cape offers an excellent example of an inadequately controlled, abuse-ridden recruiting system.[9] Throughout this period, recruiting operations remained insufficiently supervised despite mounting government concern. Officials in the Native Affairs Department, both in Cape Town and in the main recruiting centres, took their responsibilities seriously. They knew the situation was bad. The new Merriman government which came into office at the beginning of 1908 was committed to reform. Both Merriman himself and his colleague, the attorney-general, Henry Burton,[10] took a direct interest, suspected the mining companies of condoning abuses if not of actually promoting them, and called loudly for corrective action. Edward Dower, the secretary of native affairs, was a knowledgeable and active critic of mine labour recruiting, as was the Transkeian chief magistrate. They encouraged their magistrates to expose violations of the Cape Labour Agents Act 6 of 1899 and of the regulations under it.[11] In reforming the system, these men faced a number of problems, however. They were short of staff, and the close supervision of mine labour recruiting meant a heavy additional burden for the already hard-pressed resident magistrates.[12] Convictions were in any case difficult to obtain as the evidence had usually to come from other agents or runners, and they rarely informed on each other. As the Native Affairs Department pointed out, they knew too much about each other's activities, and the accuser in one case would soon find himself accused in turn.[13] The recruits also frequently refused to testify either out of fear of reprisal or because they had themselves connived at violations of the rules. In any case convictions in the magistrates' courts were difficult to obtain if the case depended mainly on the evidence of the recruits.[14] All of these problems constituted important barriers to reform but not the major ones.

During the depression in the Cape economy which continued into 1908–9, a more serious obstacle to thorough-going renovation of the recruiting system developed. The basic direction of Cape policy at the time aimed not to reform the system or to correct abuses but to enhance the flow of labour to the mines. Politicians and officials believed that the economic recovery of the colony as a whole and of its eastern districts in particular depended on this.[15] The cooperative relationship which developed with the Transvaal on labour matters derived from this common economic interest. Government encouragement of migrancy, the frantic efforts of the private recruiters, and the effects of general economic depression and consequent real hardship in the African territories had done much to produce the desired result. If Transkeian Africans regarded the Rand mines as employers of last resort they now went to them in much larger numbers than ever before. Cape Africans on the mines jumped from 16,555 on 30 June 1907 to 24,469 a year later and reached 45,769 by the end of June 1909.[16] Over a slightly longer period the increase was even more dramatic. At the end of January 1904, Cape mineworkers on the mines constituted 5.2 per cent of the total; those from the Transvaal 9.2 per cent and from Mozambique 75.4 per cent. Five years later at the end of March, 1909, the Cape share had grown to 25.5 per cent, that from the Transvaal to 14.1 per cent, while

Mozambique blacks now constituted only 45.6 per cent of a total work-force of 193,945 black miners.[17] During these years, the Cape became for the first time a major supplier of mine labour. The development of this hitherto underutilized labour pool was one major reason why the Chinese could be gradually repatriated with no diminution of the mines' labour complements.

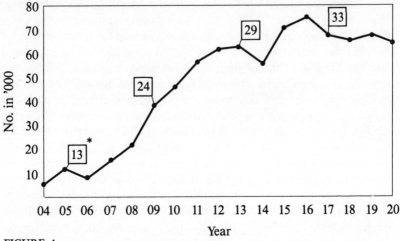

FIGURE 4
Mineworkers from the Cape, 1904–20

SOURCES: Chamber of Mines and WNLA *Annual Reports;* Native Labour Bureau estimates.
NOTE: Recruited Africans and voluntaries are included; date are approximate (see app. 1 for actual figures).
* Indicates per cent of total labour supply.

As the gold industry came to rely on the eastern Cape, so the Cape became dependent on the cash injections which the black miners provided. Wage advances in cash and cattle, on which the mines now began to spend huge sums, represented transfers to depressed rural districts from the mine economy, as did savings repatriated by returning workers and the commission fees of agents and runners. Estimates of what this meant to the rural economy are difficult to make. In 1914, H.O. Buckle concluded in the *Report of the Native Grievances Inquiry* that the mines spent £600,000 annually on recruiting and related expenses. This was exclusive of the thousands of pounds tied up in wage advances, part of which was subsequently lost as a result of desertions. In his evidence to the inquiry, Charles W. Villiers, chairman of the Native Recruiting Corporation, concluded that abolition of these advance payments, which the government was then considering, would remove £200,000 from circulation in the Transkei. Capitation fees paid to runners and labour agents amounted to another £200,000 annually.

These figures for 1912–13 are probably low in relation to actual expenditures over the previous several years. By 1913, the government had imposed a limit on the amount of wage advances which could be paid; and, through the formation of the NRC in 1912, the mining industry had begun to get some control over recruiting costs. Before that expenditures for both advances and recruiting fees must have been much higher.[18] Receipts from the mining industry had become vital to the economy of the Cape generally and to its eastern districts in particular.

Consequently, a powerful interest group made up of merchants, traders, and labour agents developed and actively opposed any government action which seemed likely to curb the flow of labour out of the area.[19] Local chambers of commerce often petitioned Cape Town on these issues, while the labour agents formed associations of their own to put pressure on government. In the eastern Cape, mine labour recruiting became a major employer, in some districts perhaps the major employer, with a substantial wage bill.[20] Governments hesitated to take any action which might jeopardize this new, obviously important, and still apparently fragile economic asset. The likely detrimental economic effects of such action and the certain political repercussions equally compelled caution. In judging whether or not to proceed even against admitted abuses, the authorities were frequently swayed by this consideration. Reforms which might lower overall recruiting levels had to be deferred. Thus in 1908, officials delayed action against the system of cattle advances in Pondoland, which all admitted was pernicious, and the government stayed its hand against the largest of the so-called labour contractors who were guilty of some of the worst abuses in recruiting.[21]

Nevertheless key officials saw that to develop the labour supply further required sweeping reform. They differed principally on timing. Priority went to establishing the system and promoting the habit of migrancy in the African population. After that was accomplished, improvements might safely be considered. In mid-1908, two men who had both been closely involved as government officials with these questions judged that the moment to consider radical change had arrived. In their different ways, they both looked toward a restoration, in whole or in part, of the labour monopsony which had collapsed in South Africa when the WNLA was virtually driven out of all of its recruiting centres except Mozambique in 1906–7. At the same time, each saw a splendid opportunity to serve his own interests. The director of the GNLB, H.M. Taberer, outlined his scheme in a confidential memorandum dated 13 August 1908. A few weeks later, A.H. Stanford, who had recently resigned as Transkeian chief magistrate, sought the support of the Merriman government for a quite different proposal.[22] Nothing came of Stanford's ideas, while Taberer and his allies needed nearly twelve years to bring their ambitious plan fully into operation. The failure of the one and the severe difficulties encountered in implementing the other revealed the complexity of the issues involved and the strength of the interests opposed to reform.

Taberer began his discussion by pointing to the success of recruiting efforts in the year which had elapsed since the formation of the GNLB. First, the system had provided nearly 30,000 additional labourers, enough to replace those Chinese already repatriated and to provide an extra 5,356 black workers. Of the total increase, 12,680 came from Mozambique, 9,330 from the Transvaal, while the Cape provided 7,914. Taberer insisted, secondly, that these figures gave no cause for optimism. Demand for labour on the mines continued to exceed supply and the contracts of the remaining 21,000 Chinese would soon expire. He suggested that although Portuguese East Africa could provide some replacements, a large proportion of the increase could only come from the Cape and the Transvaal. He warned that the situation would soon become "critical" and urged that "immediate steps should be taken to consolidate and establish sound recruiting organizations throughout British South Africa and especially in the Transvaal and the Cape colony." To achieve this, he suggested two immediate steps. The existing recruiting system had to be "cleansed," and, furthermore, measures taken to secure "fair and just treatment" for the mineworkers when they arrived on the mines. He knew, as did many other officials, that conditions on the mines powerfully affected recruiting levels. In Taberer's view, a single recruiting organization operating throughout British South Africa and backed by the "whole-hearted and active support of the leaders of the Mining Industry" was essential. The new organization should be led by a director vested with "full powers to intervene on behalf of Natives." Not surprisingly, Taberer offered himself for this position and suggested that his services could be "lent" by the government to the mining industry.

This plan aimed in short to strike at competitive recruiting and especially at the "middlemen" in the system, the "freelance" labour agents and even more the so-called "labour-contractors" who lived by "'jobbing' Natives from hand to hand and who [exploited] the Native as a chattel." He also believed that a single recruiting agency, backed by the Chamber of Mines, would have the standing to intervene with mine managements to secure redress of mineworkers' grievances and "to afford natives a sympathetic hearing." The concluding section of the memorandum described a future under Taberer's proposed system designed to appeal irresistibly both to labour-starved, cost-conscious Randlords and to officials concerned about the evils of competitive recruiting. He expected to reduce costs, to provide cheaper labour to the mines, and at the same time to bring the workers to the Rand without the charge for rail fare which most then paid. Because his costs promised to be lower, he confidently believed that competition would soon be eliminated. Since misrepresentation and fraud resulted largely from competitive conditions, the restoration of the monopsony would permit reform. Properly recruited, decently treated labour meant a contented work force, and this in turn promised increased efficiency. Even better, with the competition eliminated, the way would be clear for an assault on the "iniquitous system" of cattle and cash salary advances which jacked up labour costs and aggravated the problem of desertion. To make this case, Taberer had developed the classic arguments for labour monopsony.

The labour bureau director's boundless energy and nearly limitless self-confidence revealed themselves splendidly in his new scheme. He presented himself as the great conciliator, as the only person with the knowledge, personal charisma, and disinterested motives necessary to bring together the government and the industry to deliver increasing numbers of contented labourers to the mines. Taberer assured the government that, under his system, there would be no conflict of interest between the mines' organization and the state. If nominated to head up the recruiting industry, he would continue to serve the government "in the evolution of their Native policy, as loyally as I have in my official capacity." He assured his former colleagues in government that he had only selfless motives in putting forward these proposals: "My purpose is a higher one, more especially as I am convinced that, by reason of a unique experience, I am peculiarly capable of securing the confidence of the Natives, and, if it be humanely [*sic*] possible, of inducing them to come here to work in large numbers."[23]

His disinterested concern, he implied, could only revolutionize a recruiting system dominated hitherto by cutthroat competition and by the ruthless pursuit of self-interest. To "cleanse" the system, new men were needed, men untainted by the evil methods of the past. The established recruiters and labour contractors had completely discredited themselves, as had the WNLA in South Africa. Doubtless because he saw the WNLA as the most likely competitor to his plan, he emphasized that it should not be permitted to reestablish itself outside Mozambique. Yet there was no doubt either of the association's notorious reputation throughout southern Africa: "Its very name (Mzilikazi), in fact, conveys to a Native the idea of compulsory sale and inequitable treatment." Thus his analysis led the reader inevitably to the view that only Taberer could do the job. Singlehandedly, Taberer would restore the mine labour monopsony, save the mines from themselves, and protect the mineworkers from fraud and misrepresentation.[24]

His optimism proved irresistible. Within a few weeks, he had the permission of the Botha government to leave the bureau, and he accepted a contract to create a new recruiting organization for the giant H. Eckstein/Rand Mines firm and the Gold Fields group acting jointly. Both Lionel Phillips of the parent firm, Wernher, Beit/Eckstein, and R.G. Fricker of the Gold Fields expressed their complete support of Taberer's ideas. The former described him as a "first class man," while Fricker was equally receptive.[25] Phillips had been trying without success to bring the industry together behind one labour organization, and he definitely saw Taberer's proposals as a step toward that end. His London principals responded enthusiastically. As the main recruiter for these two groups, Taberer gained immediate control of well over half of the demand for labour on the mines. This was not a monopoly but must have seemed to him a long step toward that goal. The government did not of course "loan" his services. He resigned in December 1908, and accepted a three-year contract with the mining houses which promised salary and bonuses to a maximum of £7,000 per annum. Altruism and his self-styled "higher view" of the matter were not, clearly, to be his only reward.[26]

For several years Taberer's ideas endured a severe trial, with results immediately disillusioning both for the new recruiter himself and for his employers. The results which he obtained in the first year of operations were highly disappointing when measured against the promises which he had made and the hopes which he had aroused. Taberer's understanding of the obstacles in his way proved superficial and his optimism facile. He claimed that force of personality and better organization could transform the recruiting industry. His opponents made a joke of these assertions. They fought back savagely, and years were required to drive them completely from the field.[27]

By the time he drew up his 1908 memorandum, Taberer was probably already in touch with his future employers. The mines drew many of their recruiters and compound overseers from the government service. Certainly A.H. Stanford, who also put forward a scheme for the reorganization of mine labour recruiting, readily admitted that he had been approached by unnamed mining interests.[28] Evidently they had also made him an irresistible offer. Stanford approached the issues more cautiously and had a more realistic estimate of the problems than Taberer. On the other hand, Stanford had only the outline of a proposal in contrast to Taberer's comprehensive approach. In his letter to Edward Dower, the Cape's secretary of native affairs, Stanford explained that he wanted to become a major mine labour recruiter, but he had two preconditions. First, he required an assurance of government support – in effect a guarantee of favoured treatment against the competition – and, second, authorization to work through the chiefs. He knew what all recruiters sooner or later discovered, that, as Taberer later put it, "no matter what you do in recruiting you are bound to palm oil the chiefs."[29] In effect Stanford wanted government authorization to undercut the other recruiters by appealing directly to those whose influence counted the most – the chiefs and headmen. Current government regulations prevented the chiefs from accepting employment as runners. In fact, however, they routinely evaded the ban in practice, as Taberer indicated. Stanford proposed to allow them "a considerable percentage of the remuneration I am to receive from the Mine Managers for my services." His scheme also involved offering recruits cash advances to a maximum of five pounds and the implementation of a deferred pay proposal, working in conjunction with a deposit and remittance agency. While the former would restrict the flow of cash into the Transkei economy (since currently advances frequently exceeded five pounds), the latter, when operating effectively, would increase it. Stanford concluded his memorandum by stressing the importance of his receiving the support of the government and of "the Magistrates in the Territories lately under my charge." The former Transkeian chief magistrate was certainly naïve in thinking that the government could give to him the exclusive backing it had always declined to give to others, if only because of the political storm which such favouritism would surely generate. He had, however, identified the twin keys to the successful establishment of a monopoly. Overt support of the government and authorized access to the chiefs promised him unmatched advantages over the competition and a definite leg-up.

Stanford's colleagues in the Cape administration expressed cautious interest. Edward Dower minuted that "Mr. Stanford's proposal is admirable except in so far as reliance is placed on the Government which cannot fairly do for one licenced agent what it is not prepared to do for every other licenced agent." He sketched three possibilities.[30] Act 6 of 1899, the Cape Native Labour Agents Act, could be amended. Or the colony could designate Stanford as sole official recruiter, as the act provided (Section 22) and charge the mines for the cost of his services. Dower himself remained opposed to official, state recruiting. Third, they could encourage Stanford to go ahead but without formal government approval. This was the option which appealed to Merriman, the prime minister: "I do not see how we can do more than give him our benevolent sympathy and such assistance as may from time to time be found possible – without giving him a positive official cachet."[31] Denied the direct official endorsement which he saw was essential, Stanford abandoned his project. If Taberer had had any presentiment of the difficulties which awaited him, he might well have done the same.

Stanford's decision left the field clear for Taberer who shortly left the GNLB to establish his new agency.[32] In late 1908 and early 1909 he worked aggressively to redeem the pledges which he had made to his new employers. By late 1909, he had so far failed that one of the mining groups, the Gold Fields, was on the point of withdrawing from its agreement with him. Far from assisting in the reform of an abuse-ridden system, Taberer's activities led to an intensified struggle for labour, to more abuses, and to the spectre of increased recruiting costs.[33]

The mining companies and their recruiters probably suffered losses as a result, but the mineworkers benefited. Although misrepresentation of labour contracts by agents and runners almost certainly increased,[34] so did the size of cash advances and the presents frequently given to recruits as a bonus for signing on.[35] Traders especially often rebated all or part of their capitation fee (in trade goods) to the recruit as an inducement. They made far more from the cash advances and from interest on loans. At the beginning of 1909, a new Cape Usury Act, enacted at the urging of the new prime minister, J.X. Merriman, imposed severe restrictions on interest rates, but its terms could not readily be enforced and widespread evasion undoubtedly continued.[36] Runners and headmen would also benefit from competitive bidding for their services which promoted higher fees. Mine wages did not apparently improve very much as a result of intensified competition, but some companies eased the conditions of service. For example, several of the groups reduced the minimum "drill task" required to complete a full shift and entitle the "hammer boy" to the standard pay. The minimum was typically a hand-drilled hole for blasting of thirty-six or forty-two inches, and the standard now fell toward thirty inches on some mines.[37] The higher standard constituted a major grievance of Cape Africans especially,[38] and its speedy amendment is an indication of the greater leverage enjoyed by the recruits as competition for their services increased. Taberer's new employers, who resisted the new, easier terms, and doubtless the other mining groups were aggrieved by these developments. For its part, the Cape government saw the evils of intensified competition, not the possible benefits to the mineworkers and began to press for reform. The result was a new package of reform proposals agreed at the Cape Town Labour Conference in September 1909. Before the authorities put forward their modest suggestions, however, the rivalry between recruiters had reached destructive levels.

When Taberer left the bureau to begin recruiting for H. Eckstein/Rand Mines and the Gold Fields, he entered an already crowded field. In the Cape, dozens of agents as well as more than 2,000 runners (both white and black) scrambled for labour. Some of the agents operated independently, catching labour where they could and selling to the highest bidder. By 1908 many of the established recruiters were grouped in larger organizations set up either directly by one of the mining groups or under formal contract to them. The recruiters and runners gave only a conditional and partial loyalty to their employers, however. Resident magistrates argued that these men were totally unscrupulous. They sold their labour at the best price, ignoring their contracts whenever expedient.[39] A few of the mining groups maintained their own native labour departments as a branch of group administration and with an experienced recruiter (or an ex-government Native Affairs Department employee) at the head of it. Some of the largest agencies, the so-called labour contractors, had looser arrangements with the mines. These contractors related to the mining companies in a variety of ways. A few were very small, employed by one or two individual mines and recruiting only a few hundred mineworkers or less; others represented entire mining groups in particular districts; and in the odd case, such as Taberer's, they might represent more than one group. The terms of the contracts also varied widely. A contract might specify recruitment only, as with Taberer. In other instances, however, the labour contractor not only recruited but also arranged the transport to the Rand and fed and housed the worker after his arrival. These contractors accepted the entire responsibility and undertook to deliver a specified number of labour units to the shaft head daily in return for a fixed fee per shift actually worked. Such a contract might stipulate that the workers were to be paid at mine rates by the contractor out of the fees collected from the mining company. The contractors preferred this system rather than that where the mine paid the workers directly because it enabled them to discount wages in various surreptitious ways. Use of the labour contractor became widespread on the mines in 1907–8.

Although very little has been written about the labour contractors, information about them is readily available in the official correspondence. Anarchical recruiting conditions ensured that both native affairs department officials and the group controllers watched the contractors closely. Mining industry records concerning the formation of the NRC and the report of the select committee on the Native Labour Regulation Act (15 of 1911) are excellent sources for this little studied aspect of the mine labour system.[40] This account relies heavily on those records, especially the select committee report.

The labour contract system developed out of other forms of contracting on the mines. From an early date, mine managers let certain important jobs both underground and on the surface to contract. Much shaft sinking and development in the drives and stopes were accomplished in this way, while on the surface, other contractors handled excavations, management of tailings dumps and other wastes, and so on. Contract rates frequently included labour costs, and the contractor might supply, feed, and house his own labour force. Until after the Anglo-Boer War, few of the contractors found their living exclusively from the supply of the labour itself; they recruited usually only for their own needs; and most had few employees. However, the labour-contracting system grew out of this earlier form of contracting, as some contractors perceived that they could do better as recruiters. Their opportunity came when the decision of the Transvaal government to phase out Chinese labour threatened a major labour shortage and when, simultaneously, the WNLA structure in South Africa fell apart. Faced now with developing their own sources of local labour, several mining groups turned to the contractors, while others instead established group native labour departments. By mid-1908, various labour-contracting firms were actively competing for labour, and the rivalry between them was especially keen in the eastern Cape and northern Transvaal. Two of the largest, the Transvaal Mines Labour Company led by Col. A.E. ("Kaffir") Wilson, and the A.M. Mostert labour organization gave Taberer especially strong opposition; but the McKenzie Brothers operating out of Richmond, Natal, and recruiting for Robinson and others in the southern part of that colony and in Pondoland should also be mentioned. Baerecke and Kleudgen held an important contact with the East Rand Proprietary Mines. This very successful firm was represented in the eastern Cape by Messrs Mills and Rethman. In Swaziland and Zululand, Marwick and Morris controlled much of the migrant labour supply for the ERPM mine.

Of all the labour contractors, A.M. Mostert undoubtedly enjoyed the most success; and his company lasted the longest. It did not cease mine labour recruiting until 1919 and continued thereafter as a farm labour supplier under a new name. Mostert arrived on the Rand in 1886 and began a successful business as a contractor of surface works. To meet his substantial unskilled labour requirements, he established a small network of agents and traders supplying him with labour from the eastern Cape principally, but also from Basutoland, the northern Transvaal, and elsewhere. Like H.M. Taberer, A.H. Stanford, "Kaffir" Wilson, and others, Mostert perceived an excellent opportunity in 1907-8 to exploit divisions among the mining groups and the weakness of the WNLA by expanding into the labour supply business. As one of the first in the field, he briefly secured an important share of the market and successfully negotiated contracts with several of the leading houses. Although he could not maintain his dominance and soon lost to Taberer a vital contract with the H. Eckstein/ Rand Mines group, he remained for many years principal supplier to J.B. Robinson's Randfontein complex. He also retained lesser contracts with certain Gold Fields mines and those of other groups. In 1911, Mostert had 7,600 black miners on the Rand and planned to expand that number to 13,000.[41] Like "Kaffir" Wilson in Mozambique, Mostert probably aspired to supplant the WNLA in South Africa and to obtain a corner on the mine labour supply. While he did sign some very important contracts, his position even in 1907-8 was not as strong as it seemed. He did not secure exclusive contracts; he merely obtained authorization to recruit in competition with others.[42] With the advent of Taberer, Mostert had a special reason to be resentful because Taberer's new contract excluded him from the potentially highly lucrative H. Eckstein/Rand Mines share of the business.[43] Unlike Mostert, Taberer did receive an exclusive contract.

Despite the importance of the Mostert organization, initially A.E. Wilson was perhaps Taberer's most active opponent.[44] He had formed his company in 1906 to recruit for J.B. Robinson both in South Africa and Mozambique when the latter was campaigning actively to destroy the WNLA organization. Wilson broke into the highly competitive eastern Cape area without difficulty. As a former superintendent of the "dock native location" in Cape Town, he was well known in the eastern districts. When he left Cape Town, he brought several of his black staff with him to assist in the formation of the new company. Wilson based himself in Johannesburg but had many agents in the eastern Cape, and he frequently toured the recruiting districts. He relied not only on the trader/recruiters but also hired Africans to recruit illegally for him, sometimes sending them from Johannesburg for the purpose.[45] While Wilson soon began to do well in the Cape, he failed completely in Mozambique where Robinson quickly found other operatives.

Both Mostert and Wilson turned out to be formidable and implacable enemies of their new rival. While there were many other recruiters in the field, none of them could mount the type of sustained opposition of which the labour contractors, backed by the resources of rival mining groups, were capable. Conditions for the small, freelance recruiter became in any case more difficult at this time because the government began to act against them. The authorities believed, though they were soon disillusioned, that the larger organizations directly controlled by a mining group or at least under contract to it, would be easier to supervise. Recruiters who could not produce a letter from a bonafide employer found their licence applications refused.[46] Even when under contract to a mining group native labour department or of one of the larger labour-contracting firms, the trader/ recruiters were not easy to control. Recruiters and runners employed by rival firms easily cooperated with each other when it suited their joint interest. This could involve combination against their central employers. As a result the Johannesburg labour controllers, Taberer, Mostert, Wilson, and others, could never be certain of the loyalty of their agents in the field, which made it difficult for these big interests to pursue their rivalries with each other.[47] Just as recruiters could often be found cooperating with their counterparts in rival firms, so recruiters working for the same firm frequently pursued bitter rivalries. Taberer's representative at Indwe, C.H. Pritchard, reacted strongly when he suspected that one of his own subagents, in league with Taberer's Cape manager, M.St.V. Erskine, had agreed to take recruits from a recruiter under contract to a rival firm. This deal cost Pritchard his share of some recruiting fees, and he asked the Cape Native Affairs Department to intervene against his own colleagues.[48]

The battle between the Taberer, Mostert, and Wilson organizations and between all of them and others, opened up many opportunities for subordinate agents and runners to reap extra profits at the expense of their Johannesburg employers.[49] From their offices in Johannesburg, the labour controllers had to fight on two fronts. Locked in combat with each other, they also struggled to keep control of their own organizations and to prevent defections. The intensity of the war in the first case aggravated the problem of controlling subagents in the second. It probably also stimulated further growth in the recruiting industry as a whole. Whereas in 1908, the Cape had licensed fewer than 100 agents (excluding runners), by mid-1910, this number had jumped to over 200.[50]

The struggle between Taberer and his rivals during 1909 is well documented in the files of the Cape Native Affairs Department and the Transvaal Native Labour Bureau, and in the records of H. Eckstein/Rand Mines. This correspondence reveals not only the intensity of competition for labour, but also tells much about the actual conduct of recruiting operations. Probably the records understate the extent of the problems. Because of the reluctance of labour agents to inform on each other out of fear of reprisals and countercharges, relatively few complaints reached government. Officials found it difficult to conduct complete investigations and to bring successful prosecutions. Similarly, the mining group correspondence is more suggestive than definitive on recruiting operations. These letters concern policy making at the highest executive level, necessarily remote from what was actually going on in the field.

In their efforts to stay even with the competition, the principal recruiters and labour contractors had to contend with a series of complexities and difficulties. They needed not only to maintain the labour complements for mining groups which were notoriously impatient of failure but also to replace the remaining Chinese who were soon to depart and to supply additional labour drafts for entirely new needs. Several groups were resuming expansion in this 1908–9 period, and their demand for labour increased rapidly. Conditions of chronic labour "shortage" constituted probably the single most important barrier to eliminating competitive recruiting. Of course the shouting from mine managers cannot be taken at face value. They exaggerated their needs in order to provide a cushion against future adversity; they often used their labour wastefully; their methods of underground operation could be deplorably inefficient. However, since they so often perceived a labour shortage, their beliefs had real consequences.[51] Furthermore, the big mining houses, with possibly one exception, demonstrated an unwillingness to accept even the temporary shortages which restoration of the monopsony might have involved.[52] They invariably broke ranks whenever some temporary advantage over their rivals offered itself. Most of them seemed quite unable to see beyond next month's production except to make gloomy predictions about probable future catastrophes. Thus Taberer and the other principal recruiters had also to keep a weather-eye on their own employers whose loyalty was always conditional and frequently temporary.

The former labour bureau director launched his campaign to unseat the established recruiters confidently enough. According to the later testimony of a disaffected former employee, Taberer announced even before leaving the GNLB that "Kaffir" Wilson had been marked down for "annihilation" and that Taberer's proposed company "would practically wash out all Mostert's large contracts." At the same time, other recruiters, including the informant (who, however, soon fell out with Taberer), received the assurance that "straight" recruiters would benefit from his plans.[53] That Taberer proclaimed the doom of Mostert and Wilson is entirely believable; he aimed his plan directly at them; and Mostert in particular suffered at once. Evidently he tried to panic their subagents so that the best of them could be hired for Taberer's labour organization. By the end of 1908, at least two of Mostert's agents had joined Taberer who actively sought agents elsewhere as well.[54] Briefly these attempts to raid rival organizations seemed to have the support of the Cape authorities. At least two of "Kaffir" Wilson's recruiters found their licence renewals denied shortly after Taberer began working. They alleged that Taberer promised easy restoration of the cancelled licences if they would switch their allegiance. The Cape government backed down in this case when Wilson's company protested. Since Wilson worked for Robinson, a staunch ally of the Transvaal ruling party, Het Volk, political pressure may well have been brought to bear at the intergovernmental level. Certainly Wilson had earlier made frequent use of Robinson's political influence both in South Africa and in England.[55]

The knowledge that Taberer was leaving a key government post to join the powerful H. Eckstein/Rand Mines and Gold Fields groups must have been sufficient to upset subagents of rival companies and to tempt them to change their allegiance. As director of the bureau, Taberer had controlled the entire flow of labour from the South African territories. With the exception of Mozambique labour, all of the recruits passed through the bureau's Germiston compound. Taberer was, as he claimed, well known in the main recruiting centres which he toured frequently. Many thought him a person who "knew the native mind" and who would therefore be a formidable threat in the industry. His likely influence with his former colleagues in government together with his reputed contacts with blacks in the migrant labour system and his powerful financial backing all marked him as the probable victor in the struggle to control the mine labour supply. Many ordinary recruiters doubtless felt that to join him would be a prudent step. Certainly he managed to assemble a strong organization very quickly, hiring recruiters from Mostert, Wilson's TMLC, and others. He also took over the remnant of the WNLA organization in the eastern Cape, and the WNLA's former regional manager, M.St.V. Erskine, assumed that position for Taberer.[56]

Even at the start, however, Taberer did not have things all his own way.

He soon found his own hiring strategy turned against him and lost staff almost at once to Wilson's TMLC.[57] This case is especially instructive, since it demonstrates the extent of the rivalry among the labour controllers at the group level and also shows how individual recruiters in the field could exploit the situation to their own advantage. Shortly after leaving the bureau, Taberer managed to lure away from the A.M. Mostert depot at Indwe two of his recruiters, T.R.G. Davies and F.H. Lloyd. Taberer wanted them to work with his own principal recruiter at Indwe, C.H. Pritchard. A few weeks after this deal had been made, the parties fell out, and Davies lost his job. Taberer agreed to retain Lloyd on condition that he sever his connection with Davies. In fact, however, Lloyd continued to take recruits from Davies who now functioned as his runner. Lloyd later claimed that Pritchard had given him permission to do this. When Taberer found out, he also dismissed Lloyd whom he suspected anyway of supplying recruits to other labour companies. Taberer's next step led him to prefer charges against Davies on suspicion of his having "appropriated" recruits from still another Taberer agent and sending them on to Johannesburg "as being his own."[58] Recruiters had little option but to conduct their operations on the model of Davies and Lloyd. Since Cape Africans would normally accept contracts only for the mine of their choice, a recruiter working for a single group, however important, found his pool of potential recruits drastically reduced. Thus most recruiters made informal deals with their competition to exchange mineworkers and respect their preferences for particular mines. Because he aimed to eliminate the competition, Taberer demanded that his agents recruit only for his group.[59] Davies and Lloyd resented this since it meant that they would have to limit their recruiting to Africans who accepted employment in mines directly represented by Taberer's company. They could not hand on – and be paid for – recruits who insisted on being dispatched to mines of other groups. Lloyd, Davies, and no doubt others humoured Taberer and accepted his conditions, but simple necessity led them to carry on as before. When Taberer discovered their cheating, they found the means to defend themselves and a new benefactor in Colonel Wilson of the TMLC, who took them on as his managers. They also preferred countercharges against Taberer, accusing him of various irregularities.[60] Unable to discover the truth between these competing allegations and perhaps concerned that the principals on both sides were politically well connected, the Cape government declined to act.[61]

In this cutthroat business, even keen rivals saw the sense of certain kinds of cooperation but not Taberer. He committed his organization to total war in the hope of total victory and suffered the predictable consequences. Attempts to raid key personnel continued to be a major threat for several years. In mid-1910, Taberer almost lost the head of his Cape operation, Erskine, which would certainly have dealt a serious, if not an irreparable blow to his organization there. Only the direct intervention of Taberer's principals in H. Eckstein/Rand Mines prevented this.[62] Quite simply they also made Erskine an offer he could not refuse.

Despite early setbacks, Taberer did not give up and continued to threaten dismissal when agents broke his rules. In order to put teeth into these threats, Taberer tried to get the Cape Native Affairs Department to deny licence renewals to those whom he had banished. In this way he could also solve the problem of defections to rival companies. Although his former colleagues in government responded sympathetically, they did not act, partly because he could not provide absolute proof of misconduct and partly because, as in the case of Davies and Lloyd, those whom he accused simply replied in kind. In effect they threatened to bury the Native Affairs Department in correspondence and litigation.[63]

Taberer's difficulties with his agents may also have stemmed from his possibly more squeamish attitude toward recruiting irregularities. Since he certainly hoped to attract the support of the authorities for his efforts to dominate recruiting, he almost had to run an operation which at least appeared to be clean. Moreover, as head of the labour bureau, he had shown himself genuinely anxious to introduce reform. Thus he probably declined to wink, as the other principal recruiters routinely did, at the use of illegal methods. Almost certainly his agents nevertheless resorted to such methods – there was no other way to stay even with the competition – but they would face censure not only from the government but also from their employer when caught. Despite earlier efforts to reform the system and to control it more effectively fraudulent methods were routinely used. These included: defrauding recruits by lies and misrepresentation, ensnaring them in a nexus of trader debt and excessive salary advances, debauching them with liquor, coercing them to sign labour contracts through the systematic bribery of their chiefs and headmen.[64]

For all of these reasons, Taberer failed in the short run to carry through on his ambitious promises. After several months of effort, he remained one recruiter among many and not, perhaps, the most successful. That his progress would be slow was entirely predictable, but in this industry, wild optimism tended to march with absurd impatience for quick results. Taberer had unwisely encouraged the one; he soon began to suffer from the effects of the other. After less than a year, Taberer's employers began to grow restive. As the competition for labour became more intense, recruiting costs threatened to rise without a corresponding improvement in the supply. Taberer and the others also faced the problem of increasing demand as several groups resumed expansion.[65] By August 1909, H. Eckstein/Rand Mines companies were short five to six thousand black miners. Writing to London, H. Eckstein executives stated bluntly that Taberer had failed, yet they saw no better alternative than to support him. The London partners agreed reluctantly but noted that Taberer must soon "justify the existence of his organization which so far has proved very disappointing."[66] With less patience, the Gold Fields Company responded to the labour shortfall by withdrawing from their agreement with Taberer, first partially in July and then completely at the end of the year.[67]

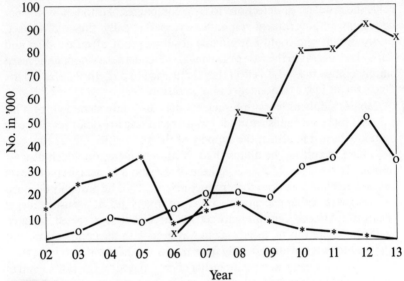

FIGURE 5
Mineworkers Received, South African Sources, 1902–13 +

SOURCES: Chamber of Mines and WNLA *Annual Reports;* Native Labour Bureau estimates.
* WNLA recruits
o Voluntaries from all sources but including new arrivals only; figures from 1902–4 are estimates.
x Contractors' and non-WNLA recruits, including NRC for 1913 only.
+ Recruited for WNLA member companies only.

Taberer's failure lay not in an inability to maintain the supply of labour at established levels. Recruiting levels improved in the first part of 1909, reaching 175,122 in April 1909. Thereafter demand outstripped supply again, and the groups considered themselves short of labour.[68] The rising demand outran the recruiters' capacity to meet it. Taberer had also to contend with the Gold Fields executives who evidently took the most short-sighted view of the labour situation. In their impatience for quick results they were not alone, however. As pressure on the recruiters intensified, raiding of rival organizations for staff (always a feature of the industry) became more severe. In mid-1910, for example, when the labour shortage was still serious, H. Eckstein and Company received word from Taberer that Erskine, his key man in the eastern Cape, would shortly resign. He had been approached with "tempting" offers. The dry prose of the official letter reporting on the situation to London retains just a hint of the incipient panic in the group's executive office. We "cannot possibly afford" to lose him now, the letter noted, he had far too much influence with "the natives." As indicated above, the group saved the situation by intervening directly with Erskine, calling him to Johannesburg and offering him "remodelled" terms.[69] Later that year, Taberer reported that rival offers to his recruiters had become "fanciful" but that he had been able to prevent defections.[70] His experience indicates a general problem faced by the industry as a whole. However able and successful – and Taberer, Wilson, Mostert, the McKenzies, and others had proven records – the principal recruiters had to contend with group controllers who were liable to panic at the first sign of labour shortage. Their subordinates gave them equal trouble by using the situation to extort better terms.

At the same time, Taberer's principals resisted his requests to ease the terms of mineworkers' labour contracts to make their mines more attractive to recruits and thus improve the competitive position of the recruits. This group clung to a forty-two inch daily drill task, well above the thirty-six inches required by many groups, notably the ERPM, which continued to fill a higher percentage of its complements than the industry average. Some of these competing groups also increased wages, an expedient that the H. Eckstein partners resisted even more firmly.[71] Unsurprisingly, Taberer and his recruiters found themselves unable to compete and could secure "hardly any boys."[72] Eventually the group controllers yielded, grudgingly, eased the drill standard to thirty-six inches and introduced a few additional, minor improvements in conditions.[73]

Intensified anarchy in the mine labour market during 1909 produced renewed pressure from government for reform. By this time, Taberer seemed unlikely to succeed in his ambitious plans to restore the recruiting monopsony in the British South African territories, especially the Cape Colony. If anything, his efforts had worsened the situation. Thus if Taberer's former colleagues in government hoped that he would be the means of the mining industry cleansing its own recruiting system, they must now have been severely disillusioned. Even before recruiting conditions deteriorated in late 1908 and early 1909, most state officials had concluded that direct government intervention was necessary. A few believed that competitive recruiting could never be adequately supervised and controlled and wanted the state to take over.[74] Although key members of the Cape government declined to consider seriously the establishment of a government recruiting monopoly at this time, they certainly began to press for closer control over the private recruiters.[75] Ultimately the chaos produced by the struggles between them acted to trigger the decision of both Cape and Transvaal governments to intervene. Many of the recruiters themselves supported this since they knew that the industry could not tolerate for long the existing situation. The two governments exchanged several reports and memoranda in the first months of 1909.[76] Officials worried about the detrimental effects of competition on the recruits themselves. They also saw earlier and more clearly than the mine controllers that further enhancement of the migrant labour supply required better recruiting methods and improved conditions on the mines.

By August 1909, both Henry Burton, the Cape's attorney-general (and acting minister of native affairs in the absence of Prime Minister Merriman in England), and S.M. Pritchard, the Transvaal's new director of native labour, had concluded independently that the moment to act had arrived. During mid-1909, Burton toured the Transkei, and his influential report led directly to the important Cape Town Labour Conference of September 1909.[77] In making the visit, Burton had several purposes in view. He wanted to investigate the administrative and legislative needs of the territories and "to make myself acquainted with the circumstances and conditions of the people." Not surprisingly, his report focused on the labour issue. The attorney-general's report of his tour coincided almost exactly with a memorandum from S.M. Pritchard, which arrived in August. Writing to Edward Dower,[78] Pritchard summarized the case for reform which he had earlier put before his own government. He believed that the origin of many of the problems could be traced to the evil influence of the labour contractors, resident in Johannesburg, who were "not as a rule personally known to natives, nor have they their confidence." These men and their agents "have no other but a monetary interest in the Natives recruited by them."[79] While Pritchard did not name specific firms, he undoubtedly had in mind the small, independent contractor to whom the mining groups often gave "speculative" contracts on no assurance beyond the claim of the contractor that he could "get boys." In the future, Pritchard proposed to license only those agents recruiting directly for a mine employer either under long-term contract or as the head of a native labour department. A labour contractor such as A.M. Mostert would fall into his first category; H.M. Taberer more into the second since he operated in effect as the head of H. Eckstein and Company's Native Labour Department. Earlier the Cape government had proposed just such a policy but dropped it at the request of the Transvaal. Pritchard felt that in the new circumstances of 1909, the proposal could safely be implemented. Largely through the cooperation of the Cape over the previous two years, the Transvaal authorities had more than made good on their pledge to replace the repatriated Chinese with locally recruited blacks. To achieve this the development of the Transkei labour pool had been critical. With the system now established and labour flowing freely, both governments stood in a stronger position vis-à-vis the mining groups. Pritchard proposed to use their greater leverage to press for another round of reform.

In both administrations, senior officials remained committed to the private system of recruiting and wanted merely to correct the more flagrant abuses. Unlike some resident magistrates and officers in the field, head office staff did not for the most part favour direct government recruiting for the mines. Still less did they challenge the system of migrant labour itself.[80] Since most officials had long since accepted the idea of the "dual economy" (based on the notion of inherent African indolence and the stagnation of traditional agriculture), virtually nobody in native affairs could see any alternative to migrancy. Even had such an attack on the system as a whole been conceivable, their perception of the strategic value of mine labour employment to the economy of the eastern Cape would still have acted to blunt fundamental change.[81] Thus the reforms proposed at the September 1909 conference aimed only to eliminate some of the worst forms of exploitation and to make the recruiting system more efficient and possibly more humane. Now that labour was leaving the eastern Cape for the Rand at gratifying rates which increased from year to year, authorities felt that they could argue for reform without fear of endangering the supply. Indeed they had convinced themselves that reforms would produce more recruits for the mines. Officials used this argument to persuade recruiters and industry controllers of the need to act against abuses.

The extensive conference records and correspondence which followed provide a clear indication of the parameters which defined the debate on black labour policy at this time.[82] On the eve of the conference, the Cape Native Affairs Department prepared a summary statement outlining the principal evils of the existing recruiting system and listing its proposals for reform. Private recruiting under close government supervision would maintain competitive conditions, desirable to maximize results, and also make possible the elimination of abuses and help carry "the gospel of work into every corner of the country."[83] Briefly, the Cape government proposed to revive a scheme, outlined in Section 59 of the Glen Grey Act, 1894, but never implemented, to establish labour bureaux in the various districts of the eastern Cape.[84] Bureau officials, rather than the magistrates as heretofore, would regulate the activities of labour agents and their runners, investigate the complaints of Africans and attest their labour contracts to ensure that they understood (and would comply with) the terms laid down. Cape magistrates already supervised the contracts and saw each mineworker when he signed on. The Cape now proposed that this work of supervision should be carried out by a new class of officials who would devote all of their time to the work. Native affairs officers aimed not only to protect the black mineworkers from the widespread misrepresentation of labour contracts, but equally to associate the power of the state with the agreement made between the worker and the particular mining groups. They proposed to finance the new bureaux by levying a tax on the so-called capitation fee paid by the mines for each recruit dispatched by a labour agent. In this way the system would finance itself. The Cape's proposal reflected the government's conclusion that recruiting for the mines was haphazard and uncoordinated, that the supply of labour was therefore subject to unnecessary fluctuations and that both the profitability of the mines and the prosperity of the eastern Cape suffered as a result. Under the new system, the labour bureaux "should be able to gauge the quality and quantity of the labour supply with almost as much accuracy as the Egyptian Government can determine the area of land irrigable from the Assouan [sic] Dam."[85] Their comparison is significant. The authors of the memorandum regarded black labour not so much as a commodity, the more usual contemporary view, but as a vital though unpredictable natural resource, akin to a great river. By providing greater knowledge about the resource, the new labour bureaux would permit maximum exploitation of it.

The conference convened in Cape Town on the 23rd of September. After a plenary session on the first day, a small committee made up of government officials and senior representatives of mine management took evidence from several leading recruiters. The whole conference then reassembled to consider various recommendations. The testimony of the recruiters amply confirmed the existence of the evils which had prompted the conference in the first place. These sessions also revealed a fair measure of agreement on the need for reform and on the changes proposed by the Cape to correct abuses. By the time the conference concluded on 28 September, the delegates had accepted a package of proposals to be recommended to the Transvaal and Cape governments.[86] Cape officials had pressed hard for agreement. They knew that circumstances in the mining industry had now combined to give the Cape greater leverage over the labour policies of the Transvaal government, the Chamber of Mines, and the individual recruiters. Before this, the mining group controllers, most recruiters, and even the Transvaal authorities had tended to resist any reforms which, however desirable, might conceivably inhibit even temporarily the flow of labour from the Cape.[87]

The conference now accepted the main recommendations which Edward Dower, the Cape secretary of native affairs, had put forward. Essentially he and his colleagues wanted to extend the measures of control which had been initiated in the negotiations with the Transvaal during 1907. The labour bureaux would exercise general supervision over the labour agents and runners. The bureaux would attest contracts and arrange for the transportation of all recruits and volunteer labour to the Rand (this would therefore no longer be the responsibility of private recruiters). A new class of officials, registry officers, would be appointed to head up the bureaux. Responsibility for labour matters would no longer fall upon the overworked magistracy. The labour registrars would work closely with the Transvaal's

Native Labour Bureau. Officials hoped the bureaux would encourage the enlistment of the mine labour volunteer. In this way, the entire system could be renovated and the role of the recruiter reduced, perhaps ultimately done away with. The bureaux would provide facilities for the transport of these volunteers to the Rand where the GNLB would assist them to find mining or other employment. The assisted voluntary scheme had been on the books since late 1907 but only a handful of Africans had taken advantage of it. Officials in the Cape Native Affairs Departments did not expect that Africans would opt for the scheme in large numbers at first. They knew that the wage advance system drew Africans irresistibly to the recruiters who used every means to thwart the assisted voluntary scheme. They hoped, however, that the advantages of this scheme would gradually become apparent to Africans. Since they also proposed to limit advances (except in Pondoland) to five pounds and perhaps eventually to eliminate them, they probably hoped eventually to eliminate the labour agent. In public, of course, they denied any such intention.

The other recommendations of the conference were designed to assist the registry officials to police the recruiters more effectively. Agents and runners should be licensed half-yearly instead of annually (the Cape later abandoned this proposal because it could not be implemented without legislation). Licences would be issued only to the nominees of employers (the freelance agents would not be licensed) and to recruit for only one employer. Runners would reside in their district and would be licensed to recruit only there. All of these measures aimed to curb the excessive competition and fraudulent practices which had previously constituted standard operating methods. These and other, more minor administrative suggestions went to the Transvaal government for approval in mid-October. The Cape estimated that £20,000 would be required annually to fund the new system. The mines would pay by the levy of a per capita fee on the recruits.

In its reply, the Transvaal Native Affairs Department accepted most of the proposals (the Chamber of Mines agreed also). The Transvaalers did suggest and the Cape later approved the attachment of the district labour bureaux directly to the Transvaal's GNLB which would also pay the operating costs.[88] The proposals of the Cape Town conference provided a blueprint for later legislative and administrative action by the Union government. These reforms marked a second tentative step toward effective state supervision of mine labour recruiting. The 1907 negotiations had endorsed the principle of interstate cooperation and established the outline of an administrative framework. Now in 1909 on the eve of Union, governments began to consider how their control could be made effective. Despite this, conditions in mine labour recruiting remained radically unsatisfactory for several years. The Union government legislated in 1911 to regulate further the operation of private recruiters. The elimination of abuses, however, required the termination of the system of advances and the promotion of industry cooperation through the formation of the monopsonistic Native Recruiting Corporation in 1912. Thus the 1909 measures constituted only another modest instalment in what became a massive administrative effort.

While the conference deliberations had revealed serious disagreements on a number of important matters, the discussions themselves had been surprisingly amiable. After the conference broke up, both the mining groups and the principal recruiters quickly gave their assent to the major administrative change which the Cape officials had put forward at the outset. All of the established recruiters could applaud the decision to restrict licences to those agents representing specific mining houses.[89] Labour registrars would take over from hard-pressed resident magistrates all work connected with the supervision of recruiting. Originally the Cape had proposed itself to appoint and supervise the work of the labour registrars, through its own Native Affairs Department.[90] At the urging of the Transvaal government, however, these new officials became part of the establishment of the GNLB which now extended the scope of its operations to the eastern Cape. A further proposal to charge the costs to the bureau rather than to the Cape probably did much to overcome any Cape opposition.[91] In the aftermath of the recruiting conference, government and industry representatives also agreed that the assisted voluntary scheme should now be revived under the supervision of the labour registrars. The scheme had been on the books since late 1907 but few Africans had taken advantage of it. The Cape Native Affairs Department hoped that the labour registrars would have the time and the energy to push the scheme against the inevitable opposition of subagents and runners in the field.

A related proposal was also adopted at this time. Except in Pondoland, a limit was placed on wage advances of five pounds.[92] Briefly, officials accepted the view of the Pondo recruiters at the conference that any departure from the cattle advance system would seriously affect recruiting. By June 1910, however, the government had ended cattle advances on the "pretext" of preventing the spread of East Coast fever.[93] Two probable motives lay behind this proposal to restrict advances. Even the recruiters could see the point of putting some limit on the competitive bidding for labour. Also a five pound maximum reduced the amount of loss to the trader/recruiter in the (all too likely) event of desertion. Although officials did not make the point explicitly, they probably had another objective in view. The prospect of wage advances constituted a major incentive for Africans to sign labour contracts. By first reducing and then eventually eliminating the wage advance, officials almost certainly aimed to make the assisted voluntary scheme (which provided rail fare and food but no cash advance) more competitive within the recruiting system. They hoped that

Africans would then become accustomed to remitting funds to their families *after* they had started work. A deposit and remittance agency had been reestablished for this purpose at the end of 1907. Most officials probably recognized that until advances were either entirely abolished or reduced still further, progress with the voluntary scheme could only be slow. They hoped, however, to make a start. Some of the more visionary among them looked forward to the day when the recruiter would fade entirely from the scene and the voluntary system provide all necessary labour.[94]

Despite sometimes heated disagreement on particular issues, the representatives of the government, the recruiting organizations, and the industry managed at least to agree on the package of basic reforms which the Cape had put forward. In the sequel, however, as the Cape and Transvaal governments moved to implement these changes, the harmony displayed at the Cape Town conference quickly evaporated. Fearing after all that the government secretly aimed to attack independent recruiting, various labour agents, including some of the big operators, who had attended the conference, began a vigorous campaign to subvert the reform program. Astonishingly, H.M. Taberer took the lead in the campaign to undo or prevent the implementation of the changes in recruiting practice agreed at Cape Town. Taberer had been a leading reform advocate at the conference and before. He had welcomed the conference and had taken an active part in it. Long before that while he was director of the GNLB he had himself advocated some of the changes finally accepted at Cape Town. By early 1910, however, his enthusiasm for reform had completely disappeared.

Taberer's shift from advocacy to opposition began to develop early in the year. He was instrumental in securing a decision of the Cape government to delay the implementation of the agreed limit on wage advances of five pounds outside Pondoland. Belatedly he discovered that his recruiting staff had already authorized the giving of advances well in excess of five pounds. This must have been severely embarrassing for Taberer who had been the leading opponent of large advances at the conference. He now confessed that his organization had approved wage advances of up to fifteen pounds in order to meet the competition. Since a number of the other recruiters had already ordered their subagents to restrict advances in anticipation of the new legal limit, they were understandably indignant at the government's decision to accept Taberer's request for delay. Although the authorities both in Cape Town and Johannesburg denied that Taberer had influenced them, they refused to name those who had. Among Taberer's rivals few doubted that the extension of the deadline was, as S.M. Pritchard put it, "engineered by Taberer who has exercised undue influence on our respective governments."[95] Pritchard denied that there had been "undue influence" but acknowledged that the request for delay was Taberer's. The suddenness of the decision coupled with the lack of warning to the other recruiters must have convinced them that Taberer had used his leverage with former colleagues to win for his agents a competitive edge just before the new limit on advances went into effect.

The delay in the implementation of the five-pound maximum advance was, however, a minor affair. Much more serious trouble erupted in February and March during S.M. Pritchard's tour of the eastern Cape. Pritchard travelled to the Cape in order to supervise the installation of the new officials, the labour registrars, who now assumed responsibility for labour matters from the resident magistrates. He also held meetings with Africans in each of the main centres of the territories in order to introduce the labour registrars and to promote the government's assisted voluntary scheme. In a confidential letter to Edward Dower at the end of February, Pritchard outlined the approach which he had taken at these meetings: "I cannot speak too highly of the very cordial co-operation which has invariably been extended to the [assisted voluntary] scheme by Magistrates ... The meetings too with the Natives have been very useful; I have naturally hidden nothing from them; on the contrary I have clearly explained to them that things are not as they should be either as regards their recruitment, transport to the Mines or their employment or terms of service. As regards recruiting I have pointed out to them the disadvantages of the present credit and advance system and the benefits which they will derive by applying to registrars for facilities to proceed to the Mines."[96]

Pritchard had, as he indicated, spoken very forthrightly at these meetings. Moreover, he now made plain what had been discreetly veiled at the Cape Town conference. The GNLB intended to promote the voluntary scheme and to encourage Africans to take advantage of it. At the conference, government officials left the recruiters with the clear impression that they aimed merely to make certain facilities available and that the labour registrars would not compete with the private recruiters. Pritchard intended now to push well beyond this modest plan. In effect he proposed to send the labour registrars into battle against the private recruiters; his own meetings with Transkeian Africans constituted the opening salvo of the campaign. Writing to the Transvaal secretary of native affairs, W. Windham, Pritchard openly condemned the entire recruiting system in the eastern Cape and all of the labour agents involved in it.[97] He argued forcefully that the implementation of the voluntary scheme would serve the interest of both the government and the mining industry itself. The mines should support the scheme, he suggested, because it promised lower recruiting costs and (since there would presumably be no misrepresentation with labour registrars running the scheme) more contented labour and less desertion. Knowing that he already faced criticism and outrage from the agents in the Cape and from their Johannesburg principals, Pritchard defended his methods in promoting the plan. With the "class of individual" running these labour agencies, he insisted, a "kid glove" policy would immediately fail. He quoted a threat from one such agent to "use any means fair or foul to break the scheme," and he continued: "You have no idea of the class of individual that deals in labour in these parts – some go as straight as they can but some are veritable 'body snatchers' – and if anything I do one day results in their general extermination I shall feel that I have at least done something for this Country."

The director had received information that his superiors might deny him their full support now that controversy had developed over his meetings with Africans in various centres. He had good reason to be concerned. His meetings in the eastern Cape aroused a storm of protest from agents and traders.[98] Several of the large recruiting agencies in Johannesburg also leaned heavily on government, hoping to force his superiors to repudiate him. Cape traders' and agents' associations went to work at the Cape Town end, while their principals tried to turn Pretoria against the GNLB director. Among the leaders of this campaign, H.M. Taberer became especially prominent. On this issue he and his arch-rival, "Kaffir" Wilson, at last found agreement.

As soon as word reached the agents that Pritchard was on tour to pro- mote voluntary labour, they denounced him bitterly, hoping to discredit him and force his recall. The agents turned their own exclusion from his meetings with Africans to advantage by simply inventing fantastic accounts of what he had said. They used these stories in turn to mobilize support from local interests which benefited from the existing system and to put pressure on both the Cape and Transvaal governments. They cleverly tailored their pitch to the two governments to take account of the special concerns of each colony. Writing to the Transvaal, the agents simply warned that Pritchard's activities endangered the labour supply to the mines.[99] If deprived of capita- tion fees and revenue from wage advances the traders would turn against government, and they could influence "the natives" to reject mine employ- ment. The headmen too would no longer promote mine labour if deprived of their "royalties." Arguments directed to the Cape stressed the political and economic repercussions of any departure from the existing system. The agents and traders would combine to fight the voluntary system; this could be politically embarrassing.[100] More importantly, any diminution of the recruiting effort and consequent reduction in the flow of labour to the mines would entail serious losses to the economy and in particular government revenues. Perceiving that Pritchard would try to line up the mining com- panies against the recruiters on the issue, they warned of another capitalist plot. This gave them a potent weapon to use with the Cape government, in particular with the prime minister, J.X. Merriman, the Cape's leading critic of Randlords. Any suggestion that the Cape government operated in cahoots with mining capitalists had to be smartly repudiated. The secretary of native affairs at the Cape, Edward Dower, wrote to one informant showing his sensitivity on this point:

Now I see that it is argued that the Government is playing into the hands of the Mine Capitalists by allowing these facilities under which voluntary Natives get free transport which the agents cannot offer and that it is all a plan to cheapen labour to the sole advantage of the Mines. And I have been assured by Labour Agents that they will withdraw all opposition if free transport is not given. But what would you think of us as Protectors of the Natives if we consented to an arrangement under which the Mines would not only be relieved of recruiting expenses but would also benefit by deducting from the wages of voluntary labourers the cost of transport? Surely that would be a one-sided arrangement which would leave the interests of the Natives entirely out of account.[101]

As the campaign against Pritchard developed, the Cape's advocacy of voluntary assisted migration to the Rand became a serious embarrassment to the government. Although ministers and officials had claimed that their reform proposals sought the welfare of the blacks, they soon found themselves accused of conspiring to maximize mining profits at the expense of the eastern Cape. The critics also blamed them for advocating a system which, if successful, would eliminate wage advances and entail serious loss to the trading community.[102] The Transvaal government did not escape. The Transvaal Mines Labour Company's local manager, Douglas McMillan, gave full vent to his fears, and warned his principals that under the new scheme "all boys will be rounded up, put under police, and in fact taken up to Umzilikazi [WNLA]."[103] "Kaffir" Wilson showed sufficient alarm to take the matter up directly with Rissik, the minister.

In fact most of these charges went wide of the mark. Neither Pritchard nor his superiors in the Cape and Transvaal administrations intended to eliminate competitive recruiting at this time. Eventually, of course, they hoped to supplant the existing system entirely but knew that years would be required to achieve this. In the short term, they aimed merely to develop the voluntary scheme as a viable alternative route to the Rand and to give it some modest publicity in the recruiting centres. Dower believed that only "a few thrifty natives" would use the voluntary route. Most of them would continue to be attracted by "the pernicious system of advances."[104] Even Pritchard did not believe that the new system could easily be established or the recruiters driven from the field overnight. By his intemperate attacks on the recruiters, however, and because of the secrecy of his first meetings with Africans he provoked the recruiters to fear the worst and to mount an all-out effort to oppose him.

Both governments found the resulting pressure irresistible and both drew back from their support of the voluntary scheme and hastened to reassure the recruiting interests. Shortly after arriving in the Cape, Pritchard received word that the campaign against him had been launched with Taberer and other principal recruiters in the lead.[105] At first Pritchard thought Taberer had simply been misinformed and that when the facts were made available, he would reaffirm the support he had given to the voluntary scheme at the Cape Town conference. Writing directly to his former colleague, Pritchard warned him not to be misled by reports from his recruiters which were "artfully calculated" to cause alarm and force the intervention of ministers.[106] This effort to win Taberer back to the cause soon failed. To his surprise and consternation, Pritchard discovered that Taberer remained firmly opposed to the plan he had originally himself designed and that his influence now prevailed in Pretoria. Pritchard's friends in the GNLB in Johannesburg wired him urgently at the end of February that the recruiters stood on the point of victory. According to the telegram, Taberer had got his way entirely. The minister pledged that the government would not compete with the private recruiters and that it would not allow bureau "native" staff attached to the labour registrars' offices to be used to promote voluntary enlistment for the mines. Taberer himself was en route to the Cape where he would attend Pritchard's remaining meetings and then retrace the director's route to inform Africans that the government scheme had been "reversed." The wire concluded that "Taberer stands apart from other recruiters here but appears to have obtained complete sympathy at Pretoria."[107] In fact the government faced severe pressure on this issue and not only from Taberer.[108] "Kaffir" Wilson also saw the minister and received written assurances that the state had no intention "of entering into the recruiting business itself," that free railway fares would not be given from official funds, that "native touts" would not be used to promote voluntary labour, and that wage advances would not be made under the voluntary plan.[109] Shortly thereafter Wilson left for the Cape in order personally to reassure his agents that government intended no serious action against them. A.M. Mostert had an interview with the minister and received similar apologies and assurances.[110] Although the Transvaal administration did not in the end completely repudiate the plan, they did bind themselves to conditions which severely limited the chances of success. At the same time, they warned Pritchard that their support for voluntary enlistment was conditional and that he must be "very discreet." Rissik very nearly ordered Pritchard's recall in the middle of his tour. Only the intervention of the Cape government prevented this.[111] Even so, Pritchard received a peremptory telegram recalling him to Pretoria as soon as he had completed his work.[112]

Why did the mining companies not rally to Pritchard's support? They stood to benefit from his reforms through much cheaper labour mobilization. In reckoning on support from the higher echelons of the mining industry, Pritchard had given insufficient weight to the timidity and shortsightedness of most of the men who made the industry's labour policy. As director of native labour in 1907, Taberer could afford to take the long view and sponsor a voluntary labour policy. He then had no responsibility to maintain recruiting levels. Later, as a private recruiter at the Cape Town conference, he could appear to be statesmanlike when the issue was posed, so to say, theoretically. His former colleagues in government expected it. Quite a different attitude prevailed, however, when the Taberers, Mosterts, and Wilsons of the recruiting industry faced developments which threatened to disrupt the labour supply–however partially and temporarily. Taberer headed the recruiting operations of the Rand's largest employers. They had emphasized their dissatisfaction with his efforts already, and their labour needs consistently exceeded the capacity of his recruiters on the supply side.

When brought to a decision on the practical question of whether to back his own men or Pritchard, Taberer had no choice at all. The statesmanlike position and his previous expressions of humanitarian concern at the abuses which private recruiting inflicted on Africans had simply to be discarded. If the flow of labour from the eastern Cape faltered even momentarily, trouble would swiftly follow. At the end of 1909, only a few months before, the Gold Fields had abandoned its contract with Taberer's Labour Organization because he had failed to recruit sufficient labour. Thus Taberer could not afford to alienate his recruiters and runners and traders in the Cape by supporting an alternative scheme which offered no guarantee of success. Quite simply he had too much at stake to take such a risk. Unless the group controllers were prepared to repudiate the heads of their native labour departments and face the possible dissolution of recruiting organizations painfully developed over several years, they too could ill afford to take risks for the voluntary system. Thus Pritchard's perception that the financial interest of the mining groups aligned them with him and against their own recruiters on the issue of voluntary labour was correct, but left too much out of account. When he tried to implement the plan, the resulting uproar soon exposed the naïvety of his thinking and the impracticality of his hopes.

Pritchard had arrived at the Cape in a confident, optimistic mood but he was soon disillusioned. The disconcerting failure of his own government to back him was especially irritating and Pritchard wrote to W. Windham, the Transvaal secretary of native affairs, expressing himself "extremely disappointed" at the line taken by his superiors.[113] Initially the politicians and Native Affairs Department officials at the Cape showed a much greater inclination to stand firm against the agitation mounted by the recruiters. Burton, Dower, and Merriman had pressed hard for the Cape Town conference and had worked tirelessly during and after the meetings to secure agreement from their more hesitant colleagues to the North. As soon as he saw the strength of the opposition ranged against the voluntary labour plan,

Pritchard wrote to Dower informing him and in effect asking for support. Cape officials backed him strongly.[114] At about this time, the Cape Native Affairs Department intercepted the telegram from Pretoria ordering Pritchard back for consultations. Smoothly Cape officials intervened to protect the threatened labour bureau director. After stating that the telegram had been read in Cape Town, the department explained to the Transvaal officials, Rissik and Windham, that the tour had been carefully prepared and the meetings which Pritchard was holding in the various centres could not be cancelled at short notice. In any case it was "very desirable" that Pritchard should meet with the resident magistrates and "leading natives" of the main recruiting centres. The Cape government expressed confidence in Pritchard and stated it was satisfied with his proposals despite the agitation which had developed. Finally the telegram urged that instructions recalling Pritchard should be cancelled.[115] Since the authorities most concerned had expressed confidence in the bureau director, the Transvaal had little choice but to comply with the request. Pritchard's tour went ahead, and he was soon joined by Dower who showed his alarm at the developing agitation by hastily leaving Cape Town for the eastern districts late on a Saturday so that he could join Pritchard at a scheduled meeting with labour agents a few days later. He arrived only a short time before Taberer and Wilson who had rushed from Johannesburg to bolster the recruiters.

The Cape prime minister, J.X. Merriman, took a very severe view of the entire affair. He believed that the agents' agitation was ridiculous and should be ignored. When the Transvaal began to waver in its support of Pritchard, however, he saw that action was required. In a long, tactful letter to Rissik he sought to give reassurance while at the same time reaffirming the need for improved methods in recruiting and expressing confidence in Pritchard.[116] Merriman agreed that government itself ought not to take direct responsibility for recruiting. In the evolution of the assisted voluntary scheme, none of the planners had proposed such a step. At the same time, he stressed the need to bring competitive recruiting under control:

It seems preposterous that large sums should continue to be wasted on the recruitment of labour and it would be far more practical if any funds that could be spared were laid out in the improvement of conditions of labour both in the mines and on the road to them ... I do not attach much importance to the opposition of the labour agents who find a very lucrative and unwholesome sort of gain slipping from them while I look forward to a large and growing increase in the number of independent labourers as soon as the improved conditions are brought home to them. There will, in my opinion, always be a field for respectable and trustworthy agents to carry on their operations.

Without the firm support of Merriman and Dower, the assisted voluntary plan would almost certainly have been scrapped. The correspondence of the Transvaal government indicates that they very nearly capitulated completely in face of the agitation of the Cape recruiters and their Johannesburg principals, especially Taberer, Mostert, and Wilson. Very probably also Cape support saved S.M. Pritchard from rough treatment at the hands of his superior officers. The telegram recalling Pritchard which the Cape was able to head off indicates that Windham and Rissik were quite prepared to sacrifice him as a means of quelling the agitation.

In relation to the issues at stake in this crisis, the uproar over Pritchard's tour was exaggerated. With the possible exceptions of Merriman and Dower all concerned overreacted. Pritchard's ill-considered "secret" meetings aroused the fears of the agents while his intemperate statements also made plain that he was no friend of competitive recruiting. However, his plans were modest and did not, immediately, pose a serious threat to the private recruiters. An examination of this agitation suggests several important conclusions. First, it indicates dramatically the atmosphere of fear, suspicion, and mistrust which pervaded all sectors of the recruiting industry. Second, it illustrates the extent and the strength of the interests which had grown up around the competitive recruiting system. Large sums of money and hundreds of careers were at stake. Organized in labour agents' associations and chambers of commerce, the recruiters and the trader/runners brought massive pressure to bear on the government as well as on their Johannesburg principals.[117] In Johannesburg, the labour contractors and the heads of the various mine labour departments had become powerful, well-connected operators. The reaction of the Transvaal government to their representations showed that they had easy access even to the cabinet and demonstrated on this occasion a notable ability to influence policy. In their reaction to the Pritchard tour, the private recruiters showed that they could overawe even the powerful mining groups and force them to repudiate the voluntary labour system through which the mines stood to make large savings on recruiting costs. Third, the agitation reveals that the independent contractors had some perception of their vulnerability. Although the state's system to encourage assisted voluntary labour never worked effectively, perhaps because of the migrants' distrust of the magistracy, the number of workers proceeding to the Rand entirely on their own without the aid of the government or the recruiters did increase steadily, especially after about 1912. By 1916 there were more volunteers on the mines from the South African territories than there were recruits from those areas. As a result, the private recruiters did find their position undermined very substantially, both in relation to the mining industry and to the government. This lay in the future, however.

Pritchard's assisted voluntary scheme survived the assaults on it, although the private recruiters had received specific assurances from the

Transvaal government that the labour registrars and their African messengers would not be competing for labour against the private agents and runners. Within this strait-jacket, the new registrars did what they could to encourage Africans to make use of their facilities.[118] They failed dismally. With dozens of agents and hundreds of runners scouring the countryside, the chances of a prospective mineworker evading "recruitment" were remote. The registrars simply could not compete with the private recruiters and the trader/runners who had wage advances to offer and (usually) the influence of local chiefs and headmen behind them. So long as the mining groups failed to combine to restore the recruiting monopsony, the private interests in the industry had a field day. Government efforts to control them remained ineffective.[119]

From the standpoint of both the Cape government and the mining industry, the competitive recruiting system had, despite the abuses discussed above, one compelling advantage: it delivered the labour. Under the WNLA, the mines themselves had tried to make the eastern Cape a major source of migrant labour. They failed completely. Within only a few years, the labour contractors were spectacularly successful in raising the participation rate of Transkei African males in the mine labour system. Not only did the absolute numbers increase dramatically, but also the proportion of the overall supply contributed by the Cape's African territories was transformed. In 1905-6, an average of 9,354 Cape workers found employment on mines and works in the Transvaal.[120] This represented just under 10 per cent of the total for the year and about 18 per cent of the average emigration from the Transkei in those two years.[121] Four years later in 1910, employment from the Cape on Transvaal mines and works had jumped to 60,509[122] or nearly 30 per cent of an average of 207,921 blacks employed on mines and works that year. Employment in these categories in the Transvaal accounted for no less than 71 per cent of the total estimated emigration from the Transkei and Pondoland in 1910.[123] This represents a huge increase whether one looks at the number of Cape Africans employed on mines and works, at the proportion of the total employed contributed by the Cape, or at the percentage of total emigration from the Transkei and Pondoland that found employment on mines and works.

The transformation of the Cape Colony into a major source of mine labour in so short a time cannot be explained by reference to any generalized process of "proletarianization."[124] There was no sudden application of government coercion or taxation levels to explain this very abrupt increase in the number of Cape workers on Transvaal mines and works. If the independence of the Cape black agriculturalists had been weakened seriously by the processes which Colin Bundy has described, most of them still avoided mining work even with the onset of the postwar depression in 1904-5. The big increase in recruiting levels for the mines occurred in

1908–10, when, if anything, the Cape government, now led by the liberal J.X. Merriman, pressed less heavily on African cultivators than it had done before. The five years after about 1904 were, certainly, years of serious depression in South Africa. Gold mining was, of course, not detrimentally affected by this downward trend in the business cycle; indeed the mines have always benefited from deflation which raises the real value of their product while helping to cut costs. Undoubtedly reduced activity in other sectors of the South African economy forced many workers who previously would not have considered the mines to seek employment on them. But this cannot have been the main reason for the sharp increase in Cape recruits on the mines, otherwise the cash and cattle advance system would not have been necessary. If Africans were so impoverished, if alternative employment was closed because of the depression, why did the mines have to bribe them with huge advances and employ hundreds of recruiters at high fees to tempt them off the land? The making of the mine labour force cannot be explained simply by reference to structural changes associated with the development of industrial capitalism in South Africa. Nor is reference to coercive government a sufficient explanation. To mobilize labour from the Cape required the mines to devise the series of measures described above. They cast aside their own instrument of monopoly, the WNLA, and embraced instead the private recruiters. They poured money into the system and allowed the real costs of their black labour to increase markedly through the wage advance system and the higher recruiting fees. It is the implementation of these specific policies which alone explains the making of the Transkei labour pool.

CHAPTER FOUR

The Native Recruiting Corporation and Its Rivals

As a result of the collapse of WNLA operations within South Africa, the mining groups had condemned themselves to several years of unrestrained competition for labour. This represented a return to the anarchical conditions of the 1890s with many of the same undesirable consequences. Recruiting costs increased sharply; independent labour contractors and recruiters captured a larger share of the business; the system of cash and cattle advances developed and cost the groups large sums; finally, the spectre of wage competition returned and differentials opened both for basic rates and for the bonuses paid principally to "drill boys." This was a direct result of the intense competition for labour which had developed in the South African recruiting zones, particularly the eastern Cape. The Chamber of Mines required four years to persuade most of the groups that the maintenance of profitable operations required that they resume cooperation in recruiting.

Despite the persistence of this wasteful competition, the recruiting industry registered some impressive successes in the decade after 1907. The size of the black labour force on the Rand increased steadily up to 1914, despite the loss of over 50,000 Chinese workers by 1910 and the later ban on the employment of tropical Africans which cost a further 20,000. The mines made these gains in South African recruiting levels without any long-term wage increases. Indeed the chamber introduced a maximum average wage agreement in 1912 which held firm despite a 250 per cent increase in the cost of living between 1911 and 1919; real wages of black workers declined drastically.[1] In Mozambique, the successful reconstruction of the WNLA in 1907 permitted the mines to maintain one of their principal sources of supply. The chamber headed off another challenge to its control there in 1911.

Outside Mozambique, the increases in the labour supply for the mines meant a corresponding loss of labour for farms and other employers. Recognizing this, the Union government intervened with regulations under

TABLE I
Earnings per Shift of Black Miners, 1911–19

Year	Earnings in Pence per Shift	Index of Retail Prices*
1911	23.3	1,081
1912	23.6	1,125
1913	`23.0	1,140
1914	23.7	1,121
1915	23.4	1,192
1916	23.1	1,245
1917	23.1	1,376
1918	23.5	1,406
1919	24.3	1,518

SOURCE: Low Grade Mines Commission, *Final Report,* 31; *Official Yearbook of the Union of South Africa, 1910–1920,* 335.
* 1910 = 1,000

the Native Labour Regulation Act (No. 15 of 1911) to close large areas of the country to mine recruiters. They found themselves excluded from the entire Free State (except Thaba 'Nchu and the Harrismith area), and from large parts of Natal, the Transvaal, and even the Cape. The antisquatting provisions of the Native Lands Act, 1913, although they affected at first only the Free State, may also be seen as an effort to release labour for farmers and offset the competitive advantage of the mines.[2] The Land Act and the earlier Labour Regulation Act should be viewed together as a package of measures deliberately designed by the first Union government to accommodate the competing labour demands of the mines and the farmers. The deal was notably generous to the mines. The state made no effort to interfere with the mining industry's hold on the eastern Cape and the northern Transvaal, then as now principal South African sources of migrant labour. In these areas, the mining groups competed with each other with a ferocity which forced up costs dramatically, drove from the field most of the farmers and competing employers, but also came to threaten the profitability of some of the mines themselves.

Competitive recruiting had differential effects on the industry and caused most trouble when recruiting levels fell during periods of "labour shortage." When labour was scarce, the shallow, outcrop mines did best because the work was easiest there, particularly the drilling, and conditions least dangerous and uncomfortable.[3] The independent labour contractors also did well (even when supplying deeper-level mines) because they generally paid their recruiters and black runners premium rates. Most of the burden imposed by shortage fell therefore on the larger, development-oriented groups which were working the lower-grade deep-level areas on a large scale. By late 1908 executives representing the two most important of these groups, Consolidated Gold Fields and the Wernher, Beit/Eckstein complex (soon to be known as the Central Mining and Investment Corporation after the partnerships were wound up at the end of 1910), had concluded that restoration of unity on the recruiting issue was essential. For the Gold Fields, R.G. Fricker worried especially that competition led the mines to agree to shorter contract periods for their workers. Since black miners on three- or six-month contracts had hardly time to learn the tasks assigned, efficiency declined and working costs tended to rise. A mine manager noted in 1909 that after such a short period, a "hammer boy" might still be struggling to accomplish his daily task. He would leave the mine resentful, and this hurt recruiting. While not as concerned as Fricker, Lionel Phillips for Central Mining agreed that the problem was serious and likely to become more so if an expected labour shortage materialized in 1909. These men tried and failed to secure industry-wide agreement on a six-month minimum contract. Just about all the groups accepted except Randfontein Estates, but in the absence of a central, controlling organization, compliance could not be enforced. The agreement did not last. During 1909, Gold Fields and Central Mining called repeatedly for restored cooperation in recruiting. At the same time, however, they pressured their chief recruiter, Taberer, to do everything possible to draw labour from the competition. [4]

Yet these two large firms found it difficult even to maintain their own joint agreement. An important difference between them developed in late 1909 over wage rates. Competition had developed in this area even among the individual mines within each group. For instance, voluntary (i.e., unrecruited) "drill boys" could command higher rates on some mines both because they generally had mining experience and because they cost the mine nothing in recruiting fees. F.D.P. Chaplin, representing the Gold Fields group's administration, and Taberer believed that the wages of the poorest paid should be levelled up. For the Central Mining head office, R.W. Schumacher, was not so sure. He asked whether Taberer could guarantee that such an increase would produce more labour and in contrast to Chaplin and Taberer revealed himself as an unreconstructed believer in the "target worker" fallacy, that labour supply moved inversely to wage increases. Very wisely, Taberer replied that he could "guarantee nothing." Recruiting levels depended not only on the state of intra-group competition, on comparative wage rates and recruiting fees, but also on the availability or not of alternative employment. The mines continued to be employers of last resort for many Africans. [5]

A related issue concerned the drill standard required by the various groups. Some specified thirty-six inches as the expected daily task of the "hammer boys" who hand-drilled the holes for blasting in the stopes. Other mines called for forty-two inches per shift. The deeper the hole, the more rock which would be broken with each charge of dynamite. The minimum required affected wage rates, both because workers failing to meet the standard received no pay and a loafer's ticker, which meant that the shift did not count toward completion of the contract, and because small bonuses became payable for each inch drilled beyond the minimum. The Central Mining group set one of the highest standards in the industry, a full forty-two inches for which their mines established a wage of 2s.6d. Disputes on these and other matters connected with recruiting proved to be irresolvable even to executives of the two groups most committed to early restoration of the monopsony. At the end of 1909, Gold Fields withdrew its exclusive contract from Taberer's labour organization which was then reconstructed as the native labour department of Central Mining. Although willing in the end to retain Taberer, Central Mining executives were far from pleased with his efforts and welcomed the opportunity to bring his organization under direct corporate control.[6]

Anxiety over growing anarchy in recruiting was not confined to representatives of these two large firms. Among some of the small groups also, executives began to express concern about the effects of the prevailing ruthless competition. In particular they feared that Taberer, with all of the resources which his organization commanded, might eventually secure a corner on the entire South African supply. This was an extravagant fear.[7] Taberer certainly had the ambition but in 1909 was far from achieving that degree of success. Still, concern regarding what he might be able to achieve probably helped to induce his rivals at least to listen when Taberer's employers renewed their efforts to bring the industry together in a cooperative recruiting organization for the South African territories. These initiatives were prompted by another downturn in recruiting levels which set in during mid-1910. More than ever before Phillips began to press "the necessity for something vigorous being done." Recruiting fees had gone up again and some contractors now paid nearly four pounds a head to their agents for mineworkers signing six-month contracts. One of Phillip's informants claimed that the black runners received fifty shillings a recruit, a huge sum.[8] At a meeting of the groups, in which Phillips and his Central Mining colleagues took the lead, the representatives agreed to establish another committee of inquiry and eventually to work out the details for a new recruiting organization for British South Africa. Phillips himself had produced a draft proposal which the committee would use as a working paper. He was not optimistic, however, and began to doubt the prospects of success even before the committee met to begin its work. As usual, the Robinson group particularly but also East Rand Proprietary obstructed an industry-wide consensus.[9]

Nevertheless, as the group representatives on the committee began their work, agreement seemed briefly possible, if not with the two dissidents then at least with the remainder of the industry. A few days after one of the early meetings, Central Mining reported to London that agreement in principle had been reached to restore industry-wide standard rates for black wages and recruiting fees. Competitive recruiting could continue for the moment, but the mining groups would bind themselves to pay both the workers and the recruiters standard rates. The firm hoped, too optimistically, that this could be the basis of restored unity. In the absence of a central recruiting organization, partial agreement on wages and recruiting charges would be inherently unstable because impossible to police. Furthermore, a number of the independent labour contractors had negotiated long-term contracts specifying recruiting fees and wage rates, especially at the ERPM where some of the contracts had as long as ten years to run.[10] Phillips thought these might be purchased, or dealt with in some other way but only at substantial cost. Moreover, the contracts entrenched powerful vested interests which could only lose from the elimination of competitive recruiting. They would fight to maintain their position.

Other, equally serious obstacles stood in the way of restoration of the mine labour monopsony. When the committee moved from drafting principles to an investigation of actual recruiting practices on the Rand, trouble quickly developed. Since chronic mistrust and suspicion characterized intragroup relations on anything to do with migrant labour, the committee met flat refusals even to supply information about present methods. No doubt the smaller groups and those employing labour contractors feared that the big employers, especially Central Mining and the Gold Fields, would use the committee as a device to discover their recruiting secrets. Since Taberer was known to be in contact with former colleagues in government, his rivals probably also feared that he might denounce them to the authorities. Whatever the reason, two of the more secretive groups refused to provide any information except to an "independent committee" which could include as members no executive from any mining house and which would delete references to particular group recruiting practices before releasing any confidential information.[11] The other houses acquiesced and somewhat reluctantly established a small "independent committee" which included the WNLA chairman, Perry, and three others.[12]

They produced an interim report in October 1910, outlining some of the rigidities and sources of rivalry which had prevented earlier efforts to restore unity.[13] It documented the very considerable involvement of all of the mining groups in the unrestrained competition among their recruiters. Since the breakup of the WNLA in South Africa in 1906-7, three distinct recruiting systems had evolved, the committee found. Some groups had established recruiting offices in the various open districts and maintained a salaried staff there which reported to group administration. The district offices received

125   The Native Recruiting Corporation

labour from the local recruiters, handled remittances, and negotiated with the recruiters on behalf of the group. Other mining houses preferred not to maintain their own district offices but instead to deal directly with a labour. agent in Johannesburg. In this case, the agent took the whole responsibility, set fees, and regulated the activities of recruiters who were his employees. He delivered labour to the mine which then put the workers under contract and arranged to pay, feed, and house them. The third system evolved as a variant of the second and by 1910 survived in only two groups, not named by the committee but certainly Randfontein Estates and the ERPM. These were the labour contractors who actually employed the mineworkers, kept them under contract, and sold their services on a per-shift-worked basis. Some of the contractors, like Mostert, paid, fed, and housed their own workers; others arranged for the mine to do this.

The committee documented the by now notorious high cost of competitive recruiting. Recruiting expenses had increased sharply especially for the contractors. Whereas under the WNLA a recruit on a six-month contract cost the mines about fifty shillings in recruiting fees and expenses, the contractors paid substantially more, even double in some cases. Finally, the committee laid down the minimum conditions required if the mines wanted cooperation rather than competition to prevail in South African recruiting. They must control the rate per shift paid to contractors, establish a schedule of recruiting fees, and devise some means of controlling and limiting the flow of labour from the competing recruiters. Any such agreement would require a central organization to police it. The mines would also have to deposit large sums which they would forfeit if caught violating their agreements.

The investigating committee issued two further reports. The first gave details of the agreements into which the two groups using labour contractors had entered, although its terms of appointment precluded the committee from naming either the groups or the contractors.[14] About two months later, the investigating committee reported on the place of the labour contractors in the system as a whole. In only a few years, these firms had become major suppliers of mine labour.[15] About 20,000 of the 100,000 South African mineworkers joined the mines under this system. Recruiting costs for these workers averaged 50 per cent higher than for those black miners recuited directly by the mining companies. Because the contractors paid so much more, they naturally had first call on what labour was available during periodic shortages; "at all times [they] are in a position to get the pick of the natives." No wonder the labour contractor system tended to spread to other mines and other groups during periods of falling recruitment. To substantiate this point the committee provided some comparative data on recruiting costs calculated on a per shift basis. Groups using their own native labour departments and those dealing through independent labour agents paid an average of about 4.5d per shift worked; the contractors paid substantially more, a minimum of 5.3d per shift to 6d and upward from there.[16] These were large premiums it is true, but the mines using contractors secured one compensating benefit, not noted by the committee. The two groups employing contractors consistently filled a higher percentage of their complements than their competitors. They rarely faced, therefore, the prospect of disrupted production schedules owing to fluctuations in the labour supply.

Why did their rivals not raise their recruiting fees to deny these two groups the benefit of the enhanced labour supply drawn in by higher fees? They knew that this advantage would persist only so long as it was enjoyed by only one or two groups.[17] The remaining houses must have realized that to enter a rate war with the Randfontein and ERPM labour contractors would result only in escalating recruiting costs with no permanent increase in the supply. Since the labour needs of ERPM and Randfontein Estates were relatively modest compared to that of the rest of the industry, to denude them completely of labour, supposing it were possible, would not meet the supply problem during periods of shortage, but it would lead to sharply increased recruiting costs. Furthermore, the industry as a whole already paid recruiting fees far higher than competing nonmining employers could pay. A higher fee schedule could not be expected, therefore, to draw more labour into the mines and away from other sectors of the economy. To allow the contractors their advantage simply resulted from a calculation that this was the lesser of two evils. An all-out recruiting war – and competition was already very keen – promised consequences far more serious.

Still, even a limited agreement was a hopeful sign. It showed that the high price of competition was beginning to outweigh the hope for increased labour supplies in the minds of at least some of the group controllers. Independently, the Johannesburg mine managers' association had reached the same conclusion, and the secretary put the case for combination succinctly in a letter to the Chamber of Mines at the end of the year:

That this Association having had three years experience of the Open Recruiting System and having regard to the state of affairs as existing to-day, viz: – increase of native pay per shift, decrease in efficiency, exorbitant capitation fees, and the alarming increase in the number of natives in the hands of labour contractors, requests your Chamber to reconsider the prohibition of independent group recruiting, and the reversion to a system of one central Labour Organization, as this Association now fully realises that its previous request for open recruiting has opened the door to all the abuses above mentioned, which state of affairs is rapidly becoming intolerable.[18]

The appointment of the investigating committee and the intergroup discussions which produced a tentative agreement on recruiting fees indicate that the mines were edging back toward monopsonistic recruiting. The mine managers, formerly among the most vocal advocates of competition, had now clearly repented, and this was promising. Still the obstacles to permanent agreement remained formidable.

Of these the presence of the independent labour contractors on the Rand was the most serious.[19] In 1911–12 they supplied not less than 20 per cent of the mines' South African labour supply.[20] From the start, these men knew that the reestablishment of the WNLA or some other official recruiting organization would be fatal to them. Their recruiters in the countryside knew it too. Restoration of the monopsony meant rationalizing the migrant labour system; there would simply be no place and no need either for the labour contracting firms or most of their recruiters and runners.[21] The position of the contractors could not have been maintained had it not been for the divisions within the industry. Clearly both Randfontein companies and the ERPM benefited from their relationship with the contractors. Consistently higher recruiting fees were more than offset by the higher percentages of mine complements which the contractors maintained for these groups.

Possibly the contractors had other allies on whom they could rely. Early in 1911 when the draft native labour regulation bill was before Parliament, Lionel Phillips hoped that at least the government would ban the system used both on the ERPM properties and by the principal Randfontein recruiter, A.M. Mostert, in which the contractor "farmed" the black workers to the mine on a per-shift-worked basis. Phillips also opposed the system where the contractor quoted a rate per shift which included wages, housing and food. He had moral objections, he said, because the contractor could cheat on the food and improve profits. More probably, he wanted to deny these rivals part of their competitive edge.[22] Finally, the ranking Wernher, Beit/Eckstein partner believed that Mostert had close political connections with Botha's South African party, was counted a "strong supporter" of the party, and could probably head off any hostile clauses in the proposed bill.

An examination of the debate on the bill and the actual content of the legislation does not produce any clear evidence of collusion between the contractors and the state. After considering the matter, the government did decline to incorporate in the bill any ban on the labour-farming system to which Phillips and others particularly objected. On the other hand, the bill as finally passed did incorporate a limit of two pounds on cash advances and confirmed the ban on cattle advances. This measure worked against all private recruiters, including the contractors, because such controls restrained competition and tended to promote the voluntary system which both the Native Labour Bureau (overtly) and the Chamber of Mines (quietly) had been trying to encourage. The restrictions did not last very long, however. Citing widespread distress in the countryside owing to drought, the government raised the limit to five pounds in 1912 where it remained for several years, partly because of political pressure brought by labour agents' and traders' associations in the main recruiting areas. In his speech introducing the debate on the bill, Henry Burton, the minister of native affairs, noted that the government wished to eliminate the labour contractor who "is really trading on the shortage of labour."[23] But the act was silent on this point. Indeed Burton himself went out of his way during the select committee hearings on the bill to praise A.M. Mostert, the leading contractor, as a popular employer.[24] Not until after 1914, when the publication of H.O. Buckle's *Report of the Native Grievances Inquiry* exposed serious recruiting abuses resulting partly from highly competitive conditions, did the government begin seriously to restrict the activities of the remaining contractors.

With only lukewarm support from the government and because the industry was itself divided, those members of the Chamber of Mines who had committed themselves to restoration of an agreed recruiting system found their efforts repeatedly stymied. Lionel Phillips continued to lead the battle for the monopsony in company with J.G. Hamilton, who served as president of the Chamber of Mines in 1912 during the final critical stages of the negotiations, and a few others. Knowing that support of the government could not be relied upon, they began to consider what other pressures and inducements might be available both to weaken the position of the contractors and to restore some semblance of unity in the industry. The search for appropriate levers intensified during 1910 and can be linked directly to recurrent failures both to maintain an adequate supply of migrant labour and to control recruiting costs. Escalation of wage rates, although not as pronounced as in the case of recruiting fees, also caused some concern. A persistent theme in the correspondence between the advocates of cooperation concerned the possibility of creating pressure from European investors to push the mining houses toward a unified labour management system: "If the European shareholders knew how we are conducting ourselves in this connection, there would be such a howl that something would be done, and as a last resort it might be possible to bring everybody into line by making a speech in the open Chamber of Mines on these lines."[25] Although tempted to proceed in this way, Lionel Phillips did not act in 1910 or later on the proposal. Such a step, he noted, would cause "squabbling" among the Johannesburg representatives of the mining groups. More importantly, it would be "a serious blow to confidence" among investors in the United Kingdom and Europe, "so that one should not dream of doing it without very mature consideration."[26] To expose publicly what amounted to serious mismanagement in the industry of its labour supply was too dangerous a weapon to use. In share market conditions which after 1908–9 were not buoyant, Phillips and his colleagues hesitated to take any step which might increase the reluctance of investors to put more money into the industry.

Another course of action which received serious consideration but which the advocates of centralized recruiting also discarded in the end concerned the possibility of taking administrative and financial control of those mining houses which consistently opposed united action. Several years before, Louis Reyersbach, a partner in the Wernher, Beit/Eckstein group, had advocated a consolidation of financial and administrative control in the industry. Known to his colleagues as "general amalgamation," this plan received attention as a way of promoting more systematic development of the gold mining areas in circumstances of investor timidity and recurrent labour shortage. If the entire industry could be brought under centralized direction, it would then be possible to direct available capital and labour to those mines which offered the prospect of high yields. Poorer mines could be closed at least temporarily, and the effect of this offset by working the richer mines at full capacity.[27] During 1911–12, Reyersbach's colleagues reconsidered the proposal as a way of overcoming intragroup competition for migrant labour.[28] The engineering department of the group prepared a report which suggested that considerable savings would result if a number of low-grade mines were closed, and the labour diverted to the richer properties: "You will see that if the companies, which took over the labour ..., were to pay the mines closed down the whole of the profits that they are now making, it would still leave a profit of nearly 1,000,000 a year which is of course enormous."[29] Despite such tempting prospects, the firm took no direct action to promote "general amalgamation." The group's partners believed that the engineering department's report had exaggerated the possibility of raising profitability in this way;[30] while in Johannesburg, Lionel Phillips argued that any attempt by his group to extend their administrative control over other firms would be fiercely resisted.[31]

In any case, such a solution constituted a rather radical approach to what was after all a more limited problem. Only two groups stood out firmly and consistently against the restoration of monopsonistic recruiting – ERPM and the Randfontein companies. The other mining houses had various detailed objections to the terms by which unity could be restored but no objections in principle. If one of the two dissident groups, probably the ERPM, could be brought into line, the other could be left to recruit on its own. By the end of 1910, the Johannesburg partners of H. Eckstein and Company believed that this result would be the best they could hope for in the short run. As long as all of the other groups came together they could, without serious risk, leave Robinson's companies "to get some advantage from being outside."[32] They continued to try to get the agreement of the Randfontein representatives, of course, right up to 1912 and after but knew that the likelihood of success was slight.

Given the probable continued intransigence of the Randfontein group, the position of ERPM became critical. George Farrar, the chairman of the ERPM controlling house, was a close associate of the Wernher, Beit/Eckstein partners over many years. The financial structures of the two groups had become closely interconnected. Representatives of Central Mining sat on the boards of the ERPM companies. As a leading Unionist in Parliament, Farrar consulted closely with Lionel Phillips. Despite this, Farrar and his colleagues proved consistently reluctant to end their relationships with the labour contractors and join the efforts to restore the monopsony. Though expensive, the contractors had been spectacularly successful in maintaining at a high level the ERPM labour complements. They led the industry in this respect.[33] Naturally, pressure was strong from within the company and from the contractors to resist proposals for noncompetitive recruiting which could only threaten their enviable record. However, unlike Robinson's representatives, the ERPM people did not decline to participate in the ongoing negotiations. Indeed they even accepted the need for cooperation in principle. Yet they raised such a host of detailed objections, declining even to provide information except on terms which would protect the absolute confidentiality of their recruiting operations, that the negotiations quickly bogged down.

Farrar and his men faced a difficult situation. They had close personal and political ties to the group, Central Mining, which had most consistently pressed for an agreed system of recruiting. Members of this group sat on Farrar's board, and they had a substantial financial stake in the company. Moreover, ERPM's financial position was weak and the management therefore vulnerable as later events were to prove. To refuse all participation in these negotiations might tempt his old colleagues to retaliatory action. Thus Farrar and his men joined the talks but did everything they could to subvert them from within. Early in 1911, when all of the groups except Robinson's seemed close to agreement on recruiting fees and wage rates, the arrangements collapsed partly because of the detailed objections of the ERPM people.[34]

This situation would in all probability have continued indefinitely had it not been for eruption of the long-simmering crisis in the ERPM management which finally became public late in 1911. As a result the board of the company was completely restructured, the old management stripped of most of its power, and the chairman, Farrar, left with the role of a figurehead. For a number of years, the group had not been well managed. Farrar himself had little day-to-day control or even knowledge of operating matters. Finally his enemies leaked information to the press that the monthly returns from the mine had been juggled to disguise the poor results obtained.[35] If he had not been a party to this, Farrar nevertheless had certainly permitted the management and the engineering staff to mislead him

131   The Native Recruiting Corporation

grievously. There is no evidence in the correspondence of Central Mining that the directors arranged for the publicity as a way of getting rid of Farrar and his opposition to cooperative recruiting. With a strong minority share-holding in the ERPM and representation on the board they had to respond to the situation, however, and saw at once the opportunity offered. To force a resolution favourable to them, the firm decided to withdraw its two representatives from the board of directors. This action by the Rand's senior house destroyed what remained of the financial community's confidence in the ERPM management. Farrar and his associates had no choice but to agree to sweeping changes and to the reconstruction of the board of direc-tors on terms which his old allies in Central Mining had virtually dictated. The new arrangement left Farrar as the chairman but gathered effective power into the hands of a new management group which Lionel Phillips and his colleagues had nominated.[36] In the evolution of a cooperative recruiting system for the South African territories this was a crucial step. It opened the way for the participation of East Rand Proprietary in the Native Recruiting Corporation from the start. The groups needed nine more months of tedious negotiation, however, to complete an agreement which in the end did not include either the Randfontein companies or the Premier diamond mine.

Intermittent discussions through 1911 achieved no results on either wage rates for black workers ("a maximum average" system) or recruiting fees. Early in 1912 the participating groups did agree to a scheme which reestablished a modest WNLA presence in the eastern Cape. The new WNLA representatives did not have authority actually to recruit labour. The idea rather was to have them provide facilities to voluntary labourers for the mines. This amounted to a Chamber of Mines version of the voluntary labour plan (or Class B scheme as it came to be known), which the Native Labour Bureau had tried with very little success to establish since 1908. The government system remained in place and the chamber simply installed these new WNLA representatives as still another set of officials attempting to mobilize labour in the Cape. That the Chamber of Mines would actu-ally attempt to implement anything so absurd is a measure of the despera-tion of those who had tried for years to restore the monopsony. In the short run, it actually impeded agreement in the industry, and this result should certainly have been predicted. The recruiters in the field, both those who worked for the contractors and those working for the various mine labour departments of the different mining groups, responded exactly as they had responded to the state's voluntary system. The recruiters employed directly by mining companies, perceiving that their employers were edging closer to agreement, became especially restive. Fearing that their jobs were in jeopardy, some of the labour agents working for Central Mining considered switching their allegiance to the contractors. This in turn alarmed Taberer, the head of the group's labour department, who now faced the defection, possibly the mass defection, of their recruiters in the field. Very probably similar developments threatened the labour departments of several other groups. With its agencies only just established, the WNLA was in no position to make good any shortfall in Cape recruiting levels which might result.[37]

Within weeks of agreement to establish the WNLA agencies, Wernher, Beit/Eckstein, under severe pressure from H.M. Taberer, had to decline to participate. Taberer warned that a large number of their recruiters might defect to the contractors if the group accepted voluntaries from the WNLA agencies on terms more attractive than those offered by the recruiters. On behalf of the company, R.W. Schumacher told Hamilton, the president of the Chamber of Mines, that half-measures of this type could not work. The new WNLA scheme left out of account the contractors who were the major obstacle to the elimination of competition and it tended to increase intra-group tensions as well as alarming the recruiters in the field. Far from reducing competition and suspicion between the mining houses, the WNLA plan actually intensified them. Within a few months the chamber withdrew these WNLA agencies.

In the campaign for the monopsony, this was a definite setback, and it was one for which the industry's leading advocates of combination had to take responsibility. Replying to Schumacher, Hamilton pointed out that unless the groups prepared themselves to confront the opposition of their own recruiters, progress in the desired direction would remain impossible.[38] Only a few of them would find positions in a new central organization, and naturally those displaced would resist the loss of their jobs. If group administrations simply collapsed, as Central Mining did, in the face of pressure, success would never be possible. Hamilton believed that under existing conditions most of the workers, "if left to themselves" without the intervention of any recruiting agency, would "gravitate" to Johannesburg. To pay any recruiting fees at all was, therefore, wasteful and unnecessary. But the fees could not be reduced unless the groups would take some risks and even accept some temporary labour shortages. As the group controllers perceived that growing poverty in the "reserves" might impel the black workers to "gravitate" to Johannesburg, the high costs generated by competitive recruiting became all the more galling to them.

Hamilton went on in his letter to suggest that circumstances were favourable to deal with the contractors. Some of them might be absorbed in the new central organization, but this could only happen if they realized that their situation was "seriously imperilled." Only when they knew that the cooperating mining groups were in earnest would they agree to settle on reasonable terms. They certainly would never settle if the mines collapsed at the slightest pressure, as Central Mining had done. Hamilton concluded by lecturing Schumacher on the evils of intragroup suspicion, using language which Schumacher's colleague, Lionel Phillips, had employed for years:

... any solution must of necessity involve some risk of temporary dislocation of labour, [and] the sooner this possibility is recognized the nearer we shall be to our goal. Any microscopic examination by the officials of Group recruiting organizations into the possible advantages to be gained by this Group or the other, under any given arrangement, can only tend towards retarding the accomplishment of our main object. It is our plain duty, in the fiduciary positions we occupy, to put a stop to the mad scramble for limited labour which, carried to its logical conclusion, must before long, and after great waste of the funds of the mining companies, result in disastrously defeating its own object.

Once again an industry leader had correctly identified the root cause of their difficulty – endemic intragroup suspicion and the fear that in any agreement reached one group or another would manage to obtain some advantage. Believing that their own livelihood might be in jeopardy, the managers of the groups' recruiting departments such as Taberer found it in their interest to play on these fears.

Nevertheless, as Hamilton had shrewdly noted, circumstances in early 1912 seemed briefly more favourable to the prospects of a restored recruiting agreement. With the Randfontein compounds momentarily full, and most of the groups doing better, competition for labour had lessened, and there had been some decline in recruiting fees. The correct move, Hamilton argued, would be to ignore the Randfontein contractors and try to buy out the others on generous terms. This proved to be the winning strategy but some months were required to bring it successfully into effect. An added push was needed and soon provided by the industry's old nemesis, F.H.P. Creswell. Early in 1912, the labour group in Parliament renewed its agitation against the use of so-called tropical labour on the mines. The group controllers knew that the object of this proposal was to produce a labour shortage and make migrant labour so expensive that the mines would have no choice but to opt for a "white labour" policy. In the midst of the parliamentary debate, Lionel Phillips wrote from Cape Town to warn his colleagues about these implications. Unless the mines acted quickly to reduce the cost of locally recruited black labour, he pointed out, they would soon face irresistible demands to employ white unskilled labour instead. These "poor whites" would swell the dissatisfied white working class already in Johannesburg and soon be swept into politics by Creswell and other dangerous enemies of the mining industry. Formerly, Phillips had advocated the employment of some indigent whites on the mines as a concession to the government and as an antidote to labour militancy after the 1907 strike. Now he saw that to do this would probably feed white labour's power.[39] Competitive recruiting within South Africa had become not only suicidally expensive but also politically dangerous. By October 1912, all of the major mining houses, except Randfontein Estates, had initialled the agreement establishing the Native Recruiting Corporation as an agency of the Chamber of Mines.

Under its new chairman, Charles W. Villiers, the Native Recruiting Corporation set out to amalgamate the various native labour departments and contracting firms belonging to or employed by the participating groups. The native labour department of Central Mining, the dominant group, constituted the core of the NRC and H.M. Taberer now became its general superintendent, a position he retained for a generation. Other leading members of the recruiting industry also found positions in the corporation, as did their best labour agents in the field. These men had much experience with the ruthless competition which had long characterized recruiting in the eastern Cape and northern Transvaal. Since Robinson's recruiters remained outside the fold, the NRC people knew that the battle would continue; and it was one they could not be sure of winning.

The NRC recruited for employment in specific member mines. In virtually every case the South African mineworkers insisted on choosing their mine. By contrast, in Mozambique the WNLA permitted only one-third of its labour force, the so-called "old mine boys" or "specials" with previous experience and a proportion of their friends, styled "brothers," to do this. Freedom of choice had always been a condition of successful recruiting within South Africa, especially in the Cape. Had the NRC not adopted this policy it would immediately have faced the mass desertion of its recruiters and agents in the field. Moreover, the NRC executive had still to reckon with the powerful contractors who continued to recruit independently for the Robinson group.

In recent years, the Randfontein recruiters, Mostert, McKenzie, and Seelig, had achieved an impressive record. Despite deplorable compound conditions and death rates which were frequently excessive, the Randfontein mines remained among the most popular on the Rand. Persistent popularity despite demonstrably adverse conditions probably resulted from several circumstances. Most of the Randfontein mines still operated at shallow depths where the rock was more friable and easily broken. Thus the job of the hand driller, the principal task underground for the black miner at this time, was easier there. Second, Robinson's recruiters could and did pay higher recruiting fees than the industry average, and they attracted some of the most successful labour agents.[40] Third, Mostert's compounds were not as rigorously supervised as most on the mines; the workers therefore had more freedom when off shift. Also they could count on some support against mine management from the Mostert supervisors and indunas. Like most recruiters, Mostert knew that reports of mine brutality quickly got back to the rural areas and adversely affected recruiting. He thus made sure that the complaints of his miners against management were investigated. These considerations helped the Randfontein contractors very materially and explain why Robinson's mines consistently filled a higher percentage of their complements than the industry average. Even two years after the formation of the NRC, during which the Randfontein labour agents had faced the united opposition of the entire industry, they still managed to provide Robinson's mines with 91 per cent of their complements as against an average for the NRC of 73 per cent.[41]

The total labour requirements of the Randfontein group constituted only a small proportion of the needs of the industry as a whole. Nevertheless the NRC could not easily tolerate the existence of this independent recruiting operation. Robinson's recruiters consistently did better than their NRC counterparts despite the incomparably greater resources available to the latter and the close and sympathetic attention which the NRC received from the Union government. Randfontein recruiters menaced the NRC because they were so successful. Their record seemed to demonstrate the superiority of independent recruiting under competitive conditions. The very existence of these contractors constituted a standing temptation to the other mining groups to break up the NRC and return to separate recruiting organizations.

From its formation, the NRC represented by far the largest proportion of the gold mining industry. Apart from the Robinson companies and the Premier diamond mine, about the only mines not represented in it were the City and Suburban GMC, Luipards Vlei Estate, and the New Heriot Company. Following the pattern of the WNLA, the Chamber of Mines constructed the new corporation as a nonprofit, joint-stock association wholly owned by the participating mining companies. Nominally the individual mines owned the NRC, but representatives of the groups, that is the holding companies, sat on the board of management. The composition of the board mirrored that of the WNLA. In both cases the executive committee of the Chamber of Mines, on which all of the groups were, of course, represented, dominated the management. When sitting in its capacity as managers of either WNLA or the NRC, the chamber executive would be augmented by the senior recruiting staff. Charles Villiers transferred from the WNLA to assume control of the NRC, and he worked closely with H.M. Taberer, the general superintendent. Naturally when the chamber executive met in its capacity as the board of the NRC, Robinson's representatives absented themselves.

Within South Africa, the NRC established a district structure in each of the main recruiting areas. Its local managers took responsibility for the conduct of operations in their respective regions, but they did not do any actual recruiting. Frequently the district managers had formerly been independent contractors or the labour representatives of the recruiting departments of particular mining groups. The NRC had many of these men under contract but certainly could not treat them as mere employees. Because the corporation feared the possible defection of these former contractors and because it also wanted to minimize the magnitude of the changes in the minds of the recruits, NRC executives tried to create the appearance of business as usual. Thus the new association continued to operate in many areas using the names of the contracting firms which it was now absorbing. For several years after 1912, for example, the NRC worked the northern Transvaal as Erskine and company even though Erskine had now become a district manager.

Almost all of the labour supplied to the NRC came from the still very independent trader/recruiters who had long dominated the business within South Africa. In 1913, the NRC listed 914 of these trader/recruiters[42] on its books, and they brought in a total of 57,100 mineworkers during that year.[43] The corporation estimated that they earned an average of about £150 each – not a large sum but a significant supplement to their income from trade.[44] Most importantly, the corporation provided the capital distributed by the trader/recruiters in the form of wage advances which supplied much of the cash circulating in the African rural areas. While many of the recruits took the advance initially in coin, most of them had necessarily to look to the trading store to provide for their families during their absence. Goods which the trader might formerly have advanced to the recruit at his own risk, he could now provide with the mine advance. Essentially, therefore, the Native Recruiting Corporation took over the rural credit system, providing the capital to the traders at no interest and absorbing the whole risk. The corporation did not invent this method of labour mobilization, of course. Widespread use of wage advances had developed over the previous decade as a result of the highly competitive conditions then obtaining and the determination of the mines to increase the participation rate in the migrant system of the rural cultivators.

The first goal of the NRC was to get control of the credit system and to reduce the cost of doing business. Two strategies emerged, of which the first predated the establishment of the NRC. By 1910, the chamber had persuaded the government to limit the size of advances to two pounds a recruit. As a result of severe distress in the countryside the maximum was raised to five pounds during 1912 and remained at that level for several years. Even five pounds represented a huge improvement over the precontrol era when advances had frequently exceeded twenty pounds. Second, the mines worked to reduce the number of recruiters and runners on the payroll. Once again the state played a significant supporting role by eliminating runners' licences for whites and reducing the number of licences which it was prepared to grant to recruiters in a given district. The number of licensed recruiters fell only slowly, but the black runners suffered almost immediately. By 1914, Taberer reported to H.O. Buckle, who was then conducting the Native Grievances Inquiry, that the NRC had begun to eliminate the use of runners, black or white.[45] The recruits now made their own way to the trading store; it was no longer as necessary to chase after them.

Since the trader/recruiters continued to receive from thirty to sixty shillings for each recruit, Buckle wondered why the NRC did not dispense with them as well.[46] Why not simply hang up a sign at the NRC regional office, Buckle asked, and wait for the workers to appear, as they were now doing at the trading stores? Taberer replied that the traders "advised" the recruits. What he meant was that the trader had considerable influence over the timing of a recruit's decision to accept mine employment and indeed over the choice of employment in the first place. He could extend or restrict credit and was an important source of information about prevailing conditions on the mines. The NRC counted on the influence of the trader/recruiter and the wage advance system to maintain the flow of labour to the mines and offset the appeal of employment at higher wages in the Cape ports or at Kimberley.[47] By contrast, the black runners in the eastern Cape were much more vulnerable to displacement once competitive recruiting eased, and they now declined as a significant factor in NRC operations. While some of the runners found employment as "messengers" or "police boys," others must have been forced to turn to mine work itself. Many undoubtedly continued to recruit, however, but illegally and outside the NRC system, as will be shown below.

The organization of the NRC reflected continuing instability in the mine labour recruiting system. Although the industry was clearly moving toward a more thorough-going cooperative system, rivalry between the mining groups and between them and outside recruiters remained substantial. Naturally this affected both the structure of the new corporation and the relationship which developed between its management and the trader/recruiters in the field. When Charles Villiers set up the NRC in mid-1912 he not only took over group mine labour departments but he also tried to buy up their contracts with outside, independent contractors.[48] He succeeded in most cases but not in all. Since his monopsony was not complete, he had to deal gently with the labour contractors lest they desert to the Robinson group or another mine outside the system. In any case, existing contracts could not be ignored; and because Villiers badly needed the services of some of the contractors he had an incentive to treat them generously.[49] Even one year after the establishment of the NRC, contractors still supplied nearly as many recruits (49,414) as the corporation did (57,100) and more than the WNLA (42,600).[50] Thus Villiers and his staff found themselves compelled to move cautiously. Although most of the labour contractors formerly supplying labour to NRC member companies now disappeared in the new corporation, a few did retain a quasi-independent existence. The Hadley recruiting company, for instance, was not formally a part of the NRC, but most of the labour supplied by Hadley's sixty recruiters went to NRC mines. Villiers claimed that he had "pretty strong control" over Hadley.[51] One or two other contractors retained a similar position under the new dispensation. Naturally Hadley's men and the others with similar arrangements enjoyed more independence than the trader/recruiters working directly for the corporation. The NRC dealt gently with Hadley and the others because they feared the consequences of not doing so. Although better placed to control the trader/recruiters directly under contract to the corporation, Villiers and the management had to be careful in their dealings with them also. In the past, these men had shown themselves adept at exploiting the divisions within the mining industry: they extorted higher recruiting fees; and they routinely deserted from employment in one group to another for high fees.

Although competitive recruiting certainly lessened with the formation of the NRC, it remained substantial for the next several years. The best NRC recruiters could continue, therefore, to work their old strategy and to play one group off against another. Their position was actually enhanced in this respect by one of the first decisions of the new corporation. Under the NRC, a "maximum average" wage system was introduced which greatly restricted the operation of piece-work rates on underground work and which severely checked the rewards of enterprise for black mineworkers.[52] The evidence suggests that the mines resisted the innovation strongly. According to H.M. Taberer, 600 mine workers left one mine in a two-week period to protest the new system.[53] With black miners leaving the Rand in large numbers, the NRC naturally became more dependent than ever on its recruiters.

Villiers and his staff were fully aware that the recruiters had enormous influence in the countryside because of their control of the flow of credit there and the other factors noted above.[54] Thus they could not openly support the government-backed "voluntary system" (on the books since 1907–8) to by-pass the recruiters by advancing rail fares and giving other limited assistance to volunteers for the mines. Villiers knew that the system promised cheap labour, and that his member mining companies did all they could, quietly, to encourage the volunteers. Because of the threat this posed to the labour agents, however, Villiers had to be very circumspect and dared not endorse the scheme publicly: "I have not got control of my recruiters ... If we were to try this voluntary system these fellows who collect would be up against me all the time. They are against me today because they say that the mines give preference to voluntary boys. The mines do it, but I dare not tell the recruiters so. They can use a great deal of influence to keep the boys back."[55] Similar considerations prevented Villiers from openly supporting the government plan to abolish cash advances to mineworkers. Such a step, he estimated, would cost the Transkei traders alone over £200,000 annually in lost business.

After the formation of NRC in the 1912, the A.M. Mostert company remained as the only really large-scale labour recruiter operating outside the monopsony. The other independents, McKenzie, Seelig, and some smaller firms, could not have maintained their position had it not been for the Mostert contracts with J.B. Robinson's Randfontein companies. Thereafter a central objective of the NRC and the Chamber of Mines was to absorb the Mostert organization. In this, mining industry policy coincided with the longstanding intention of the Native Labour Bureau to restrict and eventually to eliminate competitive recruiting in the Union. Yet the bureau should not be seen as merely the creature of the Chamber of Mines or the Union government as the captive of "Imperial Capital." Competitive recruiting led to abuses which had caused endless trouble for labour bureau inspectors in Johannesburg and resident magistrates in the recruiting districts. The resulting fraud and misrepresentation caused much discontent among the masses of impoverished Africans in the increasingly squalid reserves.[56] Officials were aware, of course, that competitive recruiting which bid up recruiting fees and even wages made no economic sense for the mines; but in acting to curb the competition the government revealed a concern not primarily for Randlord profits but rather for its own bureaucratic needs.

Competitive recruiting under the cash advance system produced a sharp rise in the cost of migrant labour. Considerable capital was tied up in outstanding advances. Charles Villiers, chairman of the NRC, estimated that the advance system contributed £200,000 annually to the Transkei economy. He cited the case of one trader who in addition to supplying advances from the mines had extended £12,000 of his own capital in credit to mineworkers. Advances and "loans" combined might run to £20 a recruit or even more. More serious were the losses experienced as large numbers of mineworkers, typically the recipients of the larger sums, deserted even before reaching the mines or at any rate well before they had worked off their debt.[57] Buckle estimated losses could go as high as 20 per cent which would mean £50,000 annually to the industry.[58] In fact the recruits became adept at working the system. If they did not desert, they would delay their departure for the mines for weeks or even months. The trader/recruiter had few levers against them. If they pressed the recruit to hasten his departure for the mines, he could simply go to a second recruiter, secure another advance, and use it to repay the first. As it was, many recruits took two or more advances, intending from the start to defraud at least one of the traders or even all of them.[59]

The large sums of money involved tempted everyone connected with the business to exploit the system in their interest. The recruits took money from the trader/recruiter and the mining companies when they could. The trader/recruiters tried to bind the mineworkers to them through the advance system and by extending credit at high and illegal rates of interest. Headmen, though prohibited by government regulation from participation in the recruiting system, were clearly an essential part of the chain connecting mining companies to the potential mineworker in the countryside. Labour agents set aside a portion of their capitation fees to keep the headmen "on side," while the black runners also had to share their profit with the local notables. Chiefs and headmen abused their power to coerce labour and maximize their personal gain from the recruiting system.

In their poverty, few parents could resist to pledge their under age children to the mines in return for large advances and the provision of credit from the trader/recruiters. A regular traffic in child labour for the mines developed into a major scandal which continued out of control for years. A.M. Mostert's recruiters alone sent forward hundreds of these "umfaans." Those who were too young, small, weak, or sick to pass the lax government medical examination at Randfontein ended up on the farm of Mostert himself or one of his neighbours to work off their contracts at low wages.[60]

From the start both the chamber and the government expressed concern over the implications of the advance system. Leading members of the mining industry recognized that like competitive recruiting itself, cash and cattle advances constituted another wasteful dimension of labour mobilization in South Africa. On the other hand there were great risks involved in any open attack on the system. Many leading recruiters and the heads of the mine labour departments believed and argued strenuously that without advances the mines would never have been as successful as they were in breaking down the resistance of Cape blacks to mine work and securing the loyalty of the trader/recruiter. As long as competition survived in the industry no single company could unilaterally repudiate the practice. To do so would simply drive the trader/recruiters into service with a rival company. Thus while Chamber of Mines and later NRC officials often spoke privately against the advances, they rarely dared to come out openly against them.

Government efforts to restrict cash advances went back to the pre-Union period and originated at the Cape and in the Native Labour Bureau for the reasons outlined above. Growing evidence of widespread exploitation of blacks in the highly competitive recruiting conditions which then prevailed led the Cape authorities shortly before Union to ban cattle advances in Pondoland and to restrict cash advances throughout the eastern Cape to a limit of five pounds a worker.[61] In regulations under the Union Native Labour Regulation Act, no. 15 of 1911, these controls were made more restrictive and extended to South Africa as a whole. The maximum permitted advance now became two pounds. Thereafter policy fluctuated for several years as the authorities found themselves compelled by various circumstances to proceed very cautiously with their declared intention of getting rid of advances altogether. Within a year of the new regulation limiting advances to two pounds, the Union government reverted to the five-pound advance on the grounds that the higher amount would help relieve widespread distress resulting from drought in the "native territories."[62] By 1913, at the prodding of the director of native labour, Pritchard, and his colleagues the limit came down to two pounds again. Early in 1914, the government announced that even the two pounds advance would not be permitted in future without special permission. The mineworker could only claim a two-pound advance once he had actually arrived on the mines and begun to work.[63]

This decision caused such an uproar that the government hastily announced that it would not be enforced until June 1914 at the earliest. To mask their rather ignominious retreat in the face of protests from members of Parliament, the Cape press, eastern province chambers of commerce, municipalities, and associations of the trader/recruiters,[64] they turned the contentious matter over to H.O. Buckle whose one-man Native Grievances Inquiry was then under way. Buckle agreed to include the whole recruiting issue within his terms of reference and to make recommendations especially on the advance question. Clearly the authorities felt compelled to seek impartial and authoritative recommendations from Buckle which might enable them to override these political pressures.

Buckle toured the Transkeian districts as part of his investigation and examined also conditions for recruits on the Rand. In his report he endorsed many of the strictures on competitive recruiting and advances which the director of native labour has been putting forward for years. The moral effects on both white and black were serious. The tout and his victim were alike tempted to commit fraud.[65] Buckle stressed the huge costs of competitive recruiting which came close to £600,000 a year. Of this no less than £200,000 went in capitation fees and large sums were always tied up in advances. Losses owing to default and desertion were large and might run as high as 20 per cent according to one informed witness.[66] Buckle recognized that the system of advances had become deeply entrenched and could only be changed gradually when an alternative way of ensuring that part of the wages of the recruit was available to his family in the countryside. Buckle agreed with much expert testimony that real economic need not the blandishments of a tout nor the prospect of an unearned advance payment drove black workers to the mines.[67] He advocated a deferred pay system modelled on the scheme already approved (although not yet operative) for Mozambique. Part of the wages would be sent home after the worker earned them. In this way the family would be provided for and the worker would not waste his money on "unwholesome food, unnecessary clothes, or such trash as concertinas."[68] Buckle did agree, however, that a considerable period would elapse before the new system could be well established.[69] In the meantime, he recommended that the limited two-pound advance be allowed in addition to rail fare and an "outfit" for the trip. The latter would continue to be necessary even after the deferred pay plan was in place.

More generally, Buckle emphasized the evils which inevitably developed when such a large number of recruiters and runners were chasing a more or less stable pool of potential labourers. He noted that opposition of the trader/recruiters had ensured the failure of the state's voluntary labour system planned in 1907-8 and introduced in 1909-10. Since they were paid by results on a per capita basis, the recruiters had every incentive both to "snatch boys" from each other and from the labour bureau's registrars.[70] In principle Buckle favoured a noncompetitive recruiting system, i.e., a complete monopsony with recruiters paid salaries instead of capitation fees.[71] But he recognized that the NRC's trader-recruiters would do all they could to defeat a plan so damaging to their material interests.[72] Furthermore, Buckle saw that abolition of capitation fees would not by itself provide a remedy. Such a ban would be impossible to police;[73] and in any case the trader/recruiters competed with each other ruthlessly not only for capitation fees but also for the opportunity to extend credit to the recruits. It was this which gave the recruiting system its hold over the blacks. Although he emphasized the resulting abuses, Buckle pointed out that the traders provided a necessary service. While the recruits paid dearly for it, the credit extended by traders enabled them to compensate for the variability of the harvest and other factors affecting their income.[74] Rather than eliminate the credit system, Buckle wanted to control it. He suggested that the Basutoland rule which made African debts to Europeans irrecoverable in the courts would put a brake on what any trader would risk lending to a recruit.[75] The commissioner argued that the evils which followed from the trader/recruiters' financial interest in capitation fees and the credit system were aggravated by the excessive number of recruiters and runners at work in the Cape. He stressed therefore that some means should be found to restrict the number of licences issued in particular districts.[76] He drew back from the proposal of some local magistrates that a single recruiter be allowed a monopoly in each district.

Buckle's report lent weight to the case for reform which the labour bureau had been pressing for some time. While competitive recruiting had clearly been necessary at an earlier stage of the development of the mine labour system, and tolerated by the state for this reason, there was much less reason for it now. Yet the political realities operating in South Africa at that time continued to frustrate government efforts to implement reform. After 1914, the Botha government several times announced plans to abolish advances only to relent each time. Following Buckle's recommendation, the cabinet indicated its approval of deferred pay systems which it hoped might eventually eliminate the need for advances. In the meantime, the two pound advance could continue to be given until 30 June 1915.[77] As that deadline approached it was extended first to the end of the year and then until the end of 1916. The extension to 1916, however, was accompanied by regulations specifying that the recruit had to proceed to work within fourteen days of receipt of the advance which could only be given with official approval and in the presence of a magistrate.[78]

Of course, much evidence available to the government indicated that restrictions on the amount and terms under which advances could be given were essentially unenforceable. An agent could exceed the two-pound maximum simply by calling the additional sum "a loan."[79] One case reported to the labour bureau was probably typical. An African, Njaja, took an advance of two pounds from a labour agent in August 1914. Subsequently he received six bags of mealies from the same agent and signed a note for twelve pounds. The acting director of native labour decided that the second transaction was not an advance but a perfectly legal loan. Action could not be taken unless the labour bureau could produce proof of intent to evade the legal limit on advances.[80] African mineworkers themselves induced agents to make advances above the two-pound maximum by threatening to sign with another recruiter.[81] Unless the system was entirely done away with, such violations would necessarily continue.

Throughout 1914–15, pressure on the government from interests behind the campaign of the trader/recruiters to maintain their lucrative position remained intense. Surprisingly little countervailing pressure developed from farmers and other nonmining employers who should have seen in this reform proposal measures which might enable them to compete more effectively with the well-financed mine labour recruiters. A few farmers wrote along these lines but their letters became swamped in the more vehement propaganda barrage from the labour agents and their friends.[82] These increased in volume and intensity every time the government sought to control the trader/recruiters more directly.[83] The labour agents also used the courts effectively to challenge the regulations. In 1916 the labour contractor, J.W. McKenzie, secured a court decision throwing out the regulation that advances could only be given in the presence of a magistrate at the time he attested the recruit's contract of service.[84] The Union's law advisers gave their view that the judgment was watertight and that an appeal had no chance. The government then withdrew the regulation.[85]

The authorities had more success in their efforts to reduce the number of labour agents and trader/recruiters licensed in the Union. Buckle had argued in the report of the Native Grievance Inquiry that many of the evils in the existing recruiting system could be traced to this situation. Simply put, there were far too many agents and runners, particularly in the eastern Cape, chasing the available recruits.[86] In its response to the Buckle report, the Chamber of Mines agreed to accept restrictions and endorsed the proposal in the report that recruiters' licences be restricted to a particular locali-

ty. The chamber also agreed that only a single recruiter should be permitted to operate in a given area. On this point at least the government did not
equivocate. Even before Buckle reported they had substantially reduced the
number of licensed recruiters. In the year following publication of the
report, the number of recruiting licences issued by the Native Labour
Bureau dropped dramatically. No doubt wartime shortages of white manpower encouraged the state to push ahead with this despite protests from
the threatened interests.

Buckle's recommendations endorsed the proposals which the labour
bureau had been pressing for years, and, in response, the politicians did
begin to move, although still cautiously. Both the NRC and the Mostert
labour contracting company, now the principal mine labour recruiters,
received warnings to this effect in 1915. As a Native Affairs Department
official later expressed it, recruitment for the mines had been "extravagantly
conducted and had been accompanied by many abuses ... The Government
could not lose sight of the fact that the system of recruiting as obtaining
to-day was calculated to seriously retard the proper administration of the
Native Territories."[87] The recruiters were told once more that unless they
set their house in order, "the Government might be forced to have to resort
to Parliament." Shortly after the Buckle report became public, officials met
with representatives of the two organizations and pressed them to accept
an agreement which put severe limits on the methods which they could use
to compete for labour.[88] After considerable prodding, the NRC and Mostert
negotiated an arrangement which came into force in 1915. It specified that
the companies would not hire away each other's agents, nor would they
employ an agent "discarded" by the other company except by agreement.
They would maintain their complements of recruiters at current levels and
would not transfer any licences without consent. The agreement bound the
parties and in effect made the director of native labour the arbiter in case
of dispute. For the next three years the new system seemed to function fairly
well and did not lead to a great deal of friction between the two companies.

Clearly many of the abuses integral to competitive recruiting which
Buckle had stressed in his report continued, however. During 1916–17, a
large number of complaints concerning misrepresentation of contracts
reached the labour bureau from individual Africans. Their allegations concerned both the NRC and Mostert's company, especially the latter. Surviving evidence in the labour bureau files indicates that the director and his
staff now began to scrutinize more closely both the activities in the field and
the conditions on the mines. The bureau continued to reduce the number
of licensed agents, on the formula that there should be more than one
licensed agent for every 200 adult males in any given district. The director
distributed the licences "as equitably as possible" between the two recruiting
companies. Even this formula provided latitude for the issue of a large

TABLE 2
Recruiting Licences Issued, 1912–18

Year	Cape	TVL	Natal	OFS	Total
1912	2,069	427	319	22	2,837
1913	1,495	237	311	5	2,048
1914	923	176	153	5	1,257
1915	542	125	83	4	754
1916	498	91	73	3	665
1917	446	79	80	3	608
1918	550	85	86	2	723

SOURCE: *Reports of the Department of Native Affairs* for the years ending, 1913–18 (UG 7-1919), 9.

number of licences and is an indication of the caution which characterized official reform efforts at this time.[89]

By the end of 1917, a more serious shortfall of black labour on the mines combined with other factors to produce another upheaval in the recruiting world. This time the Mostert organization was in trouble as a result of the 1916 take-over of Mostert's principal, Randfontein Estates, by the Johannesburg Consolidated Investment Company, a member of the NRC. For the time being, Mostert was protected by his Randfontein contracts, but as they expired the temptation for JCI to bring Randfontein Estates into the NRC would become strong. More than ever Mostert felt the pressure to justify his company by results. In fact, however, his labour complements were falling in 1917–18. This was doubly serious since penalty clauses written into his contracts entitled Randfontein Estates to large cash payments whenever the Mostert organization failed to maintain agreed recruiting levels. In what appears to have been a desperate bid to offset these losses at Randfontein, the labour contractor began to expand into the recruitment of farm labour in the Transvaal and in early 1918 established a number of new branches for this purpose. To be successful in this new endeavour, Mostert argued, he had to secure additional licences for mine labour recruiting as well. A recruiter would not agree to recruit only for farm work; he had also to recruit for the mines.[90] For a number of years, the company had been supplying under age and medically unfit Africans rejected for mine work to Mostert's own farm and others in the neighbourhood. Perhaps as a hedge against the probable future cancellation of his Randfontein contracts, Mostert decided to develop the farm labour side of the business.

When Randfontein Estates eventually did decline to renew its contracts with Mostert and became part of the NRC in 1919, the labour contractor's firm continued as Theron and Company under the control of his Transvaal manager. This lay in the future, however. In 1917–18, Mostert apparently had every intention of maintaining his position in the mine labour market.

In an aggressive move at the end of 1917, he announced that the company would not renew its agreement with the NRC. When he made this announcement, Mostert gave as a reason the company's need for many more recruiting licences to develop the farm labour side of his business against stiff competition from other companies. His next move early in 1918 was to apply to the labour bureau for even more licences in direct contradiction to Buckle's recommendations and the drift of government policy over several years. To improve the chances of success for these licence applications, he assured the authorities that the company would not raid NRC recruiters. Mostert's expansionist ambitions disguised very considerable weakness. With renewal of his Randfontein contracts in grave jeopardy and recruiting levels below required minima, he evidently felt compelled to make a bold bid to transform the situation. According to figures obtained from the Native Affairs Department from the company's own records, the efficiency of a number of Mostert's recruiters fell drastically in 1917. In certain districts, his men recruited only one-half of their previous annual total although he had more recruiters at work in some of those districts.[91]

Now he wanted to make a rapid expansion in the number of his agents to compensate for the declining efficiency of his organization. Clearly Mostert had begun to lose out, certainly to the NRC and possibly to other, nonmining employers. The real desperation he and his managers felt became obvious. By hiring these new agents on a commission-only basis he could hope to improve his results without adding significantly to the cost of each recruit. Although the Mostert organization pledged not to hire NRC recruiters, the implications of the new policy for the chamber's recruiting arm were serious. Competition promised to intensify dramatically if the authorities permitted large numbers of new labour agents to enter the field. Although he could not have been surprised, Mostert protested bitterly when the director of native labour used his discretion under Act 15 of 1911 to disallow all of these applications for additional licences. Mostert appealed to the minister, but on this occasion the Union government stood its ground and upheld the director's decision.[92]

Even before the crisis of 1917–18, A.M. Mostert's organization was in trouble and increasingly unable to compete with the more powerful, better financed NRC. He had also to contend with the high proportion of voluntaries who were coming to the Rand without the intervention of a recruiter at all. The sharp increase in the number of unrecruited Africans over the previous five years suggests that the once powerful grip of the labour companies on the main recruiting areas had weakened considerably. This at any rate is the probable explanation for the growing number of children who were showing up in the Randfontein compounds from about 1914. Child labour was the habitual resort of the unsuccessful employer and labour recruiter. Between the mines and the farms, for instance, a kind of *de facto* division of labour had grown up over the years. The farms relied heavily on ultra-low wage child labour, and these workers, once they were older, tended to move away at the earliest opportunity to mining and other employment. Children were also present in almost all of the mining compounds, however. Regulations under the Native Labour Regulation Act of 1911 prohibited the employment of those under eighteen for work underground, but recruiters would send forward anyone whom they thought would be passed by the attesting officer and the mine doctor. Since few Africans could document their age, the application of the regulation became a matter of opinion. Some attesting officers were notoriously lenient and merely took the word of the recruiter on the matter. Moreover, homosexuality was rife in the mining compounds, and adolescent boys were much in demand for such purposes there. As a result large numbers of children could be found in the compounds of almost all of the mines.[93]

In Mostert's Randfontein recruiting operations, the number of under age Africans began to grow significantly above previous levels. During 1914, the company took steps to regularize the employment of the under-eighteens. Mostert's manager, Theron, complained to the pass officer that when these workers were rejected by the authorities on the grounds they were too young, the company lost heavily.[94] In every case, an advance would have been given to the parents and it was in practice impossible to recover these monies. To prevent such losses, Theron received permission to send any recruits declared by officials to be under age to Mostert's farm, there to work off the contract and repay the advance. Mostert's standard labour contract was amended to include a clause stating that a worker rejected for mine employment could be sent to one of his farms. When Mostert's farm became over-supplied the children were sent to other farms in the neighbourhood.

Of course, many workers who were probably under eighteen were actually passed by the government inspectors and mine medical officers as fit for underground work, which they knew to be extremely demanding and onerous. It seems that the inspectors and medical officers would normally reject only those workers who were obviously under age or grossly unfit for hard physical labour. For instance, in 1919 five young boys arrived at Randfontein from Lusikisiki in the eastern Cape. They had been recruited by a Mostert agent. The magistrate at Lusikisiki passed them as suitable for mine work as did the labour bureau inspector at Randfontein.[95] Subsequently the mine medical officer rejected them. They each weighed under ninety pounds, yet were judged by the Cape magistrate and the Randfontein inspector capable of extremely demanding physical work. This case was sufficiently serious to come to the attention of the director who wrote to Mostert himself, demanding an explanation.[96] Bureau records suggest that the regulations concerning child labour were routinely breached. The farm labour clause written into the Mostert contract was simply a device to prevent losses in the case of those workers who were not passed by the inspectors or the medical officers. Its effect was to encourage the recruiters to send forward more children. A proportion, probably a high proportion, would pass scrutiny; the others would be sent to the farm.[97] Previously, rejected recruits were repatriated, and the recruiter lost the capitation fee and became responsible for any advance which he had given. Labour bureau files reveal that between 1914 and 1919, a very large number of under age males were taken by recruiters out of the eastern Cape, some of them without their parents' consent. Mostert's recruiters were not the only ones involved, but they were recruiting children on a much larger scale than most. A check of labour bureau's Randfontein office files revealed forty-two Mostert recruits rejected for mine work as under age and physically unfit in the four months, July to October 1915 alone.[98] The number recruited must have been much larger.

In recruiting these children, the Mostert organization preyed on the poverty of the parents. In 1915, for example, Harry Zihlangu of Encobo agreed to contract his three sons to the Mostert organization on six-month contracts. He received an advance of six pounds. Subsequently the children were rejected for mine work and sent by Theron to the farm of one of Mostert's neighbours to work for six months at one pound a month, well below the standard rates for underground mine work. Hearing of this the father wrote to complain and demanded compensation of about eleven pounds, the difference between the wages his sons would have earned on the mines and the money actually paid by the farmer. The labour bureau was unsympathetic, blamed the father for sending them forward in the first place and pointed out that the children had after all accepted the farm contract offered them. Theron, for his part, treated the matter as a straightforward commercial transaction. Zihlangu had accepted the advance and therefore had no complaint. His children received employment at "the very handsome wage of £1 per month." If the company had not sent them to the farm it would have lost the whole of the wage advances and rail fare paid, "because we have no single instance in the whole of our recruiting career where any father has tendered us a refund of the advance after the rejection of his child up here." Theron concluded self-righteously that "we are at a loss to find what grievance anybody has in this matter except ourselves for all the trouble and worry we have had with these children."[99] Mostert's recruiters sent forward hundreds of children for mine employment in these years.

When Mostert's organization finally left mine labour recruiting in 1919, its successor company, Theron, continued to recruit farm labour. This meant reliance on the employment of children recruited in the principal recruiting areas, the old, and the physically unfit. Not to be outdone, the NRC also began to recruit for the Transvaal farms, describing this as a gesture to help the local white farmers. The employment of the young, the physically unfit, and those too old for mine work could be much enhanced, the corporation pointed out, if railway rates for this class of worker from the eastern Cape were lowered. Wages on the farms at about one pound a month were too low to make it economic to transport the workers from a distance, if they had to find the rail fare out of their meagre wages.[100]

In combination with trader/recruiters in the countryside, Mostert and the other contractors had fought a successful rearguard action against the encroachment of the Chamber of Mines for over a decade. Their success is more striking evidence of the difficulty which the mining industry itself had in curbing destructive and very expensive competition for black labour. At every level of the management of these mining groups, from the controlling partners down to the compound managers and shift bosses of the individual mines, there were many men who could not resist the temptation to deal with the independent touts and labour contractors in the hope of at least temporary advantage over the rival houses. Most of them knew that any advantage gained in this way could only be short-lived; they knew also that competition drove costs up. Nevertheless they yielded to the discipline of a single, integrated recruiting system only slowly.

The reasons for this apparently shortsighted, even irrational behaviour relate to a fundamental contradiction in the mines' labour system. Competitive recruiting which made little sense to the industry as a whole did make a great deal of sense to particular groups or particular mines in certain circumstances. This explains the consistently independent line of J.B. Robinson. As the only group rejecting all forms of cooperation within South Africa before 1919 (the group remained a member of the WNLA), Randfontein Estates got the advantage when the other groups began to combine to lower wages and cut recruiting costs. His recruiters could pay a little more and command a proportionally greater share of the supply. Robinson's mines had other advantages but this was an important one. Testifying before the Native Grievances Inquiry in 1914, Charles Villiers gave another example of a mine benefiting from paying recruiting costs which the industry as a whole or even all of the mines of one of the groups could not afford.[101] In 1914, the Simmer Deep, a Gold Fields property, worked low-grade ore with 43 per cent of its complement of black labour. A committee of mining engineers established the complements for the WNLA and the NRC and estimated the optimum number of blacks needed to run operations efficiently at each mine. Labour allocations from the chamber recruiting companies were made on the basis of the complements which gave mine managers a motive to secure an inflated complement if they could. Discounting this inflation, a mine like the Simmer Deep could run quite well with, say, 80 per cent of its complement. At 43 per cent in 1914, however, the profitability of the mine was at risk. At that level of employment the mine simply could not supply sufficient ore to the reduction works to enable the gold to be efficiently extracted. As Villiers noted, the problem at Simmer Deep was not excessive recruiting fees or wage rates (certainly a complaint of the group as a whole) but an inability to process a sufficient tonnage of ore: "I am quite sure that if I went to the Goldfields to-day and offered them 500 boys for the Simmer Deep at 15,000 [pounds] [30 pounds a head, an enormous sum], they would pay me a cheque for it, and it would pay them handsomely to do so."[102] Thus a policy, manifestly suicidal for the gold industry as a whole, made perfect economic sense for the Simmer Deep or in a different way for the Randfontein companies in their particular circumstances.

As well as revealing the chronic divisions within the mining industry, the persistence of competitive recruiting also shows the power of the labour contractors and the trader/recruiters. Entrenched as they were at critical points in the system, they provided contacts and expertise which the mining industry could not easily do without. Moreover, they had mobilized themselves politically and could put considerable pressure on government to delay, deflect, or prevent policies hostile to their interests. The persistence of cash advances, despite attempts by the government and the mining interest to get rid of them, can be traced partly to the political influence of the recruiting lobby. In the end, the successful implementation of the deferred pay system which ensured that continued large sums of miners' wages ended up in the coffers of the traders did eventually reconcile them to the abolition of advances. However, the struggle to end the payment of advances reveals the strength of the local and regional interests which had established themselves in the recruiting system. At least before 1919, the mine owners had repeatedly to conciliate this group, and the Union government always had to be wary of its political power.

By itself the establishment of the Native Recruiting Corporation did not lead to the elimination of competitive recruiting. Indeed in the short run competition intensified. Important recruiters and labour contractors remained outside the new central recruiting organization. Rightly discerning that their livelihood was in jeopardy these men redoubled their efforts to maintain a strong presence in the principal recruiting areas. Only the growing administrative muscle of the Native Affairs Department and the Native Labour Bureau, when finally backed up by the politicians, succeeded eventually in forcing them either to submit to the NRC or, like Mostert, to leave the business. The rising proportion of voluntary labour on the mines had a great deal to do with the new strength of the NRC. With so many Africans now making their own way to the Rand, the mines had not the same need to conciliate the contractors, who increasingly were losing control of the principal recruiting areas. The NRC's victory over Mostert was the decisive step in the completion of the chamber's cooperative system.

Some contractors remained in the field; illegal touting continued to a limited extent; but the days when the independent recruiters could challenge the power of the Chamber of Mines had passed.

CHAPTER FIVE

The Recruiting Nexus: Touts, Headmen, and Their Recruits

In the Chamber of Mines' campaign to cut labour costs and to bring maximum efficiency to the management of the migrant labour supply, the establishment of the Native Recruiting Corporation at the end of 1912 marked a long step forward. Important as it was, however, this was only part of a larger plan to reorder the industry's labour system. Over the longer term, Charles Villiers and his staff counted on voluntary labour to bring recruiting costs down dramatically.[1] They hoped that, increasingly, the mineworkers would simply "gravitate" to Johannesburg, as the president of the Chamber of Mines had earlier expressed it, without the intervention of a recruiter at all.[2] In this, the interest of the mines coincided with that of the government and indeed of the black workers themselves. The Native Labour Bureau had been advocating voluntary labour since 1907. Not only was the recruiting system wasteful and expensive, but also the misinformation put about by recruiters caused endless trouble for bureau inspectors and local magistrates. The worker benefited also from a system which permitted escape from the recruiter and allowed him to search for the best available job on arrival.

Since voluntary labour was much in demand on the mines and elsewhere, the volunteer could usually count on better terms of employment than the typical recruit. NRC recruits by contrast could pick their mine but did not have the option of nonmining employment. Of course, the owners did not want a free market for labour or anything like one. The worker should be free to make his own way to the mine at his own expense, free to avoid the recruiter, but not free to change employers at will, to evade the terms of a labour contract, or to live where he liked on the Rand. Limited mobility within a coercive labour system defined the employers' objectives. Even so, the migrant who came to Johannesburg on his own got several benefits denied to the recruited worker. Only when the search for a job outside the mining sector failed would the typical voluntary turn to the mines as employer of last resort. Since the voluntaries were courted by the mines, they could secure much shorter contracts and even week-to-week work if labour was very scarce. Most mine managers disliked short-term contracts which reduced efficiency and complicated manpower planning, but they made an exception in favour of the experienced voluntary workers. The NRC recruit, by contrast, had to take a minimum six- or nine-month contract. Moreover, he might not always be given his choice of mine. Although the NRC was committed to providing this choice, the corporation would stop accepting recruits for the more popular mines when their complements (the authorized establishment of mineworkers) approached 100 per cent.[3]

In his testimony before the Native Grievances Inquiry, Charles Villiers, chairman of the NRC, explained that the "real vital difference" between the voluntary and the recruited workers was that the former had sufficient capital to get to the Rand and maintain themselves there until they found employment. By 1916, Chamber of Mines statistics indicated that slightly over 100,000 mineworkers were voluntaries. Of these about 43 per cent came from the Cape and roughly 20 per cent from the Transvaal. The mines recognized three categories of volunteer. The "local" was an African transferring from nonmining employment in Johannesburg to one of the mining firms. A "mine" volunteer was transferring from one mine to another after the expiry of a contract, while a "new" volunteer had arrived independently in Johannesburg from one of the country districts. About 70 per cent of the volunteers fell into the last category.[4] They were much in demand on all the mines since they were normally experienced workers who had *chosen* themselves to return. Shorter contracts and preferred jobs were routinely available for these workers. This rapid expansion in the number of Africans volunteering for mine employment was extraordinary and represented a 250 per cent increase over 1908 when fewer than 40,000 workers were volunteers.

The growing preponderance of voluntary labour reflected an important change in the composition of the black work-force on the mines. By 1916, a much smaller percentage of the work-force was inexperienced than had been the case ten years before when the participation rate of African cultivators in the mine economy was expanding rapidly, and many South African recruits had not previously worked on the mines. The growth of voluntary labour also reflects the work-force's extensive knowledge of working and living conditions on the Rand. The experienced South African worker normally refused the constraints involved in accepting a NRC contract. While the NRC would allow him his choice of mine, he knew that as a volunteer, he could canvass the job situation on arrival and perhaps land some congenial nonmining position. Chamber of Mines executives did not like this aspect of the voluntary system. They thought the voluntaries should "belong" to the gold mines and worked hard to counteract the activities of

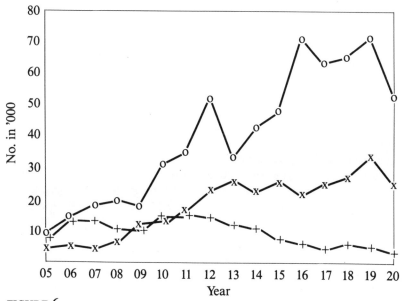

FIGURE 6

"Voluntary" Labour Employed by WNLA Member Companies, 1905–20

SOURCES: WNLA *Annual Reports.*
o New arrivals on the Rand.
+ Transfers from nonmining employment.
x Transfers from one mine to another.

those who would lure them into nonmining employment.[5]

   Although the state of research on black agriculture at this time does not permit firm conclusions, the rising proportion of voluntary labour suggests that the African rural sector, from which this labour was drawn, retained an important element of economic freedom in these years. Families supplying the voluntary workers, however hard-pressed, were able to choose the time the workers went forward, and they had to find the travel expenses involved. The really destitute had no choice but to accept the services of the recruiter in order to get the advance on wages to provide for his family and pay the rail fare.[6] Most importantly, since the volunteer worker could often secure monthly or even week-to-week work on the mines, he could more easily coordinate his period away with the seasonal labour demands of the agricultural economy. The recruited worker, locked into a much longer contract, had less freedom in this respect. This is not to deny that increasing hardship in the African reserves was an important factor in the rapid growth of the labour supply, but only to point out that the workers were making intelligent choices in order to minimize the reduction in family income from the land caused by the loss of their labour while on the mines.

It is one important indication among many of the capacity of the black workers collectively to influence, even within this coercive labour system, the terms and conditions of their employment.

At the time of the formation of the NRC, the full expansion of voluntary labour still lay several years in the future. A major factor in the growth of this component of the labour force was the limit which the Union government imposed on wage advances to the recruits. Even to the Cape workers recruitment for the mines must have seemed much more attractive when they could take part or even all of their wages in cash, months before leaving for the mines. The advance system had been central to the spectacular growth in recruiting levels from the Cape in the years after 1906. During the period of intense competition, the labour recruiters had bid up the size of advances to an extraordinary degree. By 1910, however, the Union authorities had placed a maximum, first of two pounds, then briefly five pounds a recruit before reverting to two pounds later in the decade. The effect of this was to lessen the appeal of recruitment to the potential workers who now began, increasingly, to exercise the option of going to the mines independently. As voluntary labour grew in proportion to the total labour force and more workers successfully evaded the touts, the recruiters' leverage on the system began to decline, and the mines consequently became less dependent on them. However, recruiters remained important in bringing out the first-time migrant who lacked the confidence to make his own way to the Rand and the worker who needed a cash advance before he would accept a contract.

These white labour agents and contractors had not been the only group to exploit the opportunities created by intense intra-industry competition for labour in the years after 1907. Like the voluntary labourers who found the means to evade the labour agent and to retain some independence from their employers, important groups of black collaborators emerged who were able to make the recruiting system work for them. Their crucial role in the operation of the industry rarely emerges clearly from either industry or government records. Contemporary whites had difficulty perceiving the extent to which enterprising black recruiters, runners, chiefs, and headmen could divert the profits of recruiting to their own pockets. Official correspondence focused usually on the white operators, missing the frequent reality that these whites functioned merely as front men for the black runners, touts and headmen who were often the real operators of the system. Once these misperceptions are stripped from the official record, however, the crucial role of the African recruiters becomes apparent.

Succesful mine labour recruiting depended heavily upon alliances between town and country. Although chiefs and headmen were eventually banned from licensed recruiting they remained extremely important in the system. Their involvement went back virtually to the earliest days of the mines. Under Kruger's republic, local *landdrosts* had collaborated with influential headmen to supply labour for the mines.[7] Frequently, the chiefs themselves acted as runners or they appointed agents to do this. At the Cape, the colonial government realized very early that without the cooperation of the headmen, attempts to raise the participation rate of African cultivators in the migrant system would get nowhere. In 1903 when the Sprigg government was looking to mine labour recruitment as a way of revitalizing the eastern province's economy, one of its first acts was to appoint a delegation of chiefs and magistrates to visit the Rand.

The authorities wanted the delegation to inquire "into the conditions of labour and the treatment accorded to Native labourers ... and suggest any measures by which a greater supply of labour may be induced to go to these mines."[8] At the request of the prime minister, the matter had been raised in the Transkeian general council with a view to eliciting the cooperation of black leaders throughout the territories.[9] W.T. Brownlee led the delegation of seventeen headmen which arrived on the Rand in September 1903, spent several days there, and visited about twenty of the mining compounds. The authorities wanted to persuade the headmen that conditions on the mines were good and treatment reasonable and get them to use their influence with potential recruits. While the delegation did not condemn compound conditions or the food supplied, although both were undoubtedly bad on many mines, they did complain that the WNLA operated by systematically misleading recruits as to the wages they could expect. Individual headmen also pointed to cases of brutality, and there were a number of complaints about inadequate hospital treatment. WNLA officials denied the wage irregularities, of course, but Brownlee, assisted by the headmen, was able to document a number of cases.[10] Partly as a result of the evidence provided by the delegation, the Cape government began to press the Transvaal authorities for action to improve conditions on the mines. The passage of the Coloured Labourers' Health Ordinance in 1905 owed something to the realization in the Transvaal Native Affairs Department that improved health and working conditions would help to raise recruiting levels.[11] However, the hope that the headmen would turn into loyal unpaid labour touts once they were shown what conditions were actually like proved illusory. Recruiters began to succeed with the Transkeian chiefs only when they provided a material reward for their assistance. The highly competitive conditions which followed the collapse of the WNLA in 1906–12 proved a bonanza for anyone who was thought to have influence with potential recruits in the countryside. Those headmen who did not actually become runners for one or more recruiting companies could count on presents and fees in return for their assistance.

During the years of intense competition which preceded the formation of the NRC, a piece-work system developed on several mines which operated outside industry and government labour regulations, and this provided important benefits for black mineworkers and recruiters alike. Controlled by certain "boss boys" who actually functioned as clandestine labour touts, the system flourished and eventually became the subject of a labour bureau inquiry in 1913.[12] The bureau's report revealed some of the underlying realities which governed recruiting operations at that time. During 1913, GNLB inspectors began an investigation of the contracting firm of Morkel Brothers which supplied labour to the industry's largest employer, the Central Mining group. The report showed that the techniques used by Morkel Brothers and their black associates to attract and keep labour were widely copied on the Rand. Evidence also suggested that the "boss boys" and certain acquisitive headmen in the countryside provided both the initiative and the contacts which explain the success of the Morkel Brothers. Initially the senior Morkel had made deals with black touts, living precariously on the fringes of Johannesburg's growing black urban community. Morkel provided essential cover and the appearance of legitimacy, while his "boss boys" touted illegally for labour in the city and surrounding districts. These activities violated state regulations which prohibited recruiting in labour districts, and they also contravened the efforts of the Central Mining group itself to eliminate intra-industry competition and, particularly, expensive labour thefts from the group's compounds.

By the end of 1907, Morkel Brothers had over two hundred Africans, almost all of them from Basutoland, at work on the Robinson Central Deep, an important mine which later became part of the Crown Mines amalgamation. These Africans worked on the mine under the direct supervision of Morkel's "boss boys" who were not usually mine employees. Employed exclusively for "lashing and tramming" (shovelling and transporting ore underground) under their own black supervisors, Morkel's miners could avoid the often brutal white gangers who ruled the "hammer boys" at the stope face. The mine paid one shilling per truck loaded and trammed to the shaft for haulage to the surface. The mine also supplied compound space and "medical attendance" (such as it was at the time), while the workers found their own food, candles, and grease, as well as the WNLA fee levied on member companies for every voluntary or unrecruited worker. Each worker also paid 25 per cent of his total earnings, the so-called fourth week's wages, over to his "boss boy."

The system proved remunerative to the Morkels and the "boss boys" and extremely popular with the black workers. Morkel's work force increased rapidly, and the demand for labour soon outstripped the capacity of their rudimentary illicit recruiting operation in and around Johannesburg. Consequently the "boss boys" sought other allies, and they began to recruit directly in Basutoland itself. Frequently one of the "boss boys" would himself return to the colony, take out a runner's permit and begin touting for recruits whom he would then conduct to the Rand. As the Basutoland connection developed, however, the recruiters came increasingly to rely on labour drafts supplied by chiefs and headmen. Before long the headmen, since they controlled the supply, began to dominate the system. Either a chief would himself bring a gang to the Rand and remain with it during the contract period; or he would appoint his representative to accompany the workers, to remain with them and to collect on the chief's behalf the fourth week's wages. Exercising their control at a distance, the chiefs used their representatives to supplant some of the formerly independent "boss boys." Here is one instance among many of the key role of local notables in labour mobilization and control. Morkel could not have operated without them. On the other hand, the headmen and "boss boys" who worked the system were equally dependent on Morkel who provided legitimacy, an entrée with the mine employer and some protection for the black worker from the violence of the white ganger.

This form of labour contracting spread rapidly on the Rand. By 1911, the elder Morkel had involved his brother in the business and was widening his contacts in Basutoland. Morkel himself took out a labour agent's licence there which facilitated the acquisition of runners' permits by the "boss boys" and agents of the collaborating headmen. Seeing the success of these methods, other white and black contractors began to copy them. Piece-work lashing and tramming by independent labour gangs spread from the Robinson Central Deep to other sectors of the Crown Mines and then to other mines in the Central Mining group. The system persisted after the formation of the NRC and constituted an obvious challenge to the new corporation's "maximum average" wage system which was implemented in 1912. For the first decade or more the maximum wage system did not work very efficiently. Testimony before the Mining Industry Board as late as 1922 indicated that NRC members still routinely breached the wage agreement whenever a labour-short mine manager found it expedient to do so.[13]

While statistics are not available to distinguish this form of contracting from others, it seems likely that the numbers involved were quite large, sufficient at any rate to prompt the departmental inquiry in 1913. In the period 1909–14, when piece-work contracting was spreading on the mines, recruiting levels in Basutoland, from where most of these workers came, jumped spectacularly. In 1909, the protectorate supplied less than 3 per cent of the total labour force on the mines; by 1914 this had risen to nearly 7 per cent or 13,146 workers, an increase of over 250 per cent.[14] Through piece work rates, the labour contractors evidently provided the same incentive to Sotho workers that other contractors supplied, for instance, to the Pondo through the cattle advance system.

Labour bureau officials had no trouble detecting the appeal of the system to Morkel, his headmen, and "boss boys," who were guaranteed 25 per cent

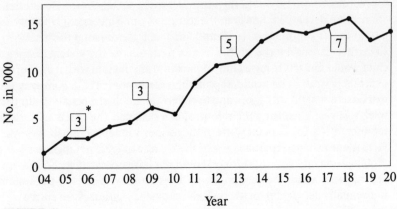

FIGURE 7
Mineworkers from Basutoland, 1904–20

SOURCES: Chamber of Mines and WNLA *Annual Reports;* Native Labour Bureau estimates.
NOTE: Recruited Africans and voluntaries included; data are approximate (see app. 1 for actual figures).
* Indicates per cent of total labour supply.

of the take. Its benefits to the workers themselves, who willingly gave up the fourth week's wages, were harder to discern. As the inquiry noted, the terms constituted a "distinct hardship" to the workers, yet they nevertheless accepted them. Mystified by this, the bureau investigators resorted to explanations which stressed the docility and gullibility of the workers and the tyranny and greed of the chiefs and the "boss boys."[15] There are better explanations. Originally the piece-work system put no limit on daily earnings. Through hard work, a gang could more than offset the loss of the fourth week's wages. Even when the NRC imposed a severe limit on piece-work rates through the maximum average, the system persisted. The black workers benefited also because they received supervision from their own "boss boys" and from the contractor Morkel. Morkel's arrangements with Central Mining gave him access to his work-force even when it was underground. He and his black collaborators shared an obvious interest in the contentment of their workers. They undoubtedly worked to protect their own contracted employees from the normal, severe discipline of the mine. At least some of the workers were also able to escape mine control when they came to the surface. The 1913 inquiry noted that many of his labourers did not live in the mine compounds. Presumably they found accommodation in the much less controlled surroundings of some nearby location, a far more congenial environment for any off-shift worker than the bleak, regimented mining compound. These factors account for the continuing popularity of Morkel Brothers and other contractors operating in a similar way, despite the eventual restriction imposed on piece-work rates.

Although the Morkels confined their operations mainly to Basutoland, their reliance on the collaboration of the local elite was typical of recruiting in all the main South African centres at that time. By 1910, virtually the entire rural elite of the eastern Cape had been swept in this way into the recruiting industry. In the King William's Town district, for example, the magistrate reported that all of the chiefs were recruiting for various companies despite a government prohibition imposed in early 1909.[16] His colleague, the labour registrar there, saw little hope for the voluntary labour system, which the government was then trying to promote, until they were removed from the system. In the view of this official, the headmen functioned as "so many auctioneers, handing the recruits to the man who pays them best."[17] In September 1909, the Cape Town Labour Conference devoted considerable attention to the involvement of the chiefs in the recruiting system. A number of the recruiters present wanted the state to recognize formally the involvement of the chiefs and to license them. Others, including the influential Taberer, opposed this. Taberer wanted the headmen excluded from the system altogether. Recruiters should be forbidden to approach them, and no one should be allowed a competitive edge.[18]

Aware of the key role of the headmen who were, in most cases, salaried government officials, the Cape authorities faced a dilemma. Prime Minister Merriman railed against the "petty tyranny" of these local despots "of whom we know so little."[19] Yet the government wanted above all to raise the participation rate of Cape blacks in the mine labour system. As Edward Dower expressed it, the influence of the chiefs could not be ignored: "it is the duty of every government officer to encourage labourers to go out to work."[20] The government wanted the chiefs to supply labour; it wanted their influence with the rural folk; but the chiefs were not to recruit for anyone in particular, nor apparently to act in a way that would bring benefit to themselves. The opportunities for profit were too large, however, for Dower's ideas to have any chance of success. Even when the Cape government formally banned headmen from holding runners' permits, their involvement in the system remained crucial. Competing recruiters would bribe them or they would extract a percentage of the wages from the mineworkers themselves as was the case with the Morkel contracting scheme.

Over the next decade mine recruiters found more sophisticated ways of keeping the chiefs and headmen sympathetic to the mines' labour needs. They developed one technique which was both highly successful and much cheaper than the old system of capitation fees and presents for recruits delivered. In fact, the mines managed eventually to shift the costs of its involvement with the chiefs directly onto the recruits just as Morkel had earlier done. In 1903, the visit of "native delegates" from the Cape to the mines had been an exceptional event, a one-time device which the government hoped mistakenly would send Cape Africans flocking back to the mines. It did not work, and the experiment was not repeated on any regular basis, although there were occasional government-sponsored visits by African chiefs to the Rand. By the second decade of the century the mines themselves were not only permitting but actively encouraging the frequent visits of the more important chiefs and headmen or their representatives to Johannesburg.

The visitor found himself treated as an important dignitary. If his district was a major source of labour, he might meet the great Taberer himself and other NRC officials. He was given access to the compounds and offered tours of underground and surface works. These tours were designed not merely to demonstrate to the chief that the recruiters considered him an important personage, nor simply to reassure the individual concerning the welfare of his people on the mines. Above all these were fund-raising visits, an opportunity for the chief to tax his dependents at a time when they still had money to give him. In the era of unrestricted cash and cattle advances, before 1910, the chiefs and headmen had not had to visit the Rand for this purpose. They and the heads of families received the money before the worker departed for the mines. The advance system had at least ensured that some of the benefits of migrancy, meagre though they usually were, accrued not to the worker himself but to his family and his chief. It is clear that the use of advances contributed very largely to the sudden jump in recruiting levels from the eastern Cape in the period, 1907–9. Pressure for them came from the black rural elite who were the main beneficiaries.[21]

Two new developments came to threaten these benefits. When the government legislated limits on the size of wage advances which could be given this reduced the flow of funds to the countryside.[22] Second, as the mineworkers gained in experience and sophistication through repeated trips to the mines, many more of them became voluntary labourers. As unrecruited workers, they, of course, received no advance of any kind, nor did the mines pay a recruiting fee, part of which in the case of the recruited African frequently would end up in the hands of his head of family or chief. Voluntary labour not only freed the worker from the recruiters but also increasingly from the bonds of family and community obligation. To counteract these new circumstances, the headmen had little choice but to come to the Rand themselves or to send a representative in order to tithe their people. Whatever the precise motives, the frequent visits of these collaborators became a regular part of the mine labour system. The labour bureau was enlisted to provide facilities and assistance to the chiefs. A department circular in 1913 required officials to give facilities to "*all* Chiefs and influential natives visiting their followers."[23]

Occasionally the bureau went further and itself solicited contributions on behalf of a particular tribal leader. In 1922, for instance, the director of native labour asked the pass officer at Benoni to contact certain workers on behalf of "Chief Lebelo" at Potgietersrust and to seek contributions for the chief's land fund. He had purchased a farm on behalf of the tribe and was heavily in debt. Forced to sell cattle to meet the interest charges, he turned in desperation when cattle prices plummeted to the local native commissioner. This officer approached the director of native labour. Given the powers of pass officials, the hapless "followers" of Chief Lebelo must have felt they had little choice but to comply.[24] Such facilities were only available to black collaborators who had the ear of the Native Affairs Department. Lesser figures were merely tolerated. Referring to the visit of one Johannes Lekoankoa, "a very petty headman" in the northern Transvaal, an officer commented: "there is no objection to his remaining on the Reef. He is probably there solely to collect enough money to pay his own taxes. It would be better if he stopped there and worked."[25] By 1921, the bureau was trying to discourage visits which were "purely to collect money," but this did nothing to reduce the number of visits nor the fund-raising.[26]

In the case of most of these chiefs, the mines provided the facilities and frequently paid the expenses of the visitor. The files of the labour bureau document dozens of visits.[27] Typically a local representative of the NRC would make the arrangements and forward particulars both to the labour bureau and to the corporation's head office in Johannesburg. On arrival in the city the headman or his induna would report to the bureau to pick up a temporary pass valid for the duration of the visit. The corporation furnished a letter of introduction to the compound managers without which he could not get access to his people.

Increasingly, the mines managed to shift the burden of keeping the headmen loyal to the system onto the workers themselves. Once institutionalized these frequent visits came to constitute a second, unofficial system of taxation. Stuck in the compounds, the workers had little chance of evading their visiting chiefs. Equipped with letters of introduction and armed with official documents, the headmen had the weight of the government and the mines' recruiting system behind them. The opportunities for successful extortion were obviously large. This continuing involvement of the rural elite in the labour system indicates very well how strategically placed local interests could extract substantial benefits for themselves from the mining economy.

Both the state and the mining industry needed the backing of the headmen even after the NRC had brought order to South African recruiting. Neither would tolerate, however, any attempt by the chiefs to interfere with mine discipline. Such intervention between the worker and management was swiftly dealt with. Headman September Gxowa of Glen Grey in the eastern Cape discovered this during a visit to the Block A, Randfontein Central compound in 1923. Shortly after his arrival in Johannesburg, he received a letter from workers at Randfontein telling him that two of his followers had died in hospital and a third was to undergo surgery. Concerned about the welfare of the surviving workers from his locality, Gxowa went to the Block A compound but was refused entry by the induna there. After waiting most of the next day, he managed to interview the compound manager who, somewhat reluctantly, allowed him to enter. He was not to hold a general meeting with his people, however, but only to visit their rooms. During his stay on the mine which continued into the following day, the compound manager concluded that Gxowa was a dangerous agitator, threatened to handcuff him, and had him ejected from the compound. Outraged by this summary treatment, Gxowa appealed to the labour bureau inspector at Randfontein who, however, sided with the management. Gxowa then wrote to Taberer but without success, and he found his appeal to the director of native labour also rejected.[28]

In sanctioning these visits, the mines and the government obviously wanted to buy the continued support of influential blacks in the countryside for the migrant labour system. In addition, they hoped that the authority of tribal society could be mobilized through the chiefs to reinforce the quasi-military discipline on the mines. In return the headmen were given access to their followers and powerful support for their fund-raising efforts, but only so long as they played according to the strict rules laid down by the mines. The authorities came down hard on Gxowa, not only because he attempted to intervene with management on a matter affecting the safety of his workers, but also because he declined to play the part of the grateful, deferential visiting chief. An articulate and forceful person, Gxowa confronted the management at Randfontein and attempted to stand up for the rights of his workers with the local labour bureau inspector. Such a potentially dangerous interloper had to be dealt with summarily. He was sent home after a severe reprimand delivered by the NRC's "head boy," speaking for both the director of native labour and Superintendent Taberer.[29]

Just as competitive recruiting gave enterprising black recruiters and workers numerous opportunities to exploit the system in their interest so the frequent visits of these chiefs and their indunas opened up other opportunities. The visits and the visitors were hard to monitor. Any African could approach a local official or NRC recruiter, claim to be representing a particular chief and seek support for a fund-raising visit to the Rand. Unless a check was made in each case there was no way to verify the authenticity of the representatives. In early 1923 two of these fund-raisers were picked up in Johannesburg and sent home after labour bureau officials received a warning from the local native commissioner that they did not in fact have permission to raise funds as they had claimed. It seems that the chief in whose name they were pretending to act got wind of their activities and complained to the magistrate. In this case, the fund raisers had a letter from a

TABLE 3
Desertion from WNLA Member Companies, 1909–20

Year	Deserters	Recruits Received	% of Recruits Received	Total Received*	% of Total Received
1909	9,856	109,971	8.96	150,837	6.53
1910	4,199	147,584	2.85	209,929	2.00
1911	3,514	138,635	2.53	208,858	1.68
1912	2,689	155,887	1.72	247,477	1.09
1913	2,479	129,363	1.92	201,496	1.23
1914	2,134	136,888	1.56	213,829	1.00
1915	2,430	167,044	1.45	252,650	.96
1916	1,606	134,946	1.19	235,061	.68
1917	1,302	116,699	1.12	213,631	.61
1918	1,447	100,154	1.44	201,105	.72
1919	1,291	123,272	1.05	233,804	.55
1920	115	121,563	.95	212,307	.54

SOURCE: Compiled from WNLA *Annual Report.*
*Includes voluntaries

local recruiter who may have been duped by them if he was not a partici-pant in the attempted fraud. Other such cases appear in the official record, and it seems likely that many more went undetected.[30]

The massive involvement of chiefs and headmen was only one conse-quence of the highly competitive conditions which remained the norm in the southern African mine labour market long after the establishment of the NRC. Since the breakup of the WNLA outside Mozambique in 1906, the independent labour contractors and the trader/recruiters had had several years to entrench their positions. Rightly fearing that their livelihood was at stake, many of them refused to yield to the discipline of a single recruiting system, even one as powerful as the WNLA/NRC combine which now represented mines employing 85 per cent of the industry's total labour needs. Because competition continued, even member mining companies of these labour organizations could afford to give them only partial and con-ditional loyalty. Many observers noted that desertion from one mine to another constituted possibly the Rand's most serious labour problem. As in the earliest days of the industry, labour touts operating in Johannesburg itself procured desertions from one firm to sell to another. They profited from the appalling conditions on many mines which led hundreds of Africans annually to flee from the Rand. Large numbers of the so-called voluntaries who were arriving in Johannesburg could also be enticed into employment by the touts.

Black workers had many reasons to desert from mine employment. Conditions were particularly bad underground and in the compounds and carried a high risk of injury, assault, serious illness, and death.[31] Mines with decent conditions and a reputation for reasonable treatment experienced little desertion. Asked to account for the absence of desertions at the Nigel GMC, one of its recruiters, James Hadley, explained that the work was comparatively easy on this outcrop mine, that, unlike most mines, the Nigel served meat daily and that, above all, the management tolerated no "rough stuff" by the white gangers.[32] Not all of the desertions can be explained by maltreatment, however. During the five years after 1907, the payment of large cash advances to South African recruits gave workers a major financial incentive to escape from an onerous, often dangerous mine contract. Many fled from the prospect of employment by leaving their train in the Free State and taking refuge on a white farm there.[33] Wages would undoubtedly be low but the worker had his advance and residence on the farm made his recapture unlikely. The highly competitive labour market led to much misrepresentation of conditions on the mines by avaricious recruiters and labour companies.[34] A brief experience with the actual situation was enough to induce flight among significant numbers of the workers who had been thus misled. With the rapid expansion of the work force during this period, many of the arrivals on the mines were first-time recruits. Among them, desertion rates were always higher, reflecting their revulsion from conditions underground and in the compounds.[35] Those who fled or were lured from the mines found an army of touts and contractors ready to help them escape from the Rand. Workers needed the services of cooperating whites who equipped them with proper documents and alternative employment – a place of refuge – away from Johannesburg.

Desertion reached a postwar peak in the period 1907–10, when the mines were making a massive effort to replace the departing Chinese. Whereas in 1905 and 1906, the mines lost respectively 64 and 68 per thousand of their workers through desertion, the rate jumped to 95 in 1907–8 and to a startling 117 the following year.[36] Of these, the labour bureau and the police managed to recover about 43 per cent, an improvement over the dismal recovery rate of 29 per cent in 1905–6, but still not sufficient to offset the alarming haemorrhage of labour.[37] According to the WNLA annual reports nearly 10,000 black miners fled their employment in 1909. As these reports included only WNLA member companies, the overall rate must have been considerably higher. Rates of default varied greatly according to territory of origin. Over 40 per cent (525 workers) of the Bechuanaland contingent decamped in 1909, while from the Cape 4,133 workers deserted that year, about half the total number of desertions which amounted to 10 per cent of the total of Cape workers on the mines. Over the two years, 1908–9, the Cape Colony supplied about 24 per cent of the mine labour force but nearly

TABLE 4
Origin of Deserters, 1909, 1914, 1919

		Year	
Territory	1909	1914	1919
Basutoland and OFS	627	318	269
Cape Colony	4,133	470	478
Mozambique, S. of 22° SL	1,492	100	138
Natal	1,460	515	84
Transvaal	1,257	248	213
Other	887	483	109
Totals	9,856	2,134	1,291

SOURCE: WNLA Annual Report, 1915, 1917, 1921.

40 per cent of the desertions, rates which were sustained into 1910 with only a marginal reduction.

For Cape Africans, the gold mines had long been employers of last resort. Many of them were now arriving in Johannesburg for the first time and the desertion rates reflected this. By contrast, few of the experienced Mozambique workers tried to flee the Rand. Far from home, many found themselves dependent on the repatriation facilities of the WNLA. It was widely believed in the recruiting industry that desertion rates varied inversely with the distance travelled by the recruits and directly with the ease of transport and facilities available to get to and from the Rand. Given the coercive labour practices which prevailed in Mozambique and the absence of alternative employment there, the gold mines, grim though they were, must have seemed places of refuge and even opportunity to many of the east coast workers. Whatever the explanation, only 2 per cent of this large work-force defaulted in 1909 (1,492 workers), a rate which fell below 1 per cent the following year. During 1914, the WNLA recorded only 100 desertions in the Mozambique contingent of over 68,000 workers.[38]

As the Chamber of Mines began to get some control over competitive recruiting, the desertion problem eased, although it remained a serious issue for another fifteen years. In 1910, the rate fell to twenty-four per thousand and the following year to nineteen. By 1912, the year the NRC was set up, only 2,689 workers defaulted, a rate of fifteen per thousand. Over the decade which followed, the annual number of desertions ranged between about 1,300 and 2,500. These figures represented a significant loss to the companies but marked nevertheless a major advance over the previous decade. Apart from less competition in recruiting, the reduction of the desertion rate owed something to an amelioration of compound and working conditions and a major improvement in the health of the black miners during the second decade of the century. Although the mines and their compounds

167   The Recruiting Nexus

remained bleak, sterile working environments, they were at least ceasing to be death-traps.

Falling rates of desertion also reflected, however, the commitment to improved methods of control on the part of both the chamber and the government.[39] With the coming of Union and the imposition of the Native Labour Regulation Act of 1911, deserters could much more easily be recovered from their home districts. The labour bureau launched many investigations designed to trace deserters, to deny them refuge in the countryside, and to ensure that they were returned, after a jail sentence, to complete the mine contracts. Even workers from the British High Commission territories did not escape, since these governments had aligned their regulations with those of the Union. Defaulting workers from Basutoland and the other territories faced fines and jail sentences on their return. Moreover, from 1910 state restrictions on the size of the cash advance which could be given to the recruited worker removed what had previously been a significant incentive to default.

Through the multiplication of individual and collective acts of desertion, the mineworkers had been able to exert considerable pressure for improvements on the migrant labour system. Labour bureau officials pressed for changes in compound and working conditions from the beginning.[40] They knew that successful recruiting depended on black perceptions of conditions on particular mines. Virtually all South African recruits specified their mine at the time they accepted a contract. They insisted on the right to avoid dangerous and unpopular employers. Without this provision, recruiting levels in the South African territories would undoubtedly have been much lower. The Mozambique blacks, two-thirds of whom enjoyed no such privilege, were used to provide a work-force for the less attractive mine employers. Almost as much as the mineworkers, the licensed labour recruiters had an obvious interest in the improvement of conditions on the Rand. Their livelihood had come to depend on the willingness of local Africans to accept employment there. At this time, the recruiters were often found collaborating with government officials to force reforms upon their reluctant mine employers.

A striking example occurred during 1913. The Native Labour Bureau commissioned an investigation of workers' grievances at Crown Mines, one of the most important of the Rand mines.[41] The charges laid were serious and the investigation important enough to be conducted by the assistant director. It arose out of complaints by H.M. Taberer, formerly head of the recruiting arm of the Crown Mines' parent house and now general superintendent of the Native Recruiting Corporation. He had evidence of maltreatment of the workers, of heavy "wastage" owing to desertion and other causes, and of a sharp fall-off in recruiting levels. The investigation which followed confirmed all of Taberer's allegations. Management followed a general policy of "hustle" (profit levels had not been adequate for several years); the white gangers as a group seemed more than usually brutal and impatient; and there had been a huge number of wage irregularities. The inquiry found a "lamentable" lack of cooperation between compound and underground officials in investigating workers' grievances. With the black work-force voting with its feet or refusing to come to the mine at all and with the intensification of pressure from the labour bureau and the NRC, the Crown Mines management began slowly and reluctantly to reform its labour practices.

Taberer's role was especially significant. After joining the NRC, he had retained close ties with his former employer, Central Mining, the Crown Mines controlling house and the dominant force in the Chamber of Mines. Taberer knew well enough about the grim financial circumstances at the Crown and the pressures on management to drive labour costs down while wringing maximum effort from the black miners. He had to be more concerned, however, with the probable effect of the situation on recruiting levels for the industry as a whole. The prospect of twelve thousand brutalized and exploited Crown Mines blacks fanning out across South Africa and spreading their tales of horror was not something the NRC or its chief recruiter could easily tolerate.[42] Despite the beginnings of reform at the Crown and other mines, desertion from mine employment continued to be significant for several more years.

Nevertheless, improving conditions on the mines and more efficient methods of control both explain the steep reduction in desertion rates which became apparent after about 1910. Although the deserters now found it more difficult to operate and the labour touts and thieves could no longer pirate labour out of the compounds with impunity, a scramble for labour continued in Johannesburg. The touts turned their attention to the so-called voluntaries, those thousands of unrecruited workers who were now seeking work along the Rand on their own. By the middle of the second decade of the century, voluntary labour constituted the largest single category of unskilled workers on the gold mines.[43] Like time-expired workers seeking to transfer from nonmining to mining employment or from one mine to another, these workers were vulnerable to hijacking by smooth-talking touts and black runners. Both the WNLA and the NRC employed black agents and "police boys" who patrolled the railway stations and the vicinity of the pass offices to try to ensure that member mines got their share at least of the voluntary labour.

As the proportion of voluntary labour grew in the years after 1912, the mines began to bid aggressively among themselves for this category of worker. The voluntary was highly prized because of his motivation (he had after all chosen to come), his experience, and his efficiency. Mine managers found ways to reward these workers despite the special fees and stringent rules applied by the NRC to prevent such competition. They paid wages and bonuses above the maximum average specified by the recruiting corporation. Very short contracts were allowed, even of a few weeks.[44] They tried to provide conditions in the compounds which would attract the work-force. The compounds of A.M. Mostert, for instance, were much less closely regulated than most and though extremely unsanitary, very popular with mineworkers.[45] During 1913 and 1914, the South African police on the Rand noticed an alarming increase in illicit liquor selling and beer brewing in and around many of the mine compounds. Officials linked this development directly to the competition for voluntary labour. All of the mines supplied a weak form of traditional African beer, but many of the workers were after the stronger stuff.

A raid on a large compound on the far east Rand in December 1913 yielded 1,500 gallons of liquor and beer. The officer in charge made thirty-six arrests and poured away "a river of skokian." He could have arrested at least a hundred workers for involvement in liquor offences at that one compound but lacked the manpower to do so. Two nights later another raid on the Knight's Central compound netted 1,100 gallons of illicit brew.[46] The labour bureau inspector at Benoni south complained that his entire district was a "hotbed" of illegal brewing.[47] Both the police and the inspectors believed that the compound managers were guilty of condoning the situation. As the inspector explained, the "wet compounds" victimized the "dry ones" in the competition for the time-expired worker who was willing to sign another contract and could sometimes be lured by the availability of liquor or beer. Certainly massive evidence was obtained for 1913 and 1914 that the mines were not enforcing prohibition effectively. Labour bureau officials and the police raided several compounds of the JCI group in 1914, and found that all of them were awash in illicit liquor and home-brewed beer. At the New Primrose, the management employed known liquor dealers, according to the bureau's inspector, and insisted on rehiring them after conviction for liquor offences. Generally the compound staff aimed "to interfere as little as possible with the Natives and exercise the least possible supervision with a view to ensuring popularity and attaching to themselves that class of voluntary labour that abominates the discipline of a well run compound."[48] Evidently the group's managers gave priority to keeping the compounds filled with voluntary labour even at the cost of having part of the work-force drunk much of the time. The Chamber of Mines had long been committed to prohibition of use on the mines of any drink stronger than the officially sanctioned traditional beer. As usual, however, the mine managers showed by their actions that they had other priorities. A work-force partly incapacitated by illicit liquor and beer was evidently better than no labour force at all. Labour bureau efforts to enforce prohibition were strenuously resisted. Repeated police raids barely kept the situa-

TABLE 5
Shifts Lost through Drunkenness, 1913–17

Month/Year	Shifts Lost	Total per 1,000 employees
1913		
January	3,510	20.2
May	3,818	21.1
September	2,961	21
Est. total	41,156	
1914		
January	1,683	12
May	2,198	15
September	2,147	14
Est. total	24,112	
1915		
January	2,812	19
May	1,870	11
September	1,885	11
Est. total	26,268	
1916		
January	2,143	12
May	1,675	10
September	1,960	12
Est. total	23,112	
1917		
January	1,900	12
May	1,659	9
September	1,671	9
Est. total	19,920	

SOURCE: GNLB 294, 238/18/D54, from Chamber of Mines data.

Note: includes mineworkers employed by mining companies but not those employed by contractors.

tion in check, and the problems on these and other mines persisted into the 1920s.[49]

The black worker arriving on his own in Johannesburg needed his wits about him. The city was filled with touts and runners bent on tempting him into work with their employers. If he was incautious or only slightly credulous, he could find himself bundled quickly into some uncongenial job at low wages perhaps far from Johannesburg. By no means all of these workers were "street-wise" and able to fend off the unwanted attentions of the touts. Many inexperienced workers became voluntaries at the expiry of their first contract. In order to sign on with another employer they had normally to leave the compound of the first and make their own way to the premises of the second. Once on their own in the streets, they were vulnerable to those who lived by preying on the weak or the merely naïve. In short, the establishment of the NRC and the rise of voluntary labour did not lessen the struggle for labour on the Rand. Moreover, actual desertions, although declining in number, by no means disappeared. The labour touts lived both by catering to the deserters and by recruiting the voluntaries once they had arrived in Johannesburg.

A serious case came to light in mid-1911 which illustrates the magnitude of a continuing problem. In cooperation with the South African Police, the Native Labour Bureau launched a major investigation into the traffic in illegal passes on the Rand. With the aid of black detectives, Native Affairs Department inspectors soon made fifteen arrests including pass sellers and some of the deserters themselves. Two black labour contractors on the George Goch mine were among those picked up. They had procured desertions from other mines, sold the deserters Orange Free State travelling passes, procured illegally from a compliant field cornet there, and promised employment at the Goch for wages which, at thirty shillings a week, substantially exceeded the NRC rates.[50] The director of native labour, S.M. Pritchard, had been attempting for some time to eliminate the large-scale traffic in forged or stolen Cape and Free State travelling passes. Would-be deserters from the mines easily acquired these documents. After absconding, they presented themselves at the Johannesburg pass office as new work-seekers from the countryside, and exchanged their illegal travelling pass for a perfectly valid six-day work-seeking permit. Following a short interval they would report to the pass office that they had been unable to find work and secure endorsement of their pass for return home. In this way the deserter could secure repatriation under the official protection of the Native Affairs Department. He stood little chance of detection since he had presented himself with hundreds of others at the pass office as a new arrival. His status as a deserter could not be exposed unless a pass official became suspicious and checked his fingerprints against the deserters' file.[51]

Although the government incorporated a ban on recruiting in "labour districts" (including the entire Rand) under the Native Labour Regulation Act of 1911, this activity went on almost uncontrolled. NRC Chairman Villiers complained of the labour contractor, Lazarus, who, although he employed not a single recruiter, managed to maintain a labour force of a thousand workers on the Rand: "he recruited every boy down at the pass office. There were 13 men recruiting [illegally] at the pass office only a few weeks ago for various contractors. I put on detectives, and we trapped this fellow Lazarus, but the Government refused to take any action at all. A large number of our boys are recruited [at the Government compound] in Germiston and sent down to Natal."[52] Lazarus was picking off the voluntaries, both the new arrivals on the Rand and those seeking to transfer from one mine to another. As his statement shows, Villiers thought these workers – "our boys" – belonged to the mines.

Labour contracting constituted only a small part of the business of Lazarus and Company. The letterhead described the company as grain brokers, commission and general agents, railway contractors, manufacturers' agents, and general store keepers. The firm had a network of trading stores in Basutoland (9), Swaziland (4), the Transvaal and Bechuanaland (2), the Cape and Natal (1 each). Although the company was certainly well placed to conduct a legitimate labour recruiting business, Lazarus and his colleagues concentrated on acquiring their labour on the Rand itself. He received permission from the Native Labour Bureau in 1914 to engage African voluntaries for the mines and other employment in Johannesburg. The bureau warned, however, that this permission did not constitute a licence to "tout." Since allowing Lazarus to engage the voluntaries gave perfect cover for illegal recruiting the bureau's warning was predictably ineffective.[53] His agents could and did use this authority to cloak their illegal touting at the Johannesburg pass office and elsewhere. Later in 1914, Lazarus applied for permission to hire voluntaries in the Boksburg, Benoni, and Germiston area as well, but the Native Labour Bureau refused the applications. Almost from the start bureau officials recognized that Lazarus and Company was "not in fact a bona fide organization endeavouring to introduce labour from native areas. Others did this while Lazarus and Co. hoped to reap the benefits on the Reef."[54] Despite this the permission to engage voluntaries in Johannesburg remained in force until 1918. Presumably Native Affairs Department officials felt that the services of the company in sweeping the streets of unemployed blacks outweighed the problems created by the touting. Lazarus may have been politically well connected although there is no evidence of this.[55]

The case of Samuel Said, another notorious tout whom the Native Affairs Department accused in 1913 of several cases of illegal recruiting, well illustrates the ruthless methods which were employed to steal labour in Johannesburg. Said operated a "kaffir eating house" strategically located near the Market Street pass office. It was one of several canteens in the area operated by predators bent on either supplying mine labour at exorbitant rates or stealing it from the mines for service elsewhere. Typically both activities went on simultaneously.[56] Because of the pass system, the entire black population working in central Johannesburg came sooner or later to the Market Street pass office. In May 1913, two unidentified informants came to the South African Police at Marshall Square to denounce Said for illegal recruiting. The investigating detective considered the charges sufficiently well based to bring before a justice of the peace, who charged Said with illegal touting in violation of regulations under the Native Labour Regulation Act of 1911. At the subsequent trial, Said won acquittal, but the evidence presented is nevertheless suggestive.

Police informants stated that in January 1913 Said had recruited 155 Africans in Johannesburg for service on railway construction near Port Elizabeth, that he received seventy-five pounds from his employers and that he used part of the money to bribe a Mr Mills, then a clerk in the Johannesburg pass office. They claimed that Said had recruited over 350 blacks for these railway contractors. Related charges held that Said also recruited for Lazarus who then had an important labour contract at the City Deep mine and that he employed "black runners" to tout for him through the city at 2s.6d. a head delivered to his eating-house.[57] In the following year Said had to defend an action in which he was accused of procuring desertions from the Crown Mines. Many of Said's recruits turned up on the collieries in the Dundee area of Natal.[58]

During 1914, the Native Labour Bureau gathered further evidence about the remarkable Mr Said, evidence which suggests, incidentally, that he was far from being the only violator of the regulations on recruiting. Bureau officials worked closely with H.M. Taberer and the NRC, which was, of course, a principal loser from the activities of men like Said. These touts could not have operated successfully had there not been a heavy demand for their services from black mine and other workers so anxious to flee from present troubles that they were willing to place themselves in the hands of recruiters of this type. The touts provided facilities without which desertion would have been much more difficult. They provided passes and the protection of their own runners and white conductors. Without this assistance most black deserters stood little chance of evading the South African Police and labour bureau dragnet on the Rand.

Writing to H.M. Taberer toward the end of 1914, an NRC informant described one case among many.[59] A few days before, he explained, a mineworker identified only by his pass number came into the pass office to request leave to return home. His father had died. The following day he was in again even more anxious for leave, for now a brother had also died. The informant approached the mine management which refused permission on the grounds that the worker was "one of the worst loafers, etc." Subsequently the black miner deserted from the mine, made his way to Said's eating-house and signed on to work at a Natal colliery. He was picked up by the police the following day, while waiting on Braamfontein station for his eastbound train, and immediately confessed the connection with Said. The labour bureau's assistant director, E.K. Whitehead, wrote to Taberer for an explanation. The bureau must have been especially concerned that the Village Main Reef from which the African had deserted belonged to the NRC. The mining groups were up to their old tricks, stealing labour from each other and employing independent labour touts for the purpose, while innocently claiming to be loyal members of the new labour cooperative. Even assisted by the state, NRC officials found themselves hard-pressed to stop the racket.

Few mine managers could resist the temptation to acquire additional labour even when it came from allied companies. The touts lived by exploiting their weakness. Said could not have operated without the cooperation of the Glencoe Colliery management and of his other employers. The colliery manager, however, denied all knowledge of the basis on which Said was supplying labour to his company. Although he admitted receiving labour from Said, he claimed that the arrangement had been made by his head office in Johannesburg. He was merely the innocent recipient of the bounty which flowed miraculously from the Rand.[60]

Said's method of operation can readily be deduced from the surviving records. Essentially he was a labour contractor who exploited his strategically placed "eating house" and his contacts in the pass office to identify deserters, round them up with his runners, and send them to his employers away from Johannesburg with new travel documents and new identities. He also recruited unemployed blacks who turned up at the pass office and weak and sick workers who had been rejected for mine employment and found themselves penniless on the Rand. Black criminals used his services and, like the deserters, saw a means to equip themselves with new travel documents and perhaps a safe place of refuge far from the Rand.[61] Said claimed to be the actual employer of the labour he sent to the Natal collieries and elsewhere, using this dodge to evade the Union government's ban on recruiting by labour agents in labour districts. A bona fide employer could hire the unemployed (though not of course deserters or fugitive offenders) and this Said claimed to be. Although the collieries paid Said's recruits their wages direct, they also paid him a fee calculated on a per-shift-worked basis and sent him the pay sheets to make it look as if he really did employ them.[62]

Samuel Said and Brother Isaac carried on their illegal traffic in black labour despite repeated attempts of the Native Affairs Department and the labour bureau to convict them of touting and other irregularities. Several charges came to trial but failed for lack of evidence. Moreover, the Saids apparently had a friend in the Native Affairs Department. The acting chief pass officer believed that this contact, a subinspector named Mills, worked actively to subvert the department's case in an action against Isaac Said. A subsequent departmental inquiry confirmed that Mills had aided the defence in the case and more generally "that there are reasonable grounds for the belief that [Mills] has been remiss in his duty where the Said brothers are concerned."[63] In connection with the same case, Isaac Said tried to discredit the department inspector who brought the action against him by accosting him in a bar and later in a restaurant to create the appearance that the inspector had accepted favours from him.[64] The machinations of the Said brothers reduced the Johannesburg pass office to chaos, and it had to be reconstructed after a special departmental inquiry.

Two circumstances favoured illegal touting on the Rand: the widespread desire by mineworkers to escape from unpopular employers and, second, the inability of the employers to control competition among themselves for labour. The touts provided a service that was much in demand; they brought voluntaries and would-be absconders together with prospective employers inside and outside of Johannesburg. Most of the mine employers, whether NRC members or not, had few scruples about employing deserters, fugitive offenders, the destitute and the sick, or anyone else obliged to work for a pittance. Not only did the number of desertions remain large in this period, but also the number of repeat offenders tended to grow. A traffic in desertion developed related to but distinct from the touting which went on on the Rand itself. Licensed labour agents in the countryside frequently connived in desertions. They stood little chance of detection and could make large profits because a deserter sent back to Johannesburg by a labour agent to a different mine was unlikely to be discovered. Hence the agent could secure a second recruiting fee from the new employer. In the case of the many multiple deserters, several fees might be paid for the same recruit by the various employers. Enterprising deserters exploited the cash advance system by taking money from several employers, while staying to complete the contract with none of them. The unscrupulous labour agent provided essential facilities for the deserter to their mutual profit.

Early in 1915, a pass office investigation identified fifty-five Africans who had deserted from two or more employers over the previous several years.[65] Because absconders remained difficult to detect, these cases of multiple offences almost certainly represent only a fraction of the total. The department officer who conducted the investigation believed that licensed labour agents routinely conspired with each other to place deserters unnoticed in new employment: "when a native has been recruited by No. 1 recruiter, deserts and returns to him he (No. 1 recruiter) instead of again putting him on his sheets, passes him to recruiter No. 2 in some other district, who enters him on his sheets and sends him up, the two or more recruiters sharing the profits."[66] Such an arrangement would probably escape detection unless the returning deserter happened to be picked up by the police for some other reason once he reached the Rand. Although all new and returning mine recruits were fingerprinted on arrival in Johannesburg, their prints were not matched against the file of deserters' fingerprints until they had actually deserted. Then their prints were added to the deserter file and a file search at that time would reveal any previous case of desertion. Still in its bureaucratic infancy, the Native Affairs Department lacked the capacity to create a master file of fingerprints and to check every arriving worker against it. As a result shrewd, fast-moving recruits, aided by compliant labour agents and even government officials, could evade detection for many years.

The case of "Libone Jack" revealed a pattern of multiple desertion often found among mine employees at this time. It is one of many documented in the files of the Native Labour Bureau. Originally recruited in Mafeking, this mineworker deserted seven times between 1908 and 1914. In each case, he returned home, reengaged for a different mine, accepted another cash advance, and returned to the Rand. According to his own testimony, he failed to complete any of the contracts. After three successful desertions, "Libone Jack" became somewhat over-confident. Following each of his last three desertions he returned to the same recruiter in his home district. This was a notorious tout named le Roux who worked in Mafeking and provided facilities for many multiple deserters. Instead of turning him in, the agent simply signed him on to a different mine under a new name, supplied him with another cash advance and dispatched him to the new employer. "Libone Jack" was only one of many deserters he helped in this way. "Libone Jack" always deserted in the company of other workers, and it seems probable that they also took advantage of the facilities of le Roux and other touts. Eventually the labour bureau became suspicious and a check of the fingerprints of this agent's recruits soon revealed what had been going on. "Libone Jack" served 123 days with hard labour and then had to return to each mine in turn to complete the contracts from which he had long since deserted. This same file documents the cases of several other multiple deserters who were tracked down by the labour bureau in 1915.[67]

As the mines' labour needs continued to increase, competitive recruiting in a situation of nearly perpetual "labour shortage" opened numerous opportunities for mineworkers abetted by touts, labour agents, and their black runners. Despite huge financial resources and increasingly sophisticated labour organizations, the WNLA and the NRC, the industry continued to experience losses from these activities. In the years after Union, the government implemented a vigorous program of control and prosecution and succeeded in reducing but not eliminating the number of defaults. Though rigorously enforced, regulations under the Native Labour Regulation Act of 1911 were still evaded, and many agile mineworkers managed to keep ahead of the law. Some of the worst excesses took place on the Rand itself where labour agents were not supposed to recruit at all. Notorious labour touts, such as the brothers Said whose activities have been outlined, were some of the most successful operators, but established, licensed labour contractors and even the NRC itself routinely ignored the law when they found it expedient to do so.

Take the case of Mozambique mineworkers, "Fokkies" and "Forage," for example.[68] Like many Mozambique blacks, these men decided to serve a second period at a different mine after their initial contract expired. They left the first mine in mid-1915, and made their way through Johannesburg intending to make a new deal at the mine of their choice through the WNLA

Johannesburg compound. En route to the WNLA depot, they fell into the clutches of a black runner working for Hadley's labour organization, which, as noted above, was linked to the NRC. They were vulnerable because of their inexperience; this was their first trip to Johannesburg. Independent labour contractors as well as the WNLA and the NRC maintained squads of black messengers and "police boys" who watched the railway stations, the pass office, and the vicinity of the offices of rival labour companies. Competition between them was incessant and unrestrained.

"Fokkies" and "Forage" became two pawns in this struggle. As they neared the WNLA compound on that day, one of Hadley's messengers spotted them, claimed to be a black detective and demanded their passes. Not surprisingly, an "irregularity" was discovered, and the messenger took them to what he said was the office of the Portuguese "curator" of labour to have the matter put right. Of course, the office turned out to be that of Hadley's agent, A. Kantor. He told "Fokkies" and "Forage" that he could not offer them work at the mine of their choice but asked them to sign on for six months at either the Simmer Deep or the Knight's Central. Although they declined the offer, Kantor put them in the charge of an induna and sent them out to the Simmer Deep anyway. Once back in the street, though in the charge of one of Hadley's men, the two recruits became fair game again. Before the small party even got out of the city, they were spotted by a WNLA "police boy" who recognized the induna as one of Hadley's touts. He secured custody and managed to deliver them to the WNLA compound which was where they had wanted to go in the first place. By itself the incident is of little significance. It requires discussion because it seems typical of a period of severe competition for labour. Furthermore the case is well documented and illustrates very clearly the methods used by even licensed labour companies to get and keep labour in Johannesburg. As inexperienced first-time mineworkers, "Fokkies" and "Forage" had little chance against the touts and runners who prowled the black areas of the city. In the end they got where they wanted to go but certainly not through their own efforts. Probably there were many like them.

The WNLA turned the case over to the Native Labour Bureau for prosecution, but Hadley's agent, Kantor, who was already well known to the authorities, contrived to escape once again: "As Mr. Hadley's Agent [Kantor] made use of an interpreter [i.e., when talking to "Fokkies" and "Forage"], who may have been in collusion with the Runner who had stopped the natives on their way to the W.N.L.A. Compound, there are good grounds to surmise that he, Mr. Kantor, was misled in thinking that he had to deal with voluntary applicants for work."[69] The reader may like to accept this fairly charitable view of a Native Labour Bureau inspector that the innocent Kantor was simply misled by his greedy black employees. More plausibly, Kantor was in the swim, working closely with the messengers and interpreters and dividing the profits with them. So long as competitive recruiting for the mines continued, raiding and counter-raiding for labour remained endemic both on the Rand itself and in the country districts.

The independent labour contractors, recruiters, and touts worked persistently to maintain their footing in the industry despite restrictive government legislation and the active efforts of the NRC to drive them from the field. A particularly revealing example came to light in 1921 fully two years after the Randfontein mining group finally joined the NRC, thus virtually completing the monopsony. J.W. McKenzie and several brothers and other relatives had served the Randfontein mines successfully as labour contractors for many years in the eastern Cape, particularly Pondoland. Since the McKenzie family had long been suspected of illegal recruiting, the labour bureau watched them closely and repeatedly tried to prosecute. The government almost always failed, however. The director of native labour told the Native Grievances Inquiry that in all of the years in which he had been concerned with recruiting the Native Affairs Department had not received a single complaint from a mineworker about the McKenzies.[70] The family used various devices to evade the regulations. For example, like many agents they sent recruits to Randfontein masquerading as voluntary labour. After clearing the labour bureau's Johannesburg compound, the supposed voluntary would report to the resident McKenzie at Randfontein for assignment to a particular employer. In this way the family evaded the labour bureau fees levied on the labour agent for each recruit reporting to the compound.

After 1919, this system was used to supply labour to cooperating Robinson group mine managers outside the NRC system. Under the new arrangement the McKenzie contract to supply labour for work in the Randfontein mines continued, but they could no longer actually recruit the labour they supplied. They had to rely on volunteers. Officials suspected strongly that not only had these "voluntaries" actually been recruited, but also that the McKenzies had paid them illegal advances of as much as seven pounds and even in one case over ten pounds, far above the legal limit. While the family obviously served its own interests in this way, it also served those of the recruits who received advances and other considerations outside what the law allowed and certainly beyond what the NRC would pay. The trader/recruiters in the countryside who supplied the labour were prime beneficiaries since the large cash advances, invariably taken in kind at the trading stores, kept the blacks in thrall to the storekeepers. Since many of these blacks had worked for the McKenzies over a long period and since they were in a sense also gainers from the family's illegal activities, evidence of violations must have been difficult to obtain.[71]

J.B. McKenzie, one of the brothers, represented the family interests at Randfontein, and he devised a version of this system to continue operating even after their contracts with the Robinson mines had expired and the latter became part of the larger NRC organization. In 1921, the Cape superintendent of the NRC, E.C. Thompson, wrote in alarm that the activities of the McKenzies were causing serious losses.[72] J.B. McKenzie had organized a clandestine network of labour touts and traders in the Transkei who supplied him with large numbers of recruits in the guise of "voluntary" labour. Some of these blacks had already accepted NRC cash advances and the corporation was thus doubly aggrieved. Superintendent Thompson complained that his recruiters had become demoralized. They could not compete effectively against unlicensed touts who had to obey no rules, who paid advances far above the limit, and who earned high fees for the risks they took. Thompson believed that the Hadley labour organization operated a similar system.

The methods employed by these men are revealed in a circular which the McKenzies distributed and a copy of which fell into the hands of the NRC's man, Thompson. The McKenzies' Transkei agent, A.E. Parkin, even sent copies of the circular to NRC recruiters in an effort to undermine their loyalty to the corporation. McKenzie did not pay recruiting fees for these workers, which would have violated the law, but real advantages still accrued to the traders who cooperated with the scheme. They could issue credit to the "recruits," send them on to McKenzie, and receive payment of their loans from McKenzie as soon as the miner started work. McKenzie, of course, recovered his remittances to the traders from the workers' wages. His circular outlined the scheme in detail.[73] The agent, Parkin, was so confident of the appeal of the scheme that he sent copies of the circular to NRC recruiters presumably in the hope that they would provide labour to McKenzie on the side, while remaining apparently loyal to their NRC contracts. As in the past the loyalty of the trader/recruiter to his employer remained conditional and frequently temporary. Despite the efforts of the NRC and the government to break the system, it still continued two years later. Recruited Africans were arriving at McKenzie's Randfontein headquarters and presenting themselves as voluntaries. He continued to assure the Native Labour Bureau that he would not let it happen any more.[74] The NRC found it impossible to drive out the labour contractors' recruiters until the last of their contracts with the mines (though no longer to recruit) had expired.

Successful recruiting for the gold mines required alliances between town and country. This was the secret of the resilience of the McKenzie organization. The most successful contracting companies were able, as the Morkel Brothers showed, to draw chiefs and headmen as well as the rural traders into their system. In the case of the NRC, contact with the local black notables was made generally through the traders and cemented by the system of regular visits which developed as a major factor in the recruiting industry after about 1910. Another group on whom the white recruiters and mining companies relied were the private black police and trusted indunas, used on every mine to maintain discipline and control. Many of these men had long service on the mines and had the confidence of the mine manager or the contractor. They were frequently used as clandestine recruiters who would operate under cover of the voluntary system. A manager would send one or more of his black police back to their home districts for "holidays" but with orders either to bring their recruits directly to the mine as "brothers" or to send them forward as voluntaries. Evidence from the Cape suggests this was a common device.[75]

As the agents of management and the front line of the mines' regimented labour system, the black police and indunas had a deserved reputation for cruelty and violence. Conditions were sufficiently bad on the eve of Union to provoke a protest from a deputy commissioner of the South African Police, who commented on the "cruel and unnecessary conditions" to which the workers were subjected. He recommended that the mines and the labour contractors be ordered to disband their private police. The government should itself provide the control with a special staff of "native police" permanently located at the main mining centres. The Native Labour Bureau rejected this proposal on the grounds that substitution of government police would weaken the compound manager's authority and "lessen his prestige in the natives' minds." The bureau did take steps, however, to supervise the compound police more closely and to secure improvements to the lock-ups which most mines used to discipline recalcitrant workers.[76] By this time the mining industry in general was notorious for the misconduct of its police, many of whom were Zulu, a group which was underrepresented in the labour force at this time.[77] Mine managements routinely encouraged ethnic rivalries and fears by this and other means in order to prevent combinations among the workers. Evidence suggests that the reputation of the Zulu police was one important factor explaining the low recruiting levels from the Cape in the years immediately after the Anglo-Boer War. To escape from the severe discipline of the mine was a major motive for desertion of those who were recruited.[78] Despite the bureau's commitment to "improving" the mine owners' police, the imposition of a brutal and arbitrary discipline continued right through the period covered by this study.[79]

Both the mineworkers and the white recruiters began to develop ways of evading this harsh system of control. Since the recruiters readily accepted what mine managements were very slow to learn, that recruiting levels were directly related to conditions on the mines, they had a common interest with the recruits in curbing violence underground and in the compounds. One very popular means to this end was to insist that each group of recruits be able, in effect, to designate one of its number as a "police boy" with responsibility for the discipline of the group and liaison with management. Sometimes the labour contractor named the individual who was to fill this role. Contractors such as Mostert or Marwick and Morris, who maintained control over their recruits throughout the employment period, employed their own "native" police and made sure that their workers were not subject to mine discipline. Very frequently the collaborating chiefs and headmen were able to impose this as a condition of their cooperation. In these cases, as the Morkel system described above shows, the induna functioned as the chief's personal representative and tax collector and the means of maintaining his traditional authority with his people while they were temporarily on the mine. In 1914, Alfred Pigg, compound manager at the giant Modder B mine, revealed how widespread this practice had become in testimony before the Native Grievances Inquiry: "we are coming down now to an average of a police boy for every twenty natives and that police boy is not appointed by us; he is a representative of his recruiter; and there it is; we cannot do anything with them; they neglect their work; they want the highest wages; and those we give them with a view to induce the native coming here."[80] Behind the recruiters stood the headmen and often the workers themselves, insisting on this as a condition of accepting employment. On many mines, therefore, whole categories of black miners developed who were not subjected to the discipline of the mine police. Here is another indication that collaboration did not at all involve passive acceptance of a coercive system. By insisting on their own police as their representatives with whom management had to deal, the workers, their headmen, and the labour contractors could exercise a measure of control over the conditions of service.

During this era of intense competition for labour, the mining industry had to condone methods of labour mobilization which, from its standpoint, were anything but efficient or cost effective. Frequently it was the workers who exploited the system in their interest, as the persistence of the desertion problem shows. Through voluntary labour, the experienced workers could make gains which were not available to the recruits. Although forced increasingly by adverse economic circumstance, natural calamity, and the tax demands of the state to seek employment on the mines, the workers did this in a way which gave them maximum mobility and choice within the coercive system. Also, in a seller's market of chronic labour shortage which characterized much of the period, opportunities opened up for enterprising chiefs, headmen, and mine police to extract important benefits for themselves. Working usually with the labour contractors or other cooperating whites, these black agents clearly provided much of the influence and expertise on which depended the flow of recruited labour and the continuing profitability of the industry. Throughout most of the period covered by this study, they demanded and got a much higher price for their services than the mining groups wanted to pay. Their advantage was temporary, however. As the NRC began to absorb the contractors, so mine managers worked to restore their control over the "boss boys" and other black supervisors. By the 1920s this process was largely complete. Until then the black workers got some protection from recruiters, headmen, and their agents whose intervention with mine managements helped to curb racial violence on the mines.

The decline of the contractors and labour touts, after their long rearguard defence, was the result of a complex process with several interacting elements. Perhaps the single most important change was connected with the rise of voluntary labour. As the more experienced workers began to see the advantages of making their own way to the Rand independently, the power of the labour contractors necessarily declined. This was the more the case when government restrictions on wage advances and on the number of recruiters which it was prepared to license removed important incentives which had previously induced many Africans to accept recruitment. Finally, the consolidation of financial control in the mining industry itself dramatically reduced intra-industry competition for labour and enabled the NRC, finally, to absorb most of the remaining independent contractors.

PART THREE

Mine Labour in the Subcontinental Economy

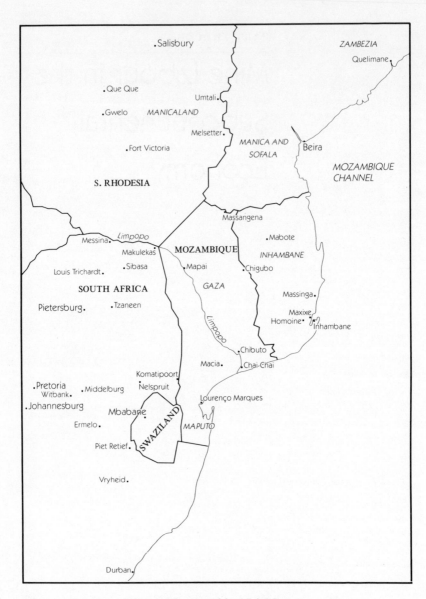

Map 3   Southern Mozambique and its Neighbours

CHAPTER SIX

The WNLA's Mozambique Connection

In developing a recruiting network in southern Mozambique which quickly made Portuguese East Africa an unrivalled source of black labour for the gold mines, the WNLA built on patterns of southward migration there which reached back at least to the 1850s. Large numbers of Tsonga migrants crossed Zululand into Natal in the late nineteenth century to find work on sugar and other estates. Tsonga were also prominent on the diamond fields from the early 1870s. Chamber of Mines recruiters located their stations and camps along the routes established by these early migrants. They involved themselves in the liquor traffic conducted on a large scale by numbers of Asian and European traders. Whole communities became dependent on fortified wine and other spirits, and to acquire them soon constituted a major incentive to seek employment outside the territory. Although continuing to enforce a ban on alcohol in mining compounds, the industry permitted its Mozambique recruiters to dispense wine to the local black population as an inducement to migracy.

Within about fifteen years of the discovery of gold, the Chamber of Mines had built an uneasy but vitally important alliance with the Portuguese colonial government which enabled it to drive out or absorb the licensed recruiters of all competing South African employers, and consequently to divert much of the supply of recruited labour from southern Mozambique to the Rand. While Mozambique officials resented the WNLA and tried continually to extract better terms, they found that they could not do without the material benefits which the association provided. The completion of the Lourenço Marques railway through to the Rand early in 1895 made large-scale organized recruiting feasible and gave the mines a great competitive advantage over other employers. The Transvaal-Mozambique agreement of 1897 formally recognized the importance of recruiting for the mines. In return for access to its territories by mine recruiters, the Portuguese government secured confirmation of customs preferences first negotiated in 1875 and guarantees that the proportion of rail traffic carried by the Lourenço Marques line would not fall below one-third of the total. At the end of 1901, Milner's Reconstruction government negotiated the so-called *Modus Vivendi* which confirmed the 1897 treaty with minor changes of detail. In the negotiations, the Portuguese showed that they had two basic objectives in view. First, they wanted to protect the competitive advantages of the shorter Lourenço Marques line to the Rand from political interference by the Cape and Natal governments on behalf of their rival railways. But second, the Mozambique government was equally determined to secure control over emigration from its territories. Its agreements with the Transvaal authorities affirmed its right to admit only recruiters licensed by the Transvaal government and to appoint a "curator" of labour in the Transvaal. This official established an office in Johannes-burg, ostensibly to provide protection for the emigrant workers, but actually to monitor the emigration, to keep full records on the Mozambique workers and to try to ensure their eventual repatriation. The inability of Transvaal governments to control clandestine immigration and their unwillingness to enforce the compulsory repatriation of Mozambique blacks at the end of their contract periods caused friction between the two jurisdictions for years.

A large flow of clandestine, unrecruited emigration continued from southern and especially from northern Mozambique because Portuguese administrative control remained weak over wide areas. Many of these ille-gal migrants fell into the hands of mining industry recruiters stationed at the main entry points along the Transvaal's northeastern border. However, the mines by no means had this clandestine emigration to themselves and faced stiff competition from Rhodesian recruiters and others in the region. On the eve of the Anglo-Boer War, the mines found about 60 per cent (slightly more than 60,000 workers) of their unskilled labour from Mozam-bique, a proportion which became even larger after the war. Sixty-five per cent of the black migrants on the mines came from southern Mozambique in 1906. Thereafter the proportion declined to the still large figure of 40 per cent and remained at about that level throughout the period covered by this study.

Further north in the tropical parts of Mozambique, WNLA agents, like others seeking labour, employed the old slaving contacts and moved the migrants to embarkation points on the coast via the well-established routes which the slave caravans had used. They also had necessarily to deal with agents of the concessionaires, the prazo holders, who dominated wide areas of the Zambesi valley, and with the chartered companies. Even by contem-porary South African standards, the prazo holders and the companies' agents were notorious for their highly coercive labour practices. Although theoretically subject to regulation by the colonial state, the prazo holders

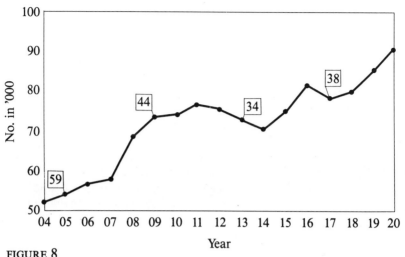

FIGURE 8

Mineworkers from Southern Mozambique, 1904–20

SOURCES: Chamber of Mines and WNLA *Annual Reports;* Native Labour Bureau estimates.
NOTES: Recruited Africans and voluntaries are included; data are approximate (see app. 1 for actual figures).
* Indicates per cent of total labour supply.

found its control ineffective and did what they liked. In the unrestrained struggle for labour which went on in these northern territories, WNLA agents had often to emulate the methods of local employers. While the WNLA achieved a monopoly of organized recruiting in large areas of the south where Portuguese officials had some semblance of control, the association was never so successful in the north. There it struggled not only against the prazo holders but also against the independent labour touts and thieves who controlled many of the migration routes and extorted large profits from southward-moving migrants. This traffic continued long after the Union government had banned employment of tropical Africans on gold mines in 1913. Conditions on South Africa's northern border with Mozambique were so bad that one hard-bitten police official felt moved to condemn the activities of the labour thieves as "nothing more or less than a kind of slave trade." Numerous government investigations repeatedly implicated Chamber of Mines' recruiters in this traffic. [1]

The successful negotiation of the Transvaal-Portuguese agreement in 1897 and the establishment simultaneously of the Rand Native Labour Association marked the beginning of a sustained effort to establish a Chamber of Mines monopoly of recruiting in Mozambique which continued over the next decade. The real work of creating a recruiting network belonged to the WNLA which succeeded the Rand Native Labour Association in 1900 and began actively to recruit in Mozambique early in 1902.

189   The Mozambique Connection

From the start, the WNLA functioned as an agency of the Chamber of Mines. Although supported by the Portuguese colonial authorities, the chamber's successful establishment of its monopsony cannot simply be attributed to government administrative support. Portuguese regulations were instrumental in excluding rival South African recruiting organizations, but many officials resented the WNLA's power and influence. They would have curbed its powers had the colony not been as dependent for revenue on the flow of labour as the gold mines themselves were. Moreover, throughout most of the colony the central government lacked the capacity to enforce its directives. Although a Mozambique statute of 1899 imposed upon Africans the obligation to seek employment and empowered both the state and private employers to requisition this forced labour, the act remained a dead letter outside the Lourenço Marques district and the Beira area. In the Zambesi valley, the prazo holders remained in control, while elsewhere in northern and central Mozambique huge territories had been leased to the three chartered companies. Whatever the legal position in most of these areas, many of them remained simply ungoverned by whites. In Barue, for example, a large territory in northwestern Mozambique along the border with southern Rhodesia, indigenous African polities successfully defied the Portuguese throughout the 1890s. A campaign of conquest led by Joao de Azevedo Coutinho at the head of nearly 16,000 troops and carriers established some semblance of control during 1902. Thereafter the Mozambique chartered company exercised a still largely nominal administration in the area until 1917 when the famous "Barue Rebellion" extinguished Portuguese authority for several years. Thus while the Mozambique government could and did support the WNLA by granting it an effective monopoly against rival recruiters from South Africa and Rhodesia, it lacked the power to control or even support the association's recruiting effort itself. For the latter, the WNLA relied on its own agents operating in the colony, and they dealt directly with the local authorities, both white and black, who did have control.[2]

Within a few years of its establishment in 1900, the WNLA put in place a recruiting network in Portuguese East Africa far more elaborate and tightly controlled than anything which the association had been able to establish in South Africa itself.[3] The greater success of the WNLA there is explained very largely by the willingness of the Portuguese authorities to grant it a *de facto* monopoly of organized recruiting for employment in South Africa. Fierce competition was encountered by the association from local employers, Rhodesian interests, and other rivals. Moreover, the WNLA was excluded from recruiting in certain parts of the territory. Nevertheless, the Chamber of Mines recruiting association established a formidable presence in the region. South of 22° SL[4] the association divided its recruiting into four distinct areas, each under the control of a principal recruiter who headed up a team including European assistants and squads of licensed

TABLE 6

WNLA Establishment in Mozambique 1906

Lourenço Marques District

1 chief recruiter, 3 assistant recruiters, 3 conductors (European staff).
European Camps
  Matugonyana, with 10 subsidiary rest camps, employing 156 licensed African runners. Total recruited,* 2,154.
  Matalla, with 5 subsidiary rest camps, employing 44 licensed runners. Total recruited,* 5,290.
  Namahasha, with 6 subsidiary rest camps, employing 25 licensed runners. Total recruited,* 273.

Gaza District, Western Area

1 chief recruiter, 2 assistant recruiters, 2 conductors (European staff).
European Camps
  Manzi Mhlope, with 5 subsidiary rest camps, employing 276 licensed runners. Total recruited,* 6,692.
  A second camp, runners included under above, no recruiting figures available.

Gaza District, Eastern Area

1 chief recruiter, 2 assistant recruiters, 1 conductor (European staff).
European Camp
  Chibuto, with 9 subsidiary rest camps, employing 296 licensed runners. Total recruited,* 5,746.

Inhambane District

1 chief recruiter, 6 assistant recruiters, 1 conductor (European staff).
European Camps
  Maxixe, with 2 subsidiary rest camps, employing 61 runners. Total recruited,* 3,998.
  Hompene, with 13 subsidiary rest camps, employing 181 licensed runners. Total recruited,* 2,910.
  Coquno, with 8 subsidiary rest camps, employing 133 licensed runners. Total recruited,* 3,183.
  Zanamella, with 5 subsidiary rest camps, "Prince Boris in charge," employing 58 licensed runners. Total recruited,* 1,109.
  Massinga, with 9 subsidiary rest camps, employing 220 licensed runners. Total recruited,* 1,225.

SOURCE: Johannesburg *Star*, 15/12/06.
*In the 12 months ending 30 April 1906.

African runners. The four principal recruiters reported to a WNLA district manager in Lourenço Marques, and he answered to the chairman and the board of management in Johannesburg.[5] Generally speaking, and except in times of crisis, the Johannesburg staff intervened little in the handling of routine operating matters in Mozambique. They required regular reports from their district manager but left him a large area of discretion. The district manager made frequent tours of inspection of WNLA camps. He decided where new camps would be sited and where to concentrate recruiting operations. In the final analysis, he controlled the recruiting staff because he had the power to dismiss them. By 1906, however, the four principal recruiters had managed to establish for themselves a very powerful position. Probably they were virtually irremoveable so long as recruiting levels held up. Very likely the board of management welcomed (if it did not actually encourage) this development. A competitive relationship between the principal recruiters and the district manager promoted good results. The WNLA hierarchy in Mozambique included one other important element. At Lourenço Marques, a third set of officials in "the Agency" handled the sensitive matter of liaison with the Portuguese authorities. The principal agent, F. de Mello Breyner, had served the chamber in this capacity since before the war. He and his partner, Wirth, and their ally, the Lisbon financier, B. Cabral, had powerful connections in Mozambique. Their appointment as agents had been virtually forced on the WNLA in the first place, and the association continued to treat them with a great deal of circumspection. The WNLA established the agency early in 1902 in response to the advice of F.H.E. Crowe, Britain's consul-general at Lourenço Marques. A few months before, negotiations with the Portuguese over the *Modus Vivendi* and the future role of the WNLA in Mozambique had bogged down. As adviser to the Transvaal authorities, Crowe traced Portuguese reluctance to conclude an agreement (they eventually signed the *Modus Vivendi* in December 1901) to the influence of Breyner, the agent of the Rand Native Labour Association at Lourenço Marques up to 1899.[6] According to Crowe, Breyner had important connections in Lisbon and virtually held the Mozambique authorities "in his hands" on labour matters. Crowe evidently feared that unless Breyner was accommodated, he might himself secure the concession to recruit in the colony. This was the view also of the then WNLA general manager, G.A. Goodwin. Acting on Crowe's advice, Goodwin went to Lourenço Marques specifically to offer Breyner his old position at an annual salary of £1,200. Crowe thought, too optimistically, that Breyner could be squeezed out later "if absolutely necessary."[7]

Given this background, the WNLA's suspicion of the agents was understandable. In early 1902, Goodwin summed up the official view. He described Breyner as proud and touchy though honest and thought that Wirth, as a "typical smart German clerk," would scheme to restore their firm as "practically the sole uncontrolled managers of the majority of the recruiting." Goodwin stressed that the WNLA had little hold on the agents, and that they should be consulted on all important decisions affecting

TABLE 7
WNLA Expenditure in Mozambique, 1902–6

Year	Amount
1902	£106,866
1903	147,446
1904	103,267*
1905	124,869
1906 (Jan. – Sept.)	92,215

SOURCE: Johannesburg *Star,* 15/12/06.

* In 1904 recruiting levels fell substantially, which accounts for the smaller expenditure. In that year, total WNLA expenditure for all districts came to about £248,000 (See SNAA 482/05).

operations. In particular, WNLA staff in Mozambique should not see Portuguese officials without the agent's approval. A breach with Breyner could not be risked without the explicit authority of the WNLA board of management.[8]

Not surprisingly, relations between the WNLA's own officials and the agents remained strained and uneasy. Late in 1906 when the whole WNLA structure was close to collapse, B. Cabral, who apparently had a financial interest in the agency, wrote to Lionel Phillips in Johannesburg, urging that the district manager's office be closed. Phillips held no official position in the WNLA or the chamber at that time. He had asked Cabral to keep an eye on the agents in the interest of his own firm should the WNLA fold up completely. As senior resident partner of the Rand's premier mining house, Phillips knew that the group's labour supply was at stake and that he could ill afford to wait upon events. Aware of this, Cabral was simply trying to squeeze out a better deal for the agency. Portuguese colonial officials resented the manager, Cabral reported. Moreover, suppression of that office would increase the profits of the agents, who required them "to keep the WNLA in the atmosphere of favour which it needs."[9] Blunt and rapacious accurately describe the suggestion. Despite the near-collapse of the association and its absolute dependence for survival on the agents and the good will of the government, this demand was not acted on. To do so would have been, in effect, to hand control of recruiting to the agents. Clearly the WNLA board of management preferred the situation where the agents watched the manager, and the manager likewise reported on the effectiveness of the agency in handling relations with the Mozambique colonial state. That the agents, like the district manager, were paid partly by commission according to the volume of recruits gave all of them an important incentive to maximize results. At least two of the agents were themselves experienced recruiters and thus well placed to give the board a knowledgeable report on the efficiency of the manager and the principal recruiters.

Important as they were at the apex of the WNLA structure in Mozambique, the district manager and the agents were not the central elements in the operation. By 1906, the key to the whole intricate network was provided by the four principal recruiters, one in each of the main recruiting districts south of 22°SL. The function of the principal recruiters, the degree of autonomy they enjoyed, and their position relative to the manager and the agents had changed considerably since the association was set up several years before. Originally they were merely salaried employees (paid at the rate of seventy pounds a month) and closely controlled by the WNLA hierachy. At an early stage, however, officials decided (in November 1902) to reduce the salary to twenty pounds a month and to pay them mainly by commission on a sliding scale varying from three shillings to ten shillings a recruit depending upon volume. Only a few months later, in March 1903, the mixed system gave way to a commission-only system at the rate of fifteen shillings a recruit with bonuses for large numbers. About a year after that, the recruiters negotiated still better terms and higher recruiting fees. As the WNLA general manager explained, the association had little choice since "there were more natives leaving [the mines] than were coming in and ... this had been going on for some months."[10] Out of their commission the recruiters had to find the salaries and fees for their European assistants, the fees paid to the African runners, food for the recruits until they reached Ressano Garcia on the Transvaal border and other "ordinary" expenses. The WNLA itself paid licence and other charges owing to the colonial government of Mozambique, all rail and boat fares, and the cost of maintaining the agency and the manager's office in Lourenço Marques. In effect, the WNLA had done what the general manager, G.A. Goodwin, had said only a year before they were determined never to allow. They had subcontracted a large part of the actual business of recruiting to the principal recruiters. Since these men depended entirely on the commission and were responsible for large fixed costs for salaries, commissions, and food, they absorbed the whole risk. The assistant recruiters continued to be paid full salaries, although they might also receive bonuses when especially good results were obtained. In a few Mozambique districts with especially bleak recruiting prospects, the WNLA paid recruiters to maintain a presence. They accepted straight salary without commission. But throughout the southern region of the Portuguese colony, the commission system dominated.

About one year after this system which assigned most of the risk to the principal recruiters came into operation, they combined to form "the syndicate" and thereafter negotiated annually with the board of management the terms which they would accept for the following year. In 1906, the contract with the syndicate stipulated that the four principal recruiters would work only for the WNLA; they bound themselves to employ at least eighteen whites at monthly salaries laid down in the agreement; they accepted the status of WNLA employees, subject to dismissal by the district manager at one month's notice; finally the recruiters agreed to pay their share of the expenses as outlined above.[11] Late in that year, the syndicate actually employed thirty Europeans as assistants and conductors and about 2,000 African runners.[12]

A committee of the WNLA board of management appointed to investigate the conduct of operations in Mozambique, noted that the syndicate had considerable autonomy in practice. Indeed, the district manager did not interfere so long as the recruiters achieved good results. When the association nearly collapsed toward the end of 1906, the response of the dominant mining house, Wernher, Beit/Eckstein, demonstrated the absolute importance of the syndicate. Practically at the first sign of trouble, the firm's partners moved hastily to make a private arrangement with the syndicate. In the event that the WNLA fell apart and individual mining houses had to recruit on their own account in Mozambique, the members of the syndicate agreed not to act without consulting first with the H. Eckstein partners in Johannesburg. Effectively, H. Eckstein and Company and an allied house, the Gold Fields group, managed to secure a first option on the services of the syndicate.[13]

There is evidence that other mining groups were bidding for the services of the syndicate. In September 1906, R.W. Schumacher reported to Wernher, Beit and Company in London that Harold Strange, a senior executive of the Johannesburg Consolidated Investment Company, had gone off to Lourenço Marques a few days before. This was ominous because Strange, who had been the first chairman of the WNLA, knew the operation well and claimed to be well connected in Mozambique. Other mining executives in the rival houses needed no great prescience to guess that he had gone there to protect the interests of his group in the event competition for labour resumed in Mozambique. Schumacher believed that Strange was "probably trying to tamper with" the members of the syndicate and that he would claim to be representing the Wernher, Beit/H. Eckstein group as well as his own. Schumacher's colleague, Sam Evans, and a Gold Fields executive, R.G. Fricker, rushed immediately to Lourenço Marques to make contact with the syndicate and the government and head off any scheming by the JCI Group.[14] In the event, all of this manoeuvring was unnecessary because the WNLA, thanks to the support of both the Portuguese and the Botha governments, managed to hold together. Their anxious plotting, however, reveals very well the fragility both of the WNLA and of intra-industry cooperation.

The competitive behaviour evident in this incident appeared frequently in the WNLA organization at every level. The mining groups plotted against each other within the organization, and WNLA employees seem also to have been at each others' throats a good deal of the time. Whether the WNLA structure with its peculiar diffusion of authority among the principal recruiters, the district manager, and the agency helped to cause this situation or emerged as a result is difficult to establish. In any case, the WNLA's set-up in Mozambique resulted from a number of considerations. Contemporary whites believed that successful recruiting of Africans depended on personal qualities. Some men had them; others did not. Frequently as well, the recruiters themselves believed that their successes as individuals were a product of their own unique attributes and methods. As Frederick Perry, the WNLA's long-time permanent chairman, noted, however, personal factors helped, but were not sufficient. He judged the WNLA recruiters to be popular because they were the only whites in their districts who had money to spend.[15]

Evidently the WNLA structure reflected these ideas. It tried to give the successful principal recruiters a good deal of latitude in running their respective districts, while still preserving the coordinating and supervisory functions of the larger organization. The system also promoted a deliberate rivalry among the recruiters: "There is a strong spirit of emulation between the different camps at present, each trying to beat its own or the other's record in output. Anything of this kind is certainly to be encouraged, because the greatest difficulty in the way of maintaining high efficiency probably lies in the slackness and depression produced by the intolerable climate and by the repeated attacks of fever to which most Europeans are subject."[16]

In contrast to the recruiting network, the agency at Lourenço Marques derived from a different set of needs and circumstances. Dealing with the Mozambique government evidently required specialized knowledge and tact as well as lots of cash. The firm of Breyner and Wirth had demonstrated a capacity to do the needful. They also had the connections. The WNLA maintained a "secret service" fund and disbursements were handled mainly by Breyner and Wirth. The Chamber of Mines probably saw the advantages of having those engaged in the sensitive – and possibly dangerous – business of doling out bribes in an arm's length relationship to the WNLA. If necessary, the agents could be repudiated. Probably also Johannesburg expected the agents to head off or at least control some of the more rapacious demands: "From sources outside the Witwatersrand Native Labour Association I am aware that at the present moment the Association is being pressed to take into its employment a certain Portuguese official, the Administrator of Lourenço Marques, who, for various reasons, is unable to live upon his salary. The association is to be asked to pay this individual £100 a month plus the same amount in expenses, and under no conceivable circumstances can it possibly get any return for its expenditure."[17] Internal rivalry between Robinson and the other houses made the industry especially vulnerable to extortion at this time.

Despite these problems, which soon became more serious, the WNLA had succeeded in establishing a commanding presence in Mozambique which alarmed some Portuguese officials:

Without having the slightest animosity against the Witwatersrand Native Labour Association and not wishing to exagerate [sic] I state in all good faith that this Association in the district of Inhambane is a "state within a state." Not that it intervenes or attempts to intervene in our political or administrative work but that it enjoys too much liberty in its relations with the natives. It has headquarters much better constructed than our Military Stations. It has under its orders a more numerous personel [sic] nearly all foreign as far as white men are concerned, and uniformed in so far as the native portion is concerned, a personel much better paid than those of the Portuguese authorities.[18]

The governor of Inhambane also noted that while he had to make do with 240 "native" troops, the WNLA employed no fewer than 750 uniformed runners in his district alone. Senior chamber staff would probably not have challenged this assessment. They knew that the association's recruiting successes depended largely on its hold on the various districts. As Frederick Perry noted after his 1907 tour of Mozambique, very often the local WNLA recruiter was the only person for miles around with money to spend: "The natives are thoroughly well acquainted with the idea of going to work on the mines, and the 'Emigration' is popular among them. Recruiters also are personally popular and have a great deal of influence, chiefly through being constantly resident, and through being practically the only white people in the country except the Commandants, and the only ones who spend money. It is by means of a liberal expenditure that they have attained and keep this position, and the natives are rather inclined to presume on it and to become more exacting in their demands."[19] Since this was a private report for the WNLA board, Perry's views cannot simply be dismissed as propaganda. At any rate, he believed that his recruiters functioned in this benign way. Going further, the situation which he described could probably be found in Mozambique at times when labour was plentiful. When labour was short, however, officials became less philanthropically inclined.

Perry's remarks can be contrasted with a report prepared in 1904 also for the WNLA board by the then general manager, T.J.M. Macfarlane. During the first months of that year, the WNLA experienced one of those periodic downward fluctuations to which recruiting in any district was prone. As the number of recruits plummeted, alarm grew and Macfarlane went to Mozambique to investigate and report. He interviewed WNLA staff there, saw the agents, Breyner and Wirth, and with them interviewed the Portuguese governor-general. He found a fair measure of agreement among all of them on the causes of the shortfall: "All our Agents are agreed that if

TABLE 8

Proportion of Returning Recruits from Mozambique, 1904-19

Year	Recruits	"Old mine boys" & "bros."	% of Total	New Recruits
1904	27,633	14,671	53	12,962
1905	38,469	21,893	56	16,576
1906	36,401	20,309	56	16,092
1907	41,134	26,549	65	14,585
1908	42,153	29,345	69	13,108
1909	39,969	25,189	63	14,780
1910	44,684	28,656	64	16,028
1911	40,894	27,650	68	13,244
1912	45,549	35,319	78	10,230
1913	35,569	23,312	66	12,257
1914	37,524	29,646	79	7,878
1915	47,985	36,899	77	11,086
1916	47,529	35,713	75	11,816
1917	41,483	32,071	77	9,412
1918	37,496	28,144	75	9,352
1919	42,648	30,359	71	12,289

SOURCE: CML, 51(2) 1920.

the natives had greater opportunities of spending a larger proportion of their earnings in the Transvaal, they would remain at work for longer periods, and in this connection it might be possible to do more in the way of establishing eating houses and stores on the mines. The question of the sale of drink to Portuguese Natives on the mines has also always been strongly advocated by our Agents who represent that these natives are accustomed to it from childhood and that the local prohibition is very unpopular."[20] This report contains possibly the most forthright statement on recruiting methods to be found in the surviving records. Macfarlane's language was deceptively bland and his manner matter of fact, but there was no mistaking his message. He was completely blunt. The prosperity of the Mozambique peasant was highly undesirable because it interfered with recruiting. Their surplus should be taxed away. The migrants who did come out to work were too thrifty and did not return often enough. They should be enticed to spend their wages at the company store and thus compelled to stay longer. If these devices failed then perhaps the recruits could simply be debauched with liquor and so parted from their cash. Evidently some of these proposals were taken up. In 1908 the Portuguese did double the hut tax, and a few years after that another report indicated that the WNLA spent "a lot of money in wine for the natives."[21] Apart from the "kaffir beer" ration, however, prohibition remained in force on the mines, although it was widely evaded in practice.

Up until early 1906 this intricate and expensive recruiting organization, developed over a prolonged period of trial and error, worked fairly well as the figures on the accompanying chart indicate. The near-collapse of the organization later that year and its difficult even painful reconstruction in 1907 show, first, how tenuous industry unity was even after several years of cooperative recruiting and, second, how vulnerable the WNLA remained to an attack mounted from within. A bitter struggle developed which pitted J.B. Robinson, the head and virtual dictator of the Randfontein group of mines, against most of the other mining houses. Robinson was publicly at odds with them in every major policy area. They argued that there was a permanent shortage in the local supply and that Chinese labour was essential. He blamed local labour shortages on WNLA deficiencies and ostentatiously offered to give up his unused importation licences, issued before the Liberals took power. His rivals stressed the impossibility of relying on unskilled white labour to any significant extent; Robinson offered to conduct further experiments with F.H.P. Creswell.[22] Robinson had the backing of the Campbell-Bannerman government in Britain, whereas the chamber loyalists sought the support of Selborne and the Transvaal administration. Selborne, Milner's successor and a Unionist appointee, did not begin to act in concert with the Chamber of Mines until about September 1906. Active personal dislike and seething resentments on both sides aggravated these policy differences and pushed them on.

The dispute originated in Robinson's persistent criticisms of the WNLA and his notorious breaches of its rules. His dissatisfaction with the chamber's recruiting arm increased at this time because the mines of the Robinson group had been especially hard hit by the prevailing labour shortage; and he now found his requests for additional labour turned down.[23] Already operating within South Africa in violation of WNLA rules, he decided to challenge the association in Mozambique as well. For years Robinson had evaded the WNLA system in South Africa itself by giving clandestine support to independent recruiters who supplied Africans masquerading as "voluntaries" to his mines. Such tactics could not be developed in Mozambique where the association had established a much stronger presence and where it continued to enjoy the backing of the Portuguese colonial administration. Thus a frontal assault became necessary, and in 1906 Robinson sought and secured the support of the British government in his campaign to unseat the WNLA in Mozambique.

The record of the Liberals in opposition showed their hostility to the Randlords whom they blamed for involving Britain in a costly, unnecessary war. During their first few weeks in office, Campbell-Bannerman and his colleagues reinforced this position by a series of decisions which demonstrated as well their determination to break with the South African policies of their Unionist predecessors. Most mining industry leaders saw the decisions to suspend the Lyttelton constitution, to move directly to full responsible government in the former republics, and above all to hold up the issue of further labour importation licences as hostile acts.[24] Alarm, even consternation marked the chamber's early reaction to the Liberals in office. For a few individuals associated with the gold mines, however, these decisions meant opportunity rather than threat. Of these, J.B. Robinson was clearly the most important. He saw himself as a victim of the crown colony administration. Close to Kruger in the prewar period, he confronted during Reconstruction a regime which was unsympathetic to his group and which regarded Robinson himself with positive distaste.[25] Robinson supported the Liberals in British politics and by 1905 had made contact also with Het Volk, the activities of which he later subsidized. In the Transvaal responsible government election, Robinson's closest associate, J.W.S. Langerman, won election as the Het Volk member for Randfontein.

Within a few months of the change of government in Britain, Robinson wrote a series of letters to the new secretary of state for the colonies, Lord Elgin, in an effort to capitalize on the support he had earlier given.[26] He first attacked the WNLA, alleging that its recruiting methods were inefficient and pointing out (correctly) that it enjoyed a *de facto* monopoly on recruiting in Mozambique. WNLA inefficiency, he suggested, was no accident and resulted from a plot to make a case for continued Chinese labour importation. Robinson went on to claim that the Chamber of Mines controlled the Selborne government and actually drafted all official dispatches on labour and mining questions. His rivals on the Rand had made a cipher of Selborne just as they had earlier controlled Milner. Robinson's remarkable cunning is nicely displayed in these dealings with Elgin. He shrewdly devised charges which pandered to the most partisan Liberal analysis of the Transvaal situation. His secret claims further undermined the already bad relations between the new government and the other mining houses, and they partly discredited Selborne and his administration, of whom the Liberals, in any case, could only be suspicious. The high commissioner was, after all, another legacy of the Unionists.

Robinson soon revealed that his real target was the WNLA. In April 1906, the leaders of several of the mining houses received identical, blackmailing letters from A.E. Wilson on behalf of his new recruiting organization, the Transvaal Mines Labour Company. He blandly informed the industry that his company had been established to recruit in Mozambique and that it had the approval of both the Portuguese and the Transvaal authorities. The company expected confirmation from Lisbon but had encountered delays which it attributed to WNLA opposition. Wilson warned that he had written to the British cabinet and his letter would reach London within the week: "we have no hesitation in stating that our presentation of the matter, coupled with the sworn testimony we have obtained and sent home, will result in free recruiting taking place in Portuguese East Africa." Wilson sadly conjured up the evils which would follow the reintroduction of free recruiting, and he reviewed the horrors of the prewar situation. The mines could prevent this by agreeing to limited competition between the TMLC and WNLA. The result, he confidently predicted, would be a doubling of the labour supply to the advantage of all concerned. Wilson concluded his letter by stating that if the WNLA ceased its opposition forthwith, the TMLC would arrange to have its report to the Liberal government "returned to us unopened."[27]

The mining houses responded warily at first and attempted to discover who was behind the TMLC and what degree of official support it actually had.[28] In the end, they decided to call Wilson's bluff and not to yield to blackmail. The TMLC did not have permission to recruit in Mozambique, but it was able to communicate with London through Robinson whose agents worked closely with the company. More surprisingly, the TMLC also had a "certificate of no objection" from the Transvaal authorities.[29] Under the *Modus Vivendi,* the Transvaal had the right to veto applications of labour agents seeking permission to recruit in East Africa. Since the certificate was routinely given, Selborne's officials acted without carefully considering the implications of the certificate. This soon changed, and in June Selborne cabled London that his government could have nothing to do with the "scoundrel," "Kaffir" Wilson.[30] The recently respectable manager of the TMLC, holder of the Transvaal's official cachet, had now become the infamous "Kaffir" Wilson.

In a carefully coordinated campaign, Selborne, his officials, and the Chamber of Mines moved to head off Robinson. They warned the imperial authorities of the evils which would follow the introduction of competitive recruiting. All of the controls which the government had laboriously built up to protect African mineworkers would be jeopardized. Moreover, the wage agreement in the industry would inevitably break down, and the poorer companies would be priced out of the labour market.[31] This last argument was certainly spurious. The wage agreement was presented as a device which protected the low-grade mines and collieries from wage competition they could not afford to meet. The richer companies which could afford higher wages (thereby securing their full complement of labour) had agreed to sacrifice themselves in the interest of the low-grade mines. The picture of the industry as a disparate collection of rich and poor independent producers was, of course, erroneous. The controllers of the rich mines were also the owners of most of the poor ones. In both capacities they benefited from the wage agreement. Moreover, this argument conveniently ignored the fact that many of Robinson's holdings were low-grade properties. According to what Selborne and the chamber wrote to Elgin, the Robinson group ought to have been the last to leave the monopsony.

In any case Robinson easily retained the initiative. In May 1906, Elgin informed Selborne that Robinson had formally applied to recruit independently in Mozambique. The secretary of state took the view that the government could not "deny to so substantial an interest the right to separate from [the WNLA] and to be placed on an equal footing with its competitors in obtaining labour."[32] Elgin asked Selborne to secure the agreement of Lourenço Marques. In an unsubtle way, he suggested that the high commissioner had not acted impartially in the matter: "[the governor-general of Mozambique] believes that he is acting in accordance with your wishes in giving the Association [WNLA] a practical monopoly."[33] Just to make sure that Selborne understood the point, Elgin passed on Robinson's charges of chamber domination of the Transvaal administration. Selborne, of course, replied with a vigorous defence of the independence of his government. At the same time, however, he adopted a new strategy in dealing with Robinson which coincided precisely with the chamber's. He first called for delay. Such complex issues, Selborne argued, required careful consideration. Any policy changes should be preceded by a thorough inquiry – perhaps a joint inquiry of the British and Portuguese governments.[34] This ploy also failed. Elgin replied that the imperial government favoured a joint inquiry but only after Robinson had been granted his recruiting licences by the Portuguese.[35]

Robinson meanwhile had switched horses and disengaged "Kaffir" Wilson from Mozambique. In Wilson's place, he sent G.G. Holmes, a Robinson group manager, to Lourenço Marques.[36] In the face of Elgin's peremptory instructions, the Transvaal government had little choice but to grant Holmes his certificate of no objection.[37] After some delay, the Mozambique authorities also capitulated and issued a licence to Holmes.[38] The response of the members of the WNLA was immediate and dramatic – *sauve qui peut*. They now forgot the rhetoric which just weeks before had been used to defend the monopsony: the WNLA as the guardian of the Africans; the WNLA as protector of the poor mines. With the association's monopoly breached, each group immediately demanded for itself what the Liberals had apparently acquired for Robinson. They all wrote to the high commissioner urging that London secure the same privileges for their companies. Otherwise, as the Rand Mines letter expressed it, the mines of their group would be "deprived of their just proportion" of Mozambique labour.[39] The president of the chamber reiterated the arguments the industry always used when adverse government action threatened: "the position of many producers is today already sufficiently serious. We are convinced that their position will become precarious, and in many cases impossible, if the cost of production is further increased by reason of the increased cost of native labour."[40] The Transvaal government continued to do what it could to deflect Elgin and the Liberal government from its course, including frantic efforts to discredit Robinson: "the experience of the Native Affairs Department is that the mines of the Robinson group will take no measures involving any expense for the welfare of their coloured labourers which cannot be enforced by law." This was true. On the other hand, the contrasting depiction of the WNLA as virtually a humanitarian organization was mere chamber rhetoric.[41]

J.G. Baldwin, the British consul-general at Lourenço Marques, raised another matter with Selborne which he promptly passed on to the secretary of state. Reporting a conversation with the governor-general of Mozambique, Baldwin explained that the Portuguese authorities opposed competitive recruiting, fearing it might disturb the colony. The governor-general himself favoured government recruiting for the mines, and Baldwin pointed out that in Mozambique this meant forced labour.[42] Government recruiting would also give the Portuguese an even firmer stranglehold on the Transvaal.[43] With the Transvaal still more dependent on Mozambique, Selborne warned, his government might be forced to amend the *Modus Vivendi* and to grant further concessions to Mozambique on railway and customs policy. This in turn could only exacerbate bad feeling between the Transvaal and the Cape and Natal. The Cape in particular already used every opportunity to complain that under the present arrangement her ports got far too little of the vital Witwatersrand railway traffic.

Both the chamber and the Transvaal government tried to impress upon the secretary of state the disastrous consequences for the mines, for the Transvaal, and for British South Africa which his continued support of Robinson would involve. None of this should be taken at face value. There was more than an element of contrivance in the indecent haste with which the other mining groups rushed to abandon the WNLA when the Liberal decision to back Robinson became known. Moreover, when they demanded similar privileges for themselves, they wrote virtually identical letters. Here is evidence of an orchestrated disunity – an organized campaign to create the appearance of chaos in the hope that the Liberals would recoil from the consequences of their support for Robinson and drop him.

Lord Elgin yielded neither to the bizarre threat of the chamber to wreck its own recruiting organization nor to Selborne's various alarmist warnings. The British government continued to press the Portuguese on behalf of Robinson,[44] while warning the other mining houses that similar treatment for them could not be considered until after the proposed joint inquiry with the Portuguese had taken place: "The Secretary of State accordingly requests his Excellency [the high commissioner] to warn the members of the Witwatersrand Native Labour Association against taking precipitately any irrevocable step for the breaking up of the Association."[45] Thus the chamber found itself neatly checkmated and its plans to produce anarchy in the labour market neutralized.

The transparently hostile attitude of the secretary of state, together with the inability of Selborne to exercise much leverage upon him, forced the chamber and the WNLA back upon their own resources. Late in 1906 they compelled Robinson to leave the WNLA, and he then resigned from the Chamber of Mines. Knowing that the battle was only beginning, they also put pressure of their own on the Portuguese to counter that of Robinson's agents and the diplomatic activities of the imperial government on his behalf. Yet by the end of 1906, Robinson seemed to be winning. Through the intervention of the imperial government both in Lisbon and at Lourenço Marques, his agent, G.G. Holmes, had been granted a licence to recruit in Portuguese East Africa. Holmes went off immediately to Lourenço Marques and began to construct a separate recruiting organization. Very likely the Robinson group also had former black employees touting for it illegally in the Portuguese colony.[46] This was as close as he ever got to over-turning the WNLA in Mozambique. By early 1907 a stalemate had developed which opened the way for a successful mediation effort by the new Botha-Smuts government of the Transvaal which took office in March. Robinson had been granted only a single licence, and the Portuguese, under heavy countervailing pressure from the WNLA and its friends, resolutely refused to grant Holmes the additional licences for subrecruiters and African runners without which he could not operate effectively.[47]

Nevertheless the threat posed to the WNLA could not be lightly dismissed. By himself Holmes could do substantial damage, and the association also had to fear much increased illegal touting by blacks in Robinson's employ. F. Perry, the WNLA chairman, explained the possibly serious consequences of these activities: "When the recruiter [in Mozambique] had enlisted the natives, he could send them on from one rest house to another and be confident that they would reach their destination. But with the advent of competition, all this changed. A gang of natives travelling even for a short distance without a white man in charge, may be snapped up by any opposition recruiter who happens to meet them."[48] The WNLA would need to hire many more whites, he noted, and this would be expensive. In addition, the cost of African runners would almost certainly go up. In a competitive situation they would soon demand much more than the 2s. or 2s.6d. capitation fee then paid. Perry warned that fees could go as high as one pound a head, the rate before the Anglo-Boer War: "this factor alone would mean an increase in the expense of our east coast recruiting by 30,000 pounds a year."[49] Many of those who sat listening to Perry's warning could remember the prewar situation when a Mozambique recruit cost seventy shillings "per boy for the bulk landed at Johannesburg" and sometimes as high as ninety shillings under competitive conditions.[50] Perry noted, in an earlier memorandum, that many companies could ill afford higher recruiting costs: "to one of the older and richer outcrop mines, it might have been merely a question of a slight reduction in the dividend whether their native wages were 3 or 5 [pounds] a month, but to new enterprises which contemplated working low grade reef on a huge scale, it was a question of life or death."[51]

Fortunately for the WNLA the Portuguese remained adamantly opposed to further concessions to Robinson, despite persistent pressure on them from the British Foreign Office. They yielded only to the extent of agreeing to a joint inquiry into the system of recruiting in Mozambique. The basis of Portuguese intransigence in the face of such severe diplomatic pressure is not easy to establish. J.G. Baldwin believed that the Portuguese feared the disruptive effects of competitive recruiting on their relations with the African population. Portuguese pride must also have been aroused by the rather crass interference to which they were subjected by the British Liberal government. However, there were other considerations involved which were equally important in the explanation of Portuguese loyalty to the WNLA. The contacts which the WNLA had built up in Mozambique and the influence of the association's agents, Breyner and Wirth, were certainly crucial.

In addition, the Rand's leading mining house, Wernher, Beit/Eckstein, was acting against Robinson, independently of the Chamber of Mines. This group had excellent connections both in Lisbon and at Lourenço Marques. The ranking Johannesburg partner, Lionel Phillips, wrote to London in March 1907 about the good work being undertaken by Dr Balthazar Cabral. A Portuguese banker, Cabral had come to Mozambique for the first time in 1897. Phillips described him as a "sort of Pooh-Bah with bank mortgages upon the steamers of Abreu," who was very well connected in the Portuguese colony.[52] A former WNLA employee, Cabral had been dismissed from the association for unexplained reasons, but he apparently retained his interest in the Breyner and Wirth Agency. Cabral claimed to have great influence with the governor of the colony whom he described as "the same as a Brother."[53] Later a brother of Cabral's actually became a district governor. Given Cabral's unhappy record with the WNLA, Phillips's renewed contacts with him at this time are suggestive. The association's survival could no longer be assured, and the individual mining groups now moved to protect themselves in the event that competitive recruiting resumed. Phillips' negotiations with Cabral doubtless reflected as much a desire to protect his own group as to defend the interests of industry at large.

The nature of Dr Cabral's interest and the role he played in the crisis emerge in the following extract from an official letter from H. Eckstein and Company to their London principals: "the Board of Management of the WNLA have given very careful consideration to the request contained in Dr. Cabral's cables for a loan of 40 000 pounds for the provincial government of Mozambique and have decided to give their consent. At the same time, they considered it advisable to point out to Dr. Cabral that the transaction if it ever became public might be misconstrued, particularly as Mr.

Massinghame [*sic*] has alleged in the 'Daily News' that the mine owners have bribed the Portuguese authorities."[54] Later, they decided not to proceed with the "loan."[55] The evidence shows, however, that Cabral in association with Breyner and Wirth did much to stiffen the resistance of Lourenço Marques to the demands of J.B. Robinson. Cabral also played a role in efforts to put pressure on the Portuguese minister in London, de Soveral.[56] At the first intimation that Robinson's agents had tampered with the WNLA establishment in Mozambique, Lionel Phillips had gone immediately with Frederick Perry to Lourenço Marques to interview the governor-general. He agreed to refer the matter to Lisbon, and Phillips then urged his principals to "get at" de Soveral.[57] Apparently the London firm did not try to influence de Soveral because they were warned that he was sympathetic to Robinson's Liberal friends.[58] As expected, de Soveral did eventually recommend that his government grant the recruiting licence to Robinson's agent, G.G. Holmes. Lionel Phillips also made contact with the Portuguese minister of marine in Lisbon, Capt. Ayres d'Ornellas, and claimed to be on "very friendly" terms with him.[59] The correspondence indicates that these efforts contributed to the ultimate victory of the WNLA but were not sufficient by themselves to drive Robinson completely from the field. Thus Robinson's agent Holmes remained in Lourenço Marques throughout 1906 and into 1907, and he continued to threaten the WNLA's hold on the territory.

Moreover, during early 1906, Robinson's senior Johannesburg associate, J.W.S. Langerman, had begun working on another tack to win over the Portuguese. Like Robinson a supporter of Het Volk (and later Het Volk MLA for Randfontein), Langerman had promised the Portuguese to use his influence with the Transvaal party on railway matters. Lionel Phillips heard an alarming rumour that Langerman had offered to persuade the Botha-Smuts party, should it come to power, to have the new Mozambique-Swaziland Railway pushed through to Ermelo and on to the Rand. This project had strong support in Lourenço Marques because of the additional competitive edge (the gradients on the proposed line were much lower) it would give the Mozambique line over the Cape and Natal government railways.[60] If the rumour was correct, Langerman's offer constituted tempting bait for the Portuguese. Recently Selborne's government had opened negotiations with Mozambique on the question of the preferential rates guaranteed to the Delagoa Bay line under the 1901 *Modus Vivendi*. The Cape and Natal had bitterly attacked the *Modus Vivendi* for years, and at the intercolonial railway conference of 1905, the Transvaal authorities finally agreed to seek a downward revision from the Portuguese. In these circumstances, Langerman's offer to deliver the support of Het Volk, the probable successor to Selborne's crown colony administration once responsible government was conceded, must have been very tempting indeed. Cape and Natal efforts to win better terms for their railways could thus be frustrated.

Given the Liberal government's support for Robinson and the offers which Robinson's agents had dangled before the Portuguese, the position of the WNLA in Mozambique remained perilous into 1907. With the Transvaal election pending, there seemed every prospect that the political balance would shift against the recruiting organization. Contacts which the WNLA and the Chamber of Mines had carefully nurtured both in Lisbon and Lourenço Marques over several years had bought time for the organization but could not alone guarantee final victory. Generally, the London representatives of those groups which continued to back the chamber were less sanguine about defeating Robinson than their Johannesburg offices. These London houses put some pressure on their colleagues in South Africa to make concessions to the Randfontein group in the hope of avoiding a complete rupture.[61] Late in 1906, a meeting of George Farrar, the ERPM chief, and F. Eckstein, for the Wernher, Beit group, with Robinson was forestalled only by the decision of the Chamber of Mines in Johannesburg to expel his companies. Eckstein continued to urge that a compromise be reached, but Lionel Phillips and the other Johannesburg partners remained opposed to any "kow-towing" to Robinson.[62]

During the first months of 1907, the immediate threat to the WNLA came from a proposed joint-inquiry which the British government was now pressing on the Portuguese. The idea of an inquiry into WNLA operations in Mozambique had originally been put forward by the backers of the association as a means of delaying hostile action by the Liberal government.[63] But Lord Elgin's advisers in the Colonial Office had taken over the inquiry idea and refashioned it into a weapon against the WNLA. If the Portuguese agreed to an inquiry which then turned up evidence of inefficiency and mismanagement, clearly the survival of the WNLA would become doubtful. Given the methods which the association had used over the years to get and to keep favour at Lourenço Marques, methods which were bound to come out in any real inquiry, one can imagine the anxiety of the Chamber of Mines to head off this dangerous proposal. Though presented by the Liberal government as a kind of compromise, the proposed inquiry was actually a ticking bomb planted at the centre of the structure of monopsonistic recruiting in Mozambique. That the friends of the WNLA had initially proposed the inquiry is simply a measure of their desperation at an earlier stage of the crisis. At that time delay was the only weapon to hand, and they wrongly hoped they could buy time with the proposed inquiry. Not only did they fail to win delay – the licence for Holmes went ahead – but also they now faced the threat of a real inquiry into their establishment in Mozambique.

Robinson was also in a difficult position. Holmes still languished in Lourenço Marques without the means to make his licence effective. He and Robinson's former agents, the Transvaal Mines Labour Company, had exaggerated their ability to operate successfully in the Portuguese territories.

As Dr Cabral noted in a letter to Phillips, there was the possibility already, which Robinson must have recognized, that he had missed his chance: "Robinson did not know how to formulate his request [for recruiting licences], but for this he alone is to blame. When he awakens to his mistake, he will have to ask for his concession to be amended; but when this happens, the British government will no longer be in such haste to see him served because it will not have another [Transvaal] Constitution to publish, nor will Mr. Robinson have more Chinese to give up."[64] In any case, even with the support of the imperial government, Robinson had been unable to do more than disrupt the WNLA operation. Specifically he had failed to establish firmly his own labour supply from Mozambique. Although the independent recruiting operations of the Randfontein group and its labour contractors were undoubtedly successful within South Africa itself, and although these mines were less dependent on Chinese labour than most, they could certainly not afford to remain largely cut off from the prime recruiting territories in Portuguese East Africa.

There was no speedy resolution to the crisis. Though Robinson was in practice excluded from Mozambique, his agents competed vigorously for labour elsewhere in southern Africa. Exploiting the weakness of the WNLA and divisions within the mining industry, private labour-contracting firms and independent recruiters rushed to secure a share of the South African business. The TMLC concentrated its attention on the Cape and joined the other contractors who had been fiercely bidding for labour in defiance of the WNLA. Moreover, Robinson still hoped that imperial pressure would win for his companies a foothold in Portuguese East Africa. In early 1907, therefore, the conflict was still far from resolution. Both sides had reason to entertain a compromise because neither could be certain of ultimate victory. In their different ways, the contending forces were evenly balanced. With continuing deadlock probable, an opportunity arose for the successful mediation of the new Botha government in the Transvaal.

Within weeks of taking office, Botha and Smuts made contact with Robinson and his enemies in an effort to bring the two sides together. The prime minister also informed Selborne and Elgin that his government believed recruiting in Mozambique must be carried on "through a single organised body [and] the Witwatersrand Native Labour Association must be kept in existence for this purpose."[65] Furthermore, the Transvaal government opposed the planned joint British-Portuguese inquiry on the labour issue and wished to negotiate directly with Mozambique. Elgin agreed to go along with this.[66] Responding warily to the unexpected election victory of the Afrikaner-dominated Het Volk-Nationalist coalition, the Liberals wanted above all to be sure that the new administration would carry through the decision to end Chinese labour. By contrast the altercation over Mozambique and the demands of J.B. Robinson probably meant little to them.

The Het Volk cabinet's intervention in the dispute over the future of the WNLA followed from many of the same considerations which led this government at about the same time to establish the Native Labour Bureau. The bureau's responsibilities included both the inspection of mine labour conditions on the Rand and the supervision of private recruiting with South Africa. Committed as they still were to the prompt repatriation of Chinese labour, Botha and his colleagues had an important incentive to ensure maximum exploitation of the local labour supply, particularly the supply from the industry's most important labour pool in Portuguese East Africa. Throughout the election, they had campaigned for "repatriation and replacement." With the Chinese about to go, it made little sense to allow the disruption of South African supplies. Het Volk also had the greater debt to Robinson who had been able to threaten the WNLA in Mozambique but had not established an effective organization there himself. Moreover, if the WNLA failed, anarchical conditions would certainly return to Mozambique recruiting, and the Transvaal government could easily find itself forced to take direct responsibility for the labour supply. This was something all South African governments had hitherto avoided. In the case of Mozambique, any involvement of the Transvaal authorities in recruiting operations there would also require an unpalatable partnership with the Portuguese. The kind of charges which the WNLA had attracted of participating in forced labour practices, and of systematically corrupting Portuguese officials, would then be directed toward the government. No doubt the politicians preferred to avoid this.

Apart from all of these considerations, the Botha government, like every South African government before and since, could not afford indifference to massive instability in its leading industry, particularly at a time of general economic depression in South Africa and high white unemployment. As it happened, the ability of the government to carry through with Chinese repatriation and yet avoid disruption of the gold output depended as much on their good fortune as on good management. Despite all of the recruiting problems which plagued the industry in early 1907, the black labour supply became "consistently abnormal," increased at a fast rate throughout the year and more than compensated for the loss of the Chinese. During January 1908, for example, the total nonwhite labour supply on the mines and works in the Transvaal increased by 3,911, despite the loss of 4,196 Chinese. In that month more than double the number of Africans (16,004) registered for the mines than had registered six months before, during June 1907 (7,920).[67]

The improving labour supply situation could only have facilitated the administration's successful settlement of the WNLA dispute. Intra-industry competition naturally lessened when supply problems eased after a period of shortage. Sensible political tactics also promoted the mediation effort.

Despite the political ties which linked J.B. Robinson with Het Volk, Botha and his colleagues, unlike the British Liberals, tried at this critical juncture to draw back from too partisan identification with one side in the dispute. The priority which these men gave to the mines' labour problems is indicated by the meetings which the Transvaal colonial secretary, J.C. Smuts, convened with a special Chamber of Mines committee during April 1907. Smuts took the initiative and met the committee in order to canvass the prospect of reconciliation between the WNLA loyalists and Robinson. If Smuts did not have the prior agreement of Robinson, he had certainly consulted him.[68] At a meeting on 25 April, Smuts presented the chamber representatives with a package of proposals for a settlement. The thirteen clauses of the draft agreement reconstructed the WNLA almost completely and gave the government large supervisory powers over its operations and even its membership. At Smuts's urging and with few amendments but with much hesitation and backsliding, the contending parties finally accepted the package.[69] It constituted in effect a government charter for the WNLA in which the state confirmed the association's monopoly position in Portuguese East Africa subject to good behaviour and compliance with the terms which Smuts had established.[70] If in the judgment of the government, the WNLA failed at any time to conduct itself efficiently or if it discriminated against one or more members (both of these requirements echoed Robinson's earlier charges), the government reserved power to break the monopsony and to issue separate recruiting licences to the different groups for East Africa; the WNLA agreed to allow government inspectors access to its books on demand. In disputes between member companies, the state would mediate directly or at its discretion appoint a single arbitrator. The revised articles of association bound member companies to the results of such mediation. Smuts proposed and the chamber agreed that the WNLA waive control over membership. It had to accept as members companies approved by the Transvaal government. These critical clauses relating to state supervision had been carefully devised so as to exclude the Native Affairs Department or the labour bureau from any responsibility to maintain recruiting levels or to supervise routine operations.[71] Several clauses in the draft agreement referred to these points of detail and set out general principles governing, for example, the important matter of the distribution of labour between member companies. Both sides secured amendments on matters relating to internal questions, but on the issue of government control, the final settlement differed little from Smuts's original draft.

Negotiations were prolonged and difficult and nearly broke down on at least one occasion. Apart from controversy on issues of principle, agreement nearly foundered because of bitter personal hostility within the industry, hostility which erupted in the public press during the dispute. When Robinson published a letter "in which he referred to all the principal mining houses here as a gang of Tammany thieves," some chamber members sued. In reply the Johannesburg *Star,* which the Wernher, Beit/Eckstein group controlled financially through the Argus Company, described Robinson as "an imposter and a fraud,"[72] and Robinson threatened a counter-suit. Longstanding personal antipathies constituted a major barrier to agreement.[73] Even after both sides had accepted Smuts's terms, suspicion and hostility remained considerable. For a time, Robinson convinced himself that his enemies in the chamber were behind an abortive shareholders' revolt against his management.[74] On the other side, feelings ran strongly as well. In London, the normally phlegmatic and undemonstrative Julius Wernher wrote with (for him) unprecedented venom: "I feel very bitter abt. J.B.R. – he is a black hearted cur." With slightly more detachment, Lionel Phillips attributed Robinson's attitude "to politics, personal vanity on his part and hatred and jealousy, particularly of us."[75] Although clearly founded in business rivalries reaching back to the earliest days of the industry, these hatreds and jealousies developed a life of their own and greatly impeded agreement in the industry on labour and other matters. Robinson's lack of business principle and vindictive determination to retaliate against any slight, real or imagined, prevented really full cooperation on labour and other issues until he sold out his interest in 1916. Robinson was one of the last of the buccaneers, and his eventual departure opened the way for the final triumph of a managerial rather than an entrepreneurial approach to the organization of the migrant labour supply. In 1907, that development, long anticipated by his business rivals, still lay nearly a decade in the future.

Despite these complicating personal considerations agreement was finally reached in the WNLA dispute largely thanks to the patience and persistence of J.C. Smuts. As a result the state became involved to an unprecedented degree in the control of east coast recruiting. The Randlords became so alarmed at the cost implications of their dispute that both sides actually welcomed the supervisory role of the Transvaal government. The politicians intervened first to restore unity in the WNLA and then to keep the groups together through the supervisory functions which they continued to exercise under the revised WNLA articles of association.

Although neither the Transvaal government nor its Union successor tried to exercise day-to-day control over the WNLA, the state did intervene, usually reluctantly, in particular cases of abuse. During 1911, for example, the new Union government launched a major inquiry into WNLA activities on the east coast and in the northern territories.[76] This was part of a review of mine labour policy which preceded the passing of the Native Labour Regulation Act in the same year. But the investigation was triggered by concern over the continuing high death rate among "tropical" Africans recruited from territories lying north of 22°SL. (This issue is discussed separately in chapter

7.) The general review of WNLA activities followed from a meeting of the Union minister of native affairs, Henry Burton, and leading members of the Chamber of Mines executive in July 1911. Burton informed the chamber that the government had received applications from certain interests, well established, he said, in the recruiting world, for permission to recruit outside the WNLA structure. Under the Mozambique convention of 1909, the Portuguese had agreed to license labour agents approved by the Union government. Moreover, the revised articles of association of the WNLA transferred to the state broad powers to modify or even end the association's monoposonistic control of recruiting in Mozambique. Thus the WNLA enjoyed its unique position on sufferance, and the minister's reference to new recruiting applications was extremely ominous.

Burton declined to name these aspiring competitors, but he did say that they were people of "respectability and standing in the recruiting world."[77] He added that some of them were concerned with certain mining groups which he also declined to specify. The chamber representatives would have required little imagination to guess from which quarter the attack originated. They were almost certainly representatives of one or more of the large labour-contracting firms which had established an important position both in the eastern Cape and the northern Transvaal in the years since the WNLA organization had collapsed there in 1906. Very probably the principal contractor for the Randfontein group, A.M. Mostert and Company, led the pack, and Mostert may well have had the backing of the group's controller, J.B. Robinson. The WNLA's old adversary, "Kaffir" Wilson, may also have been involved. Replaying the struggles of 1906–7, the interests aspiring to supplant the WNLA had claimed that the association was inefficient and had failed to exploit fully the labour supply of Portuguese East Africa. Apparently some Portuguese officials had themselves expressed dissatisfaction.[78] Burton proposed to investigate these charges and suggested that a joint WNLA-Native Affairs Department commission to be set up to go to Mozambique and to report on all phases of the WNLA operation. Recognizing that this was the best deal they were likely to get, the chamber representatives quickly accepted. Burton particularly wanted the commission to investigate the charges that recruits entraining at Ressano Garcia were mistreated both by the WNLA officials and the railway personnel.

These initiatives by the private labour contractors followed from two new developments which seemed to leave the WNLA vulnerable. Considerable publicity had been given to the prevailing high rates of mortality among the "tropical" recruits on the mines and government's mounting concern was known. Second, the republican revolution in Portugal at the end of 1910 seemed to undercut the labour association's position. With new officials in place or en route to Mozambique by mid-1911, the WNLA's competitors must have thought the moment opportune to act. Presumably they hoped that the association had been discredited in the Portuguese colony because of its connection with the ousted monarchy. This at any rate was the view of senior Chamber of Mines officials when Burton interviewed them in July. The minister himself added that the new Portuguese team in the colony had expressed dissatisfaction with the WNLA, thought recruiting levels should be higher, and should therefore be receptive to the idea of open recruiting.

The mining industry had little choice but to agree to the minister's proposal, and by the beginning of August, an inquiry commission had been named and dispatched on its tour of inspection in Mozambique. P. Ross Frames and Julius Jeppe represented the WNLA, while the director of native labour, S.M. Pritchard, and one of his associates, H. Bell, a Native Affairs Department official, acted for the government.[79] Frames and Jeppe wrote a report, Bell submitted some notes,[80] and Pritchard, who had to leave the tour early because of illness, could contribute very little. In their report, the two WNLA representatives had few criticisms to make of the conduct of the association's recruiting operations.[81] They had toured extensively in southern Mozambique, visited twenty of the rest camps and interviewed chiefs, headmen, and numerous workers as well as the association's principal recruiters, their white assistants, and African runners. They confirmed the official WNLA view that the labour supply there could not be significantly augmented. If anything, the association had too many employees. Migrancy was so well established in these districts that most of the workers did not need to be recruited at all. Seventy-five per cent of them showed up of their own volition at the association's camps. Those who did so received the same payment as would be given to a runner who brought in a recruit. Just because of the current charges of WNLA inefficiency, however, the commissioners thought it would be inexpedient to reduce the establishment at that time.

Although its language was somewhat muffled and the phrasing oblique, their report did uphold the minister's charges of poor conditions in the WNLA's compounds and hospitals in Mozambique. Large facilities existed both in Lourenço Marques and Ressano Garcia on the Transvaal border and neither was satisfactory. The compound at Lourenço Marques had been badly sited and was "very dirty and in a disgraceful condition." They recommended construction of an entirely new facility there. At Ressano Garcia, the association had belatedly undertaken the construction of a new compound, but the hospital was in bad shape. The medical officer nominally in charge lived across the border in Komati Poort, as did the only trained person regularly in attendance, a white orderly who came to the hospital for a few hours each day. Otherwise untrained African staff looked after the patients with the results which the minister had criticized so severely. This complete neglect of basic hospital good practice was also typical of most of the mine hospitals at that time. Only continuous prodding from the government produced very gradual, grudging improvements. In the case of the hospital at Ressano Garcia, a full-time medical officer and other trained staff were appointed even before the commissioners had left the town. When threatened with drastic action, as Burton had done, the WNLA could move to correct deficiencies very speedily indeed. Frames and Jeppe also condemned the facilities provided for mineworkers on the South African railways between the border and Johannesburg. Despite all this, they concluded that "the boys are well cared for, and properly fed by the officials of the Association" and that "the boys returning from the mines are usually in a very much better state of health than when they leave their country."

A less charitable view of the condition of returning migrants came from a WNLA official at Maxixi whose comments did not get into the official report. He gave them privately in a letter to Pritchard: "No boy should be allowed to leave the hospitals on the Rand with a disease curable within a reasonable time (I think he is worth nursing for a year?). Out of a boat-load of twenty returning natives who were dumped on the shore here on one occasion – all from the Premier Mine – only one could walk upright, the other nineteen being all crippled either temporarily or permanently – I recorded this at the time in my diary."[82] His letter suggested that this was no isolated occurrence. Pritchard's informant believed that the WNLA's critics – and the director himself – were correct in "assuming that more labour could be squeezed out of the country." WNLA officials proceeded with too much "calm assurance, with the result that the business is of far too listless a kind." Nevertheless he thought that to permit competition would be too costly and "the worst kind of policy from all points of view."[83] His idea was to deploy modern advertising techniques. The migrants, he said, were all totally familiar with conditions on the mines: "they go up to the Rand and return throughout each year and form a moving circle, and, like circus animals, require whipping up at points around the ring." The recruiters should be on tour continuously to "breathe the word" and to prevent the migrant from resting too long at his kraal and neglecting the requirements of European and other investors. Labour for the gold mines should be marketed in Mozambique in the same way that a certain company advertised the benefits of Pears soap. This advocate of modern business enterprise in Africa believed, finally, that WNLA activities should be more closely monitored by an independent inspector reporting to the Chamber of Mines but outside the WNLA structure.[84]

Both in the formal reports and in private correspondence with WNLA officials, the inquiry provided the government with a great deal of information about the conduct of recruiting, much of it very critical of the association. Despite this, few changes resulted. Burton did not carry through with his implied threat to open the colony to independent recruiting, and the WNLA structure was not significantly altered as a result of the charges of its "inefficiency." Tropical mortality continued to be extremely high and the government demanded and got further changes and improvements in the compounds and hospitals both from the association and the mining groups themselves. As before these improvements were too slow and grudging to forestall a government decision to ban recruiting north of 22°SL which finally occurred in mid-1913.

From the standpoint of the WNLA itself, one of the most important results of the Frames-Jeppe report was the information provided about the attitude of Portuguese officials. High officials in the colony, they thought, generally favoured noncompetitive recruiting for the mines. Certain district commandants, it was true, disliked the WNLA, but this was because they saw the association as a competitor to the government in their districts. The WNLA had more money to spend, a more visible presence, and more influence over the local black population than the Portuguese administration had. A few officials wanted to see recruiting ended entirely and the labour used locally for development. Knowing conditions in Mozambique, the WNLA commissioners did not think that this constituted much of a threat. All of the officials they interviewed at every level argued strenuously that if recruiting was to continue, and most thought that it should, the system of deferred pay should be extended and made compulsory. If all the migrants were forced to defer half of their wages for payment on return to the colony, as was already the case with those from the tropical territories, then the economic payoff from migrancy to the state and the white population generally would be much enhanced. In 1903, the Zambezia Chartered Company and the Nyassa Company had made this a condition of recruiting in territories administered by them.[85] During the few years that recruiting was permitted in Nyasaland, authorities there imposed a similar condition, as did certain prazo holders in Quilimane and Tete when they permitted recruiting in 1905.[86] The Mozambique government itself had negotiated a deferred pay arrangement in one of the northern territories under its direct control.[87] The Union government estimated that in 1911, 18,000 out of 96,000 Mozambique recruits arrived under contracts of this type. A total of £320,764 from their wages had been deferred for payment in the colony.[88] Just because the Portuguese were so anxious to see the system extended to the southern districts, Frames and Jeppe argued, the policy could be used to extract "important concessions" from them.[89]

However, they also pointed out that there was a negative dimension to be taken into account. Deferred pay would probably be very unpopular with the mineworkers themselves and could lead at least temporarily to a falling off in recruiting levels. Payment of the deferred wages due should be arranged through WNLA agents only. Experience suggested that if the funds went to the Portuguese authorities, very little of it would ever reach the mineworkers. This was not only because of the venality of Portuguese officialdom, but also because they were so feared and hated by the local population that most returning workers would never put in a claim for the wages due. The WNLA commissioners based this conclusion on the experience with payments owing as compensation to the families of deceased mineworkers. These sums were administered by the Mozambique government. Only 15 per cent reached the Africans concerned as contrasted with a rate of 90 per cent in the Cape Colony.[90] Despite these potential difficulties, Frames and Jeppe recommended the policy, and, within a year, the WNLA Board of Management had begun negotiations. An agreement with the Portuguese on deferred pay was successfully concluded in December 1912.

The WNLA commissioners made their suggestion at a time when both the government and the chamber had been considering the attractions of deferred pay for the industry as a whole. Within South Africa itself they saw it as a possible alternative to the prevailing system of granting cash advances to the intending migrants. Not only was this expensive but also it led to widespread abuses by recruiters and considerable loss through workers deserting before repayment had been made. The authorities had limited the size of advances, but their measures were difficult to enforce. Everyone recognized, moreover, that the cash advance met a real need in the African community. Many hard-pressed peasants would not accept a mine contract until provision had been made for their families while they were away. From the mines' standpoint, deferred pay offered a cheaper, safer way of providing for the families without the risks of fraud and desertion which were inescapable under the present system.

The advance system had resulted directly from the advent of competitive recruiting in South Africa during 1906–7. Because the WNLA's control over recruiting in Mozambique remained in the end unaffected, advances never became established there. Recruiters in Mozambique could give small advances to intending workers in cash or clothing but on nothing like the scale prevailing in the main South African recruiting centres. Thus the appeal of deferred pay for the Portuguese colony lay exclusively in its potential to lever better terms from the authorities. At the same time, chamber officials may have realized that a successfully running deferred pay system throughout Portuguese East Africa would have a useful demonstration effect in South Africa itself.

Whatever their thinking, they soon began negotiations with Lisbon once Ross Frames had secured Burton's informal permission to proceed.[91] The procedure was unusual in that talks were held directly with the minister for the colonies without at first even the knowledge of the Mozambique governor. Nor were Union officials, including the minister, kept informed of the substance of the talks until an agreement had been reached and signed. The latter seems not to have been intentional, while the decision to approach Lisbon direct was taken on the advice of one of the WNLA's agents at Lourenço Marques, Wirth.[92] The reasons do not appear in the correspondence but may have had something to do with the complexities of postrevolutionary politics in Portugal.

The agreement which was eventually reached provided for the compulsory deferral of part of the pay of all Mozambique mine workers.[93] During a transitional period ending 30 June 1914, migrants from south of 22°SL would receive all of their pay during the initial contract period of twelve months paid in the Transvaal as was currently the case. Those who accepted a six-month or longer extension of the contract (as most did) would have half of the additional wages deferred. Workers from the tropical territories would continue to receive half of their wages on return to the colony as before. After the transitional period, the agreement provided that the initial contract period for all Mozambique workers would be extended from twelve to eighteen months and that half of the wages for the first twelve months would be deferred. The same would apply to wages for any extension of the contract beyond the initial eighteen months. Before paying the deferred wages the WNLA would deduct amounts to cover any advances paid and repatriation costs. Payments would be made in the workers' home districts by the nearest WNLA official in the presence of a designated Portuguese representative. In the event the official failed to appear after due notice, the association could proceed with the payments.

The Portuguese government expected substantial benefits from the new arrangement. Estimates varied widely of the actual amount of additional stimulus which would result to the Mozambique economy by the specie transfers necessary to meet the deferred wages. After all, roughly one-sixth of the migrants already had part of their wages deferred, and most of the others saved substantial sums on their own to take back with them. Somewhat extravagantly, the governor of Inhambane and a local Lourenço Marques newspaper estimated that an additional sum of over one million pounds sterling would be involved. Fearing serious loss of business to the Rand traders, the *Rand Daily Mail* and the Johannesburg Chamber of Commerce echoed these probably inflated figures.[94] Most agreed, however, that the economic impact of the new arrangement would be large. One exception was the president of the Chamber of Mines who claimed that the workers already took back with them more money than would be involved in the new agreement.[95] This left the problem of explaining why Mozambique wanted the agreement so badly if it gave them no additional benefits. In any case the chamber was responding to a mounting agitation in the press and in Parliament against their agreement. After taking account of the conflicting estimates, the government's mining engineer, Robert Kotze, concluded that: "the new scheme will assist the thrifty to save more and the thriftless to save at least the instalment to be paid on their return, so that on the average the amount spent here will be less than before."[96] Contrary to Kotze, however, much mineworker expenditure on the Rand was not discretionary but used to supplement the bland, still inadequate mine diet.

Whatever the actual figures, the Mozambique government had high hopes and made a number of strategic concessions to get the agreement. Most important was the extension of the initial contract period to eighteen months, effective mid-1914. Although a large proportion of the workers already stayed for the longer period, the agreement meant that the mines could now count on all doing so. This would greatly assist planning and the smooth meshing of the monthly outflow of time-expired workers with the inflow of those newly recruited. Uncertainties created by short contract periods resulted in sometimes violent fluctuations – up and down – in the size of mine labour complements with a consequent loss in efficiency. Moreover, everyone connected with the industry agreed that the longer a worker stayed on the mines the more efficient he became. With roughly 100,000 Mozambique workers each serving a minimum of eighteen months as now proposed, the mines could be sure of a core of stable, highly efficient black workers. This would offset the more volatile South African part of the work-force, the majority of whom would only accept a six-to nine-month contract and often as short as three. This agreement to lengthen the contract period constituted a major concession on the part of the Portuguese who from the very beginning of large-scale migrancy to the mines had realized that a large number of the time-expired workers never returned.[97] Since the Union government and the mines would not agree to compulsory repatriation, they feared that the longer a worker stayed on the mines the less likely was his eventual repatriation.

Portuguese concessions to the WNLA negotiating team extended much further than this. They agreed to protect the association's recruiting pool from further inroads by the prazo holders in the northern part of Mozambique.[98] These concessionaires had already closed large areas of Tete and Quelimane provinces to South African recruiters at the cost to the WNLA of a substantial amount of tropical labour. In particular, the WNLA had been actively competing with the London magnate J.P. Hornung, who had huge sugar and other interests in the area, both for local and emigrant labour from Nyasaland. The association had tried and failed to get the Union government to intervene against Hornung.[99] Now they persuaded the Portuguese colonial officials at least not to create new obstacles of this type to their recruiting effort. During the term of the agreement, Lisbon agreed to grant no new prazos or similar leases beyond those in force on 1 September 1912. In return for this restraint, the chamber representatives undertook to pay annually the fairly modest sum of £6,000 as compensation. The WNLA could now be assured that at least in territories directly administered by the Mozambique colonial state, the prazo system would not be further extended. The agreement did not affect the position of the existing leaseholders but only confirmed that the association could negotiate directly with them for recruiting rights.

Furthermore Lisbon protected the WNLA's prime recruiting area in another way. Except in the Maputo district, the government would no longer issue passes to Mozambique Africans permitting them to seek work independently outside the colony. To the extent that this could be enforced, it meant that intending emigrants would increasingly have to deal with WNLA recruiters and accept employment on the mines as the only legal way of reaching the Union. In addition the Portuguese government decided to open an entirely new area to the gold mines' recruiters. At the option of the WNLA, its agents could now operate in Angola, east of 19°EL and south of 10°SL, a huge area encompassing roughly one-quarter of the giant colony. Easy access to the region was possible from the association's bases in the southeastern part of northern Rhodesia. Finally, the Lisbon government also eased certain administrative requirements which would have permitted the WNLA to make some staff reductions had the new arrangements come into effect. Since the deferred pay agreement did not come into force for many years and since the Union government soon banned the employment of tropical Africans on the gold mines, most of these concessions remained inoperative. They do show, however, just how anxious the Portuguese were to secure an agreement on deferred pay.

The Chamber of Mines executives who had negotiated the deferred pay proposal certainly did not expect the protests which erupted both in Johannesburg and in the Union Parliament as soon as the terms became known. The Rand trading interest feared, of course, a serious loss of business and argued that the whole economy of the Transvaal would be seriously weakened. At least one city newspaper, the *Rand Daily Mail,* supported the merchants, and, in Parliament, F.H.P. Creswell, always on the lookout for issues embarrassing to the mine owners, took up their cause. Here was just another instance of a bunch of largely expatriate Randlords sacrificing South Africa's whites to the interests of a foreign colonial state.[100] Had the owners anticipated the degree of opposition which arose, they would have done more to secure the prior approval and support of the Union government. Ross Frames had, it is true, approached Henry Burton and received his informal approval to begin negotiations, but there was no contact with the labour bureau or the Native Affairs Department during the negotiations and no attempt to get prior approval of the various provisions. Once the agreement became known, the Union government received severe criticism for allowing the negotiations to go forward. Under pressure from the chamber to make good on Burton's implied pledge of support and having to deal with the criticisms of the traders, Botha and his colleagues temporized.

Native Affairs Department officials approved the principle of deferred pay. Indeed, they were promoting it in South Africa itself as an alternative to the abuse-ridden advance system. However, they disliked the longer contract period, both because it contravened technically the Mozambique convention of 1909, providing for an initial twelve-month contract, and because of the likely detrimental effects of the eighteen-month period of service on the workers' health. The logic here was somewhat obscure since the convention permitted reengagement for successive six-month periods and most Mozambique blacks remained at least eighteen months on the mines. The health worries and the quibble about the legality of the proposed contract period gave the government reasons to delay and to inform Lisbon that implementation could not be considered until after a report of the miners' phthisis commission. Then the war intervened, and in 1915 the two governments accepted that the extension of deferred pay in Mozambique would be held over until the end of hostilities in Europe.[101] In the event, the Portuguese had to wait until the negotiation of the 1928 Convention to get agreement.

Even though this extended version of deferred pay was not implemented for some years, the negotiations helped to cement the same close relationship between the WNLA and the new Lisbon government as had existed under the monarchy. Evidently the arrangement which brought massive numbers of black workers to the gold mines on long-term contracts in return for huge injections of cash into the Mozambique economy was too mutually beneficial to be much affected by the vagaries of Lusitanian politics.

CHAPTER SEVEN

Tropical Recruiting and the Bid for the Labour of the Hinterland

During 1902, the Chamber of Mines began to consider development of a recruiting network in central and east Africa, particularly northern Mozambique, Nyasaland, and northern Rhodesia. Before the war, tropical migrants in some numbers had found work on the mines, but apart from the activities of independent labour touts no recruiting had been undertaken by the Rand Native Labour Association, the official arm of the Chamber of Mines until the wNLA came into existence in 1900. Consideration of recruitment north of 22°SL reflected the same motives which led to the decision to import Chinese labour in 1904. With the restart of mining operations at the conclusion of the Anglo-Boer War, Africans had been very slow to return to the mines. Disturbed conditions in many districts together with the continuing availability of alternative employment, especially in military projects, help to explain this. A major factor, however, was the decision (soon rescinded) of the Chamber of Mines to reduce wage rates by about one-third as compared with the already low prewar levels. Unable as a result to compete for migrant labour in South Africa itself, the mine owners were forced to explore possibilities in the very low-wage northern territories on the periphery of the subcontinent.[1]

At the request of the mining industry, the new Transvaal Reconstruction government sought permission from the Colonial Office and the Foreign Office to recruit in the British colonies and protectorates of central and east Africa.[2] Replying to an inquiry by the Colonial Office in August 1902, the Foreign Office reported that the commissioners of Uganda, British East Africa (Kenya), and the British Central African Protectorate (Nyasaland) had expressed strong and unanimous opposition to any recruiting for the Rand gold mines.[3] Pressure on Foreign Office officials to reconsider was immediate and intense. At the Colonial Office, Chamberlain, urged on by Milner in South Africa, did everything he could to persuade Lord Lansdowne, the foreign secretary, of the urgency of the situation,[4] while,

221

in South Africa, the WNLA dispatched its general managers, Macfarlane and Nourse, to east and central Africa respectively. Despite Macfarlane's enthusiastic reports about the prospects in Uganda and Kenya and Milner's urgent representations to London on behalf of the WNLA, the mines never did succeed in overturning the Foreign Office ban on recruiting in East Africa.[5] The staff of the protectorates were not anxious to have their territories stripped of labour. Concern arose also that to permit the flow of labour south could promote the spread of sleeping sickness.[6] Joseph Chamberlain himself decided after talks with Sir Charles Eliot while en route to South Africa that the EAP could not supply any large amount of labour "for a long time."[7] He did, however, urge that the WNLA be permitted to send agents to Uganda to investigate and report on recruiting prospects there.[8] On his return to London Chamberlain's pessimistic telegram to Milner in effect closed the issue of recruiting in East Africa: "After full consideration and in view of sleeping sickness in east Africa and strong objections from Administrator and others, His Majesty's government find themselves obliged to await results of experiment in British Central Africa, where circumstances are more favourable, before considering question of recruiting in British East Africa or Uganda. My personal opinion is that no supply of least importance could be obtained from East Africa at present."[9]

As the secretary of state indicated, the Chamber of Mines experienced more success in its efforts to open the central African territories to WNLA recruiters. Milner's government also strongly backed these initiatives and tried to induce the Nyasaland authorities to agree. Initially commissioner Sharpe in the British Central African Protectorate opposed WNLA recruiting, fearing that the drain of labour would be large and adversely affect the development of the protectorate. Sharpe was responding to two memoranda by Sir Harry Johnstone, the former proconsul, who had enthusiastically advocated migrant labour as a way of raising government revenue through hut and other taxes.[10] Later in 1902, Johnstone became an informal consultant to the chamber through Wernher, Beit in London. Johnstone's enthusiasm for the potential of Nyasaland and Uganda as sources of mine labour seemed to stimulate the imaginations of these normally cautious men. The London partners reported eagerly to Johannesburg that Sir Harry "states ... there is a practically inexhaustible source of supply to draw upon and that it is only a question of careful organisation and good management to find in those regions a solution of the Native labour difficulty."[11] Despite Johnstone's optimism and the continuing efforts of the WNLA and the chamber, progress toward an agreement to recruit in Nyasaland was slow. The Foreign Office, which administered the territory, remained cautious, and the protectorate government unenthusiastic at best.

These officials had also to consider white opinion in Nyasaland. Missionary groups, planters, and commercial interests united to condemn the prospect of recruiting for the South African mines. As a Nyasaland governor later explained, local wages for blacks averaged three shillings a month, and the white planters, wanting to preserve this state of affairs, vigorously opposed emigration to the mines where employment was available at many times local rates.[12] They put continuous pressure on protectorate officials and on the Foreign Office over the next several years.[13] Initially the Foreign Office cast a veto but by late 1902 indicated a willingness to reconsider. Through the Colonial Office, Milner had repeated his urgent plea that the need for labour on the Rand was "a very pressing matter" upon which depended the "return of prosperity to the country generally."[14] In the Transvaal, the commissioner of native affairs pointed out that failure to approve recruiting for the mines in the tropical territories would inevitably produce demands from the industry for Chinese labour.[15] When Chamberlain arrived in South Africa, the chamber successfully persuaded him to request that the Foreign Office reconsider.[16] Responding to the renewed pleas from South Africa, Lansdowne reopened the matter and again sought the advice of Sir Alfred Sharpe in Zomba. By this point in late 1902, Sharpe had become less hostile to the prospect of mine recruiting. Migrant labour would bring much needed cash into the local economy; it would certainly help the revenue, as well as alleviate the effects of a famine then under way in the protectorate. There was "a certain surplus" at present, and he did not doubt that "considerable numbers" would agree to go south on six month contracts. Still he worried that the long-run interests of Nyasaland whites would be jeopardized by a large-scale exodus of labour. If construction on the railway would begin soon, Sharpe added, all of the territory's labour would certainly be needed at home.[17]

Despite Sharpe's rather equivocal views, the Foreign Office finally withdrew its earlier veto and somewhat reluctantly granted permission for the WNLA to import 1,000 labourers from Nyasaland on an experimental basis. Intense lobbying by the Colonial Office certainly contributed significantly to the decision, and the personal intervention of Chamberlain was probably decisive. In authorizing the "experiment," Lansdowne established explicit conditions concerning wages, recruiting arrangements, health care, and accommodation and specified that a portion of the wages should be deferred and paid to the workers on their return to the protectorate.[18] The deputy commissioner, Major Pearce, worked out the details with WNLA representatives who had been dispatched to the protectorate.[19] Total monthly wages of thirty shifts came to forty-five shillings, 25 per cent of which the mines paid in the Transvaal and the balance to the workers on their return to Nyasaland. The protectorate administration also collected a ten-shilling fee for each recruit accepted by the WNLA. T.M.C. Nourse, the joint general manager, signed bonds of indemnity which would be forfeit to the Nyasaland government in the event that the association defaulted on the terms of the agreement.[20] Sharpe seconded a protectorate official, C. Knipe, to accompany the recruits to Johannesburg and his salary with a cost of living allowance became a charge on the recruiting association. Finally, Sharpe permitted the WNLA to bring 200 headmen from Nyasaland to tour the mines in the hope they would promote enlistment on their return.[21] The workers whom the WNLA brought to the Rand under this arrangement turned out to be very expensive to recruit and transport. By June 1904, the association had imported only 921 at a cost which when repatriation expenses were included reached eleven pounds for each individual, not including the protectorate government's ten-shilling fee for each recruit. WNLA officials hoped to reduce these charges substantially once they secured permission to recruit larger numbers.[22]

The experiment began as it ended ten years later with persistent reports of endemic illness, high death rates, and chronic complaints by the workers about the terms and conditions of service. The first group of several hundred workers arrived on the Rand at the very worst time of the year, in the middle of winter. They were completely unused to the frosty climate, did not receive adequate clothing and were sent immediately to work underground at the Robinson Deep. An influenza epidemic broke out at once. Of those who remained fit about 300 refused to go underground, stating they had accepted contracts only for surface work. When Native Affairs Department officials warned of the consequences of breach of contract, all but eighty-four did go into the mine. A magistrate sentenced the recalcitrants to fourteen days' hard labour, but Lagden had the sentence remitted a few days later when the eighty-four asked to be sent back to the mine.[23] Despite these and other problems the imperial government permitted the recruitment of an additional 5,000 Nyasaland workers in February 1904, but specified that they should not be brought to the Rand in winter. At the same time, the new colonial secretary, Lord Lyttelton, wrote to Milner and delivered a blunt warning. Mortality rates approaching one hundred per thousand per annum could not be defended. Parliament had expressed its concern, and the government must be able to show that the mines were taking precautions to safeguard the Nyasas. He also pointed out that if the Chinese, when they came, began to die at this rate, it would be "fatal" to the whole labour importation scheme.[24] Despite these expressions of concern and the introduction in 1905 of a Coloured Labourers' Health Ordinance, establishing minimum standards for compound accommodation and food, death rates persistently exceeded one hundred per thousand per annum. Yet the Transvaal governments urged that the "experiments" continue, and the Colonial Office acquiesced.

Pneumonia, meningitis, influenza, and various diseases related to diet deficiencies were the main killers. WNLA officials argued that these workers died in large numbers in their own countries. Since premature death was the way of life in Africa, according to this explanation, one need not be too concerned about mortality in the mining compounds. The ingenious C. Knipe, an official whom the protectorate government had seconded to the WNLA, argued that recruitment for the mines actually protected Nyasaland blacks since they died at home in even greater numbers than on the Rand. Thus to ban recruiting for the mines would only increase mortality among them.[25] The WNLA came to appreciate Knipe's qualities and later made him their district manager in northern Mozambique. Even the high commissioner was half persuaded by the argument, but the imperial government refused to lift the restrictions on numbers and on their employment in winter.[26] Chamber of Mines medical officers tried to explain the horrifying mortality by reference to the generally poor physical condition of the recruits and their consequent inability to stand the rigours of the Rand's winter climate at an altitude of 5,000 feet. Less interested contemporaries had no trouble seeing that bad food, cold, drafty compounds, and grossly inadequate clothing were major causes of illness and death. Moreover, the tropical recruits had developed no natural resistance to most of the diseases, especially pneumonia, which were endemic in the compounds. Since the mines had not yet built change houses at the shaft heads to protect the work-force (as they were later required to do), the miners faced daily a frequently long march to the compounds, dressed often only in the ragged shorts which were the typical uniform of the underground worker. Naturally these working conditions increased the vulnerability of the workforce.

After repeated warnings had failed to reduce mortality to tolerable levels, the imperial government banned recruiting in Nyasaland for underground work on the gold mines in 1906. Two years of persistent government efforts to persuade the WNLA and the mines to take more care had failed totally. The death rate actually increased. For the year ending 30 June 1906 it reached 166 per thousand per annum.[27] The government continued to permit limited recruiting for surface work on the mines, but the Randlords declined most of these permits, since they rarely had a shortage of volunteers for surface work. Those who did arrive died at a rate of about sixty-seven per thousand per annum.[28] In any event, large numbers of migrants from north of 22°SL continued to find their own way south to the mines, using the overland routes which skirted the eastern edge of Rhodesia's border with Mozambique. Independent recruiters established themselves in the adjacent parts of Mozambique to promote this, and WNLA agents there also took recruits who left Nyasaland either voluntarily or upon inducement by runners infiltrating the border areas.[29]

The tropical northern part of Mozambique which became an important region of WNLA operations presented different problems to the recruiters.

Over wide areas, the Portuguese had delegated powers of government to the chartered companies and particularly in the Zambesi valley to the prazo holders. At first, the Chamber of Mines argued that the *Modus Vivendi* gave the mines access to recruits throughout the colony, and that the Portuguese government as signatory to the agreement should enforce its terms on the chartered companies and the prazo holders. Quite naturally the companies and leaseholders affected resisted this interpretation and put counter-pressure on the colonial government in Lourenço Marques. Once again the Chamber of Mines sought the backing of Milner's administration, which through the Colonial Office requested the Foreign Office to intervene with Lisbon.[30] The WNLA sent one of its peripatetic general managers into the northern territories, and he managed to convey through not so subtle threats that the association intended to break into these areas by whatever means. Colonel Arnold, the local watchdog at Beira for British interests in the Mozambique company, wrote in protest to Milner:

Mr. Nourse, in discussion, maintained that the co-operation of British Authorities with the Administration of this territory in the prevention of illicit recruiting of labour by unauthorized agents is practically dependent upon permission being given to the authorized agents, viz., the Witwatersrand Native Labour Association, to recruit here. By this he managed to convey to the Governor [of the Company] and Director of Mines something which they uneasily regard as a threat that with or without their permission the labour supply of this territory will be tapped for the benefit of the British Hinterland.[31]

Nourse denied the charge, of course, and Milner replied placatingly that he was sure the WNLA had been misunderstood. In any event Nourse's "threat" became a remarkably accurate prediction.[32] The company declined to permit recruiting, and the illicit touts and bandits, both white and black, continued to ensure that for many years there would be large southward flows of labour from and through the Mozambique company's territories.

Of course the WNLA in partnership with the Transvaal government did not merely threaten. The association could offer substantial inducements to cooperating jurisdictions as the initial agreement to recruit in Nyasaland showed. In northern Mozambique both the Nyassa Chartered Company and the Zambesia Company signed agreements with the WNLA in 1903. The WNLA contracted with the Zambesia Company to pay its representatives two pounds for each recruit supplied to the association's depots at Quilimane and Chinde. The association agreed to defer most of the recruits' wages which would be paid through the Zambesia Company to the workers' families or used to meet the cost of repatriation at the end of the twelve-month contract. Opportunities for profit were thus large both to the Zambesia Company itself and its agents. In 1909 this agreement was extended to give WNLA recruiters access to the labour of the chartered company's prazo holders. Certain of the leaseholders, notably the London sugar baron, J.P. Hornung, put up a stiff resistance, however, and prevented the WNLA from making much use of the agreement before the ban on recruitment and employment of workers from tropical territories went into effect in mid-1913.[33]

The WNLA's treaty with the Nyassa Company included a number of similar features. Substantial direct and indirect benefits accrued to the company for each recruit removed from its territories. In this case WNLA agents did the recruiting but had to be licensed (at £100 pounds per licence per year; £10 for a runner) by the company. As in the case of the agreement with the Zambesia Company, the WNLA held back half of the wages from the twelve-month contract for payment in the home territories after the workers' return. The terms provided less opportunity for chartered company agents to defraud the workers of their deferred pay, since the WNLA itself paid the money directly to the worker at his place of embarkation for home. A Nyassa Company official certified that the wages had been paid. The direct fees payable by the WNLA to the company for each recruit amounted to thirteen shillings for a twelve-month contract and twenty-five shillings for the longer contract.[34] After 1911, Nyassa Company officials themselves did the recruiting and delivered to WNLA agents along the coast.

Before about 1908, relatively few workers from the Nyassa company's territories went to the Rand. The WNLA intensified its efforts in 1907-8 as part of the major push to replace the departing Chinese. Barry Neil-Tomlinson pointed out that South African mining firms were prominent in the capital restructuring which took place at about that time. Additional capital amounting to £250,000 was provided, which the company used to finance its "brutal campaigns of conquest." Neil-Tomlinson argued that the contributing companies, with strong financial ties to the Rand, conceived of the Nyassa Company primarily as the manager of a labour reserve and saw their contributions to its refinancing in these terms. Of the companies he names, however, only one, Johannesburg Consolidated Investment, was at all prominent in the WNLA. Whatever the motives of those who provided the capital of the company, there is no doubt that the WNLA did mount a major recruiting operation there during 1909.[35]

Africans recruited in northern Mozambique did not die on the mines at quite the same rate as those from Nyasaland, but the mortality was still terrible and far higher than that experienced by migrants from the South African territories.[36] By 1905, tropical Africans constituted about 10 per cent of the labour force but contributed 28.2 per cent of the total number of deaths. They died at the rate of 127 per thousand per annum as compared with the overall death rate of 46.[37] Africans from northern Mozambique experienced death rates of 75.99 per thousand in 1907 and 78.11 in

1908. Nearly 1,200 of these workers died in the two years out of a work-force of 6,856 in 1907 and 8,572 in 1908. The ban imposed on Nyasaland recruiting in 1906 did not apply in the tropical parts of Mozambique. The labour supply from these districts, while not a large percentage of the total, increased steadily and in 1910 reached 17,577.[38]

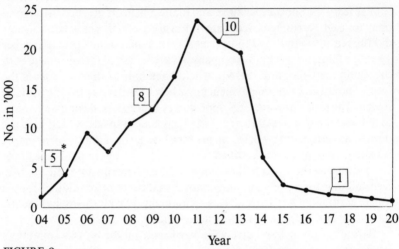

FIGURE 9

Mineworkers from Northern Mozambique and Nyasaland, 1904–20 +

SOURCES: Chamber of Mines and WNLA *Annual Reports*; Native Labour Bureau estimates.
NOTE: Recruited Africans and voluntaries are included; data are approximate (see app. 1 for actual figures).
* Indicates per cent of total labour supply.
+ Tropical recruiting was banned in 1913; figures for tropical workers on the mines after that date do not include the many Africans from tropical territories employed illegally on the gold mines.

During 1907, the Transvaal government, now in the hands of Het Volk, renewed efforts to secure access for the mines to the labour of Nyasaland: "[Ministers] regret His Majesty's Government decision not to sanction the employment of natives from tropical territories. . . . Ministers again call attention to probability of natives in British Central Africa finding their way down to gold mines independently without supervision and resultant increased danger to health."[39] Determined to end the importation of Chinese labour, Botha and his colleagues had to tap every available southern African source, particularly the potentially important tropical territories, in pursuit of their policy of "repatriation and replacement." To its credit, the Liberal government in Britain, though equally determined to end Chinese labour, declined to permit a resumption of recruiting in Nyasaland. It did relax the ban to the point of permitting the WNLA to arrange transport for voluntaries who informed the magistrates of their intention to leave.[40]

The justification of this was that since the voluntaries were going anyway and the government lacked the power to stop them, it was preferable that they go under WNLA discipline, using the associations's established land/sea route south to Lourenço Marques and then by rail to the Rand. There were also the obvious revenue benefits for the colonial government. Elsewhere, especially in tropical Mozambique, recruiting had continued and by 1909 slightly over 12,000 blacks from those territories had found employment on the mines. The Transvaal minister of native affairs considered that this number was too small and left "a large margin for development."[41] His colleague, J.C. Smuts, urged London to intercede with Lisbon and overturn the Mozambique chartered company's ban on recruiting for the gold mines in its huge territories north of 22°SL. Milner had tried but failed to do this in 1902. Now the Botha government was no more successful.[42] Given the compelling need to develop local sources of supply, so that the Chinese might be speedily replaced, the Transvaal government persuaded itself with little difficulty that the WNLA would be able to correct the problem of excessive mortality.

In throwing its support behind tropical recruiting for the gold mines, the Botha government disregarded the private advice of the WNLA chairman, F. Perry. Shortly after the new government came into office at the beginning of 1907, Perry prepared a memorandum on the whole question.[43] He reviewed the difficulties which had accompanied efforts to develop these sources of supply. The workers died in large numbers, recruiting costs were high, and the survivors tended to be quite inefficient. Despite this, Perry believed that large numbers of these workers could ultimately be obtained: "If a Mozambique, or a British Central African survives one season and comes down a second time, he will probably survive that also, and if we ever reach the stage when fifty per cent of these boys are Old Mine Boys ... the mortality rate among them will probably show a considerable decrease ... The rate of mortality will depend mainly on the number of 'salted' as compared with the number of raw boys." Perry's memorandum displayed crude racialism and social Darwinist assumptions. He attributed tropical mortality almost exclusively to the supposed inherent biological weakness of the workers and their poor physique, which were important factors, but he ignored the demonstrably dangerous and unhealthy conditions on the mines. In a private note to the minister accompanying the memorandum, however, he did show an awareness of the human issue. Despite the view expressed in the memorandum that the tropical labour supply could be significantly developed, he argued in the private communication against continuance. A death rate in excess of 100 per thousand per annum was not "a thing which should be tolerated ... by any modern government." But the state must take the responsibility for the decision; it could not "fairly or safely" be left to the employers. When the mines experienced labour shortage, they could not be expected to abstain from the employment of tropical workers unless compelled to do so by legislation. When Rissik, the minister, and his colleagues took their decision to support continued access to Nyasaland and the other northern territories, they let short-run political needs overrun the moral issue raised by Perry.

With the coming of Union, however, the situation changed once more. By 1911 the government had demonstrated the success of its policy of "repatriation and replacement" and the last of the Chinese were leaving the mines. Local recruiting levels jumped spectacularly in 1908–10, particularly in the eastern Cape which only recently had developed into a major recruiting centre second only to Mozambique. Concerning the tropicals, the WNLA had failed to make good on its pledges, and the death rate constituted an obvious scandal. With local Africans and recruits from south of 22°SL offering themselves in larger numbers, the case for continued importation from the northern districts became harder to make. Thus when F.H.P. Creswell began to attack the policy in Parliament and when his charges attracted widespread publicity, the authorities found themselves compelled to act.[44] Creswell simply used the issue in his campaign for an all-white Rand, but there was no denying the essential truth of his attack. The Creswell campaign was one important element in the government's decision to look more closely at the WNLA operation.

As a result Henry Burton convened his important meeting with the Chamber of Mines executive in July 1911. After discussing various matters connected with recruiting in South Africa itself, the minister turned to the problem of tropical mortality on the mines; and he castigated the chamber for its grossly inadequate measures to protect the health of the mineworkers. He had recently toured several of the mines, found a horrifying situation, and now bluntly informed the mining executives that "all I can say is that it is a regular slaughter that is going on."[45] Chamber spokesmen replied with the arguments which they had used for years to justify the continuation of tropical recruiting. They said that they were working on the problem: "We want to say that we have done a great deal, but it is not the best we can do: we are going to do better." They asked about the death rates in the home areas of the recruits, as if to suggest that a high death rate in the African countryside excused a high death rate on the Rand. And they speculated that perhaps "those who die here might be of such a low physique that they would have died in any case." Although in 1907 the Transvaal government had solemnly repeated similar arguments when attempting to persuade the imperial authorities to relax their ban on Nyasaland recruiting, the Union government was no longer prepared to be so complacent. Indeed Burton issued a blunt warning: "What I want to bring to your notice is that this is not simply a talkee talkee about things. The Government is most seriously concerned about the thing; and exactly what immediate steps we will take we have not decided yet, but I am bound to tell you that it seems to me to be as grave as it possibly can be, and mining industry or no mining industry we have to answer [to] the country."[46] Finally, Burton gave the chamber representatives a stern lecture: "You see how this whole thing strikes me. I came down here for as much time as I can give. I make a casual visit to some of these mines, and on the very surface of it a poor lay man like myself is struck with these things. You say you are going to inquire: how is it that these things have not struck the mining people years ago? Here are these fellows lying in their beds and dying off like a lot of rats. Nobody does a thing. It is very hard indeed for the Government to show sympathy with regard to matters of this kind when that is the state of affairs. I saw it myself."[47]

Despite the minister's evident shock at the conditions he saw on his tour and despite the declared intention to act, tropical recruiting continued for another two years. The inquiry commission was set up immediately, however, and it toured Mozambique later in 1911. The commission recommended a number of improvements in compound conditions at Ressano Garcia and condemned the inadequate medical supervision at the WNLA hospital there.[48] Concerning the conduct of actual recruiting operations, the committee reported very favourably on the WNLA system and recommended strongly against any breach in the monopsony. This was accepted by the government without much discussion. That the authorities dropped the matter so readily may indicate that they were merely using the threat of competitive recruiting as a lever to force changes from the WNLA on the health problem.

Even on the immediate issue of tropical recruiting, the administration drew back in the end from the drastic action which Burton had threatened. However, the Native Affairs Department did begin to monitor more closely the new steps taken by the mining industry to protect the health of the tropical labour force. It seems that government health regulations were themselves partly responsible for the death rate. The Coloured Labourers' Health Ordinance of 1905 required the installation of large ventilators at both ends of the compounds. These could not easily be closed and the resulting cold, draughty conditions in winter increased vulnerability to pneumonia and related diseases.[49] Prodded by the government, the mines introduced change-houses at the shaft heads so that the overheated mine workers coming off shift would be properly dressed before going out into the cold of the high veld winter. Sometime before the interview with the minister, the WNLA had appointed an official to make regular tours of inspection and to check on the performance of individual mines on health matters. He reported to a special committee of the Chamber of Mines which in turn sent regular assessments to the minister of native affairs.[50] Over the next eighteen months, the association made an undoubted effort to protect

TABLE 9

Shifts Lost through Accident and Illness, April 1913

Group	Average Number Employed	Shifts Lost
Central Mining	38,145	32,172
Consolidate Mines Selection	4,729	5,503
ERPM	23,626	24,105
General Mining	17,816	13,225
Goerz and Co.	6,357	6,468
Gold Fields	21,905	31,448
JCI	16,857	13,663
S. Neumann	14,159	15,765
Randfontein	32,322	19,408
Rand Mines*	29,029	26,556
Other	5,254	3,030
Totals	210,199	191,343

SOURCE: NTS 205, 2782/473.

* Administered as part of the Central Mining group.

the health of tropicals more effectively, as the director of native labour acknowledged.[51]

Despite these inquiries and other government pressures, conditions on a number of the mines remained very unsatisfactory and resulted in a large number of deaths monthly. In many cases apparently, individual mine managers and their compound overseers simply stalled and failed to respond when the WNLA recommended improvements. The WNLA management worked actively to secure reform; the Chamber of Mines executive had received blunt warnings from the minister; but none of this became translated into adequate action at the level of the individual mine. Doubtless callous indifference and racialist unconcern constitute part of the explanation. However, there were also countervailing pressures. Mine managers faced continuous scrutiny from their group administrators obsessed with the imperatives of cost minimization. Group mining engineers and even the occasional Randlord himself could always be found prowling the mines, checking for signs of waste and inefficiency. Group accountants pored over the books with similar zeal. Some of the highest mortality rates were experienced on mines of the Central Mining group. As long-time leaders of the chamber, Lionel Phillips and his colleagues had accepted the need to address the health problem. However, they failed to communicate this adequately to the individual managers. What they did communicate very effectively was the group's relentless zeal to drive down costs and increase profits.

Small wonder that improvements which interfered with efficiency, which required capital expenditure, or even some additional white supervision seem often to have been ignored or forgotten.[52] Thus the WNLA reform efforts failed, and the government acted in mid-1913 to enforce a ban not merely on the recruitment but also on the employment of tropical labour.

Before taking this final step, however, the authorities made one last effort to secure effective action. They now publicly exposed and condemned the situation in Parliament.[53] Criticisms which the minister had made privately to the industry in mid-1911 he repeated in the House of Assembly debate on the Creswell motion (he introduced it annually) in March 1912. Henry Burton spoke plainly of his visit to the mines several months before, and he condemned a situation which "speaking with a full sense of reponsibility could only have existed because of a cynical disregard of human life and ordinary common humanity." The Chamber of Mines had been bluntly told, he explained to the House, that unless there was further improvement, importation would be stopped completely. He acknowledged that there had been some reforms but pointed out that the industry could take no credit for this: "the damning thing is that since this warning has been given, this improvement has taken place." In any case, the change for the better was modest and confined to certain mines. There were others, including some of the Rand's largest employers, Central Mining and the Randfontein group among them, where the mortality remained enormous. Burton agreed that the responsibility rested with management at the highest level: "all the information in his office showed clearly that there was a distinct connection between the high rate of mortality and the management of these mines." There was no medical mystery here, just hard, ruthless group administration which drove the individual mine management to ever greater cost-cutting measures at the expense of the work force. Burton mentioned some of the positive steps which had been taken. The chamber had commissioned an inquiry by the British medical expert, Sir Almoth Wright; the search for an antipneumococcal vaccine had begun. All this was hopeful, but the death rate remained far too high and the government had determined to act. With Burton's speech, the cabinet tried to capture the moral ground of humanitarian concern now occupied, egregiously, by Creswell. The minister's indignation would have been more impressive if several of members of the government had not themselves earlier supported the reintroduction of tropical labour, despite the known health risk, and if the authorities, including Burton himself, had been quicker to act than they were. It took repeated parliamentary exposure of what was, by contemporary standards, an industrial health scandal of grave proportions to prompt the minister's public expression of indignation.

A few months after the debate in the House of Assembly, the Native Affairs Department moved a step closer to complete prohibition of the use

TABLE 10
Mortality Rate on Gold Mines, 1910–11

Category	Average No. Employed	1910 Deaths	Rate/1,000	Average No. Employed	1911 Deaths	Rate/1,000
Nyasaland	3,718	366	98.4	1,925	152	78.9
All Tropicals	19,278	1,465	76.0	23,903	1,550	64.8
Non-Tropicals	171,505	4,220	24.6	189,538	4,354	23.0

SOURCE: NTS 190, 377/473, acting DNL to SNA, 31/1/12.

of this labour. As a result of discussions with the director of native labour and other officials, the WNLA agreed to deny tropical labour to mines where the death rate remained high. WNLA officials had themselves privately suggested this when their own impotence to force improvements from the mining companies became obvious.[54] The association also pledged to withdraw such labour from any mine should the Native Labour Bureau request it to do so. During April 1913, shortly before the ban went into effect, the labour bureau conducted an intensive review of the health situation in the compounds of the principal mining groups.[55] This showed that the results of the reform effort had been far from satisfactory. During the month, the mines employed an average of 210,199 workers. Of these nearly 10 per cent were sufficiently incapacitated as a result of illness or accident to remain off shift on each working day during April. In total this represented a loss of 191,343 shifts for that month alone. Since rates of illness and death remained much higher among the tropical workers, they must have contributed a very disproportionate share of this alarming total.

The director concluded that most of the groups remained callously indifferent to the fate of these workers, despite years of intense government pressure and efforts by the chamber and the WNLA to bring the gravity of the situation to the attention of individual mining groups. Describing conditions in the mine hospitals, Pritchard estimated that the medical officers averaged about an hour a day with the black patients. There were exceptions – doctors who "devoted themselves" to these workers – but they were very rare. He agreed with the view of his inspectors on the Rand that the standard of medical care remained "shockingly inadequate." Where proper medical care had been given and careful nursing, particularly with the pneumonia cases, "comparatively low rates of mortality" were always found.

Given the continuing gravity of the health situation and the damaging publicity which it was now receiving, the state had little choice but to act on its pledge to terminate the use of the "tropicals" entirely. The new minister of native affairs, J.W. Sauer, made the announcement in Parliament and only two days later wrote to inform the WNLA.[56] Despite the endless threats and warnings repeatedly given over the previous months, industry officials were still shocked that the axe had finally fallen and did not disguise their hostility. The director of the labour bureau suspected that the chamber doubted the government's resolve and hoped that the minister could somehow be persuaded to reconsider.[57] Once finally brought to a decision, however, the Botha government refused to reopen the matter even when, toward the end of World War I, the Low Grade Mines Commission argued for a new round of experiments. Immediately after the original ban was announced, the WNLA briefly considered a legal challenge to the government's action. There was in fact some doubt that the authorities had the legislative power to ban the "tropicals," but an amendment to the emigrants' restriction bill then before Parliament put the matter beyond question.[58]

During the decade which followed, the industry did put its medical services in order. Centralized, properly equipped and staffed hospitals were set up, in place of the frequently unsatisfactory facilities provided previously by the individual mining groups. Change-houses for workers coming off shift were universally introduced. The establishment of the South African Institute of Medical Research, jointly by the state and the industry, and the later development of the Lister antipneumococcal vaccine represented major triumphs. These undoubted successes should not obscure, however, the record of the first thirty years when a ruthless and short-sighted drive for maximum labour mobilization and efficiency led the mines to persist in the employment of workers from the tropical territories without regard to the horrifying incidence of serious illness and death. Callous neglect and indifference characterized the response of most of the mining groups to a mortality rate which was shocking even by the standards of the age. According to one estimate, nearly 50,000 black mineworkers died during the single decade, 1902-12.[59]

Most of the migrants from north of 22°SL did not enter South Africa through the facilities provided by the WNLA before the ban was imposed. They made their own way south and often fell into the hands of clandestine recruiters operating on and beyond the northern Transvaal border. This part of the migrant labour flow from the northern territories was little affected by the government decision to prohibit their employment on gold mines. To bring the clandestine traffic in black labour under control required a prolonged and costly administrative effort. South Africa's northern frontier areas made an ideal infiltration point for those migrants and labour touts bent on evading the restriction. This wild, inhospitable country where South Africa's borders intersected with those of Mozambique and Rhodesia had never been effectively controlled by any colonial government. Infested with the tsetse fly and malarial mosquito, the border area contained only scattered African communities and practically no resident whites. None of the three governments maintained any permanent police or administrative presence in this difficult wasteland; they merely sent the occasional police patrol which would soon withdraw again. On the South African side of the Limpopo, a sub-native commissioner resided at Sibasa, perhaps three days' ride to the south. The nearest police post of any size was the district commandant's headquarters at Pietersburg, over two hundred miles further west. He sent a patrol along the river boundary from time to time but lacked the men to do anything more substantial to police the area. The Portuguese and Rhodesian presence in their respective sectors of the border area was equally insubstantial.

Since the 1890s, the far northeastern Transvaal had been the most notorious centre of illegal recruiting in the entire subcontinent. Its importance in this respect derived not from the size of the local black population, which was small, especially close to the border, but from its strategic location on the main route used by large numbers of the black migrants from the far north, especially Nyasaland and northern Rhodesia. According to a Nyasaland official, the movement of Nyasas south to the Rand began in about 1898 when Tsonga residents on the west bank of Lake Malawi began to migrate in large numbers. This informant stressed the horrors of the journey and the privations suffered by these early migrants. Many died along the way. Some fell ill and were "left to the mercy of wild beasts." Others again were robbed by the touts and thieves who infested the migration routes and lived by preying on the traffic. Although this officer was making a case for WNLA recruiting in Mozambique (claiming this would protect the migrants from the touts), all of the evidence supports his conclusion that conditions along the way were "terrible."[60]

They remained bad throughout the period covered by this study. Despite the risks of the journey by the unpopulated routes south from Nyasaland along the Rhodesia-Mozambique border to the Limpopo, many migrants preferred it to travel via the established Rhodesian transport system. Use of the latter meant a real possibility of coercion into low-wage employment. Equally important, few Nyasa Africans could afford the stiff rail fares charged for travel through to the Rand. Given the risks of death or serious illness by the border route, the migrants' preference for it was a notable comment about Rhodesian wage rates, the reputation of its employers, and the high cost of transport.[61] As late as 1935, 90 per cent of Nyasaland migrants still travelled south on foot.[62] The early migrants had much to fear from wild beasts. Later the more serious danger came from those in human form. During the period 1917–20, Nyasaland emigrants suffered severely from reprisals by the Barue and other insurgents against the Portuguese in Tete and adjacent provinces along the Zambesi. Large numbers of them were caught and killed as Portuguese collaborators during the Makombe rising.[63]

As elsewhere in southern Africa, recruiting for the gold mines from beyond the Limpopo became an elaborate, highly organized business. For most of this period it belonged to unlicensed touts and their black runners. Not until they had crossed into South Africa itself did the intending mineworkers become attached to the NRC or one of the licensed labour contractors. Because their writ did not run in Rhodesia or the adjacent parts of Mozambique, most of the South African recruiters had to work with unlicensed touts and even white bandits who did operate there. Since ruthless competition for labour was the rule in these transborder regions and because no government exercised effective supervision, the mine labour recruiters could not be squeamish about their methods or their allies. A recruiter could expect that few workers indeed would reach his depot at Pietersburg or Sibasa if he did not make a deal with one of the touts operating across the border. A rival agent would surely get them or they would end up in nonmining employment in the Transvaal or under severe discipline on some mine or farm in Rhodesia or Mozambique. Since the touts offered their services to southward-moving migrants frequently at gunpoint, all of the established agents perceived that they needed allies across the Limpopo who were equally persuasive.[64]

Charles van Onselen has argued that the ability of many thousands of black migrants to evade low-wage employers in Rhodesia and Mozambique testifies to their own enterprise. He also pointed to the sophisticated intelligence network developed by these workers which enabled them to identify the safest routes south and to sell their labour in the best market. Van Onselen emphasized the organized recruiting carried on by the Rhodesian Native Labour Bureau but did not stress the key role of the labour touts and brigands, operating outside the formal recruiting structures.[65] These men had critical advantages in the struggle to control the stream of migrant labour and few migrants could avoid their "services." They operated frequently outside the law; they often went armed and lay in wait at the various junction points along the routes through which most migrants had necessarily to pass. A recruit from Nyasaland faced a journey of six to eight weeks or more through the most difficult territory where he was usually a stranger. Few recruits had adequate food or other supplies for the journey, and they had to make the trip in the shortest possible time. Poorly equipped, unarmed or carrying only a spear, travelling in small groups or even alone, the migrants were naturally vulnerable to the touts and thieves who waited for them along all of the main routes. New, unexpected hazards could develop at any time along the way, and this increased the vulnerability of the migrants.

When recruiting in Nyasaland by the WNLA for the Rand mines was banned on humanitarian grounds in 1906, migration did not stop or even slow down. It carried on as before but now almost completely unregulated.

Nyasaland employers paid meagre wages even by the abysmal standards of neighbouring colonies. Conditions on most estates were also grim; in the adjacent province of Mozambique, Hornung's sugar estates paid higher wages and provided superior living conditions for the work-force, many of whom were emigrant Nyasas.[66] Since the Nyasaland government could not adequately police its borders, it had little if any control over the flow of labour south. Nor did the ban in any way stop recruiting; the labour agents, including WNLA representatives, simply moved their camps across the frontiers into the adjacent parts of Mozambique.[67] WNLA representatives picked up as many workers as they could, forwarded them to Beira on the coast, and then by the sea/rail route to Lourenço Marques and on to Johannesburg. Since they now lacked privileged access to Nyasaland, the association's agents faced severe competition from their many rivals within the mine labour system and outside it.[68] On the overland journey south, a network of touts apparently developed, and the migrants were passed from hand to hand. Just as the migrants moved south in this way, so the money and recruiting fees moved north. The last tout in the chain who sold his labour to the NRC agent or Seelig representative at Makulekas or Pietersburg in the northern Transvaal collected, in effect, for each link in the system. This overland route along the Rhodesia/Mozambique border developed as an alternative to the safer WNLA route, and the touts did everything they could to promote it..

This is not to suggest that the WNLA record was in any way distinguished. Like its sister organization, the NRC, later the WNLA could not ignore the prevailing methods in the business. Thus its agents were right down there with the worst of them. Take the case of E. Compton Thomson who was operating on the Zambesi during 1909.[69] He was a failed "native storekeeper" from Rhodesia who became a recruiter for Hornung's Chimbwe sugar estates in northern Mozambique during 1907. The Nyasaland government gave him permission to recruit 1,500 workers for this employer in the following year. According to the Nyasaland superintendent of native affairs, Thomson simply took another 1,200 recruits without bothering to secure permission. Denied further permits to recruit in Nyasaland, Thomson left the sugar estates and moved into Chimbwe itself, ostensibly to grow rice but really to tout illegally for labour. He had apparently made a deal with the WNLA recruiter at Beira. Before long, Thomson began to entice labour away from his former employers in order to sell them a second time to the WNLA.[70]

When the Nyasaland authorities asked the Mozambique government to stop the flow of Nyasa labour through Beira, Thomson, always with an eye to the main chance, demanded compensation from the Colonial Office for loss of business. According to Sir Alfred Sharpe, the governor of Nyasaland, Thomson was only one of many touts established "round our borders." They sent runners into the protectorate and lived by enticing blacks across the border. Under pressure from Nyasaland planters to keep local labour at home, Sharpe stressed that "there is absolutely no guarantee that such men as they succeed in obtaining will be put under definite agreements, properly cared for, returned to their homes, or fed on the journey."[71] C. Knipe, the WNLA district manager, stated that he had refused to employ Compton Thomson, but the Nyasaland authorities suspected that the association was taking recruits from him. [72] The Union government also made inquiries to the WNLA head office in Johannesburg on this subject.[73] While the Mozambique Chartered Company in northern Mozambique did not allow the WNLA to recruit in its territories, the recruiting company did maintain an office in Beira which forwarded voluntaries, including Nyasaland blacks, to Johannesburg.[74] Despite intensified efforts by the Nyasaland government to discourage emigration, efforts which included fining and jailing returning migrants who had left as clandestine emigrants, the exodus continued at a high rate.[75] Apparently the lure of high wages more than offset concern about the dangers and rigours of the journey. Agents for the Rand gold mines took advantage of this and competed actively with local Mozambique employers – the nearby sugar estates – and Rhodesian farms and mines for the labour which the Nyasaland government lacked the means to keep at home. This could be a risky business. Writing to London in 1910, Lionel Phillips remarked that the WNLA had set up its agencies in these areas "with a good deal of trepidation." Fortunately, he added, "so far nobody has been wiped out."[76] The main competitors of the WNLA for Nyasa labour were the Manica and Sofala Labour Bureau, an agency of the Mozambique Chartered Company, the Rhodesian Native Labour Bureau and the Zambesia Chartered Company, all of which kept touts and agents at the main exit points from Nyasaland.[77] Local Mozambique employers, notably the nearby sugar estates, also sought every available Nyasa worker.[78]

A few years later, in 1912, a new Nyasaland governor, W.H. Manning, acknowledged that large numbers of blacks left as work-seekers annually. Only total prohibition of their employment on the Rand would halt the flow, he believed. Merely to continue the ban on recruiting for the Rand would not be enough. Of course, when the Union government took this step a year later, in mid-1913, it did not stop the movement of labour south.[79] Tropical Africans continued to find employment illegally on the gold mines and legally on the coal fields and sugar estates of Natal. Because the ban on the employment of tropical labour included one of the most popular and important groups of mineworkers, the Mozambique Shangaans, recruiters quite naturally worked assiduously to evade the law. Both the NRC and the Randfontein recruiter, H. Seelig, almost certainly connived in their unlawful employment on the Rand. When they arrived at the native commissioners' offices to have their contracts attested, these illegal immigrants had been well schooled to claim residence in some Mozambique district south of 22°SL.[80] THE 1913 restriction did end the system, however, through which the WNLA had arranged transport for volunteers from Nyasaland via Beira. This left the overland routes as the main paths of southward migration and threw the migrants even more into the hands of the unlicensed agents and thieves who infested these areas. The migrants benefited little if at all from a measure aimed to promote their interests. High mortality prompted the ban on their employment in gold mines, but the migration continued and so did the mine employment. The ban acted not only to make the southward journey more hazardous, but it also had another unfortunate effect.

Because the employment of tropicals had been declared illegal, the substantial numbers of such workers who continued to find employment on the mines lost the partial protection which official recognition and control, haphazard and inefficient though it was, had provided. State regulation of their conditions of service naturally ceased, but even this was not the worst effect of the ban. Once the last of the pre-1913 tropicals had left the mines, this category of worker no longer appeared in the Chamber of Mines statistical returns of illness and mortality. Officially, tropical labour was no longer "a problem." The mines continued to employ them; presumably they died as before; but now they disappeared statistically in the much larger numbers of Union and southern Mozambique workers who were far less vulnerable to poor health and working conditions on the Rand. The lower overall mortality rate diluted the very high rate experienced by the Nyasaland and northern Mozambique workers. On the other hand, these clandestine tropicals did benefit like all mineworkers from the rapidly improving health conditions and medical supervision on the mines in the second decade of the century. The South African state lacked the capacity to enforce its ban on the recruitment and employment of tropical labour; it succeeded only in driving the issue out of the public view. This in itself was a major gain both for the government and the mining industry. For years Creswell and the Labourites had embarrassed them both in Parliament by publicizing the tropical mortality scandal; the ban at least denied these persistent critics a potent weapon. However, there is some evidence that the government was not motivated only by political considerations, that it did genuinely want to see a reduction of the extremely high mortality rate experienced by the tropical workers. Henry Burton's various pronouncements on the subject certainly suggest as much.

By 1913, most of the mine labour recruiting organizations and labour contractors were operating in the northern Transvaal, either openly or in clandestine fashion. From their district headquarters at Pietersburg or Sibasa, they sent out licensed agents and touts, most of whom based themselves near the trading store at Makulekas. This place was close to the border, and lay on a route favoured by many of the illegal immigrant work-seekers. The agents had little to fear from the very occasional police patrol. One native affairs official estimated in 1913 that 16 recruiters operated in the Makulekas area. Of these only four held Union recruiting licences and even they were in cahoots with the touts.[81] Since many of the work-seekers arrived on the Transvaal border in a starving condition, they had little choice but to seek out the store at Makulekas and thus almost inevitably to fall into the hands of one gang of recruiters or another.[82]

Clearly a very large traffic in illegal immigrants had developed. In the immediate vicinity of the virtually uncontrolled border, thousands of recruits annually crossed into South Africa. Further south at Sibasa where the Union government had authority, and where the Native Affairs Department was represented, the native commissioner could not control recruiting or identify very many of the prohibited immigrants after they were swept into the mines recruiting system. He complained about the "undesirable and immoral gang" of touts who controlled recruiting in his district and implied that even here police supervision was ineffective.[83] He had little to propose beyond the obviously limited suggestion that the government deny these men rights of residence on land it controlled.

Conditions at Sibasa and other established northern Transvaal centres gradually improved, something which did not happen in the remote corner of the northeastern Transvaal at Makulekas. Throughout the period covered by this study, it remained a zone of illegal touting and lawlessness. Government regulations not only failed to arrest the flow of clandestine immigrants and to end touting, but also the abortive efforts to control the situation may actually have promoted anarchy. Officials at Sibasa, who were closest to the problem, took this view. After noting the prohibitions on the employment and recruitment of tropical labour in 1913, the native commissioner explained that the restrictions "have [actually] been favourable to the illicit man who made it evident to the tropical labourer that but through him he could not get to the Rand to work."[84] In this way also the ban on the employment and recruitment of tropical labour for the gold mines had serious unwanted consequences.

Competition was so great that the few established employers in the area had great difficulty getting and keeping labour for their enterprises. Agents in the employ of the gold mines and other large-scale businesses elsewhere in South Africa scoured the region for every available black worker. The Messina copper mine near the Limpopo River employed several hundred miners, almost all unrecruited voluntaries, many of whom crossed the river from Rhodesia. Mine management employed no recruiters and relied totally on the workers making their own way to the company's compounds. As competitive recruiting intensified in the area, the mine began to lose its labour supply, and the manager, J. Allan Woodburn, wrote in alarm to the director of native labour to complain.[85] Labour agents lay in wait in the vicinity of the mine to intercept his workers and to divert them for employment in the south. Not content with this, the touts also invaded his property and stole labour right out of the Messina compounds. Woodburn demanded that the whole region be declared a labour district under the Native Labour Regulation Act of 1911 and recruiting there prohibited entirely. This was eventually done, but the mine continued to experience very serious labour theft.

Conditions governing recruiting on and beyond the northern border deteriorated to the point where Union government officials began to press more vigorously for remedial action. Late in 1912, H.J. Kirkpatrick, the district commandant of the South African Police for the Zoutpansberg area, toured the Limpopo during his annual leave. A few months later, C.A. Wheelwright, the long-time chief native commissioner for the region, prepared a report for Edward Dower, the Union secretary for native affairs.[86] Kirkpatrick wrote strongly urging reform. A deplorable situation had arisen and could not be allowed to continue. Throughout the northern Transvaal, he explained, "most of the country Store Keepers, and even many of the farmers are in the swim, and are the wheels within wheels by which the recruiting machinery is worked." Virtually the whole white population, he suggested, lived by "exploiting the native with the object of making money on his labour."[87] Recruiters and touts attracted very large fees which, according to Kirkpatrick, might go as high as seven to nine pounds. Their runners in turn received bounties of up to five pounds for recruits agreeing to twelve-month contracts. The police commandant saw social reasons for reform. The system was demoralizing both for "the natives," who received an exaggerated view of their own worth, and for the white recruiters who "live familiarly with the natives and their women, living with and no better than the natives themselves." Kirkpatrick had toured the whole border but thought conditions along the Limpopo in the vicinity of Makulekas the most alarming. Licensed agents camped along the river, purporting to recruit local blacks but actually to pursue "the profitable illegal recruiting trade" in Rhodesian, Nyasaland, and Mozambique tropicals. He met black runners in the pay of these agents who brought migrants to the river from the Mozambique or Rhodesian side and sold them to the highest bidder. Kirkpatrick condemned this "disgraceful state of affairs" which constituted "nothing more or less than a sort of slave trade." He thought the evil would grow uncontrollably unless recruiting both of local and foreign blacks was completely banned in the region.

Responding to Kirkpatrick's report, H.S. Cooke, the acting director of native labour, had some sympathy with the idea of a total ban but argued that it would not address the underlying problem.[88] Until adequate police supervision was provided at Makulekas, touting would continue whether or not the state had legislated to ban it. Without a continuous police presence reliable evidence of illegal activities could not be obtained in "these practically uninhabited wildernesses." Cooke was among the first to suggest that a permanent police post be established in this area, but the idea was rejected on grounds of expense.

C.A. Wheelwright, the native commissioner of the Zoutpansberg district, based his report on an earlier trip through the border regions and on talks with the NRC's northern Transvaal manager, David Erskine.[89] Wheelwright argued that the real source of the trouble lay far to the north of the Union's borders near the confluence of the Sabi and Lundi Rivers in Mozambique. The topography forced most travellers past this point, and a number of "irresponsible and lawless white men" had established themselves there to traffic in the migrant labour moving south. These men captured most of the workers and "sold" them to licensed recruiters on the South African side of the border. Fierce competition bred violence, and several murders had occurred. Because government authority was as poorly established in western Mozambique and the eastern Rhodesian border as it was in the northern Transvaal, the touts could "elude" the Rhodesian police and "defy" the Mozambique authorities. Believing that neither of these governments would pay the cost in money and in the lives of policemen (a high rate of deaths through disease could be expected) required to bring order to the area, Wheelwright suggested that private enterprise be mobilized to provide a solution. He wanted the WNLA to work with the Mozambique Chartered Company which nominally controlled the worst affected areas. For instance, a WNLA post near the Sabi-Lundi junction would siphon off much of the southward moving labour and undercut the touts. The problem had always been, however, to get the chartered company to agree. Alternatively, the Union government could try to deny residence to any black without a proper Portuguese pass. For this to work, the Portuguese would have to provide a police post at the Sabi-Lundi confluence and another one at the Limpopo corner, something they had shown absolutely no inclination to do. In any case the South African government itself lacked the staff even in the major centres to apprehend and then to identify any substantial number of illegal immigrants from the north. All it had been able to do was divert some of the flow to the mines and farms of Natal where conditions for tropicals seemed to be less unhealthy.

S.M. Pritchard, the director of native labour, who had meanwhile returned to duty, did not think much of Wheelwright's ideas.[90] A WNLA post at the point suggested by the native commissioner might divert migrants away from the illicit touts but it would also drain labour from bona fide northern Transvaal employers, notably the Messina Copper Mine. Greater police supervision was advocated for years by just about everybody who looked at the problem. The director thought the key to a solution lay in the recent formation of the Native Recruiting Corporation. If the NRC survived and succeeded in at least reducing if not eliminating endemic intra-industry competition, the most important root cause of anarchy on and beyond the border would fall away. This was obviously true, but Pritchard was far too sanguine about NRC prospects in the short run. The corporation needed over ten years to drive out or absorb its competitors completely.

Until 1919 and even after that date, the NRC had to contend with the labour contractors employed by the Randfontein mines. These contractors were long established and included some of the most able men in the business. Men of the experience and expertise of J.W. McKenzie, A.M. Mostert, and H. Seelig were not intimidated by the formation of the new recruiting organization. Just as they had earlier driven the WNLA out of South Africa, they now set out to defeat the NRC. In the short run, the emergence of the NRC probably produced intensified competition for labour. On the Union's Limpopo border, the NRC confronted the firm of H. Seelig. Seelig had established himself in the northern Transvaal as a recruiter in the 1890s.[91] Twenty years later he retained all of the contacts and intimate knowledge of the region and its people which made him a formidable rival. His company had recruited for the Robinson group, the Premier diamond mine, and other employers over many years and was not finally ousted until the eventual sale of the Robinson group to Johannesburg Consolidated Investment Corporation finally brought the former's recruiting operation into the NRC. So long as his recruiters remained in the field, the struggle for labour along the Union's borders continued unabated.[92]

Across the Limpopo, Rhodesian authorities became equally concerned about the growth of uncontrolled recruiting and lawlessness on their eastern borders. They knew that huge numbers of emigrants from the north who might at one time have found employment in Southern Rhodesia now used the eastern route to reach the higher wages on the Rand and elsewhere in South Africa. During 1915–16, the BSA Company police identified eighteen or nineteen illegal recruiters operating between the Limpopo and the Sabi-Lundi rivers, amply confirming Wheelwright's earlier comments.[93] Africans in the area had been terrorized for years, and the situation was plainly out of control. Of these illegal recruiters, three of the worst operated together and constituted a notorious gang, well known along the entire Mozambique border from the Limpopo to Melsetter far to the north. Charles Diegel was a German national, one accomplice, Barnard, an Afrikaner, and the other, Roux, was described by the authorities as a "Transvaal half-caste."[94] Repeated police patrols failed to pick up this unwholesome trio but found plenty of evidence of their work. The gang was armed, of course, and had thoroughly cowed the local population by burning kraals and systematically flogging and assaulting the inhabitants. There had been several murders in the area. In this heavily wooded region, Diegel and his associates easily evaded the police. They had good intelligence from their black collaborators and were familiar with all "the little known paths and water-holes used chiefly by recruiters and natives hunting."[95] At one stage the BSA Company police sent in a plainclothes patrol but with the same lack of success.[96] Only concerted action by the three governments could put a stop to these criminal gangs. Both the Rhodesian chief native commissioner and the commandant of police made this point in separate letters to the administrator, F.D.P. Chaplin.[97] Chaplin wrote to the Union government, pointing to the seriousness of the situation and proposing both to set up a new police station in the Chibi district and to strengthen the existing posts elsewhere along the border. He also noted that the root cause of the problem was the unrestricted competitive recruiting which South Africa continued to tolerate in the northern Transvaal.[98] Writing also to the governor of the Mozambique Chartered Company at Beira, Chaplin proposed to send another strong police patrol to try to apprehend the Barnard gang. He wanted to send the police twenty miles inside the Mozambique border and suggested that a Portuguese official accompany his men to make any arrests that might be possible.[99] This suggestion was accepted but met with no more success than the many earlier patrols.

Meanwhile, the Union government had also been reconsidering the situation, once it became clear that the establishment of the Native Recruiting Corporation by the Chamber of Mines in 1912 had done nothing to reduce competition for labour along the Transvaal's northern border. As early as 1913, the Union banned the recruitment of nonresident blacks for work outside the northern Transvaal area but could not enforce the restriction.[100] Recognizing this, local officials tried to bring the principal competitors in the NRC and Seelig organizations together in an effort to curb illegal activities. Through the good offices of the local notable, H. Mentz, MLA, E. Stubbs, the sub-native commissioner, Zoutpansberg, convened a meeting between the NRC's local manager, David Erskine, and H. Seelig himself. They met in Mentz's office and surprisingly made an agreement. Stubbs wrote in elation:

There was complete agreement on the following points, viz: (a) that competition be eliminated; (b) that no recruiting take place across the frontier, only boys presenting themselves voluntarily at Makuleka being accepted; (c) that the representative or representatives at that place be paid by salary and not commission; (d) that all recruits be forwarded to Pietersburg to be dealt with by the principals as to attestation, etc.; (e) that the fees, capitation money, etc. be pooled. The only point left undecided was that whereas I strongly urged the appointment of only one Agent for both organisations, Messrs. Erskine and Seelig preferred each to have a representative. I aim at abolishing competition altogether, but even the latter arrangement would be a great advance, as no further Police surveillance would be required.[101]

The acting director of native labour, H.S. Cooke, also held talks with officials of the NRC,[102] and after a good deal of further discussion, the recruiting corporation did enter into a formal contract with the H. Seelig organization.[103]

The parties agreed to limit their establishments at Makulekas to one white recruiter supported by ten black runners each. The contract also stipulated that Seelig and the NRC would receive volunteers only through the channels established at Makulekas. Neither side would recruit at Makulekas nor beyond the borders, and they agreed not to deal with the independent touts and bandits who roamed freely in the neighbouring parts of southeastern Rhodesia and the border areas of Mozambique. The two authorized recruiters received salaries rather than a commission, a step designed to remove a major incentive to cheating. The runners worked for a commission of ten shillings a recruit, which represented a sharp reduction of the extravagant rates paid by the companies under competitive conditions. The parties agreed to pool the total number of workers taken on at Makulekas on the basis of 65 per cent to the NRC and the balance to H. Seelig and Company.

Essentially this contract represented another small step toward the completion of the mine labour monopsony. Initially it involved only one company outside the NRC, H. Seelig, and it applied only in one area, the northeastern Transvaal. Moreover, the contract did not extend even to all of the recruits from that area but only to immigrants from across the northern borders. Because the two recruiting companies retained their separate organizations, though now on a much reduced scale, and because the illicit labour agents remained active in the field,[104] the agreement removed neither the ability nor the incentive of the parties to break it. Despite this, sub-native commissioner Stubbs, who had done much to bring the parties together, was sanguine at first that their compact would by itself eliminate the recruiting scandal in the area. A few months after the contract was signed, he noted that a number of the worst touts had vacated their "favourite haunts" around Makulekas because the licensed companies would no longer deal with them.[105] Yet Stubbs soon learned, as others had before him, that the industry's good intentions and self-policing by mine labour recruiters were worthless instruments to bring order to the labour market. Within less than two years, the NRC-Seelig agreement had collapsed completely, and illegal recruiting became once again a major problem for the authorities.

NRC officials were largely responsible for the breakdown. Certainly at the corporation's head offices in Johannesburg, officials called loudly and incessantly for the maintenance of honest methods in recruiting and for cooperation rather than competition between the agents; but such noble sentiments got short shrift from the NRC's own employees in the field. Early in 1918,

Stubbs reported from Sibasa that the NRC's man at Makulekas was apparently using the services of Barnard, now described as "a notorious body snatcher."[106] Like many of the touts, Barnard, Diegel, and Roux lived by stealing recruits at gunpoint, in this case from the unarmed runners employed by Seelig and another recruiter, Fischer, who had meanwhile joined the NRC-Seelig agreement. In 1918, the Rhodesian authorities finally managed to get Barnard into court on charges of assault and violation of the game laws. In view of Barnard's activities, which almost certainly included murder, the outcome of his trial was remarkable. He won acquittal on the assault charge and escaped with a five-pound fine for the game law violation. Evidently in that part of Rhodesia, the state could protect the animals more easily than the people.[107] The Rhodesian administration knew that Barnard was wanted by the Portuguese on serious charges, but in the absence of an extradition treaty declined to hold him. Barnard's main base lay fifteen miles inside the Mozambique border, forty miles from the Sabi River. Most of the migrants passed this point and could easily be rounded up by the touts and delivered to licensed agents across the Limpopo; and they could just as readily evade the periodic patrols from both the Rhodesian and the Portuguese sides of the border.[108] Everyone acknowledged the ineffectiveness of these feeble efforts to extend control over the area. Eventually the Portuguese did manage to apprehend Diegel on charges of stock theft when a serious wound inflicted by a charging buffalo left him immobilized in camp and unable to slip over the Rhodesian side of the border.[109]

This lay in the future, however. In 1917, Barnard and Diegel still worked their labour racket and did so in informal partnership with the NRC. They sold their illegal catch to the NRC representative at Makulekas who in turn sent them to the mines outside the pooling arrangement earlier agreed with Seelig. Barnard needed the connivance, at least, of the NRC's district headquarters staff at Pietersburg. The NRC head office may well have known what was going on. These dealings with Barnard, apparently no isolated occurrence, were both a violation of the contract with Seelig and Fischer and also illegal. To deal with an unlicensed agent was itself unlawful, and regulations under the Native Labour Regulation Act, as amended, disallowed the recruiting of foreign blacks in the area. Although NRC employees were the major offenders in this case, Seelig's men can certainly not be described simply as victims. Seelig's runners ran afoul of Barnard and other thieves because they were working illegally beyond the borders of the Union in violation both of the law and of their principal's contract with the NRC. Nevertheless the primary fault lay with the NRC. In his report on the situation at Makulekas, Stubbs, the nearest resident government official, wrote plainly of the implications:

The employment of this man [Barnard] by the Recruiting Corporation is a disgrace to that organization which must know of his methods. By taking over gangs of boys from him and no doubt making it worth his while by paying a substantial capitation fee, they are encouraging a system which the NRC representatives condemned and pretended to remedy by their agreement with Messrs. Seelig and Fischer. It would appear that the NRC never intended to discontinue the payment of capitation fees [to labour agents as required under the 1916 agreement] because it is reasonable to suppose that someone is paying Barnard, and as all Barnard's boys are handed over to the NRC, his employers must be the NRC[110]

Stubbs did not doubt that the NRC's deal with Seelig was a mere sham from the start, and he implied that even senior officials must have known that their employees were conniving with the touts. He warned Pretoria that still more trouble could be expected in the future. Seelig and Fischer would not sit still while their business was shamelessly plundered. Moreover, a number of other illegal agents had joined Barnard so that the self-regulation of the industry involved in the 1916 agreement stood now revealed as a hopeless failure. By 1918, Stubbs could see no remedy short of the establishment of a strong police post at Makulekas.[111]

Throughout the first post-Union decade and beyond, clandestine immigration and large-scale illegal recruiting remained a major problem in the northern Transvaal. Even the 1919 take-over of the mine labour supply of the Robinson group by the NRC did not immediately achieve the expected remedy. Both continued at a high rate until the state gradually achieved better police supervision during the course of the 1920s. In 1918, when the Native Affairs Department discovered that the NRC was itself one of the main violators of the recruiting regulations, officials began to look at further steps to achieve effective government supervision. As they had frequently done in the past, they now consulted their counterparts in Salisbury. An important conference resulted later in the year.[112] Before that could take place, however, the Union government looked again at the whole question of self-regulation by the mining industry.

Ideology need not be invoked to explain this touching and totally misplaced faith in private enterprise; nor had the entire Native Affairs Department and its allied agencies been suborned by the Randlords. Neither of the two stock explanations for what goes on in South Africa work in this case; instead, the explanation is even simpler. Officials shrank from the expense which they knew direct state control would require. More importantly, they did not want (and had long struggled to avoid) responsibility for the maintenance of the mines' labour complements. While any alternative remained, however unlikely it might be to bring order, they put aside the idea of a strong police detachment along the Limpopo. Such a force would necessarily be very expensive, and the policemen could be expected to die in large numbers from the unhealthy conditions which obtained there.

Since the NRC had shown itself to be a main cause of illegal recruiting rather than the hoped-for remedy, officials once again looked briefly to its sister organization, the WNLA, for an alternative solution. Despite so much evidence since 1900 of the gold mines' incapacity to clean their own house even when to do so promised higher profits for the industry as a whole, officials never abandoned their hope that the recruiters would somehow learn to discipline themselves at no cost to the state. On this occasion they dusted off an earlier suggestion[113] that a WNLA post be established beyond the border to compete with the illicit touts.[114] Using the WNLA, migrants proceeding independently toward the Transvaal's borders could be siphoned off, and the supply of labour which nourished the touts would thus be diverted eastward through WNLA channels to Lourenço Marques and then under proper supervision to the Rand.

With its large staff, sophisticated organization, and excellent contacts in the Mozambique colonial state, the WNLA ought to be able to wrest control of the labour traffic from the handful of vagabonds and thieves who now controlled it. Such must have been the reasoning of the secretary of native affairs and his officials in renewing the suggestion. On the earlier occasion, the proposal to deploy the WNLA against touts based further north in the Portuguese colony failed partly from lack of cooperation from the Mozambique Chartered Company. This time the Rhodesian administration protested and for obvious reasons. The last thing they wanted was the formidable WNLA camped on their borders; the flow of labour toward the south was already deplorably large. Their farmers and mine owners moaned incessantly about chronic "labour shortage," though the problem resulted directly from their own bad wages and harsh conditions of service. The British South Africa Company's administrator had previously complained that no "serious attempt" was made to prevent Rhodesian blacks from north of 22°SL from crossing the Limpopo. When informed of the proposal to involve the WNLA, the chief native commissioner in Salisbury asked for "an explicit assurance" that Rhodesian blacks would not be recruited.[115] Plainly Rhodesia preferred to tolerate the touts rather than to accept a remedy of this sort, especially since the Union suffered most of the consequences. However, even had the scheme gone ahead and a WNLA post been established near the intersection of the three colonial borders, the objective would probably not have been achieved. When given the opening, WNLA recruiters would likely have been as susceptible as NRC people to the blandishment of touts and brigands with labour to sell.

This was not the view of H.S. Cooke, the acting director of native labour, who defended the proposal to involve the WNLA in his letters to the Rhodesian chief native commissioner. Indeed he forthrightly upheld the record and good intentions of both the WNLA and the NRC: "The Witwatersrand

Native Labour Association and the Native Recruiting Corporation are fully aware of the policy of this Administration ... and have emphatically dissociated themselves with the action of unscrupulous persons who ... endeavour to make capital out of [illegal] recruitment, and I have every reason to believe that these Associations will cordially cooperate in any additional measures which can be inaugurated for the improvement of the position.[116] Since the NRC had just been implicated by a Native Affairs Department official in the grossest kind of recruiting irregularity and since WNLA methods in similarly remote and unpoliced areas were equally suspect, Cooke's view was extravagant and unjustified. Officials continued to cling to the idea of self-regulation by the mining industry long after the industry had demonstrated its incapacity to do the job. There was another element in his thinking, however. Cooke had little sympathy with Rhodesian efforts to keep their own blacks at home. Concerning those who regularly crossed the Limpopo to work at the Messina Copper Mine and for other northern Transvaal employers, Cooke thought it "unreasonable to debar Natives from selling their labour with such obvious advantage to themselves." Of course, the acting director of native labour, who enforced the highly restrictive labour regulations operating within the Union, had not become a sudden convert to the idea of a free market for labour. South African officials had their own labour shortage to worry about, and this affected their view of the recruiting situation at every stage.[117] Cooperation with Salisbury was no doubt desirable but not if it meant acquiescing in further barriers to the flow of labour into the the Union from Rhodesia itself. A WNLA depot was later established just beyond the border in southwestern Mozambique.

Nevertheless, the Union government decided not to proceed immediately with the proposal to involve the WNLA. Instead they continued with their round of consultations among Native Affairs Department officials and between them and their Rhodesian counterparts. In September 1918, the officials most directly concerned met at Pietersburg to consider means to enforce a recent government decision to ban the immigration of blacks from the north.[118] The Union cabinet had decided that the immigration of tropical labour must be "absolutely stopped." They left officials to achieve this without additional expense, a hopeless task.[119] After extended discussion, the officials who met at Pietersburg concluded that the migration of blacks across the Limpopo could not be stopped with the means available. They reaffirmed the ban on recruiting of these migrants but could suggest no new means of enforcement. As a gesture to Salisbury, they suggested that "machinery be created for the registration of all Southern Rhodesian natives within the Union."[120] But this would in no way meet the Rhodesian government's main concern that too many of its blacks secured entry to South Africa, nor would it do anything to root out recruiting irregularities.

The recruiting scandal yielded only slowly to reform. With the adherence of the Robinson group in 1919, the NRC's monopsony was finally completed, and this certainly removed a major incentive to the use of illegal recruiting methods. It did not provide a complete solution, however. NRC recruiters continued to deal with illicit touts and labour thieves who delivered labour to the border. Only gradually during the 1920s as South African and Rhodesian police extended supervision on both sides of the Limpopo, did touting for labour become first more difficult and then impossible to mount on any scale.

Map 4   Northern Mozambique and Nyasaland

Conclusion

This investigation of the origins of the gold-mining industry's labour systems has suggested a pattern of development very unlike that depicted in earlier accounts. From Sheila van der Horst writing in the early 1940s to Norman Levy in 1982, historians and social scientists of the mining industry have seen in its early policies an inexorable drive to monopsony.[1] Despite some important differences in interpretation, writers of both a liberal, centrist perspective and those taking the newer, radical approach have shared a view which stressed the monopoly power of the gold-mining industry. Eventually, a highly centralized recruiting system under Chamber of Mines control did emerge, and most accounts of the industry's early history either did not notice or thought it unimportant to explain the persistence of competition and disunity, despite the best efforts of the chamber, during the first thirty years of expansion after 1886.[2] While the Chamber of Mines called repeatedly for an end to wasteful and destructive competition for limited labour, many mine managers and recruiting personnel consistently flouted these directives. If the mining groups were as powerful as most historians think they were, if they had *de facto* control of the state as the radicals argue, if their economic welfare and even survival required monopoly control as many have suggested, why did the industry require so long to secure its interests?

Some of the reasons for this have been advanced in earlier chapters, and they suggest a few general conclusions. At least before about 1912, competition for unskilled black labour was not dysfunctional to gold-mining profitability. To pay too high a price for this labour was bad in the eyes of the Randlords, but not to get the labour at all was much worse. If the managers were often found violating their recruiting agreements and paying the high fees and wage advances demanded by the independent labour agents and contractors, this was simply because the independents repeatedly showed that they could deliver the workers. In consorting with the independents in this way, individual mines indicated a necessary priority to maintain production levels. Without adequate black labour they could not raise sufficient tonnage of ore from underground to supply their reduction mills. Many of the managers showed by their actions that, when the alternative was severe shortage, they were willing to pay a high price for their black labour. At such moments the target worker argument was quickly discarded. A manager could raise wages when, in the short run, he was able to offset higher labour costs by juggling his ore reserves and raising the yield of gold per ton. Over an extended period, such a policy might drastically shorten the working life of a mine, as long as the gold price remained fixed. Few managers could afford the long view, however. In an office of group administration or in the boardroom of the chamber, senior staff could stress the advantages of monopsony over the long term; they could even accept, in principle, a temporary cost in reduced labour supplies and constrained production which this might entail; but at the level of the individual mine, the manager knew that his job depended on what he could get out of the mine next week or next month.[3]

For many years the dominant groups in the Chamber of Mines wrestled with two interrelated problems. First, if the rapidly expanding labour requirements of the industry were to be met, some means had to be found to raise the participation rate of African cultivators in the migrant system. This was particularly the case once the political decision was taken in 1906–7 to repatriate the 50,000 Chinese workers. To sustain the drive for expansion the labour supply had to be increased by 400 per cent in the twenty years after about 1890. Second, the industry's commitment to the maximum exploitation of its huge reserves of low-grade ore required that labour costs be driven down. Not to do so meant leaving unworked large deposits of the lowest-grade ores. Driven to this wasteful expedient in the 1890s, the owners were determined after the Anglo-Boer War to get control of their wage bill, the largest single element in mining costs. In these years, the mines needed a huge increase in the labour supply but insisted at the same time that wages must not increase. Higher wages were also ruled out by the target worker theory which stated that mineworkers would respond to higher wages by working for shorter periods to the detriment of the overall labour supply. Consequently the chamber, unlike many individual mine managers, convinced itself that the industry simply could not go into the labour market and bid for its additional requirements with higher wages or more attractive terms of service.

Almost from the start, leading members of the chamber's executive committee began to develop a multifaceted but coherent strategy to achieve simultaneously a vast expansion of the black labour force and a reduction of unit labour costs.[4] As early as 1890, they knew what had to be done to achieve this but consistently underestimated the difficulties in the way of implementation.[5] When their policies resulted in diminution rather than enhancement of the supply, various mines and mining groups would invariably break ranks and return to competitive recruiting. The chamber wanted the state to use its power to restrict land available to Africans, to tax them and thus to force the labour they required into wage economy. At the same time, centralized recruiting institutions under industry control would reduce costs, stabilize wages at a low level, end wasteful labour competition among the mines, and forestall the emergence of an open labour market in which the chamber would have to compete with other employers and with the African rural economy for its requirements.

The mines had these policies in place for the first time by 1893. Blacks had lost most of their land in the preceding one hundred years; hut and other taxes had been imposed long since; South African governments were beginning to act against the so-called squatting problem, which had permitted thousands of black cultivators to maintain their independence by negotiating share-cropping and leasehold arrangements on white-owned land. Within the mining industry itself, a wage reduction agreement had been negotiated and steps taken to establish a Native Labour Department of the Chamber to coordinate policy among the big mining houses. With this cluster of strategies, the chamber worked to achieve a rapid expansion of the labour force at lower unit cost.

The first bid for monopsony in 1890–3 was an abject failure for the reasons which were set out in chapter 1. Taxation turned out to be too blunt an instrument to direct significant amounts of labour to the mines. Anti-squatting measures could not be effectively enforced for many years. And the chamber's wage reduction agreement and Native Labour Department both collapsed ignominiously. Labour touts flourished and extracted large fees for their services. Black wages proved highly resistant to reductions and many mines simply ignored chamber schedules and made clandestine payments far above agreed levels. Under the leadership of the more development-oriented mining groups, the industry tried again in 1896–7. Most of the houses cooperated in the formation of the Rand Native Labour Association and accepted a new round of wage reductions imposed in that period. Again the result was disappointing. State regulations designed to direct labour to the mines and control it once it was there fell well short of the industry's minimum requirements. Independent recruiting continued; the mines persisted in stealing labour from each other. Costs remained well above levels acceptable to the chamber. When the RNLA showed that it could not deliver sufficient labour to meet the needs of an expanding industry, individual managers simply reverted to their previously independent methods. Cutthroat competition continued right up to the outbreak of war in October 1899.[6]

More significantly, during this time some companies began to experiment with alternative labour systems. A few of the mines tried to stabilize a higher proportion of their labour force as permanent residents with their families on company property.[7] Others set up "labour farms" at a distance from the mine on land bought earlier for speculative purposes and made available small acreages to blacks and their families in return for an agreed period of mining work. In this way they could reduce their dependence on uncertain migrant labour supplies in competitive conditions. Unit costs would rise with stabilization but so presumably would the efficiency and productivity of the work force. (Later, during the crises of 1906–9 and 1918–22, the industry again showed a willingness to consider radical alternatives to migrancy although it did not, in the end, need to implement these.)

Once war began in 1899 key mine controllers hoped that the expected British victory would produce conditions favourable to centralized, low-cost labour mobilization on a large scale. By late the following year, the mining groups had developed their industrial strategy for the new era which would follow the conquest of the republics. They expected the Milner administration in the Transvaal to be both more competent and more sympathetic to their needs than the Kruger regime had been. When Milner refused to run the recruiting system as a public work, they proceeded to reconstitute the RNLA as the Witwatersrand Native Labour Association and to adopt a new schedule of ultra-low wages. The new wage reduction agreement did not long survive the resumption of large-scale mining in 1902, and the mines found themselves compelled to revert to the higher 1896–7 schedule. Investigations showed that many companies continued to pay above even these rates. Despite the higher wages, the WNLA failed to deliver sufficient labour and dissatisfaction with its lack of performance grew rapidly. The arrival of 50,000 Chinese in 1904–6 led the WNLA to reduce its efforts in the South African territories – it remained very active in Mozambique – which caused much dissatisfaction among those groups not receiving significant amounts of Chinese labour.[8] They began to recruit outside the association's rules in the eastern Cape and elsewhere and made contracts with some of the most effective recruiters in the business. When the new Transvaal government announced in 1907 that Chinese labour would definitely not be continued, the most powerful groups, which depended heavily on the Chinese, found that they could not now fall back on the discredited WNLA. Consequently all of the groups had to set up independent recruiting operations for the South African territories. Supported by the Portuguese colonial authorities, the WNLA did best in southern Mozambique, but even there the labour supply was prone to fluctuations.

The chamber's third bid for monopsony under the WNLA, in 1900–6, failed for essentially the same reasons which had defeated it in the 1890s. The mines remained bitterly divided on labour matters; the major houses could not agree to rally together behind the WNLA; and the industry exaggerated the capacity of the state to deliver labour to the mines through its tax policies, coercive pass laws, and restrictive land arrangements. Despite the best efforts of government and despite recurrent drought and cattle disease, black cultivators in South Africa itself retained an important degree of independence in these years. Although increasing numbers were, of course, forced into the wage market, most avoided the mines. The process of "proletarianization" was slower, more uneven in its effects and less capable of delivering labour to the large, low-wage employers than some earlier studies have indicated.[9] The resilience of the African cultivator and the determination of those who did seek wage employment to get the best wages is a major factor accounting for the Chamber of Mines' persistent over-optimism concerning the labour mobilization potential of centralized recruiting at low wages. Communities of African cultivators in the eastern Cape particularly were surprisingly successful both in resisting government labour-mobilizing policies and in coping with the effects of natural calamity.

It is true that these were years of serious depression in South Africa, and the decline of economic activity elsewhere in the economy undoubtedly assisted the mines by weakening competition from nonmining employers and undermining the position of independent African cultivators. More Africans than before found themselves with no alternative to mining employment. There is no doubt either that the amount of labour arriving on the mines from the principal South African recruiting zones increased very dramatically in the decade after about 1906. However, this much-increased flow of labour, particularly from the Cape to the mines, which enabled the industry to replace the departing Chinese and to maintain production levels while pursuing ambitious development plans in new mining areas, was not the result of any mere windfall. The mines got this labour mainly not as the result of a fortuitous decline in business activity elsewhere in the economy but because they went out vigorously to recruit it. Temporarily shelving their bid for a labour monopsony, the large mining groups now began again to compete aggressively with each other for labour. Recruiting costs increased dramatically; hundreds of whites and thousands of blacks were drawn into the industry as recruiters and runners; the government service was plundered for the talent needed to head up the recruiting services which the individual mining groups were now forced to establish. They made allies of the country traders and local headmen without whose influence successful recruiting could not be carried on. More than this, the industry's principal recruiters devised powerful incentives to tempt blacks into mine employment and the country traders into service as recruiters. In the years after about 1906–7, the mining industry supplied huge sums to the eastern Cape economy in the form of cattle and cash advances on wages. If, as Colin Bundy and others have argued, most Africans in the eastern Cape had been totally impoverished and without alternative means of livelihood than migrancy, none of these incentives should have been necessary.[10] The evidence suggests unquestionably that without these inducements and without the massive recruiting effort which the labour agents and contractors now launched, much less labour would have gone to the Transvaal from the Cape.

To consider these workers only as victims is to ignore the substantial benefits which they extracted from the industry in this period. In a sellers' market for labour, the workers took full advantage and forced the mine labour recruiters into a frantic competition which horrified government officials and alarmed the mine controllers.[11] Officials resented an economic situation in which roles were reversed and the white man was now having to "chase after" the black. In 1906–7 top executives in the Chamber of Mines watched helplessly as the escalating demand for labour completed the collapse of their third bid for a labour monopsony. A marked increase in desertion levels, as Cape workers in growing numbers took their cash advances and then fled from mine employment, is another indicator of their leverage on the system at this time.

Much as they might deplore this, neither the mining industry itself nor the various colonial governments could do much about it in the short run. The overriding need for more labour threw power temporarily to the supplying districts, to the periphery of the subcontinental economy at the expense of the mining heartland. The eastern Cape received a powerful stimulus to its economy in the form of the wage advances and recruiting fees which did much to offset the impact of depression. In case Cape Town was ever inclined to forget this, a strong political lobby of country traders, labour contractors, and allied Chambers of Commerce in the major centres emerged to remind them. For several years after 1906, therefore, both the mines and the Transvaal government were forced to tolerate a costly, highly competitive recruiting system for the gold mines. Experience had shown that there was no other way to increase the participation rate of the African cultivators.

In the evolution of the gold mines' recruiting system, this era of intense competition played a crucial role. It was no mere prelude to the mining industry's inevitable assertion of hegemony, as some have argued.[12] At high cost to the industry, the independent labour agents and contractors succeeded in doing what the chamber and its agencies, the RNLA and the WNLA, had earlier failed to accomplish, what natural calamity, market forces, and government coercion could not by themselves achieve: they delivered the labour. Thus, at this particular stage, competition was highly functional to industry expansion and the foundation of its later prosperity. By tempting a much larger proportion of rural cultivators into migrant labour for the mines, they created in the key South African recruiting districts a pool of industrial labour sufficiently large to supply the basic requirements of the mines. Their power in the system proved to be short-lived, however. Although the private recruiters fought hard to defend the lucrative business which they had established, they soon began to suffer the consequences of their own earlier success.

By 1912, a large number of South African blacks had at least some mine experience. Knowledgeable about working conditions in Johannesburg, they began to make their own way there without the intervention of a recruiter. Voluntary labour had been a significant element in migration from the Cape at an early stage, but the proportion of voluntary workers of the total supply from that province increased dramatically in the second decade of the century. Some of the voluntaries were clandestine recruits, but an increasing number were independent work-seekers. Many factors were involved in this change. It may have reflected a diminishing aversion to mine work as health and working conditions improved. Conditions in the rural areas were particularly bad in 1911–2 as a result of severe drought and out-breaks of East Coast fever among the cattle. The resulting poverty would certainly swell the numbers of migrants for the mines, but few of the poorest Africans, those most affected by agricultural calamity, would be voluntaries. They were the workers most in need of the wage advance for family support which only the recruiter could provide. More important in explaining the sharp increase in the number of volunteers was the freedom which these workers enjoyed to seek out the best available job on arrival in the Johannesburg area. Moreover, since voluntary workers were much sought after by the mines, they could get work on short contracts, month-to-month or even week-to-week. This was important since it enabled the cultivator-miner to withdraw from the mines at important times in the agricultural cycle in order to tend his crops and beasts. The recruited worker, locked into a six- or nine-month contract, did not have this flexibility. Independence was more important to the voluntary workers than the wage advances and other inducements which the recruiters could offer.

The rise of voluntary labour from the Cape, had, however, some unintended consequences for the rural economy and the families of the workers. As more of them refused recruitment in order to make their own way to the mines, the mines' dependence on the private recruiters and con-tractors declined, and the state found it could begin to achieve by 1910 what its officials had long been advocating, a statutory limit on wage advances. Previously the wage advance, paid in cash or cattle (in Pondoland), had been an indispensable inducement to migrancy and powerful factor entrenching the power of the labour recruiters. Governments had earlier been constrained from such action out of fear that to curb wage advances might seriously hurt recruiting levels and arouse the wrath of the recruiters and their political allies. Now as the phenomenon of the voluntary mineworker emerged, such concerns had much less weight. As a result of

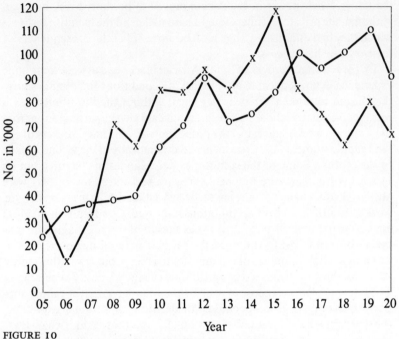

FIGURE 10

Mineworkers Received by WNLA Members, South African Sources, 1905–20

SOURCES: WNLA *Annual Reports*.
x Recruited from South Africa and the High Commission territories
o Voluntaries from all sources

the maximum imposed on advances, the cash flow into the rural areas from the mining economy declined. It now depended much more heavily on the voluntary remittance of workers' savings. Voluntary labour also obviously strengthened the hand of the Chamber of Mines against the independent suppliers of labour. Thus the advocates of restored monopsony were able to respond with a renewed effort to absorb or eliminate the independent recruiters.

The new bid for monopsony under the Native Recruiting Corporation (1912) could not have worked if the chamber had not been able simultaneously to put its own house in order and successfully eliminate by stages the intra-industry competition which had defeated earlier efforts to secure cooperation in labour matters. The *de facto* take-over by Central Mining, the most consistent advocate of noncompetitive recruiting, of East Rand Proprietary Mines, previously one of the most independent of mining groups on labour matters, established the preconditions in 1911 for the renewed effort to curb the power of the labour contractors. Shortly thereafter Central Mining absorbed the smaller S. Neumann group. Equally, it was the 1916 acquisition of the Randfontein complex by the powerful JCI group which enabled the advocates of combination in the chamber to complete the monopsony by 1919. In short by the second decade of the century conditions both in the countryside and on the mines had begun to swing decisively in favour of the mining industry.

The remaining obstacle to the reconstruction of the mines' cheap labour policy was, of course, the politically powerful independent recruiters and contractors. Their role in the successful campaign to replace the Chinese with South African blacks had been crucial, but with this achieved by 1910, the independents now constituted a serious barrier to the rationalization needed if the industry was to achieve further reductions in labour costs. Here the support of the government for the chamber was slow to develop. The contractors used their political influence to defend the competitive recruiting system. Although dwarfed in size and financial strength by the Chamber of Mines' recruiting arm, the WNLA and the NRC, the independents had some crucial advantages which enabled them to maintain their position for many years. Most of these men had worked the business from its earliest days; they knew their respective districts; often they controlled the contacts with the chiefs and local notables which were essential to successful recruiting. Frequently well connected in the mining industry itself, a number of them became adept at exploiting the rivalries which flourished there.

In the more remote parts of the Union, particularly along the northern frontier where administration and police supervision scarcely existed, the independents operated entirely outside the law or on the fringes of it. The Chamber of Mines recruiting arms could not as easily do this. Under pressure from the state, head office staff had committed itself against the use of illegal methods which, in any case, tended to subvert the monopsony they were trying to create. But their agents in the field who competed with the unscrupulous independent recruiters and bandit elements could ill afford the luxury of a clean operation. An NRC recruiter who explained his lack of success by reference to the restrictions imposed on him by law knew he could expect little sympathy from the mine controllers, whatever propaganda was currently broadcast by the Chamber of Mines and orchestrated by the industry's press. Still, the mine labour controllers dared not publicly admit involvement with illegal methods, and when these were exposed, the chamber could only condemn them. NRC recruiters had, therefore, to be careful. The very fact that a recruiter worked for the NRC meant greater scrutiny of his activities and increased the likelihood of an investigation should suspicions arise concerning his methods. The NRC's vulnerability to goverment scrutiny gave the independents and the touts an advantage against it.

Another fundamental reason for the success of the independents lay simply in the demand for their services. Had black mineworkers in large numbers not been willing to seek out the independents, they could not have remained a persistent threat to the industry's recruiters. Various factors account for this. Up until 1919, a labour contractor such as Seelig or Mostert working for the Robinson group had the advantage that these were popular mines for many blacks. However improbable, the perception was real and so, therefore, were its consequences. In the case of an operation such as that of the McKenzie family which had been in business in Pondoland for so long, clearly an element of trust between the contractor and his recruits had grown up. Within the context of a dependent, exploitative relationship, many of the recruits must have thought that they had been reasonably dealt with. Though this company promised little, it did apparently make good at least on that.

Even this limited type of honesty was rare. Many of the touts were violent opportunists who coerced their labour and lived by deception. As a group they continued to attract recruits, however; and, although many used force, this alone cannot account for persistent success. In fact, these men offered services which were much in demand among black migrants. On the Rand itself, the tout provided the deserter with new documents, rail tickets, money and food, and, of course, alternative employment – some safe haven out of reach of his former employer or a labour bureau inspector. In the countryside, an enterprising labour agent could also find new employment for the returning deserter with a different mining group back on the Rand, and supply the recruit with another cash advance. Such arrangements were obviously jointly beneficial; furthermore, each side needed the other. When conniving to despoil the mines, the tout and his recruit had often to act together, and they shared the resulting profit, though unequally. Beyond the Union's northern borders, many long-distance migrants must have had little choice but to use the services of the gangs of desperadoes who lurked in the vicinity of all of the main migration routes. Putting oneself into the hands of one such gang might provide some protection from the others. Those recruits with little food or money would also seek out these camps. Not to do so could mean starvation.

In a limited and partial way, a kind of alliance had emerged against the mining groups during these years. Perhaps surprisingly, the independent recruiter and the black worker – the tout and his victim – shared some common interests. The latter struggled to get to the mines; the former made his profit by facilitating this. Both aimed to secure better terms from the mining companies. Some of the means to this end, desertion for instance, required recruiter and recruit often to conspire actively together against the mines. All recruiters had an interest in promoting better wages and working conditions on the mines because both had an important effect on recruiting levels; but the independent agent occupied a structurally stronger position to press for change than the NRC people. He could threaten to offer his workers to another employer.

An important contractor such as A.M. Mostert could be very active indeed against an employer on behalf of his work-force.[13] Of course, Mostert was no humanitarian; conditions in his compounds were grim. As one of the largest labour contractors, he simply had an interest in securing redress of grievances from the mining companies on behalf of the work-force which he had recruited. Complaints against his own organization received no such consideration. One of the most successful of the contractors, J.S. Marwick of Marwick and Morris, the Swazi and Zululand recruiters, expressed succinctly the common interest which bound recruiter and recruit together:

The want of consistency and very often the want of intelligence that is prevalent in the handling of natives underground is astounding. Our constant concern is to try and see that we keep faith with these natives throughout the period of their contract, but our task is rendered most difficult by the peculiarities of the underground management. The indifference about raising natives [promptly] from the lower levels [at the end of the shift], the apathy with regard to the constant cancellation of shifts ["loafer ticket system"], the stolid refusal to transfer a native from one gang to another who complains that his miner has a grudge against him, and the failure to realise that the natives have been persuaded to come to the mines on the promise of fair treatment are among the difficulties we have to contend with.[14]

That self-interest rather than any disinterested desire to "keep faith with these natives" explained Marwick's concern only strengthens the conclusion. Above all, the tout and his recruit shared a common interest in opposing the completion of the mine labour monopsony. For the labourer, centralized recruiting threatened lower wages and the likely elimination of cash advances; for the recruiters, it meant probable unemployment for many and lower agents' fees for the rest.

These shared interests promoted alliances of convenience; they did not certainly lead to any kind of coalescence of class interest between petit-bourgeois white recruiters and black workers. Colour prejudice conditioned their basic relationship which remained exploitative. The touts and their recruits simply revealed in their actions a limited number of shared interests against the mine employers. Cooperation was mostly piecemeal and spontaneous, and it can only be understood in the context of a profoundly unequal relationship, the recruiting nexus, which bound them together. No common consciousness united them. Moreover, as the mineworkers gained in experience, they found that they had less need for the services of the labour agent and began in large numbers to seek work independently. Yet their coooperation was nonetheless important. As individuals, only the strongest of the recruiters and the most daring of the recruits could defy the mining industry for long. When acting in the ways outlined in this book, however, they demonstrated impressive collective strength. To bring them to heel required the work of many years. Industry and government succeeded only when they began to deploy the modern, quasi-totalitarian instruments of control which now characterize one of the world's most regimented labour systems.

Appendix 1

Average Number of Africans Employed on Mines and Works, Transvaal, 1903–20

Year Ending 30 June (excl. Africans employed by contractors)		Union of South Africa					British Protectorates				Mozamb. south of lat. 22°S	TOTAL	Nyasa-land Prot.	North. Rhod-esia	South. Rhod-esia	TOTAL	Portu-guese Trops.	All Trops.	Un-classified	GRAND TOTAL
		Cape Prov.	Natal & Zulu.	Orange Free State	Trans-vaal	TOTAL	Basuto-land	Bechu-analand	Swazi-land	TOTAL										
1903–4	No.	5751	2365	244	12157	20517	1398	842	438	2678	52169	75364	923	–	411	1334	–	1334	869	77567
	%	7.4	3.1	.3	15.7	26.5	1.8	1.1	.6	3.5	67.3	97.3	1.2	–	.5	1.7	–	1.7	1.0	100.00
1904–5	No.	11835	3145	228	12331	27539	3057	896	742	4695	54364	86598	1725	–	2632	4357	–	4357	693	91648
	%	12.9	3.4	.3	13.5	30.1	3.3	1.0	.8	5.1	59.3	94.5	1.9	–	2.9	4.8	–	4.8	.7	100.00
1905–6	No.	9354	3365	288	10808	23813	3034	1091	1011	5136	57264	86213	2531	–	4083	6614	3055	9669	667	96549
	%	9.7	3.5	.3	11.2	24.7	3.1	1.1	1.1	5.3	59.3	89.3	2.6	–	4.2	6.8	3.2	10.0	.7	100.00
1906–7	No.	15643	5348	485	10985	32461	4257	1072	787	6116	58298	96875	1607	–	1104	2711	4417	7128	505	104508
	%	15.0	5.1	.5	10.5	31.1	4.1	1.0	.8	5.9	55.7	92.7	1.5	–	1.1	2.6	4.2	6.8	.5	100.00
1907–8	No.	21470	6726	608	18062	46866	4848	1053	1943	7844	69360	124070	730	224	1517	2471	7912	10383	501	134954
	%	15.9	5.0	.5	13.4	34.8	3.6	.8	1.4	5.8	51.4	92.0	.5	.2	1.1	1.8	5.9	7.6	.3	100.00
1908–9	No.	39535	9732	857	21574	71698	6256	1631	1786	9673	73448	154819	541	183	1009	1733	10778	12511	413	167743
	%	23.6	5.8	.5	12.9	42.7	3.7	1.0	1.1	5.8	43.8	92.3	.3	.1	.6	1.0	6.4	7.5	.2	100.00
1909–10	No.	46869	12145	749	18837	78600	5246	1587	1738	8571	73892	161063	2394	122	928	3444	13174	16618	467	178148
	%	26.3	6.8	.4	10.6	44.1	2.9	.9	1.0	4.8	41.5	90.4	1.3	.1	.5	1.9	7.4	9.3	.3	100.00

SOURCES: Chamber of Mines and WNLA *Annual Reports*.

Average Number Continued

Calendar Year (incl. Africans employed by contractors)		Cape Prov.	Natal & Zulu.	Orange Free State	Transvaal	TOTAL	Basutoland	Bechuanaland	Swaziland	TOTAL	Mozamb. south of lat. 22°S	TOTAL	Nyasaland Prot.	North. Rhodesia	South. Rhodesia	TOTAL	Portuguese Trops.	All Trops.	Unclassified	GRAND TOTAL
		Union of South Africa					*British Protectorates*													
1910	No.	60509	14419	1149	22137	98214	7877	1797	2800	12474	77454	188142	3735	121	1033	4889	14359	19248	531	207921
	%	29.1	6.9	.5	10.6	47.2	3.8	.9	1.4	6.0	37.3	90.5	1.8	.1	.5	2.4	6.9	9.3	.2	100.00
1911	No.	57901	17267	1312	21331	97811	8992	1718	3089	13799	77825	189435	1925	104	1167	3196	20379	23575	451	213461
	%	27.1	8.1	.6	10.0	45.8	4.2	.8	1.4	6.5	36.4	88.8	.9	.1	.6	1.5	9.6	11.0	.2	100.00
1912	No.	61938	17971	1243	25269	106421	10600	2451	4104	17155	75938	199514	2110	89	1792	3991	17072	21063	297	220874
	%	28.1	8.1	.6	11.4	48.2	4.8	1.1	1.9	7.8	34.4	90.3	1.0	—	.8	1.8	7.7	9.5	.1	100.00
1913	No.	62621	16249	1063	22956	102889	11041	3226	3969	18236	73366	194491	1110	50	1569	2729	16665	19394	144	214029
	%	29.2	7.6	.5	10.7	48.1	5.2	1.5	1.9	8.5	34.3	90.9	.5	—	.7	1.3	7.8	9.1	.1	100.00
1914	No.	56867	14787	1282	21649	94585	13146	4350	3751	21247	70463	186295	694	40	1350	2084	4648	6732	100	193127
	%	29.4	7.7	.7	11.2	49.0	6.8	2.2	1.9	11.0	36.5	96.5	.4	—	.7	1.1	2.4	3.5	.1	100.00
1915	No.	71443	13592	1292	21300	107627	14332	4507	3977	22816	76780	207223	565	48	724	1337	1791	3128	70	210421
	%	34.0	6.5	.6	10.1	51.2	6.8	2.1	1.9	10.8	36.5	98.5	.3	—	.3	.6	.9	1.5	—	100.00
1916	No.	76109	13522	1262	26714	117607	14092	4031	4655	22778	81125	221510	682	45	638	1311	1397	2708	55	224273
	%	33.9	6.0	.6	11.9	52.4	6.3	1.8	2.1	10.2	36.2	98.8	.3	—	.3	.6	.6	1.2	—	100.00

Average Number Continued

Calendar Year (incl. Africans employed by contractors)		Union of South Africa					British Protectorates				Mozamb. south of lat. 22°S	TOTAL	Nyasa-land Prot.	North. Rhod-esia	South. Rhod-esia	TOTAL	Portu-guese Trops.	All Trops.	Un-classified	GRAND TOTAL
		Cape Prov.	Natal & Zulu.	Orange Free State	Trans-vaal	TOTAL	Basuto-land	Bechu-analand	Swazi-land	TOTAL										
1917	No.	69388	12393	1291	22114	105186	14711	3640	3807	22158	78816	206160	646	40	618	1304	1045	2349	45	208554
	%	33.3	5.9	.6	10.6	50.4	7.1	1.8	1.8	10.6	37.8	98.9	.3	–	.3	.6	.5	1.1	–	100.00
1918	No.	66700	12932	1340	20003	100975	15195	2934	4784	22913	80126	204014	598	55	555	1208	841	2049	39	206102
	%	32.3	6.3	.7	9.7	49.0	7.4	1.4	2.3	11.1	38.9	99.0	.3	–	.3	.6	.4	1.0	–	100.00
1919	No.	69723	10796	1195	19599	101314	13397	2468	4170	20035	76209	197558	474	46	385	905	658	1563	38	199159
	%	35.0	5.4	.6	9.9	50.9	6.7	1.2	2.1	10.1	38.3	99.2	.3	–	.2	.5	.3	.8	–	100.00
1920	No.	65650	8840	1120	18260	93870	14285	2580	3684	20549	90592	205011	469	46	334	849	506	1355	28	206394
	%	31.8	4.3	.5	8.9	45.5	6.9	1.3	1.8	10.0	43.9	99.3	.2	–	.1	.4	.3	.7	–	100.00

Appendix 2

Mine Workers Received, WNLA Member Companies, 1902-20

Year	Recruited Workers		Voluntary°	Total
	WNLA +	Non-WNLA*		
1902	54,838		3,423	58,261
1903	70,721		14,656	85,377
1904	60,969		26,924	87,893
1905	77,042		24,482	101,524
1906	49,132	4,541	36,564	90,237
1907	61,517	17,909	38,565	117,991
1908	66,962	54,070	39,620	160,652
1909	57,900	52,071	40,866	150,837
1910	67,555	80,029	61,445	209,029
1911	58,271	80,364	70,223	208,858
1912	63,568	92,319	91,590	247,477
1913	42,628	86,735	72,133	201,496
1914	37,524	99,364	76,941	213,829
1915	47,985	119,059	85,606	252,650
1916	47,549	87,397	100,115	235,061
1917	41,484	76,215	95,932	213,631
1918	37,496	62,658	100,951	201,105
1919	42,648	80,624	110,532	233,804
1920	53,650	67,913	90,744	212,307

SOURCE: WNLA *Annual Reports.*

+ Recruited from throughout southern Africa, 1902-6; thereafter from southern Mozambique only.
* Includes NRC recruits after 1912.
° Includes some clandestine recruits, hired outside WNLA/NRC rules and presented as voluntaries, especially 1902-6.

Appendix 3

"Voluntary" Labour on Transvaal Gold Mines, 1905–20

Year	New*	Local+	Mine++	Totals
1905	9,246	9,113	6,123	24,482
1906	14,910	14,814	6,840	36,564
1907	19,237	13,152	6,176	38,565
1908	20,245	11,352	8,023	39,620
1909	18,614	10,464	11,788	40,866
1910	31,239	15,117	15,089	61,445
1911	35,181	17,357	17,685	70,223
1912	51,629	15,856	24,105	91,590
1913	34,297	11,724	26,112	72,133
1914	42,030	11,259	23,652	76,941
1915	49,578	9,042	26,986	85,606
1916	70,300	7,545	22,270	100,115
1917	63,873	6,164	25,895	95,932
1918	65,014	7,769	28,168	100,951
1919	70,783	6,531	33,218	100,532
1920	59,266	4,849	26,629	90,744

SOURCE: WNLA *Annual Report.*

* New arrivals on the Rand.
+ Transfers from nonmining employment on the Rand to the mines.
++ Transfers from one mine to another.

Appendix 4

Territorial Analysis of Desertion, WNLA Member Companies, 1909-20

	Cape			Tvl			BBS			Moz.		
	Ttl	Des.	%	Ttl	Des.	%	Ttl	Des.	%	Ttl	Des.	%
1909	38,146	4,133	10.8	14,026	1,257	9.0	6,557	1,257	19.2	69,614	1,492	2.1
1910	48,280	1,582	3.3	16,341	328	2.0	9,393	518	5.5	73,496	878	1.2
1911	46,793	1,103	2.4	16,181	304	1.9	11,057	477	4.3	73,303	955	1.3
1912	44,841	692	1.5	19,830	358	1.8	13,956	579	4.1	71,621	450	.62
1913	45,919	631	1.4	17,910	203	1.1	15,367	579	3.8	68,943	440	.63
1914	42,521	470	1.1	16,150	248	1.5	18,078	772	4.3	68,332	100	.14
1915	56,064	749	1.3	16,090	290	1.8	19,795	877	4.4	75,258	140	.18
1916	60,799	645	1.1	20,797	197	.9	19,706	605	3.1	79,862	85	.10
1917	56,180	459	.81	16,709	190	1.1	19,819	381	1.9	77,646	121	.2
1918	54,708	480	.9	14,273	193	1.4	20,720	430	2.1	79,292	152	.2
1919	61,005	478	.8	13,942	213	1.5	18,236	370	2.0	75,662	138	.2
1920	59,813	474	.8	11,710	104	.9	18,641	330	1.8	90,137	174	.2

SOURCE: WNLA *Annual Report.*

270

Notes

INTRODUCTION

1 See John Taylor, "Mine Labour Recruitment in the Bechuanaland Protectorate," University of York, Centre for Southern African Studies, *Collected Papers* 4(1979): 115–30.
2 W. Beinart, "Joyini Inkomo: Cattle Advances and the Origins of Migrancy from Pondoland," *JSAS* 5(1979): 199–219; also F. Cooper, "Peasant Capitalists and Historians: Review Article," *JSAS* 7(1981): 284–314.
3 Overviews from a radical standpoint are M. Legassick, "South Africa: Forced Labour, Industrialization and Racial Differentiation," in *The Political Economy of Africa*, ed. R. Harris, 244-70; the influential G. Arrighi, "Labour Supplies in Historical Perspective ..." in *Essays on the Political Economy of Africa*, ed. Arrighi and J.S. Saul, and the older but still important H.J. and R.E. Simons, *Class and Colour in South Africa*. For the liberal perspective see F. Wilson, *Labour in the South African Gold Mines, 1911–1969*, 2–5; S.E. Katzenellenbogen, *South Africa and Mozambique*, esp. 36-44, 57-8; S.T. van der Horst, *Native Labour in South Africa*, 160–72; G.V. Doxey, *The Industrial Colour Bar in South Africa*, chaps. 3,4; R. Horwitz, *The Political Economy of South Africa*, 238-62; D.H. Houghton, "Men of Two Worlds: Some Aspects of Migratory Labour," *South African Journal of Economics* 28(1960): 177–90.
4 F.A. Johnstone, *Class, Race and Gold*, 34–45; R. Davies, "Mining Capital, the State and Unskilled White Workers in South Africa, 1901–13," *JSAS* 3(1976), and his *Capital, State and White Labour in South Africa, 1900–60*. For some instructive East African parallels see J. Lonsdale and B. Berman, "Coping with the Contradictions: The Development of the Colonial State in Kenya," JAH 20(1979): 487–505.
5 P. Richardson, *Chinese Mine Labour in the Transvaal*, 8–26; also P. Richardson and J.J. Van-Helten, "The Gold Mining Industry in the Transvaal, 1886–99," IN *The South African War,* ed. P. Warwick.

6 "The great reputation these fields justly have for security and regularity is in gold mining merely relative and based on the law of averages," in "A Descriptive and Statistical Statement of the Gold Mining Industry of the Witwatersrand," annexure to *CMAR,* 1902.

7 *The Economist,* 16 November 1897; F.H. Hatch and J.A. Chalmers, *The Gold Mines of the Rand,* 74-6; C.S. Goldmann, *South African Mines,* vol. I, *Rand Mining Companies.*

8 The concept of the "pay limit" is discussed in F. Wilson, *Labour in the South African Gold mines,* 39-40. See also T. Gregory, *Ernest Oppenheimer and the Economic Development of Southern Africa,* 77.

9 In 1902, a committee of consulting engineers, surveying the history of seventy-nine producing companies, identified thirteen which had paid in dividends an average of only 4.5d per ton of ore crushed. A further twelve companies paid average dividends of 9.1d per ton of ore crushed. "A Descriptive and Statistical Statement," 10.

10 *ICI,* evidence of F. Raleigh, 86-7; W. Dalrymple, 95-6; A. Brakhan, 183; *TLC,* evidence of J.N. de Jongh, 631; S. Jennings, 646-63.

11 The obsession of the majority of the members of the Mining Industry Commission, led by F.H.P. Creswell, with proving that mining with white unskilled labour was an economic proposition, distracted them from full attention to the question of financial malpractices. *MIC,* Majority Report, 2-19, 29-31. One member of the commission signed a minority report.

12 See P. Richardson, "Coolies and Randlords: The Structure of Mining Capitalism and Chinese Labour, 1902-10" (Seminar paper, Oxford University, n.d.) and his *Chinese Mine Labour in the Transvaal,* chap. 1; also van der Horst, *Native Labour.,* 205n1.

13 S.H. Frankel, *Capital Investment in Africa.*

14 For example, J.P. FitzPatrick, *The Transvaal from Within* ; Lionel Phillips, *Transvaal Problems;* and more recently, A.P. Cartwright, *The Corner House* and *Gold Paved the Way.* The annual reports of the Chamber of Mines, of course, are an excellent source of self-congratulatory statements.

15 Cf. Heribert Adam, *Modernizing Racial Domination,* 29.

16 G.A. Denny, *The Deep Level Mines of the Rand,* 149. Denny suggests that black labour costs averaged 24 per cent of total costs. See also ICI, evidence of C.S. Goldman, 110-16.

17 G. Fredrickson, *White Supremacy,* 220.

18 TAD, Secretary of the Transvaal Labour Commission Archive, vol. 2: statement of W.E.M. Stanford, 25/8/03; memorandum of W.T. Brownlee, 15/8/03; memorandum of R.J. Dick, 2/9/03; evidence of F. Suter, 23; D.H. Fraser, 219-20; F. Hellmann, 614-17; Nathaniel Umhalla, 855. SANAC, Minutes of Evidence, 2: evidence of H.T. Lowry, 1063-4; W. Waddell, 1087; P.K. Kawa, 616; W.N. Seti, 563; J.T. Jabavu, 727-8; vol. 4; evidence of J. Ellenberger, 239; Solomon Plaatje, 268. Cape of Good Hope, Department of Native Affairs,

Report of Native Delegates together with Correspondence relating to visit of Native Representatives to Johannesburg ..., a very useful source on this issue.

19 On the concept of a regional economic system, see C. van Onselen, *Chibaro,* 227-9.

20 Ibid.

21 J.M. Mackenzie, "Sambo and Economic Determinism: A comment on Charles van Onselen's 'Black Workers in Central African Industry'," *JSAS* 2(1975): 98-101; C. van Onselen, "Black Workers in Central African Industry," *JSAS,* 1(1975): 228-46. Mackenzie gives a useful reminder that mine wages should not be viewed, as van Onselen tends to do, in isolation from prevailing rates in other sectors of the economy, especially farming.

22 See chap. 7.

23 Practically nothing has been written on the labour contractors. These were independent companies which supplied migrant labour to the mining groups under contracts which usually specified a wage rate per shift, an allowance for recruiting costs, and sometimes transport and housing as well. A good place to start on this important issue is Union of South Africa, House of Assembly, *Reports of Select Committees,* 1910-11 (First Session, First Parliament, vol. II), *Select Committee on Native Labour Regulation Bill, 1911*, Minutes of Evidence, passim. And also chapters 3 and 4.

24 See chapters 1 and 2.

25 M. Fraser and A.H. Jeeves, eds., *All That Glittered: Selected Correspondence of Lionel Phillips, 1890-1924,* sec. 2.

26 See the reference in n. 23.

27 S. Marks and S. Trapido, "Lord Milner and the South African State," *History Workshop* 8(1979); some of them have trouble recognizing it, however: see A.H. Duminy, "The Capitalists and the Outbreak of the Anglo-Boer War" (booklet, University of Natal, Durban, 1977).

28 C. Bundy, *The Rise and Fall of the South African Peasantry,* 134-45.

29 D.J.N. Denoon, "The Transvaal Labour Crisis, 1901-6," *JAH,* 8 (1967): 481-94; and the chapter on labour in his *A Grand Illusion.*

30 N.G. Garson, " 'Het Volk': the Botha-Smuts Party in the Transvaal, 1904-11," *Historical Journal* 9(1966): 101-32.

31 A.H. Duminy and W.R. Guest, eds., *FitzPatrick, South African Politician,* J. Wernher to J.P. FitzPatrick, 6/2/06, 420-1, discussing an important meeting in London between Smuts, Wernher, and Wernher's colleague, Alfred Beit.

32 A.H. Jeeves, "The Control of Migratory Labour on the South African Gold Mines in the Era of Kruger and Milner," *JSAS,* 2(1975): 3-29.

33 J. van der Poel, *Railway and Customs Policies in South Africa, 1885-1910,* and Katzenellenbogen, *South Africa and Southern Mozambique,* 78-100.

34 Cf. Johnstone, *Class, Race and Gold.,* 20-45; P.C.W. Gutkind et al., eds., *African Labor History,* 20-1; Denoon, "The Transvaal Labour Crisis," and *A Grand Illusion* and "Capital and Capitalists in the Transvaal in the 1890's and 1900's,"

Historical Journal, 23(1980): 111-32; H. Wolpe, "Capitalism and Cheap Labour Power in South Africa: From Segregation to *Apartheid," Economy and Society* 1(1972): 429-30; M. Legassick, "South Africa: Capital Accumulation and Violence," *Economy and Society* 3(1974): 260-1; S. Marks and Trapido, "Lord Milner"; B. Bozzoli, "Capital and State in South Africa," *Review of African Political Economy* 11(1979): 40-50. Nonradical perspectives on this issue include: A.A. Mawby, "Capital, Government and Politics in the Transvaal, 1900-1907: A Revision and a Reversion," *Historical Journal* 17(1974): 387-415; and "The Transvaal Mine Owners in Politics" (seminar paper, University of London, c. 1973). Also A.H. Duminy, "The Political Career of Sir Percy FitzPatrick, 1895-1906" (PHD thesis, University of Natal, Durban, 1973).

35 *ICI,* evidence of George Albu.

36 C. Bundy, *Rise and Fall of the South African Peasantry;* also T. Ranger, "Reflections on Peasant Research," *JSAS* 5(1978): 99-133.

37 E.H. Brookes, *The History of Native Policy in South Africa,* 87-118; W.D. Hammond-Tooke, *Command or Consensus,* 88-9.

38 See chap. 3.

39 For instance, regulations under the Native Labour Regulation Act, 1911, barred recruiters and their black runners from operating in specified white agricultural districts.

40 GNLB 12, 2255/10

41 SNAA 1616/07 and 1825/09.

42 GNLB 3, 313/09, "Memorandum on the Position of the Native Labour Supply in the Proclaimed Labour Districts of the Transvaal as at March 31, 1909" by DNL.

43 GNLB 6, 4007/09.

44 NTS 186, F473, vol. 9.

45 GNLB 6, 4007/09.

46 SNAA 3749/09.

47 GNLB 12, 2255/10; 111, 1376/13/D154, Crown Mines Investigation, 6/8/13.

48 GNLB 12, 2255/10.

49 GNLB 1, 3885/08.

50 *Rand Daily Mail,* 7/7/14, clipping in GNLB 116, 1759/13/243.

51 GNLB 2, 614/07 and 2245/07.

52 GNLB 203, 1622/14/D104.

53 GNLB 110, 1328/13/07, DNL to SNA, 7/6/13.

54 NTS 185, F473, vols. 7 and 8.

55 NTS 196, 3657/F473, reporting the Burton visit.

56 See, for example, NGI, passim and the comment on the Native Grievances Inquiry in the *Rand Daily Mail,* 7/7/14, clipping in GNLB 116, 1759/13/243.

57 On the harsh discipline typical of most of the mines, see, for example, GNLB 111, 1376/13/D154, Report of the Crown Mines Investigation, 6/8/13.

58 GNLB 1, 3147/09, memorandum of H.M. Taberer, 1908.

59 GNLB, 111 1518/14/D104 contains the report which is discussed in chap. 5.

60 The labour bureau and Native Affairs Department archives contain very extensive records of assaults and brutality on the mines. See, for example, GNLB 1, 3885/08; 12, 2255/10; 109, 1238/13/D48; 198, 1518/14/D54; and NTS 186, F473, vol. 9.

61 The desertion issue is discussed in chap. 5.

62 *Cape Times*, 2/7/14, clipping in GNLB 116, 1759/13/243.

63 GNLB 197, 1440/14/48, contains many files on worker "unrest" during the war. For the 1920 strike, see P. Bonner, "The 1920 Black Mineworker Strike: a Preliminary Account," in *Labour Townships and Protest*, ed. B. Bozzoli, 273–97. See also van Onselen, *Chibaro*, 218–26, 237–44.

64 Van de Horst, *Native Labour*, 191–2. See also G. Hunter, ed., *Industrialization and Race Relations*, 97–140, 220–53, and D. H. Houghton, "Migrant Labour," in *Africa in Transition*, ed. P. Smith.

65 Davies, "Mining Capital, the State," 44.

66 Frederickson, *White Supremacy*, 210–20; and S. Greenberg, *Race and State in Capitalist Development*, esp. chap. 8.

67 Davies, "Mining Capital, the State."

68 See the discussion in chap. 1.

69 Johnstone, *Class, Race and Gold;* Davies, *Capital, State and White Labour;* M. Lacey, *Working for Boroko.*

70 L.M. Thompson, *The Unification of South Africa*, 16–17, and see also J.S. Marais, *The Fall of Kruger's Republic.*

71 M. Lacey, *Working for Boroko*, 299.

72 For J.A. Hobson see his *The War in South Africa.* Creswell's standpoint is considered in chap. 2. When stripped of its white racialism, his thinking bears some striking similarities to the modern radical analysis.

CHAPTER ONE

1 G.A. DENNY, *The Deep Level Mines of the Rand*, 50, estimated that £590,000 were required to develop and equip a first-row deep-level (not very deep) property. Also S.H. Frankel, *Capital Investment in Africa*, 100.

2 R.V. Kubicek, "The Randlords in 1895: A Reassessment," *Journal of British Studies* 11(1972): 91–2, 97–8.

3 F.H. Hatch and J.A. Chalmers, *The Gold Mines of the Rand*, viii–xi (preface by John Hays Hammond), 97–8, 271–2. Also annual report of Rand Mines, *Standard and Diggers' News*, 19/3/97.

4 *MIC*, evidence of L. Reyersbach, 93–7. Working costs in 1906 averaged 22s. 1d. for sixty companies. Ibid., 100.

5 *ICI*, evidence of W.L. Hamilton, 74–5; *The Economist*, 13/2/97. JCI paid no dividends at all in 1897–8. R.R. Mabson, *Statist Mines of the Transvaal*, 137–8.

6 *ICI*, evidence of E. Brochon, 178–812. See also *Standard and Diggers' News*,

3/5/97, R.V. Kubicek, "The Randlords in 1895," 99–101.

7 BRA, HE, G. Rouliot letterbook, to J. Wernher, 27/3/97, 19/4/97.

8 The sharp fall in the average grade of ore extracted in 1906 as compared with 1897 suggests that this policy may have been followed. See *MIC*, evidence of L. Reyersbach, 93–7.

9 *South African Mining Journal*, 5/12/96. For background on Kruger's policies see C.T. Gordon, *The Growth of Boer Opposition to Kruger*, 28–57, 86–111, and his "Aspects of Colour Attitudes and Public Policy in Kruger's Republic," in *African Affairs*, ed. K. Kirkwood (St. Antony's Papers, no. 21).

10 HE, G. Rouliot letterbook, to J. Wernher, 8/2/97.

11 D.J.N. Denoon, *A Grand Illusion*, 191.

12 Thirty mines withdrew from the chamber early in 1896, leaving over one hundred companies in it. *CMAR*, 1896, 3, 32.

13 R. Robinson and J. Gallagher with A. Denny, *Africa and the Victorians*, 422; J. van der Poel, *The Jameson Raid*, 8, 80.

14 The *Standard and Diggers' News* for 1896 contains many examples. See also HE, G. Rouliot letterbook, to J. Wernher, 1/2/96.

15 HE, G. Rouliot letterbook, to J. Wernher, 11/6/97.

16 *South African Mining Journal*, 2/1/97.

17 HE, G. Rouliot letterbook, to J. Wernher, 19/4/97.

18 J.S. Marais, *The Fall of Kruger's Republic*. On the evidence of the Colonial Office Records, Marais argued that the British agent in the Transvaal, Conyngham Greene, was instrumental in bringing the industry together at this juncture. Mining industry records do not support this interpretation and suggest that Greene exaggerated his own ability to control the mine owners.

19 *CMAR*, 1890, 61, Chamber of Mines to secretary of state, 23/1/90. See also Rhodes House, Oxford, Charter Consolidated MS, Box 50, draft statement of industry grievances, February 1897.

20 *CMAR*, 1890, 61, 66, 75; 1891, 50.

21 Ibid.,1891, 49–50; 1892, 52; 1893, report of Committee of Mine Managers' Association.

22 Ibid., 1893, 31, 41–2.

23 Ibid., 1894, 48–50; 1895, 26; S.H. Barber et al., trans., *Laws, Volksraad Resolutions, Proclamations and Government Notices Relating to Natives and Coolies in the Transvaal*, 76–86.

24 *CMAR*, 1896, 104–5. Law 23 of 1895 was amended in 1896 and again in 1899. See Barber et al., trans., *Laws, Volksraad Resolutions*, 58–60.

25 *South African Mining Journal*, 24/10/96.

26 *CMAR*, 1896, 5–6; 1897, 4–5.

27 *ICI*, evidence of F. W. Kock, Chief Pass Office, Johannesburg, 294–5. *TLC*, evidence of T. Maxwell, 31–3 and M.S. Erskine, 265. Erskine was giving evidence on the prewar situation. In 1903, he was a WNLA district manager. See also, *Transvaal Administration Reports for 1902*, pt. I, A31.

28 *CMAR* 1896, 156-7, 168-9. *South African Mining Journal,* 1/5/97.
29 *CMAR* 1897, 4-5.
30 JPFP, H. Eckstein and co. to Wernher, Beit, 8/1/98.
31 *CMAR* 1899, 41-2, government labour agent, Cape Colony (L.H.S. Tainton) to Chamber of Mines, 31/1/99.
32 Ibid. 1897, 118-19. JPFP, H. Eckstein and co. to F. Sander, 25/11/97; J.P. FitzPatrick to A. Beit, 27/9/97; to Wernher, Beit, 31/1/98. See also *South African Mining Journal,* 6/2/97.
33 *CMAR* contains many examples.
34 HE, J.B. Taylor to Wernher, Beit, 23/9/93; G. Rouliot to J. Wernher, 20/7/97.
35 TAD, Leyds Argief, no. 670, Briewebook Lionel Phillips, Phillips to A. Beit, 12/8/94; HE, Phillips to Beit, 26/11/92; J.B. Taylor to Wernher, Beit, 28/10/93.
36 A.H. Duminy and W.R. Guest eds., *FitzPatrick,* FitzPatrick to Wernher, 23/10/97, 8/11/97; JPFP, H. Eckstein and co. to Wernher, Beit, 4/12/97; CO 879/55/532, nos. 130, 132 at 135-41.
37 *ICI,* evidence of George Albu, 14; W.L. HAMILTON, 85; J.H. Johns, 261; SNAA, [261], G. Lagden to A. Wheelwright, 20/10/02. Note: Since the research for this chapter was completed, the Transvaal Archives has reorganized the SNAA collection. Some of the references here to SNAA (in square brackets) refer to volume numbers now superseded and can be traced through the new inventory of the collection.
38 *TLC,* evidence of William Grant (native labour commissioner of the chamber, 1893-7), 490.
39 *Report of the Superintendent of Natives of the ZAR for the Year 1897,* app. D: First Volksraad Resolution no. 2260, 8/12/96; translation in SNAA 2012/04. See also *CMAR,* 1899, 83.
40 S.T. van der Horst, *Native Labour in South Africa,* 165.
41 On labour supply problems in the immediate postwar period, see D.J.N. Denoon, "The Transvaal Labour Crisis, 1901-6," JAH 8(1967): 481-94, an excellent, pioneering article; Also P. Warwick, "African Labour during the South African War, 1899-1902," ICS, 7(1975-6): 104-16.
42 *CMAR* 1900 and 1901, 106-11, Chamber of Mines to Milner, 21/8/00. Generally, on the subject of the mining industry's expectation from the new dispensation, see J.A. Hobson, *The War in South Africa;* G. Rouliot's presidential address to the Chamber of Mines, 3/4/02, printed in the Johannesburg *Star,* 4/4/02; Leo Weinthal, *Memories, Mines and Millions.*
43 Stephen Koss, ed., *The Pro-Boers,* xxxvi, 54-8.
44 A. Mawby, "The Transvaal Mine Owners in Politics" (Seminar paper, University of London, c 1973), 11. Also A.H. Duminy, "Political Career of Sir Percy FitzPatrick, 1895-1906" (PHD thesis, University of Natal, Durban, 1973).
45 Duminy, "Political Career of Sir Percy FitzPatrick."
46 *Transvaal Administration Reports for 1902,* A32-A33.
47 Ibid., A4. South African Native Races Committee, *The South African Native*

Races: Their Progress and Present Condition (London, 1908), supplement to *The Natives of South Africa* (London, 1901), 21-2.

48 SNAA 2451/05, Chamber of Mines to G. Lagden, 16/7/06; 2944/05, secretary of native affairs [hereafter, SNA] to secretary, Law Department, 11/10/05; also file 664/06, passim.

49 Mawby, "The Transvaal Mine Owners."

50 SNAA [5], H. Strange to Lagden, 8/1/02.

51 GOV, 753/PS50/03, report of the chief inspector, Native Affairs Department, for the year ending 30/6/03. There were exceptions, of course. Archibald Grant, the compound manager at the Lancaster GMC, was dismissed at the request of the director, Foreign Labour Department, when it was found that "he and the Chinese interpreter on the mines were in the habit of selling opium to the coolies, gambling with them and at the same time receiving a percentage of all stakes." See HC, 17/956, Selborne to Elgin, 24/9/06.

52 SNAA 1458/04. It must be added that by 1904, partly as a result of adverse criticism in Britain, the inspectors were maintaining a closer watch on the mines.

53 SNAA [7], C.W. Spencer, General Manager, Consolidated Main Reef GMC, to G.A. Goodwin, 4/4/02; 1308/02, report on strike of natives at Langlaagte Estate GMC, 7/7/02; 1342/02, report on strike of natives at Geldenhuis Estate GMC, 22/8/02; 1480/02, report on strike of natives at Durban Roodepoort GMC, 7/8/02.

54 TLC, evidence of R. von Harnach, 681-2. On compounds generally at this time see South African Native Races Committee, *The Natives of South Africa* 139-40., and the supplement, *The South African Natives,* 25-8.

55 *TLC,* evidence of E. Croux, 12-14.

56 SNAA [261], H.W. Lloyd [?] to Lagden, 30/6/06.

57 Cf. Denoon, *A Grand Illusion,* 171, who suggests that Lagden did nothing in this area.

58 SNAA 1200/02, report by V.M. Pietersen, Native Affairs Department inspector; 1761/02, passim; and 2135/02. Cf. *Transvaal Administration Reports for 1902,* pt. I: report of chief inspector, Native Affairs Department, A29f, which minimized deficiencies in the mine compounds.

59 SNAA 2195/02, SNA to Chamber of Mines, 8/10/02.

60 Transvaal Native Affairs Department, *Annual Report for the Year Ending 30 June 1904,* annexure B, B19-B21.

61 See *TLC,* "Report on the Mortality of Natives [on the mines]," 557-65. The report was the work of a committee of mine doctors commissioned by the chamber at the suggestion of Lagden. For improvements effected and the fall in the death rate see Transvaal Native Affairs Department, *Annual Reports for the Year Ending 30 June 1904 and 30 June 1905.* The introduction of African mineworkers from the British Central African Protectorate led to a rise in the death rate again, ibid., A10-A12 and chap. 7 below.

62 SNAA [5], secretary of state to high commissioner, 18/11/01. The Colonial Office kept a close watch on mine labour conditions and several times urged vigilance

on the Transvaal Native Affairs Department. See, for example, GOV 753/PS50/04, A. Lyttelton to Milner, 25/3/04.

63 *TLC,* 295-6 and 810-11; Cape of Good Hope, Department of Native Affairs *Report of Native Delegates together with Correspondence relating to visit of Native Representatives to Johannesburg* ... (G 4-1904, Cape Town, 1904); SNAA [7], WNLA fortnightly report, 10/11/02; 1794/03.

64 SANAC, Minutes of Evidence, vol. 4: evidence of Harold Strange, 778.

65 SNAA 1308/02; 1124/03; 1280/05.

66 SNAA 1280/05.

67 ON THE *Modus Vivendi,* see J. van der Poel, *Railway and Customs Policies in South Africa, 1885-1910,* and especially R.E. Ellsworth, "Economic Regionalism and Political Centralism and South African Union" (Research essay, Queen's University at Kingston, 1981). On the Transvaal government's knowledge of the secret WNLA-Mozambique agreement see SNAA 3513/05, C. Rodwell, imperial secretary, to W. Windham, SNA, 2/12/05; and CO 879/89/801, governor-general of Mozambique to high commissioner, 22/11/05, encl. 1 in no. 50, 36-7. Apart from the BCAP, the chamber and the government were also involved in correspondence concerning possible recruiting in North Africa, Gold Coast, East African Protectorate, Uganda, Hungary, southern United States, Barbados, and Japan among other places. A sampling of the correspondence can be found in GOV 731/PS37/04.

68 SNAA, [1], secretary of state to Milner, 24/8/01; Milner to Chamberlain, 6/12/01 (Transvaal, no. 312); and Lagden to high commissioner, 5/12/01.

69 SNAA [261], A. Wheelwright to Lagden, 12/9/03.

70 Ibid., Lagden to Windham, 16/11/06.

71 Ibid., Lagden to Selborne, 31/1/07.

72 For example, SNAA 12/04.

73 SNAA, [261], Lagden to Selborne, 28/11/06; 1282/05, Lagden to Windham, 8/5/05, on other alleged breaches of the monopsony by the Robinson group.

74 The thirty-shilling agreement was actually negotiated late in 1900 in Cape Town. SNAA 1234/02, Chamber of Mines circular, 25/10/00.

75 "A Descriptive and Statistical Statement of the Gold Mining Industry of the Witwatersrand," annexure to *CMAR* 1902, 25. On the target worker idea see F. Wilson, *Labour in the South African Gold Mines,* 75-6; E.J. Berg, "Backward Sloping Labor Supply Curves - the African Case," *Quarterly Journal of Economics* 75(1961): 468-92.

76 SNAA 2361/02, Chamber of Mines circular, 13/11/02. The agreement was amended again early in 1903.

77 HC 17/86, employment statistics, Transvaal gold mining industry; CS 1085/3142/05, "Influx and Exodus of Natives from Mines and Works, July 1904-June, 1905," encl. in Asst. SNA to P. Duncan, 17/8/05. Cf. Denoon, *A Grand Illusion,* 134-5.

1 Complaints about the shortage of development capital were widespread at this time. See, for example, the *Transvaal Leader,* 13/12/06, reporting the speech of Raymond Schumacher to the annual meeting of the South Nourse GMC; and R.V. Kubicek, *Economic Imperialism in Theory and Practice,* 72–85.

2 BRA, HE 152, Lionel Phillips to J. Wernher, 4/12/05; also, *South African Mines, Commerce and Industries,* 1/9/06.

3 HE 144, Wernher to Phillips, 10/11/05, on the tube mills.

4 Reported in the Johannesburg *Star,* 20/11/07.

5 HE 253/134/741, H. Eckstein and co. to Wernher, Beit 5/3/06; also HE 134, S. Evans to F. Eckstein, 24/9/06 and 19/11/06. The reorganization of the industry at this time is considered in P.C. Grey, "The Development of the Gold Mining Industry of the Witwatersrand, 1902–1910" (D.Litt. et Phil. thesis, University of South Africa, Pretoria, 1969).

6 HE 253/148/932, "Notes on the Development of the Mining Industry," prepared by the engineering department of Consolidated Mines Selection, June 1907.

7 M. Fraser and A.H. Jeeves, eds., *All that Glittered, sec. III; South African Mines, Commerce and Industries,* 9/2/07.

8 *Transvaal Leader,* 13/12/06, reporting Raymond Schumacher's speech to the annual meeting of the South Nourse GMC.

9 *South African Mines, Commerce and Industries,* 1/9/06, reported the speech. This journal, a spokesman for the industry in Johannesburg, was specializing in gloomy reports on "the out-look." This was part of a press compaign mounted by the mines to "educate" public opinion and governments both in South Africa and in Britain on the detrimental effects of political uncertainty and especially on the need to reduce mining costs. HE 90, Phillips to Wernher, 23/7/06.

10 On the politics of this period see A.H. Duminy and W.R. Guest, eds., *Fitz-Patrick,* pt. 12; W.H. Hancock and J. van der Poel, eds., *Selections from the Smuts Papers,* vol. 2, pt.7; Fraser and Jeeves, *All that Glittered,* sec. 3.

11 *South African Mines, Commerce and Industries,* 20/1/06.

12 HE 152, Phillips to Wernher, 10/3/06.

13 Ibid., Phillips to Wernher, 24/12/06.

14 Fraser and Jeeves, *All that Glittered,* Phillips to Wernher, 28/1/07, 171.

15 HE 134, S. Evans to F. Eckstein, 25/2/07.

16 HE 152, Phillips to Wernher, 18/3/07. In 1906, the chamber installed a mining industrialist named de Jongh as president. They hoped that his Dutch name "might save us something at the hands of the Liberal govenment," but as Phillips laconically later noted, it did not seem to have had "much effect." Ibid., 11/2/07.

17 HE 144, Wernher to Phillips, 5/1/06.

18 On the interview see ibid. and Duminy and Guest, *FitzPatrick,* Wernher to J.P. FitzPatrick, 6/2/06, 420–1.

19 Duminy and Guest, *FitzPatrick,* Wernher to FitzPatrick, 23/2/06, 422–3.

20 Ibid., 423, emphasis original.
21 At the climax of the election campaign, FitzPatrick, who was deeply committed against Het Volk and the Nationalists, asked permission to make the interview public as a means of discrediting Smuts. Wernher declined to permit this possibly dishonourable breach of confidence. He was also taking a longer, less romantic view politically than his fiery colleague. See HE 152, Phillips to Wernher, 28/1/07.
22 Duminy and Guest, *FitzPatrick*, 423; HE 152, Phillips to Wernher, 10/3/06.
23 HE 152, Phillips to Wernher, 10/3/06, emphasis original.
24 Duminy and Guest, *FitzPatrick*, Wernher to FitzPatrick, 23/2/06, 422–3.
25 W.K. Hancock, *Smuts*, vol. 1, *The Sanguine Years*, 224–5; and Smut's speech at Middelburg, reported in the Johannesburg *Star*, 17/12/06.
26 Johannesburg *Star*, 15/12/06, leader on "Creswellism."
27 HE 252/136/708, Chamber circular 22/05, 1/9/05; PM 35, 73/9/07, acting secretary to the prime minister to secretary of the Chamber of Mines, 28/3/07.
28 *Transvaal Leader*, 3/5/07, and the Johannesburg *Star*, 2/5/07, extracted in CO 879/94/866, 110–15.
29 CO 879/94/866, Selborne to Elgin, 6/5/07, no. 86, 108–10.
30 *Standard and Diggers' News*, November 1898 to March 1899, passim.
31 *MIC*, majority report, accurately reflected Creswell's thinking. See also his letter in the *Transvaal Leader*, 15/12/06.
32 *MIC*, 115.
33 Ibid., 29–30.
34 Ibid., 115.
35 *Smuts Papers*, 2: 338–9, Smuts to J.X. Merriman, 10/4/07.
36 CO 879/94/866, encl. 1 in no. 96, 133. On the standpoint of the white workers see E. Katz, "White Workers Grievances and the Industrial Colour Bar, 1902–13," *South African Journal of Economics* 42(1974): 127–56.
37 The government estimate is in CO 879/94/866, encl. 1 in no. 98, 137; Reyersbach's estimate is deduced from his statement during an interview with the prime minister, PM 36, "Report on an Interview ... ," 7/6/07.
38 HE 153, Phillips to Wernher, 13/5/07.
39 Lionel Phillips wrote to London during the strike that "the Dutchmen" are "flocking in" to the mines. After the trouble ended, there would be "no places for known agitators" and "a good many others" would find their places filled. Ibid., 154, Phillips to Wernher, 25/5/07.
40 R. Davies, "Mining Capital, the State and Unskilled White Workers in South Africa, 1901–13," *JSAS* 3(1976); and F.A. Johnstone, *Class, Race and Gold*.
41 HE 90, Phillips to Wernher, 3/9/06.
42 Reported in the Johannesburg *Star*, 30/5/07.
43 HE 154, Phillips to F. Eckstein, 13/4/08.
44 HE 90, Phillips to Wernher, 3/9/06.
45 R. Davies, "Mining Capital, the State," 60, and his *Capital, State and White*

Labour in South Africa, 1900–1960, 61, 89n42 and 141n122; for a more convincing discussion of the relations between the mining industry and the state in South Africa, see D. Yudelman, *The Emergence of Modern South Africa.*

46 HE 152, Phillips to Wernher, 30/7/06, his emphasis. See also 7/8/06 and 11/8/06 in the same letterbook, and in HE 90, Phillips to Wernher, 3/8/06.

47 HE 152, Phillips to Wernher, 25/2/07.

48 Ibid.

49 HE 253/148/24, notes of meeting of mining deputation with General Botha in London, 6/5/07.

50 The numbers of recruits began to increase dramatically early in 1907 and was attributed to depression in other sectors of the economy, to crop failures in the northern Transvaal and Swaziland, and to certain developments in Portuguese Gazaland which made many Africans "feel that they will be safer on the Rand than in their own country." Given death rates on the mines at this time, the last factor was remarkable evidence of conditions in Mozambique. HE 134, S. Evans to F. Eckstein, 14/1/07; and HE 253/148/889, H. Eckstein and co. to Wernher, Beit, 14/1/07.

51 HE 152, Phillips to Wernher, 19/4/07.

52 Transvaal Legislative Assembly, *Debates,* statement by J. Rissik, 18/6/07 cols. 122–5; 13/8/07 col. 2251; 15/8/07 col. 2387.

53 On Transvaal government policy toward Nyasaland labour see ibid. and Johannesburg *Star,* 19/6/07. Partly owing to the intercession of the Botha government, the imperial authorities reluctantly sanctioned a second "experiment" with Nyasaland labour but they refused to allow any actual recruiting. See below, chap. 7.

54 Lionel Phillips addressing the annual meeting of the Village Main Reef GMC in London, 15/7/07, reported in the Johannesburg *Star,* 16/7/07; J. Wernher's speech to the annual meeting of the Central Mining and Investment Corporation in London, reported in the Johannesburg *Star,* 9/8/07.

55 HE 152, Phillips to Wernher, 19/4/07.

56 Ibid.

57 Transvaal Legislative Assembly, *Debates* 14/6/07, cols. 49–54. Also GNLB 206, 1705/14/110, Papers on formation of the government native labour bureau. On the collapse of the WNLA, see chap. 6.

58 CO 879/94/867, minute by Transvaal ministers, 29/5/07, encl. 1 in no. 84, 83–4.

59 SNAA 3875/10, "Constitution and Rules and Regulations of the 'Rhodesian Native Labour Bureau'," Government notice 169, 1906, 19/7/06.

60 NTS 182, H.L. Phooke to J.X. Merriman, 10/1/08.

61 SNAA 2803/10, Proclamation 375 of 29/7/07, "Amendments to Labour Agents' Regulations." See also CO 879/94/867, encl. 1 in no. 84, 83–4.

62 Transvaal Legislative Assembly, debates, J. Rissik statement, 1/8/07, cols. 1882–5.

63 HE 253/134/822, H. Eckstein and co. to Wernher, Beit, 30/6/06.

64 HE 253/134/790. See also 253/134/807, H. Eckstein and co. to Wernher, Beit, 11/6/06.

65 HE 90, H. Eckstein and co. to Wernher, Beit, 20/8/06.

66 HE 134, S. Evans to F. Eckstein, 22/10/06.

67 *South African Mines, Commerce and Industries,* 25/8/06.

68 NTS 191, /596 [SNAA file 3625/1907], "Memorandum on the Unskilled Labour Question" by F. Perry, 27/5/07. Official figures for January 1907 showed 148,076 unskilled labourers on the mines: 94,221 blacks, and 53,856 Chinese. Transvaal Legislative Assembly, *Debates,* J. de Villiers statement, 30/7/08, col. 1277.

69 F. Perry, "Memorandum on Unskilled Labour."

70 Minute by Cape ministers, 1/754 of 13/12/05, cited in PM 35, 73/04/07.

71 Ibid., minute by G. Lagden on Cape minute cited.

72 NTS 181, minute by Cape ministers 1/116, 19/2/07. On the private views of officials, see, for example, ibid., W.E. Stanford to L.S. Jameson, secretary to the prime minister, Cape Town, 21/03/07.

73 PM 35, 73/04/07, secretary to prime minister to SNA, 28/03/07.

74 NTS 181, minute by L.S. Jameson for the governor, 13/5/07.

75 IBID., F. Sparg, Indutywa to Messrs. Malcomess (copy), 17/4/07; W.H. Fuller to Col. Crewe, MP, 20/4/07; "Tembu" to "Natives," Cape Town, 23/4/07 and 24/4/07; East London Chamber of Commerce to Jameson, 24/04/07; "Griqua" to "Natives," Cape Town, 26/4/07; E. Dower to secretary, East London Chamber of Commerce, 22/5/07.

76 Ibid., minute by Louis Botha for the governor, 11/6/07.

77 Ibid., W. Stanford (Johannesburg) to "Natives," Cape Town, 5/4/07.

78 Ibid., [SNAA file 87/07], "Memorandum of Native Labour Scheme ..." 20/6/07.

79 HE 252/136/646, L. Reyersbach to Wernher, Beit, 20/2/05; see also 252/136/652, same to same, 6/3/05. The evidence in the second letter suggests that the estimates of the labour needs of the mines given to the Transvaal Labour Commission in 1903 resulted not, as is usually argued, from a deliberate effort to mislead the commission but rather from the competitive inflation of mine complements which the WNLA system produced. The WNLA adopted revised complements in April 1905 which at a stroke reduced total labour needs by 23,000 men. The mines simply resumed the inflation from the new, lower base. HE 252/136/656, H. Eckstein and co. to Wernher, Beit, 10/4/05.

80 HE 144, J. Wernher to L. Phillips, 31/7/08.

81 SNAA 1615/07. By April the mines were apparently unable to provide work for several hundred Africans on hand in the Braamfontein depot. See also HE 253/148/901, H. Eckstein and co. to Wernher, Beit, 4/2/07 and HE 253/148/911, H. Eckstein and co. to Wernher, Beit, 8/4/07, which indicate that the WNLA was having trouble "disposing" of Cape recruits. The association finally waived the recruiting charges in order to induce the mines to take them.

82 On the registry offices see PM 35, 73/4/09, J. Rissik to J.X. Merriman, 10/3/10; and SNAA 683/10.

83 *NGI,* 85/642–4.

84 SNAA 4317/07, passim; CO 879/94/867, enclosure "B" in no. 84, 89–90.

85 See S. Marks, *Reluctant Rebellion,* chap. 12.

86 In December 1907, the Transvaal government secured unanimous agreement from the other South African colonies for the reestablishment of such an agency. Because it was poorly supported the original deposit and remittance agency had closed in 1906. CO 879/94/866, Selborne to Elgin, 9/12/07, no. 118, 114.

87 SNAA 496/08, Transvaal Chamber of Mines, report of the Executive Committee for 1907, vii.

88 Johannesburg *Star,* 19/9/07.

89 The figures are as follows: for 1908 – Cape, 28,532 – Natal and Zululand, 7,289; for 1909 – Cape, 42,941 – Natal, 11,366. GNLB 265, 568/16/243, "Territorial Analysis of Natives in Proclaimed Labour Districts of the Transvaal."

90 See the extensive report on recruiting abuses in the *Cape Times,* 19/11/09.

91 *Smuts Papers,* vol. 2, pt. 8; P. Lewsen, ed., *Selections from the Correspondence of J.X. Merriman,* vol. 4, chap. 3; Fraser and Jeeves, *All that Glittered,* sec. 3.

92 "Closer union is necessary, if only to take control of the immense native population out of the hands of the handful of incompetent people in Natal." HE 154, Phillips to F. Eckstein, 12/10/08 and passim in this volume.

CHAPTER THREE

1 This was particularly the case in the eastern Cape and on the northern border of the Transvaal. For the Cape see CAD, CNA 708, which contains many examples, and vol. 1150 which contains the proceedings of the Cape Town Labour Conference of September 1909 where the situation was fully discussed. For the northern Transvaal see, for example, SNAA 2714/09, native commissioner, northern division to SNA, 16/8/09.

2 CNA 1150, proceedings of the Cape Town Labour Conference.

3 In the Cape, the runners were often whites, usually traders, taking advantage of the lower fees and acting as subagents for fully licenced recruiters. Elsewhere, runners were blacks.

4 CNA 1150, statement of Mr Dix, 35.

5 CNA 708, Dower to J.X. Merriman, 17/8/08, encl. in Dower to RM, Dordrecht, 21/8/08.

6 CNA 718, vol. 1, RM, Molteno to SNA, 4/5/10, and passim in this volume.

7 CNA 721, vol. 2, asst. chief magistrate, Transkei, to SNA, 2/12/09 and enclosures.

8 On the worsening situation, see, for example, CNA 708, E. Barrett to S.M. Pritchard, 19/12/08, and the enclosures.

9 See the extensive report in the *Cape Times,* 19/11/09.

10 By arrangement with Merriman, Burton toured the eastern Cape in August 1909 and his report was an important factor in the government's decision to press for reform. See PM 38, 81/2/09, "Memorandum on Visit to Native Territories"

by H. Burton, 3/9/09.

11 See, for example, CNA 710, department circular, 8/12/09.

12 This was recognized in 1909 when a new set of officials, the labour registrars, was appointed in the Cape recruiting centres to handle matters connected with the migrant system.

13 CNA 1150, proceedings of the Cape Town Labour Conference, comments of E. Dower; *Cape Times,* 19/11/09.

14 This conclusion is based on the large number of cases in which the Native Affairs Department declined to prosecute or failed to secure convictions. For instance, see CNA 708, RM, Nqamakwe, to SNA, 29/8/08, and minutes by Stanford (16/9/08) and Dower (28/9/08); also CNA 725, correspondence on the cases of Klaas Pitshi and George Katshwa.

15 CNA 1150, H. Burton to J.F.B. Rissik, Transvaal SNA, 11/09/09, annexure C in papers relating to Cape Town Labour Conference.

16 *Cape Times,* 19/11/09. By 1909, the Cape had outstripped the northern Transvaal and Natal as a source of mine labour. Only Mozambique provided more.

17 BRA, HE 254/137/1153, "Memorandum on the Native Labour Supply in Proclaimed Labour Districts of the Transvaal," 31/03/09.

18 *NGI* 74/546, 559; JPL, NGI, Charles W. Villiers; earlier in 1909, one mining executive estimated that the Cape was receiving about £300,000 annually from wage advances and recruiting fees paid to their agents and miners by the gold mines. CNA 1150, proceedings of the Cape Town Labour Conference.

19 See below, pp. 113–20.

20 In 1907, the Cape had licensed about 100 agents and over 2,000 runners. In 1908, there were about 72 licensed agents in the colony. CNA 708, Dower to RM, Dordrecht, 21/08/08, enclosing Dower to Merriman, 17/08/08; and Dower to controller and auditor-general, 11/04/08.

21 On the problem of advances, see CNA 708, minute by Dower, 29/8/08 and E. Barrett to Transkeian chief magistrate, 21/9/08, reporting the reluctant agreement of the prime minister, J.X. Merriman, to the continuation of cattle advances. On the labour contractors, see CNA 708, department circular, 21/9/08. At this time the department began actively to discourage the so-called intermediary agents who were the "agents of agents" and had no direct agreement themselves with a mine employer.

22 Taberer's memorandum is in GNLB 1, 3147/08; for Stanford's proposal see CNA 708, A.H. Stanford to Cape SNA, 3/9/09.

23 GNLB 1, 3147/08, Taberer memorandum.

24 Ibid.

25 HE 154, Lionel Phillips to F. Eckstein, 12/10/08; and HE 254/149/1006, H. Eckstein and co. to Wernher, Beit, 19/10/08.

26 HE 254/149/1004, H. Eckstein and co. to R.G. Fricker, 16/11/08; also HE 280 227/1, memorandum of agreement between Rand Mines, H. Eckstein central

administration, and the Gold Fields group.

27 HE 254/149/1137, H. Eckstein and co. to Wernher, Beit, 26/7/09; 254/149/1138, H. Eckstein and co. to Wernher, Beit, 31/7/09; 254/149/1141, H. Eckstein and co. to Wernher, Beit, 16/8/09; and especially 254/137/1186, H. Eckstein and co. to Wernher, Beit, 22/11/09.

28 CNA 708, Stanford to Dower, 3/9/08. Apart from Stanford and Taberer, a Mr Jenner, labour bureau inspector, left government service to become head of recruiting for the Neuman group. F.Perry, for many years chairman of the WNLA, had been a senior official in Milner's Reconstruction administration. For Jenner see CNA 709, circular no. 13, 31/12/09.

29 CNA 1150, proceedings of the Cape Town Labour Conference, evidence of H.M. Taberer.

30 CNA 708, Dower's minute on Stanford's letter, 3/9/08.

31 Ibid., Merriman's minute, 18/9/08.

32 There is no evidence that they were aware of each other's proposals.

33 HE 254/137/1186, H. Eckstein and co. to Wernher, Beit, 21/11/09.

34 CNA 710, file 4709.

35 HE 254/137/1186, H. Eckstein and co. to Wernher, Beit, 22/11/09; CNA 714, T.R.G. Davies to SNA, Cape Town, 19/12/08.

36 CNA 708, F.2/6543, E. Barrett to S.C. Harding, 7/12/08.

37 HE 254/149/1128, H. Eckstein and co. to Wernher, Beit, 28/6/09.

38 On opposition to the thirty-six and forty-two-inch minima see PM 38, 81/2/09, Burton memorandum.

39 CNA 708, RM, Nqamakwe to SNA, 29/08/08; CNA 713, SNA to Civil Commissioner, Fort Beaufort, 6/9/09.

40 Union of South Africa, House of Assembly, *Reports of Select Committees,* 1910–11 (First Session, First Parliament, vol. 2).

41 *Select Committee on Native Labour Regulation Bill,* minutes of evidence, 113, 120.

42 On Mostert's contracts see CNA 714, authority to recruit for the Robinson group, 25/8/08, and for the H. Eckstein/Rand Mines group, 23/7/08.

43 The H. Eckstein/Rand Mines organization revoked their authority early in 1909. CNA 713, F. Raleigh to A.M. Mostert, 10/3/09.

44 On Wilson's background see CNA 712, Dower to SNA, Pretoria, 12/10/07; on his relations with Robinson see A.H. Jeeves, "The Control of Migratory Labour on the South African Gold Mines in the Era of Kruger and Milner," *JSAS* 2(1975): 3–29.

45 CNA 714, SNA to RM, Engcobo, 27/2/09 with enclosures, and RM, Engcobo, to SNA, 4/3/09 with enclosures.

46 CNA 708, E. Barrett to W. Carmichael, secretary-treasurer, Transkeian General Council, 22/8/08, and department circular, 21/9/08, encl. in Dower to Taberer, 23/9/08.

47 CNA 713, minute D30/443/09 by SNA, 6/3/09, and enclosures.

48 CNA 709, C.H. Pritchard to Asst. RM, Indwe, 1/1/10, encl. in E. Barrett to RM, Dordrecht, 18/2/10.

49 CNA 714, RM, Engcobo to SNA, 4/3/09.

50 SNAA 2803/10, Cape Native Affairs Department notice, 23/6/10.

51 When evaluating the industry's continual complaints of labour shortages, these considerations need always to be kept in mind.

52 With its huge resources and ability to be more flexible in the allocation of labour between production and development, the H. Eckstein/Rand Mines group consistently took a longer view. Senior executives in this group were almost alone in calling persistently for restoration of the monopsony in South Africa itself, and of course they played a leading role in the formation of the NRC in 1912.

53 CNA 713, T.R.G. Davies to Asst. RM, Indwe, 5/6/09, encl. in RM, Dordrecht to SNA, 4/8/09.

54 CNA 713, Transvaal Mines Labour company to Cape SNA, 18/8/09, and enclosures.

55 CNA 710, chief magistrate, Transkei to SNA, 18/2/10, and enclosures, especially TMLC to E. Dower, Cape SNA, 9/12/09 and 19/1/10, and E. Dower to secretary, TMLC, 5/2/10.

56 For documentation on the early rounds of the struggle, see CNA 713, passim, especially undated memorandum on the cases of Davies and Lloyd, and minute by RM, Dordrecht, to SNA, 4/8/09.

57 CNA 713, H.M. Taberer to acting director, GNLB [S.M. Pritchard], 2/3/09.

58 Ibid.

59 Ibid., minute by RM, Dordrecht, 4/8/09, and enclosures. He did allow them to *accept* recruits from other companies, however.

60 Ibid., SNA to RM, Dordrecht, 30/4/09.

61 The entire episode can easily be traced in CNA 713, especially TMLC to SNA, 18/8/09, and enclosures.

62 On the Erskine case, see below, p. 104.

63 CNA 713, H.M. Taberer to acting director, GNLB, 2/3/09, and minute by RM, Dordrecht, 4/8/09, and enclosures. The latter is a thick file, documenting the extent of intra-industry competition for labour in the Cape.

64 CNA 725, contains extensive records of recruiting irregularities. See also CNA 720, clipping from the *Church Chronicle* on illicit recruiting, 27/1/09.

65 HE 254/149/1128, H. Eckstein and co. to Wernher, Beit, 28/6/09.

66 HE 254/137/1186, H. Eckstein and co. to Wernher, Beit, 22/11/09; and 254/1137/1214, Wernher, Beit, to H. Eckstein and co., 31/12/09.

67 HE 254/149/1138, H. Eckstein and co. to Wernher, Beit, 31/7/09, and no. 1141, H. Eckstein and co. to Wernher, Beit, 16/8/09; HE 254/137/1198, H. Eckstein and co. to Wernher, Beit, 6/12/09.

68 HE 254/149/1137, H. Eckstein and co. to Wernher, Beit, 26/7/09.

69 HE 255/139/1281, H. Eckstein and co. to Wernher, Beit, 20/6/10.

70 HE 264/177/7, H.M. Taberer to H. Eckstein and co., 29/12/10.

71 HE 254/149/1128, H. Eckstein and co. to Wernher, Beit, 28/6/09.
72 Ibid.
73 HE 254/139/1337, H. Eckstein and co. to Wernher, Beit, 26/9/10.
74 *Cape Times,* 19/11/09.
75 CNA 708, RM, Nqamakwe, to SNA, 29/8/08, and memoranda by A.H. Stanford, 16/9/08, and E. Dower, 28/9/08 in the same volume; CNA 721, civil commissioner, King William's Town to SNA, 22/12/08.
76 CML NIO of 1912, Johann Rissik, Transvaal minister of native affairs, to J.W.S. Langerman, president of the Chamber of Mines, 10/6/09.
77 PM 38, 81/2/09, Burton memorandum.
78 CNA 1150, S.M. Pritchard to E. Dower, 13/8/09. Pritchard was responding to a set of confidential reports from the Cape which had reached him several months before.
79 The trader/recruiter, permanently resident in an African area, might have an interest in maintaining a reputation for fair dealing which the transient contractor obviously did not have.
80 See Edward Dower's remarks at the opening session of the Cape Town Labour Conference. CNA 1150, proceedings of the conference.
81 Ibid., "Memorandum on the Supply of Cape Labour for the Transvaal Mines" by E. Muller, Cape Native Affairs Department, 17/9/09.
82 The conference records are conveniently grouped in CNA 1150. See also the extensive report on the conference in *Cape Times,* 19/11/09, clipping in the same file.
83 CNA 1150, "Memorandum on the Native Labour Question."
84 Ibid., memorandum on "A Cape Native Labour Bureau," prepared for the Cape Town conference, September 1909.
85 Ibid., "Memorandum on the Supply of Cape Labour" by E. Muller.
86 Ibid., "Memorandum of Proposals discussed."
87 See S.M. Pritchard's remarks in ibid., conference proceedings, minutes of evidence, 24/9/09.
88 CNA 719, W. Windham to E. Dower, 26/10/09, encl. in Dower to Transkeian chief magistrate, 31/1/10.
89 CNA 1150, conference digest of proceedings.
90 Ibid., memorandum on "A Cape Native Labour Bureau."
91 Ibid., conference proceedings, W. Windham to E. Dower, 26/10/09, and the accompanying memorandum outlining the Transvaal's alternative scheme.
92 CNA 710, department circular, 8/12/09.
93 W. Beinart, "Joyini Inkomo: Cattle Advances and the Origins of Migrancy from Pondoland," *JSAS* 5(1979): 210.
94 CNA 721, Dower to Pritchard, 13/10/09. In addition to the reforms mentioned here, the Cape and Transvaal also agreed that rail facilities for Cape mineworkers were bad and terribly overcrowded. Authorities promised improvements and ordered S.M. Pritchard to investigate.
95 CNA 711, "Natives," Johannesburg to "Natives," Cape Town, 15/1/10;

"Natives," Cape Town to Heitzman, Johannesburg, 11/1/10; also E. Dower to J.X. Merriman, -/12/09.

96 CNA 719, vol. 1, Pritchard to Dower, 25/2/10, attached to Pritchard to "Indaba" [Native Affairs Department], Pretoria, 11/3/10.

97 GNLB 12, 2259/10, Pritchard to W. Windham, 27/2/10.

98 CNA 719, vol. 1, passim. This volume contains a large number of letters and telegrams from labour agents, traders, commercial interests, and others, protesting Pritchard's activities.

99 GNLB 12, 2259/10, F. Douglas McMillan to secretary, TMLC, 14/2/10. McMillan was a local manager for the TMLC in the eastern Cape. "Kaffir" Wilson passed this letter to the Transvaal authorities and used it in his efforts to induce ministers to repudiate Pritchard. See also SNA to A.E. Wilson, 23/3/10, and a second letter of the same date, also in this file.

100 GNLB 12, 2259/10, McMillan to secretary, TMLC, 14/2/10.

101 CNA 719, vol. 1, Dower to G. Whitaker, 31/3/10.

102 Ibid.

103 GNLB 12, 2259/10, F. Douglas McMillan to secretary, TMLC, 14/2/10.

104 CNA 719, vol. 1, Dower to Whitaker, 31/3/10.

105 GNLB 12, 2259/10, Taberer to Pritchard, 18/2/10.

106 Ibid., Pritchard to Taberer, 19/2/10 and 28/2/10.

107 Ibid., "Natives," Johannesburg to Pritchard, 28/2/10.

108 Ibid., Rissik to Merriman, 10/3/10.

109 GNLB 13, 2259/10, Wilson to Rissik, 17/3/10; GNLB 12, 2259/10, SNA to Wilson, 23/3/10, and a second letter of the same date.

110 GNLB 13, 2259/10, A.M. Mostert to Rissik, 17/3/10.

111 GNLB 12, 2259/10, "Natives," Cape Town to "Indaba," Pretoria, n.d., and CNA 719, vol. 1, Merriman to Rissik, 17/3/10.

112 GNLB 12, 2259/10, "Natives," Cape Town to Pritchard (at Muizenberg), 18/3/10, relaying the message of recall. Pritchard left for Pretoria so quickly that he had to cancel a scheduled meeting with Merriman.

113 Ibid., Pritchard to Windham, 27/2/10.

114 CNA 719, vol. 1, Pritchard to Dower, 25/2/10.

115 GNLB 12, 2259/10, "Natives," Cape Town to "Indaba," Pretoria, n.d.

116 CNA 719, vol. 1, Merriman to Rissik, 17/3/10.

117 *Cape Mercury,* 8/4/10, clipping in CNA 1150.

118 See the weekly reports of the labour registrars in CNA 719, vol. 1 passim.

119 *NGI,* 73/537; 74-5/545-9; 85/644, 649.

120 See the table in app. 1.

121 Calculation from C. Bundy, *The Rise and Fall of the South African Peasantry,* table 3, 121.

122 App. 1.

123 Bundy, *Rise and Fall,* table 3, 121; R. Palmer and N. Parsons, eds., *The Roots of Rural Poverty in Central and Southern Africa,* 1-15; and compare an impor-

tant new study, P. Lewsen, *John X. Merriman,* 305-29.

124 Bundy, *Rise and Fall,* 109-45; M. Legassick, "Gold, Agriculture and Secondary Industry in South Africa, 1885-1970: From Periphery to Sub-Metropole as a Forced Labour System," in *Roots of Rural Poverty,* ed. R. Palmer and N. Parsons, 175.

CHAPTER FOUR

1 C. Bundy, *The Rise and Fall of the South African Peasantry,* 125, 142n7. Bundy correctly notes the fall in real wages over the whole period. Between about 1907 and 1912, however, the cost of black labour to the companies tended to increase as a result of higher recruiting fees to recruiters and runners, better piece work rates for the "hammer boys," and an easing of the daily task required of the workers. See BRA, HE, 254/149/1128, H. Eckstein and co. to Wernher, Beit, 28/6/09, and passim in this volume.

2 On the closing of certain districts see *Union Gazette,* 7/5/12, Government notice, no. 627, 2/5/12. For the Land Act see T.R.H. Davenport and Keith Hunt, eds., *The Right to the Land,* sec. 3; W.M. Macmillan, *Complex South Africa,* 117-43; E. Hellmann, ed., *Handbook on Race Relations in South Africa,* 171-90; Marian Lacey, *Working for Boroko,* 120-47.

3 HE 254/149/1119, H. Eckstein and co. to Wernher, Beit, 22/5/09.

4 HE 254/149/1102, R.G. Fricker to Lord Harris, 10/10/08; HE 154, Lionel Phillips to F. Eckstein, 6/11/08.

5 HE 254/137/1141, report of a meeting of representatives of Rand Mines, H. Eckstein central administration, and Consolidated Gold Fields, 28/10/09.

6 HE 155, Phillips to Wernher, 6/12/09.

7 HE 254/149/1147, H. Eckstein and co. to Wernher, Beit, 6/9/09.

8 HE 155, Phillips to F. Eckstein, 8/7/10.

9 Ibid.

10 HE 255/139/1300, H. Eckstein and co. to Wernher, Beit, 11/7/10.

11 HE 255/139/1324, report of committee to look into combination on recruiting in British South Africa, 13/8/10. See also no. 1294.

12 HE 255/139/1331, notes of meeting of group representatives, 31/8/10.

13 CML, N10, 1911, "Interim Report of Recruiting Investigation Committee," 15/10/10.

14 Ibid., "Further Interim Report," 25/10/10.

15 Ibid., "Further Report," 19/12/10.

16 HE 255/139/1374, H. Eckstein and co. to Wernher, Beit, 28/10/10, and see 255/139/1350, H. Eckstein and co. to Wernher, Beit, 31/10/10.

17 HE 155, Phillips to F. Eckstein, 28/10/10.

18 CML, N10, 1911, secretary, Association of Mine Managers, to secretary, Chamber of Mines, 31/12/10, enclosing unanimous resolution passed on 23/12/10.

19 GNLB 55, 1356/12, J.G. Hamilton, president of the Chamber of Mines, to R.

W. Schumacher, 19/3/12.

20 Twenty thousand of 100,000, according to the interim report of the chamber's recruiting investigation committee, 24/12/10. HE 255/139/1378. Early in 1911, S.M. Pritchard testified before the select committee on the native labour regulation bill that about 14 per cent of a total of 206,536 black labourers on the mines (including non-South African) were employed or recruited by independent contractors. Select committee evidence, 29-32.

21 Select committee evidence, 29-32.

22 HE 155, Phillips to Wernher, 16/1/11.

23 Henry Burton's notes in NTS 186, /473, vol. 9, n.d.

24 Select committee evidence, 132-3, statement of the chairman, Henry Burton, during testimony of A.M. Mostert, 22/2/11.

25 HE 155, Phillips to F. Eckstein, 8/7/10.

26 Ibid.

27 M. Fraser and A.H. Jeeves eds., *All That Glittered,* 216.

28 Ibid., letter 110, 238.

29 Ibid., letter 111, 240-1.

30 Ibid., 277n31.

31 Ibid., letter 113, 243.

32 HE 155, Phillips to F. Eckstein, 10/10/10.

33 HE 255/139/1332, Wernher, Beit to H. Eckstein and co., 12/8/10.

34 HE 255/139/1386, H. Eckstein and co. to Wernher, Beit, 23/1/11.

35 Fraser and Jeeves, *All That Glittered,* letter 118 to F. Eckstein, 254.

36 HE, Lionel Phillips letterbook, 1911-16, to L. Reyersbach, 22/1/12.

37 GNLB 55, 1356/12, R.W. Schumacher to J.G. Hamilton, president of the Chamber of Mines, 16/3/12.

38 Ibid., J.G. Hamilton to R.W. Schumacher, 19/3/12.

39 Fraser and Jeeves, *All That Glittered,* to R.W. Schumacher, 6/3/12, letter 119, 257.

40 HE 255/139/1332, Wernher, Beit to H. Eckstein and co., 12/8/10.

41 NTS 1, 3242/2, statement by F.S Malan, minister of native affairs, 1/10/14, cited in memorandum by S.M. Pritchard, 6/10/14.

42 JPL, NGI, Charles W. Villiers. This typescript in the Johannesburg Public Library contains a small part of the testimony given before Mr Justice H.O. Buckle who conducted the Native Grievances Inquiry.

43 Ibid., S.M. Pritchard.

44 Ibid., Charles W. Villiers.

45 NGI CA, 1, H.M. Taberer.

46 *NGI,* 74/545.

47 NGI CA, 1, H.M. Taberer.

48 The contractors certainly knew that they held the whip hand. Testifying at the Native Grievances Inquiry in 1914, Villiers complained bitterly that some of them "did us down an enormous sum of money" during the take-over. In one

instance, he claimed, the corporation was defrauded of £13,000. JPL, NGI, Charles W. Villiers.

49 Ibid., S.M. Pritchard.
50 Ibid.
51 Ibid., Charles W. Villiers.
52 F.A. Johnstone, *Class, Race and Gold,* 41-5.
53 JPL, NGI, H.M. Taberer.
54 Ibid., Charles W. Villiers.
55 Ibid.
56 W. Beinart and C. Bundy, "State Intervention and Rural Resistance: The Transkei, 1900-1965," in *Peasants in Africa,* ed. M.A. Klein, 271-316.
57 JPL, NGI, Charles W. Villiers; CNA 1150, proceedings of Cape Town Labour Conference, evidence of Mr Shulz, 1-11.
58 *NGI,* 74/546.
59 CNA 1150, proceedings of Cape Town Labour Conference, evidence of Mr Mills, 4-16 and passim.
60 GNLB 53, 1239/12/53, contains a file on under-age Africans recruited in 1915 by the Mostert organization and refused attestation of their contracts or rejected by the local medical officer. By 1915, the state had extended more effective control over the mines' recruiting and employment practices. A major problem identified in 1915 must have been considerably more serious several years earlier when competition for labour was unrestrained and government controls very lax. The child labour issue is discussed below.
61 NTS 6, 2390/2, A.H. Stanford, Chief Magistrate Transkei, to SNA, 6/9/12.
62 SNAA 2803/10, "Labour Agents Licences and Regulations," unsigned, n.d. [7/8/10].
63 *East London Daily Despatch,* 2/2/14; *Cape Mercury,* 30/1/14; and Johannesburg *Star,* 3/2/14; clippings in NTS 6, 2390/2.
64 See the following in NTS 6, 2390/2: *Transkeian Gazette,* 12/2/14; DNL to Secretary, King William's Town Chamber of Commerce, 16/2/14; *Transvaal Leader,* 18/2/14; petition from Kaffrarian Labour Association and others, 4/3/14; Chief Marelane to Native Affairs Department, 6/3/14; resolution of King William's Town chamber of commerce, 9/3/14; petition from labour agents' association, East Grigualand; resolution of the Alice municipality; "Natives," Cape Town, to "Natives," Pretoria, 18/3/14, referring to a delegation of MPs which interviewed Botha at this time to oppose abolition of advances.
65 *NGI,* 74-5/549; 76/561-36. For a summary of the report see Charles Diamond, "The Native Grievances Inquiry, 1913-14," *South African Journal of Economics* 36(1968): 211-27.
66 *NGI,* 74/546.
67 Ibid., 82/615-7.
68 Ibid., 80/595.

69 Ibid., 83/628.

70 Ibid., 85/642-8.

71 Ibid., 87/667.

72 Ibid., 86/652.

73 Ibid., 86/655.

74 Ibid., 86/657.

75 Ibid., 86/658.

76 Ibid., 87/668.

77 NTS 6, 2390/2, copy of minister's statement to Parliament, n.d. [1914].

78 Ibid., SNA minute, 20/5/15, cited in acting DNL to SNA, 29/11/15, and draft circular from DNL, n.d. [late 1915].

79 Ibid., S.M. Pritchard to E. Dower, 11/2/14.

80 GNLB 46, 1159/12/38, RM, Nggeleni to acting DNL, 3/11/15, and reply from H.S. Cooke, 19/11/15.

81 Ibid., magistrate, Harding, Natal to DNL, 4/6/15.

82 NTS 6, 2390/2, E. Barrett, Native Affairs Department to A.W. Leslie, 7/7/14, covering a letter from a Natal farmer, n.d., which called for abolition of advances, and a second letter from an East London group, 28/5/14. The East Londoners wanted advances restricted to a two-pound maximum in order to minimize the loss of labour from the area.

83 See, for example, GNLB 45, 1159/12/38, acting DNL to SNA, 24/8/16, concerning the regulation that advances be given in the presence of a magistrate.

84 GNLB 262, 482/16/38, J.W. McKenzie vs. Union government, 30/8/16.

85 NTS 8, 1308/2.

86 NGI, 87-8/668-71; 94/761.

87 NTS 1, 3242/2, SNA to secretary for justice, 8/8/18.

88 Ibid. The meeting was held on 1 October 1914.

89 See n. 109.

90 NTS 1, 3242/2, A.M. Mostert to minister of native affairs, 12/7/18 and 22/7/18.

91 Ibid., acting DNL to SNA, 31/7/18.

92 Ibid., A.M. Mostert to minister of native affairs, 12/7/18 and 22/7/18. The basis of Mostert's appeal is set out in minutes by secretary for justice, 14/8/18, in ibid. See also minutes by the acting DNL, H.S. Cooke, in the same file, 31/7/18 and 13/8/18.

93 GNLB 229, 583/15/D145, concerning bureau investigations of "unnatural vice" in the mining compounds.

94 GNLB 53, 1239/12/D53, pass officer, Randfontein to DNL, 4/6/14, reporting a request of Theron's.

95 GNLB 51, 1239/12/D53, DNL to magistrate, Lusikisiki, 24/3/19.

96 Ibid., A.M. Mostert to DNL, 20/3/19.

97 GNLB 53, 1239/12/D53, pass officer, Randfontein to DNL, 4/6/14; 229, 599/15/310, and 227, 522/15/87, passim.

98 GNLB 53, 1239/12/D53. This is a huge file, documenting the traffic in under-

age workers.

99 GNLB 229, 599/15/310, acting DNL to Harry Zihlangu, 24/12/15; A.M. Mostert, contractor, to DNL 3/12/15; statement by Harry Zihlangu, 18/11/15.

100 GNLB 339, 81/22/243, NRC statement to the Mining Industry Board, 1922.

101 JPL, NGI, Charles W. Villiers.

102 Ibid.

CHAPTER FIVE

1 JPL, NGI, Charles W. Villiers.

2 GNLB 55, 1356/12, J.G. Hamilton to R.W. Schumacher, 19/3/12.

3 CML, Low Grade Mines Commission Files, vol. 4: "Native Recruiting Corporation, Statement of Evidence ... 1919."

4 *WNLA Annual Report*, 1921.

5 JPL, NGI, Charles W. Villiers.

6 Ibid.

7 See chap. 1.

8 "Report of Delegates Together with Correspondence Relating to Visit of Native Representatives ... to Johannesburg ..." (Cape Town, G.4-1904), 1.

9 Ibid., 4.

10 Ibid., 9-12.

11 These matters are discussed in chap. 1.

12 GNLB 3, 313/09, contains the report on which the following account is based.

13 GNLB 339, 81/22/243.

14 *WNLA Annual Report*, 1916.

15 GNLB 3, 313/09.

16 GNLB 1, 3476/08, acting RM, King William's Town, to civil commissioner, 3/3/10.

17 GNLB 10, 1238/10.

18 CAD, CNA 1150, proceedings of the Cape Town Labour Conference, September 1909, passim.

19 Ibid., Merriman minute on Dower to Merriman, -/5/10.

20 Ibid., proceedings.

21 W. Beinart, "'Joyini Inkomo': Cattle Advances and the Origins of Migrancy from Pondoland," *JSAS* 5(1979): 199-219.

22 See chapter 3 for an estimate of the contribution of advances to the Cape economy.

23 Cited in GNLB 150, 136/14/37(3), DNL to sub-native commissioner, Sibasa, 17/9/24 (emphasis original).

24 GNLB 150, 136/14/37(48), DNL to pass officer, Benoni, 15/6/22, and sub-native commissioner, Potgietersrust, to DNL, 12/6/22.

25 GNLB 150, 136/14/37(50), sub-native commissioner, Sekukuniland, to DNL, 12/7/22.

26 GNLB 149, 136/14/37, DNL to SNA, 17/10/21.

27 GNLB 149, 136/14/37(19), and 151, 136/14/37.

28 GNLB 149, 136/14/37/(19), September Gxowa to DNL, N.D [1923].

29 Ibid., Inspector, NRC, to DNL, 8/5/23.

30 Ibid., "Natives," Haenertsburg to GNLB, Johannesburg, 23/4/23.

31 JPL, NGI, S.M. Pritchard. A helpful perspective on the desertion issue is C. Perrings, *Black Mineworkers in Central Africa,* 165-73.

32 CNA 1150, proceedings of the Cape Town Labour Conference, September 1909, evidence of James Hadley.

33 See, for example, GNLB 220, 283/15/35, documenting a large number of desertions of "Mostert natives" while en route to the Rand.

34 JPL, NGI, S.M. Pritchard.

35 This is the probable explanation of the high number of desertions of mineworkers from the Cape. During this period recruiting levels were increasing much more rapidly in the eastern Cape than in any other South African territory.

36 GNLB 4, 927/09 and 2330/09, labour bureau reports for 1907-8 and 1908-9.

37 Ibid.

38 *WNLA Annual Report,* 1915, 25.

39 GNLB 20, 1101/11.

40 The labour bureau director, S.M. Pritchard, had fought for improvements since first appointed to succeed Taberer in 1908. See his evidence before the Native Grievances Inquiry: JPL, NGI.

41 GNLB 111, 1376/13/D154, 6/8/13.

42 Twelve thousand black workers constituted the complement at Crown Mines, the largest of the amalgamations of the previous several years. This labour force would turn over completely in less than two years.

43 NGI, 77/578-9.

44 NGI, CA, 1, J.G. Millar.

45 On the Mostert compounds see, for example, GNLB 228, 558/15/D100. An inquiry into conditions in these compounds was held in 1911 and found much to condemn. Few improvements seem to have been made, however. See Union of South Africa, House of Assembly, *Reports from Select Committees,* 1910-11, vol. 2: appendix to the report on the Native Regulation Act.

46 GNLB 136, 2756/13/54.

47 Ibid., inspector, Benoni south, to DNL, 9/12/13.

48 GNLB 198/14/D80, bureau memorandum, 1914.

49 GNLB vols. 135, 136, 137 contain extensive files.

50 GNLB 33, 1756/11, report of E.E. Mills, 27/7/11.

51 Ibid., S.M. Pritchard circular, 1/6/11. See also the report of E.E. Mills, 12/5/11, in this file, concerning a black gang on the Rand which was selling large numbers of stolen passes to would-be deserters.

52 JPL, NGI, Charles W. Villiers, 54. In the second case mentioned by Villiers, the touts in Germiston were operating on behalf of Natal collieries, some of which

were subsidiaries of NRC member groups.

53 GNLB 188, 1246/14/53, S.M. Pritchard, DNL, to SNA 29/8/82. The bureau had a tendency to invite trouble of this sort. Between 1913 and 1918, labour agents' licences were issued to messengers and deputy messengers of the magistrates' courts, a standing temptation to these whites to tout illegally for labour.

54 NTS 3, 1940/19, acting DNL to SNA, 16/4/19.

55 Ibid.

56 GNLB 133, 2570/13/53, papers connected with investigations of the activities of Samuel Said in 1913.

57 Ibid., statement by Detective Broekman, 27/5/13. The City Deep contract was soon cancelled by the NRC. See JPL, NGI, Charles W. Villiers, 33.

58 GNLB 133, 2570/13/53, statement of R.H. Thomas, 28/9/14.

59 Ibid., information bureau, NRC to H.M. Taberer, 9/11/14.

60 Ibid., statement of Lindsay Douglas Normand, 4/1/15.

61 Ibid., Magistrate R.M. Thomas, Dundee, to DNL, 28/9/14.

62 Ibid., Normand statement, 4/1/15; DNL to deputy commissioner, Johannesburg CID, 14/1/15, rejecting the fanciful notion that Said was the actual employer.

63 GNLB 212, 1/15/C, "Report on the evidence taken at the Berg-Mills Enquiry," June 1915. The department soon transferred Mills out of the city to the City and Suburban Mine. After war broke out in Europe, he left South Africa to return to Britain. See also GNLB 133, 2570/13/53.

64 GNLB 212, 1/15/C, "Report on ... the Berg-Mills Enquiry."

65 GNLB 209, 1827/14/35.

66 Ibid., acting chief pass officer, E. Berg, Johannesburg, to DNL, 5/2/15.

67 Ibid., statement by "Libone Jack," 18/3/15, encl. in secretary, NRC, to DNL, 5/8/15. Both the department and the Native Recruiting Corporation conducted inquiries into this and several similar cases of multiple desertion.

68 GNLB 223, 378/15/53, statement of "Fokkies," 9/7/15; of "Forage," 9/7/15; of "police boy English," 15/7/15; and A. Kantor to asst. DNL, E.K. Whitehead, 8/7/15.

69 Ibid., labour bureau inspector, Johannesburg (town), to DNL, 15/7/15.

70 GNLB 104, 927/13/53; JPL, NGI, S.M. Pritchard.

71 Ibid.

72 GNLB 100, 585/13/53, E.C. Thompson to NRC, 5/3/21.

73 Ibid., enclosure, n.d.

74 GNLB 104, 927/13/53, sub-native commissioner, West Rand to DNL, 25/9/23.

75 See chap. 3.

76 GNLB 10, 1238/10.

77 S. Moroney "Industrial Conflict in a Labour Repressive Economy" (BA hons. dissertation, University of the Witwatersrand, 1976), 43–7; C. van Onselen, *Studies in the Social and Economic History of the Witwatersrand, 1886-1914*, vol. 2, *New Nineveh*, 171-201; and F.Z.S. Peregrino, *Life among the Native and Coloured Miners of the Transvaal.*

78 *NGI,* 19.

79 NGI, CA, 1, J.S. Marwick.

80 Ibid., Alfred Pigg.

CHAPTER SIX

1 On the early development of migrancy from Mozambique, see P. Harries, "Labour Migration from the Delagoa Bay Hinterland to South Africa, 1852-1895," ICS 7(1975-6): 61-77; M. Newitt, "Migrant Labour and the Development of Mozambique," ICS 4(1972-3): 67-76; R.J. Hammond, *Portugal and Africa, 1815-1910,* 311-34. The clandestine emigration from Mozambique to South Africa is discussed below.

2 On the weakness of Portuguese colonial authority in Mozambique at this time see J. Duffy, *A Question of Slavery,* 139-43; M. Newitt, *Portuguese Settlement on the Zambesi,* 330-1, 337-8; A.F. Isaacman, *The Tradition of Resistance in Mozambique,* 49-74, 156-85.

3 Except as noted below, this outline of the WNLA system is based on the following: NTS 191, /596, report on east coast recruiting prepared by a committee of the board of management of the WNLA in 1906; BRA, HE 253/134/793, WNLA memorandum on the investigating committee, 18/5/06; Johannesburg *Star,* 15/12/06, report on Mozambique recruiting issued by the Chamber of Mines; and F. Perry, "Portuguese East Africa and South African Union," *The State* 1(1909): 551-2.

4 North of 22°SL a quite different situation obtained. The WNLA dealt with the so-called chartered companies. See chap. 7.

5 In practice, the WNLA board of management was the executive committee of the Chamber of Mines augmented by the senior WNLA staff.

6 Amendments to Mozambique recruiting regulations in 1899 required the Rand Native Labour Association to appoint a Portuguese national acceptable to the government as agent. Breyner's appointment was gazetted on 30/9/99, a few days before recruiting operations ceased. CO 879/98/901, encl. in no. 36, 48.

7 SNAA 15/02, F.H.E. Crowe to A. Milner, 17/10/01, and report of a conference on Portuguese labour, 22/10/01, in this file.

8 SNAA 30/02, G.A. Goodwin to T.M.C. Nourse, 15/2/02.

9 HE 253/148/866, B. Cabral to L. Phillips, 12/10/06. Cabral later changed his mind when Breyner and Wirth decided that they wanted the manager left in place. HE 253/148/895, Cabral to Phillips, 29/12/06.

10 SNAA 2020/04, T.J.M. Macfarlane to the chairman and board of management, WNLA, 17/8/04.

11 HE 291/257/202, contains a memorandum on the contract with the syndicate for 1906 and the changes proposed for 1907.

12 HE 290/242/162, H. Eckstein and co. (Sam Evans) to Wernher, Beit, 8/10/06.

13 Ibid. Three other groups had been invited to participate in this arrangement

also should the WNLA actually collapse. See also HE 290/242/161, R.W. Schumacher to J. Wernher, 29/9/06.

14 Ibid.

15 NTS 191, /596, report of F. Perry on visit to Portuguese East Africa, 11/9/07.

16 Ibid.

17 CO 879/94/866, Major J.G. Baldwin, consul-general, to Selborne, 5/2/07, encl. in no. 31, 31-2.

18 SNAA 2162/07, extracts from the annual report of the governor of Inhambane, translations enclosed in J.G. Baldwin to Selborne, 19/10/07.

19 NTS 191, /596, report by F. Perry on his tour of Portuguese East Africa, 11/9/07.

20 SNAA 2020/04, T.J.M. Macfarlane to the chairman and board of management, WNLA, 17/8/04.

21 NTS 193, /596, E. Macdonell, British consul-general at Lourenço Marques to foreign secretary, 21/9/15, encl. in A. Bonar Law to Viscount Buxton, 4/11/15; GNLB 32, 2558/11/53, notes on a visit to Mozambique by S.M. Pritchard [1911].

22 HE 253/148/831, H. Eckstein and co. to Wernher, Beit, 27/8/06.

23 *South African Mines, Commerce and Industries,* 4/8/06.

24 See above, chap. 2.

25 Robinson's enemies were legion, most with long memories. The *Cape Times* spoke for them at his death, referring to the "loathsomeness of the thing that is the memory of Sir Joseph Robinson" (7/11/29). Imperial officials also disliked J.W.S. Langerman, Robinson's key associate. Joseph Chamberlain once described him as "touchy, unreasonable and wild," and did not think his presence on the Legislative Council would be "useful." HC 106, Chamberlain to Milner, 10/3/03.

26 CO 879/89/801, Robinson to Elgin, 27/4/06, no. 87, 89-92; 8/6/06, , no. 132, 126-7; 11/6/06, no. 14, 135-6; 18/6/06, no. 149, 147-50; 14/9/06, no. 205, 212-3. Robinson's exact relationship with the British Liberal party requires investigation. In 1908, he was created a baronet on the recommendation of H.H. Asquith. Later he was to be raised to the peerage by the same government. It seems he had purchased one of Lloyd George's titles. The outcry, not least in the House of Lords, was so great that Robinson had to be asked to decline the honour. See *The Times,* 31/10/29.

27 The letter is reprinted in *CMAR,* 1906, 14-5. The firm of Lewis and Marks was already recruiting in Mozambique outside the WNLA monopsony but in a very small way. See GOV 210/224/06, Selborne to Elgin, 11/6/06, and Elgin to Selborne, 7/7/06.

28 Lionel Phillips of Wernher, Beit/Eckstein carried on extensive negotiations with Wilson, apparently on behalf of the chamber. See SNAA 989/06, Wilson to Phillips, 19/5/06; Phillips to Wilson, 23/5/06; Wilson to Phillips, 24/5/06, encl. in Selborne to Elgin, 26/5/06; Phillips to Wilson, 26/5/06, encl. in

Selborne to Elgin, 28/5/06; Wilson to Phillips, 29/5/06, encl. in Selborne to Elgin, 11/6/06.

29 Ibid., C.H. Rodwell, imperial secretary, to A.E. Wilson, 29/3/06, encl. in Rodwell to Lagden, [6] /4/06.

30 Ibid., Selborne to Elgin, 24/6/06.

31 Ibid.; CO 879/89/801, Selborne to Elgin, 21/5/06; GOV 210/59/06, Lagden to Selborne, 30/10/06, encl. in Selborne to Elgin, 5/11/06; and 210/227/06, F.D.P. Chaplin to Colonial Office, 3/7/06, encl. in Elgin to Selborne, 14/7/06. *CMAR*, 1906, central administration of Eckstein group to high commissioner, 29/10/06, 24 (and several other nearly identical letters from other groups and individual mines). These are examples only of a torrent of protest which poured in upon Elgin from the Transvaal government, various mining houses, and the chamber.

32 SNAA 989/06, Elgin to Selborne, 21/5/06. For a discussion of the role of the imperial government, based largely on Foreign Office sources, see Duffy, *A Question of Slavery*, 148–54.

33 SNAA 989/06, Elgin to Selborne, 29/5/06.

34 Ibid., Selborne to Elgin, 5/7/06.

35 Ibid., Elgin to Selborne, [?] 1906.

36 CO 879/89/801, J.B. Robinson to Elgin, 4/6/06, no. 141, 136–8.

37 SNAA 989/06, Selborne to Elgin, 28/9/06.

38 Ibid., J.G. Baldwin to governor-general, Mozambique, 19/11/06.

39 *CMAR*, 1906, 22–3, Rand Mines to high commissioner, 29/10/06.

40 Ibid., 29, president of Chamber of Mines to high commissioner, 1/11/06. This letter and the preceding one were of course written for the secretary of state and were forwarded immediately to him.

41 SNAA 989/06, governor, Johannesburg, to secretary of state, 1/12/06.

42 Ibid., Baldwin to Selborne, 27/11/06.

43 Ibid., Selborne to Elgin, 3/12/06.

44 CO 879/89/801, Fred. Graham (Colonial Offie) to J.B. Robinson, 21/9/06, no. 206, 213. GOV 210/61/06, J.G. Baldwin to Selborne, 19/11/06, and Baldwin to governor-general, Mozambique, 19/11/06, enclosures in Selborne to Elgin, 3/12/06.

45 *CMAR*, 1906, 37–8, private secretary to high commissioner to president of the Chamber of Mines, 10/11/06. See also J.N. De Jongh (president of the chamber) to private secretary to high commissioner, 19/11/06, which came as close to an outright attack on Elgin as it was safe to come in official correspondence.

46 HE 253/148/850, H. Eckstein and co. to Wernher, Beit, 22/10/06; and 253/148/857, same to same, 29/10/06.

47 HE 253/148/864, B. Cabral (in Lisbon) to J. Wernher, 13/10/06. Cabral reported that Lisbon confirmed the decision to grant Holmes only the single licence. See also the enclosures with this letter, undated telegrams exchanged

between Lionel Phillips and Cabral.

48 CML, chairman's speech to the fifth ordinary general meeting of the WNLA, 11/4/07, 78–9, *WNLA Annual Report, 1906.*

49 Ibid.

50 SNAA 15/02, report of a conference on Portuguese labour, 22/10/01.

51 HE 253/148/918, unsigned memorandum on the "Unskilled Labour Question" [by F. Perry], 27/5/06.

52 HE 152, Phillips to Wernher, 4/3/07.

53 Ibid. See also HE 253/148/866, B. Cabral to Phillips, 12/10/06.

54 HE 253/148/883, H. Eckstein and co. to Wernher, Beit, 7/1/07.

55 HE 253/148/894, H. Eckstein and co. to Wernher, Beit, 21/1/07.

56 HE 253/148/866, B. Cabral to Phillips, 12/10/06.

57 HE 253/134/795, Phillips to F. Eckstein, 15/4/06.

58 See HE 152, Phillips to F. Eckstein, 7/1/07.

59 HE 90, Phillips to F. Eckstein, 1/6/06; HE 290/142/176, Phillips to Ayres d'Ornellas, 8/10/06; HE 152, Phillips to F. Eckstein, 7/1/07.

60 HE 253/134/795, Phillips to F. Eckstein, 15/4/06.

61 HE 90, H. Eckstein and co. to Wernher, Beit, 29/10/06; same to same, 5/11/06.

62 HE 152, Phillips to F. Eckstein, 3/11/06; HE 290/242/180, R.W. Schumacher to F. Eckstein, 5/11/06.

63 SNAA 989/06 passim; HE 134, S. Evans to J. Wernher, 3/7/06.

64 Robinson had ostentatiously offered in 1906 to abandon Chinese labour, and this gave credence to the Liberal/Het Volk claim that ample labour was available locally. Because his mines were less dependent on Chinese labour than most, he could well afford his own "magnanimous gesture" – at once a way of toadying to the Liberals and putting a knife into his rivals in the chamber. HE 253/148/866, B. Cabral to Phillips, 12/10/06.

65 CO 879/94/866, Selborne to Elgin, 17/6/07, no. 105, 158-9; NTS 191,/596, J.C. Smuts to L. Reyersbach, 29/5/07.

66 CO 879/94/867, H.W. Just (Colonial Office) to Foreign Office, 18/4/07, no. 43, 36.

67 SNAA 630/08, minute by S.M. Pritchard, 22/2/08.

68 HE 291/257/226, "Suggestions Put Forward by Mr. Smuts ... ," 25/4/07; HE 152, Phillips to Wernher, 19/4/07.

69 See also NTS 191, /596 [SNAA file 3625/07], "Notes on the proposals put forward for the re-entry of the Robinson group into the W.N.L.A.," by F.P.[Perry], 11/5/07.

70 According to Lionel Phillips, the Chamber of Mines had itself originally proposed for the government a supervisory role in relation to the WNLA. HE 152, Phillips to Wernher, 19/4/07.

71 NTS 185, vol. 7, memorandum on "Recruitment of Native Labourers in Portuguese East Africa ... ," n.d. [early 1910].

72 Quoted in HE 253/148/842, H. Eckstein and co. to Wernher, Beit, 29/9/06.

73 See the exchange of letters printed in the *Transvaal Leader,* in which the parties retracted their respective charges and composed their differences. Reprinted in CO 879/94/867, encl. in no. 83, 82, Selborne to Elgin, 28/8/07.

74 HE 153, Phillips to Wernher, 3/6/07.

75 HE 144, Wernher to Phillips, 1/9/07; HE 154, Phillips to F. Eckstein, 25/11/07.

76 See n. 79.

77 NTS 196, 3657/473, report of meeting between Henry Burton and Executive Committee of Chamber of Mines, 13/7/11.

78 Ibid.

79 GNLB 32, 3384/11, "Witwatersrand Native Labour Association Limited: Report of the WNLA Enquiry Commission," 7/9/11.

80 Ibid., 2558/11, "Notes," n.d. [September 1911].

81 "Report of the WNLA Enquiry Commission."

82 GNLB 32, 3384/11, W.W. O'Shannessy to S.M. Pritchard, 16/8/11.

83 Ibid.

84 Ibid.

85 See the contracts negotiated with the Zambesia Company and the Nyassa Company in 1903. SNAA 2905/03, encl. in WNLA to G. Lagden, 20/11/03.

86 NTS 193, 596/473, C.W. Dix, secretary of the WNLA to DNL, 7/2/13; GNLB 32, 3384/11, "Memorandum Regarding the Witwatersrand Native Labour Association's Position in the Tete District," n.d.

87 NTS 193, 596/473, Dix to DNL, 7/12/13.

88 Ibid., "Memorandum on Mr. Creswell's motion re Deferred Pay for Portuguese Natives," 20/3/13.

89 "Report of the WNLA Enquiry Commission."

90 Ibid.

91 NTS 193, 596/473, see paper entitled "Motion, House of Assembly," 25/2/13.

92 BRA, Lionel Phillips letterbook, Phillips (in Cape Town) to R.W. Schumacher, 30/5/12.

93 "Report of the WNLA Enquiry Commission."

94 *Rand Daily Mail,* 29/1/13, clipping attached to MNW 162, 293/13, R.N. Kotze, government mining engineer to secretary for mines, 23/1/13.

95 Ibid., R.N. Kotze letter.

96 Ibid.

97 See, for instance, SNAA 1406/02.

98 Leroy Vail and Lanteg White, *Capitalism and Colonialism in Mozambique,* 179–83, describe the interests of J.P. Hornung but completely ignore the role of the WNLA.

99 See n. 77.

100 NTS 193, 596/473, memorandum on the "motion Tabled by the Honourable Member for Jeppe [F.H.P. Creswell] in the House of Assembly," 25/2/13.

101 Ibid., and governor-general of Mozambique to Union governor-general, 30/4/15, and DNL to SNA, 9/6/15, both in the same file.

CHAPTER SEVEN

1 C. van Onselen, *Chibaro,* 95-6.
2 *CMAR,* 1902, 18; NTS 190, 377/473, vol. 2, "Memorandum on the Introduction of Tropical Natives ... ," n.d.[1911].
3 CO 879/80/721, Foreign Office to Colonial Office, 29/8/02, no. 26, 28-9, and Milner to Chamberlain, 19/7/02, no. 20, 26.
4 Ibid., Colonial Office to Foreign Office, 10/9/02, no. 31, 32.
5 Ibid., Milner to Chamberlain, 3/10/02, no. 41, 58, repeating a telegram from Macfarlane.
6 CO 879/90/716, Chamberlain (at Mafeking) to Earl of Onslow, 24/1/03, no. 94, 34.
7 CO 879/80/721, Chamberlain (at Mazeras, East Africa) to Earl of Onslow, 16/12/02, NO. 65, 85.
8 Ibid., Milner to Earl of Onslow, 7/3/03, no. 89, 107, referring to a letter of Joseph Chamberlain published in the *Transvaal Leader,* 27/1/03.
9 Ibid., Chamberlain to Milner, 3/4/03, no. 114, 129.
10 Ibid., Sir A. Sharpe to Lansdowne, 10/3/02, encl. 1 in no. 17, 23-5.
11 BRA, HE 250/139/36, Wernher, Beit, to H. Eckstein and co., 3/10/02.
12 CO 879/104/947, governor, Nyasaland, to secretary of state, 5/3/10, no. 88, 73-4.
13 CO 879/80/721, George Wemyss, chairman, British Central African Company, to Sir Clement Hill, Foreign Office [early 1903], encl. in no. 70, 89; Church of Scotland Mission council to Sir A. Sharpe, 20/1/03, encl. in no. 98, 118-19, and passim in this volume.
14 Ibid., Colonial Office to Foreign Office, 10/9/02, no. 31, 32.
15 SNAA 1408/02, memorandum by G. Lagden 31/10/02, covering Chamber of Mines, to Lagden 22/10/02.
16 SNAA 1402/03, Lagden to Milner, 16/3/03. See also SNAA 1408/02, passim.
17 CO 879/80/721, Sir A. Sharpe to Lansdowne 16/12/02, encl. 1 in no. 63, 84-5; Lansdowne to Sharpe, 19/3/03, encl. in no. 95, 116.
18 SNAA 1402/02, Lansdowne to Sharpe, 23/3/03.
19 CO 879/80/721, Major F.B. Pearce (Zomba) to Lansdowne, 25/3/03, encl. in no. 104, 123; Pearce to Lansdowne, 31/3/03, encl. 1 in no. 115, 130.
20 SNAA 1402/02, Nourse to acting secretary, WNLA, 19/6/03.
21 SNAA 197/03, Sir A. Sharpe to F.B. Pearce, 12/4/03, encl. in F. Perry, chairman, WNLA, to Lagden, 17/4/03.
22 Ibid., secretary, WNLA, to SNA, 30/6/04.
23 SNAA 1714/03.
24 CO 879/90/743, Lyttelton to Milner, 22/2/04, no. 125, 58; S.T. van der Horst, *Native Labour in South Africa,* 221.
25 CO 879/89/801, D.O. Malcolm to Selborne, 12/3/06, reporting the views of C. Knipe, encl. in Selborne to Elgin, 2/4/06, no. 80, 75-6.

26 Ibid., Selborne to Elgin 18/6/06, no. 168, 158.

27 Ibid., Selborne to Elgin, 25/8/06, no. 197, 199–200.

28 NTS 190, 377/473, vol. 2, "Memorandum on Introduction of Tropical Natives ... ,"n.d. [1911].

29 CO 879/98/901, Sir A. Sharpe to secretary of state, 7/6/08, no. 53, 67–8. See also PM 52, 106/6/09. The WNLA, of course, denied that its agents recruited surreptitiously in Nyasaland but independent evidence indicates that they were doing so. NTS 190, 377/473, vol. 1, C.W. Dix, WNLA secretary, to SNA, 14/4/09, and passim in this volume.

30 CO 879/80/721, Milner to Chamberlain, 8/9/02, no. 30, 31–2.

31 Ibid., Arnold to Milner, 22/4/02, encl. 11 in no. 34, 43–4.

32 Ibid., Milner to Arnold, 14/5/02, encl. 15 in no. 34, 45–6.

33 SNAA 2905/03, "Agreement Between the Zambesia Company and the Witwatersrand Native Labour Association," encl. in WNLA to G. Lagden, 20/11/03. GNLB 32, 3384/11, "Memorandum Regarding the Witwatersrand Native Labour Association's position in the Tete District," n.d. [1911].

34 SNAA 2905/03, contract dated 6/10/03 and enclosed in WNLA to Lagden, 20/11/03; also SNA 855/08, extract from Mozambique Boletim Official, 12/12/03.

35 Barry Neil-Tomlinson, "The Nyassa Chartered Company, 1891–1929," JAH 18(1977): 109–29.

36 For the years ending 30 June 1905 and 30 June 1906 the rates per 1,000 workers per annum were: Nyasaland, 118.3 and 166.3; Mozambique District, 128.2 and 65.8; Quilimane District, 163.9 and 71.6. NTS 190, 377/473, vol. 2, "Memorandum on the Introduction of Tropical Natives ... , " n.d. [1911].

37 SNAA 459/04, memorandum by S.M. Pritchard, 2/1/06; CO 879/98/901, encl. in no. 52, 67.

38 Compiled from CMAR 1910, 378–9.

39 CO 879/106/874, Selborne to Elgin, 22/8/07, no. 437, 149.

40 Even this limited concession was made reluctantly after heavy Transvaal government pressure over a period of nearly eighteen months. See CO 879/101/931, Crewe to Selborne, 5/2/09, no. 20, 32–3.

41 GNLB 3, 1912/09, J. Rissik to president of the Chamber of Mines, 28/9/09. On the eve of the ban on tropical recruiting, the number employed had reached about 25,000.

42 CO 879/98/901, minute by J.C. Smuts, 5/2/08, encl. in no. 23, 21.

43 NTS 191, /596 [SNAA file 3625/07], "Memorandum on the recruiting of Tropical Natives" by F. Perry, 7/5/07.

44 NTS 185, /473, vol. 7, minister's statement on the introduction of the Creswell motion, 7/2/11. There was also renewed pressure from the imperial government. CO 879/108/970, governor-general (Lord Gladstone) to Union ministers, 5/4/11, encl. 2 in no. 121, 139.

45 NTS 196, 3657/473, transcript of H. Burton interview with Chamber of Mines,

July 1911.

46 Ibid.

47 Ibid.

48 GNLB 32, 3384/11, report of WNLA inquiry commission, 7/9/11.

49 Minute by Henry Burton 28/9/11, on E. Dower to Burton, 26/9/11, NTS 199, 4752/473; also NTS 185, /473, vol. 8, Sir A. Sharpe to Crewe, 24/7/10.

50 NTS 197, 3694/473, secretary, WNLA, to minister of native affairs, 24/7/11 and 9/8/11.

51 CML W16, 1911, and NTS 197, 3694/473.

52 While a senior executive of group administration might express concern for tropical mortality in, for instance, a Chamber of Mines discussion, the orders he gave to his mine managers could frequently contradict this.

53 NTS 184, /473, vol. 5, extract from Hansard, 5/3/12.

54 NTS 199, 4752/473, S.M. Pritchard to acting secretary of native affairs, 10/6/12. This had occasionally been done earlier. For instance, at the end of 1910, the government banned the employment of tropical recruits on the Randfontein mines where health conditions were bad and the standard of medical care extremely low. See also NTS 185, /473, vol. 8, Dower to DNL, 25/2/11; and NTS 343, 7201/1131, H. O'K. Webber to H. Burton, 25/12/11: "Private/I would like to tell you that we must welcome them making an example of any mine whose death-rate of tropicals is persistently high - We have had much trouble with some."

55 NTS 205, 2782/473, DNL to SNA, 7/6/13.

56 NTS 197, 3694/473, extract from Hansard, statement of J.W. Sauer, 8/5/13.

57 Ibid., secretary, WNLA, to minister of native affairs, 17/5/13; and director's minute in the same file.

58 Ibid., secretary, WNLA, to DNL, 2/6/13.

59 MNW 194, 2718/13.

60 CO 879/80/721, C. Knipe to Foreign Office, 25/11/03, encl. 1 in no. 229, 230-1.

61 C. van Onselen, *Chibaro,* 74-115.

62 E.P. Makambe, "The Nyasaland African Labour 'Ulendos' to Southern Rhodesia ... ," *AA* 79(1980): 548-66, n. 12.

63 Ibid., and T.O. Ranger, "Revolt in Portuguese East Africa: The Makombe Rising of 1917" in *African Affairs,* no. 2, ed. K. Kirkwood (St. Anthony's Papers, no. 15).

64 On the methods used, see, for example, GNLB 123, 1950/13, passim. The following deal with labour migration from Nyasaland in this period: B.S. Krishnamurthy, "Economic Policy, Land and Labour in Nyasaland, 1890-1914," in *The Early History of Malawi,* ed. B. Pachai, 384-404; J.L. McCracken, *Politics and Christianity in Malawi, 1875-1940,* 114-16; L. Vail, "The Making of an Imperial Slum: Nyasaland and its Railways, 1895-1935," *JAH* 16(1975): 89; E.P. Makambe, "Nyasaland African Labour"; F.E. Sanderson, "The Development of Labour Migration from Nyasaland, 1891-1914," *JAH* 2(1961): 259-71.

65 C. van Onselen, "Worker Consciousness in Black Miners: Southern Rhodesia, 1900-20," *JAH* 14(1973): 237.

66 L. Vail and L. White, *Capitalism and Colonialism in Mozambique,* 181.

67 For an illustration see CO 879/101/931, deputy governor, Nyasaland, to general manager, British Central Africa Company, Blantyre, 3/3/09, encl. 4 in no. 161, 234. On forced labour practices in this area see A.F. Isaacman, *The Tradition of Resistance in Mozambique,* 84-5, 87-9.

68 CO 879/101/931, governor of Nyasaland to secretary of state, 13/11/09, no. 277, 323. Briefly after 1907, the Nyasaland government authorized the WNLA to arrange transport for a limited number of voluntaries who had received official permission to seek work on the mines. Large numbers of other blacks left Nyasaland without such official sanction.

69 On the Compton Thomson case see ibid.., memorandum by J. Charles Casson, n.d. [1909], encl. 1 in no. 277, 325-7; E.H. Compton Thomson to G.E. Vicary, 4/5/09, encl. 1 in no. 161, 232-3.

70 Ibid., Sharpe to secretary of state, 13/11/09, no. 277, 323.

71 Ibid.

72 NTS 190, 377/473, vol. 1, C. Knipe to C.W. Dix, 21/6/09; E.H. Compton Thomson to C.W. Dix, 25/4/09.

73 Ibid., SNA to C.W. Dix, secretary, WNLA, 22/10/10.

74 CO 879/111/994, secretary of state to governor of Nyasaland, 3/1/12, no. 2, 2-3; NTS 190, 377/473, vol. 1, C.W. Dix, secretary, WNLA to deputy governor, Nyasaland, 29/3/09.

75 GNLB 265, 551/16/240, curator of Portuguese labour to DNL, 18/10/16. From the start, several mine labour recruiters evaded the ban. GNLB 123, 1950/13/240, SNA DNL, 8/10/13.

76 HE 155, Phillips to L. Reyersbach, 18/4/10; also, GNLB 123, 1950/13/240, Stuart Erskine for the NRC to SNA, 5/10/13.

77 ZA, BSA Co. archive, A3/18/30/25. See the informative letter from the Rhodesian Native Labour Bureau agent at Chemba to the chairman of the bureau, 18/4/12.

78 Ibid.

79 NTS 314, 826/814, unsigned memorandum on tropical labour, n.d. [May 1914]; also GNLB 123, 1950/13/246, extract from a letter from the sub-native commissioner, Sibasa, 13/8/13.

80 ZA A3/18/30/22, sub-native commissioner, Sibasa, to DNL, Johannesburg, 14/6/15; GNLB 38, 198/1912/75, this file covers the period 1912-26.

81 GNLB 123, 1950/13/240, extract from a letter from the sub-native commissioner, Sibasa, 13/8/13.

82 NTS 2, 5766/1(1), reports and papers connected with the clandestine immigration of "tropicals"; statement of H.S. Cooke, acting DNL, 10/9/18.

83 SNAA 2714/09, native commissioner, northern division, to SNA, 16/8/09.

84 GNLB 123, 1950/13/240, sub-native commissioner, Sibasa, to DNL, 14/6/15.

85 NTS 188, 135/473, J. Allan Woodburn to DNL, 10/8/11; see also H.S. Cooke to acting SNA, 14/11/10 and 13/9/11 in the same file.

86 NTS 2, 5766/2(2), H.J. Kirkpatrick to secretary, South African Police (Transvaal), 18/10/12; C.A. Wheelwright to E. Dower, 6/1/13.

87 Ibid., Kirkpatrick letter.

88 Ibid., H.S. Cooke to SNA, 26/11/12.

89 See n. 86, Wheelwright letter.

90 NTS 2, 5766/2(2), S.M. Pritchard to SNA, 22/4/13.

91 For Seelig's early activities, see SNAA 1380/05, H. Seelig to G. Lagden, 29/12/02.

92 For a short summary of the government's efforts to control illegal recruiting in this area see GNLB 123, 1950/13/240, E. Stubbs to DNL, 26/10/15.

93 ZA, A3/18/30/22, list of touts attached to J.M. Scallon to "ADSP," Melsetter, 18/8/15. For BSA Co. labour policies generally see J.M. Mackenzie, "African Labour in the Chartered Company Period," *Rhodesian History,* 1(1970): 43-58, and "Chartered Africans: Colonial Office, Settlers and B.S.A. co, Rhodesia, 1890-1923," ICS, 4(1972-3): 77-86.

94 ZA, A3/18/30/22, governor, Mozambique Chartered Co. to administrator, BSA Co., 8/11/16.

95 Ibid., report of G. Pierce, corporal, BSA Co. police, Chibi, 7/2/16, of a patrol which attempted to arrest Barnard.

96 Ibid., J.M. Scallon, trooper, BSA Co. police, to "ADSP," 18/8/15.

97 Ibid., chief native commissioner, Salisbury to administrator, 27/1/16, and commandant-general, BSA Co. police, to administrator, 13/3/16.

98 Ibid., administrator, BSA Co., to high commissioner, 16/2/16; administrator to governor, Mozambique Co., 20/3/16; and governor, Mozambique Co., to administrator, 7/8/16.

99 Ibid., governor, Mozambique Co., to administrator, BSA Co., 8/11/16.

100 NTS 197, 3694/473, E.R. Garthorne to imperial secretary, Cape Town, 24/6/14.

101 GNLB 123, 1950/13/240, E.T. Stubbs to DNL, 26/10/15.

102 Ibid., H.S. Cooke to SNA, 24/11/15.

103 Ibid., deed of agreement, 28/1/16.

104 See, for example, GNLB 245, 201/16/53, sub-native commissioner, Potgietersrust, to DNL, 29/2/16 (and enclosures), concerning the activities of the notorious tout, "Jakals" van der Merwe.

105 GNLB 123, 1950/13/240, E.T. Stubbs to SNA, 20/3/16.

106 Ibid., Stubbs to native commissioner, Zoutpansberg, 7/2/18, encl. in native commissioner, Zoutpansberg to SNA, 11/2/18.

107 ZA, A3/18/22, staff officer, BSA Co. police, Salisbury, to secretary to the administrator, 15/8/18.

108 Ibid., passim in this file.

109 ZA, A3/18/30, P. Forrestal, native commissioner, Chibi to superintendent of natives, Fort Victoria, 18/1/17.

110 GNLB 123, 1950/13/240, E.T. Stubbs to native commissioner, Zoutpansberg,

7/2/18, encl. in native commissioner, Zoutpansberg, to SNA, 11/2/18.

111 Ibid.

112 GNLB 123, 1950/13/240, H.J. Taylor, chief native commissioner, Salisbury, to SNA, Pretoria, 14/5/18, in reply to the latter's letter of 26/4/18.

113 NTS 2, 5766/2(2), H.S. Cooke to SNA, 26/11/12.

114 GNLB 123, 1950/13/240, H.J. Taylor to SNA, Pretoria, 14/5/18, in reply to the latter's letter of 26/4/18.

115 Ibid.

116 Ibid., H.S. Cooke to SNA, 16/7/18.

117 Ibid.

118 Ibid., notes of a conference held at Pietersburg, 10/9/18.

119 Ibid., remarks of H.S. Cooke.

120 Ibid.

CONCLUSION

1 S. van der Horst, *Native Labour in South Africa,* 163-7; N. Levy, *The Foundations of the South African Cheap Labour System,* 28.

2 Levy, for instance, noted the extent of industry disunity on labour matters but stressed at the same time the emerging monopoly power of the Chamber of Mines. He left the reader to sort out the apparent contradiction. Levy, *Foundations,* 84, 94, 116.

3 JPFP, H. Eckstein and co. to Wernher, Beit, 8/1/98.

4 M. Fraser and A. Jeeves, ed., *All that Glittered,* letters, 7, 8, and 11.

5 *CMAR,* 1890, 61.

6 This paragraph summarizes an argument developed in chap. 1.

7 *ICI,* evidence of E.J. Way, A. Brakhan, H. Jennings, G.A. Denny. See also Isongesit S. Ibokette, "Labour Strategies in the Transvaal Gold-mining Industry, 1890–1910" (MA thesis, Queen's University, 1983), 26-58.

8 P. Richardson, *Chinese Mine Labour in the Transvaal,* 177-8.

9 C. Bundy, *The Rise and Fall of the South African Peasantry,* 109-145, and cf. W. Beinart, "'Joyini Inkomo': Cattle Advances and the Origins of Migrancy from Pondoland," 218, which showed how effectively Pondo families could extract benefits from the advance system for investment in the rural economy.

10 C. Bundy, *Rise and Fall,* 109-45.

11 See the statements at the Cape Town Labour Conference, September 1909, especially those of the Cape prime minister, J.X. Merriman, and the secretary for native affairs, Edward Dower. CAD, CNA 1150.

12 See above, n. 2, and R. Davies, *Capital, State and White Labour in South Africa,* 3-4.

13 See Union of South Africa, House of Assembly, *Reports of Select Committees,* 1910–11, vol. 2, app. B: "Report of an Enquiry Held by Direction of the

Minister of Native Affairs Regarding Native Labourers Employed by Mr. A.M. Mostert."

14 NGI, CA, vol. 1, evidence of J.S. Marwick.

Bibliography

MANUSCRIPT SOURCES

In Southern Africa

Barlow Rand Archives, Johannesburg, Archives of H. Eckstein and Company, 1890–1910
Cape Archives Depot, Cape Town, Native Affairs Department Archive, 1890–1910
Chamber of Mines Archives and Library, Johannesburg, Records, 1899–1920
Johannesburg Public Library, Typescript of Evidence Led before the Native Grievances Inquiry, 1913–14
National English Documentation Centre, Grahamstown, J.P. FitzPatrick Papers

Rhodes University, Grahamstown, Consolidated Gold Fields' Collection.
Transvaal Archives Depot, Pretoria
a) Official Archives
  South African Republic
      Leyds Argief
  Transvaal Colony
      Colonial Secretary, 1900–10
      Governor, 1900–10
      Governor-General
      Prime Minister, 1907–10
      Secretary of Native Affairs, 1902-10
  Union Government
      Native Affairs Department, 1910–20
      Native Labour Bureau, 1907–20
      Secretary for Mines and Industries, 1910–20
b) Accessions
      J.C. Smuts Collection
c) Great Britain, Colonial Office, Confidential Print: African South co 879,
      1895–1914 (microfilm)

80/721	90/743	97/897	106/900
85/755	90/747	98/901	106/925
89/792	90/760	101/927	106/934
89/800	90/765	104/947	106/952
89/801	93/849	106/807	108/970
90/715	94/866	106/820	111/994
90/716	94/867	106/874	

d) Commission Archives
      Transvaal Labour Commission, 1903
      Mining Industry Commission, 1907–08
      Native Grievances Inquiry, 1913–14
      Economic Commission, 1914
      Low Grade Mines Commission, 1919–20

Zimbabwe National Archives, Harare.
      Administrator's Office, Labour, 1912–20; Private Secretary's Papers,
      1912–20

In the United Kingdom

Rhodes House, Oxford
  Central Mining and Investment Corporation, Ltd., Collection

OFFICIAL PUBLICATIONS

Chamber of Mines of South Africa
  Annual Reports, 1890-1920
  Evidence and Report of the Industrial Commission of Inquiry, 1897
  Witwatersrand Native Labour Association, *Reports,* 1903-24
Great Britain
  Report of the Transvaal Labour Commission. London, Cd. 1897, 1904
Transvaal Colony
  Transvaal Administration Reports, 1902-1910
  Evidence and Reports of the Mining Industry Commission, 1907-8. Pretoria,
  TG 1, 2, 1908.
  House of Assembly Debates, 1907-9
Union of South Africa
  Hansard, House of Assembly Debates, 1910-14
  Official Reports
    Reports from Select Committees, 1910-14.
    Report of the Native Grievances Inquiry, 1913-14. Pretoria, UG 37, 1914.
    Report of the Economic Commission, 1914. Pretoria, UG 12, 1914.
    Reports of the Department of Native Affairs for the Years Ending, 1913-18.
    Pretoria, UG 7, 1919.
    Interim Report of the Low Grade Mines Commission, 1919. Cape Town, UG
    45, 1919.
    Final Report of the Low Grade Mines Commission, 1920. Cape Town, UG 34,
    1920.
    Native Economic Commission, 1932. Pretoria, UG 22, 1932.
    Official Yearbook of the Union. Pretoria, No. 4, 1921.

PUBLISHED CORRESPONDENCE

Duminy, A.H., and Guest, W.R., eds. *FitzPatrick: South African Politician: Selected Papers, 1888-1906.* Johannesburg: McGraw Hill, 1976.
Fraser, M., and Jeeves, A., eds. *All That Glittered: Selected Correspondence of Lionel Phillips, 1890-1924.* Cape Town: Oxford University Press, 1977.
Lewsen, P., ed. *Selections from the Correspondence of J.X. Merriman.* 4 vols. Cape Town: van Riebeeck Society, 1960- .
Van der Poel, J. ed., *Selections from the Smuts Papers,* 7 vols. Cambridge: Cambridge University Press, 1966- .

NEWSPAPERS AND PERIODICALS

Cape Times, 1909, 1911–12
The Economist, 1897, 1899
Johannesburg *Star,* 1890–1914
South African Mines, Commerce and Industries, 1907–9
Standard and Diggers' News, 1890–99
Transvaal Leader, 1907–9

CONTEMPORARY SOURCES

Bryce, J. *Impressions of South Africa.* London: Macmillan 1897.
Denny, G.A. *The Deep Level Mines of the Rand.* London: Lockwood 1902.
FitzPatrick, J.P. *The Transvaal from Within.* London, W. Heinemann 1899.
Goldmann, C.S. *The Financial, Statistical and General History of the Gold and Other Companies of Witwatersrand, South Africa.* London: Effingham, Wilson 1892.
– *South African Mines.* 3 vols. London: Effingham, Wilson 1895–6.
Hatch, F.H., and Chalmers, J.A. *The Gold Mines of the Rand.* London: Macmillan 1895.
Hobson, J.A. *The War in South Africa, Its Causes and Effects.* London: James Nisbet 1900.
Peregrino, F.Z.S. *Life Among the Native and Coloured Miners of the Transvaal.* Cape Town: printed by Hodgson and Denne 1910.
Perry, F. "Portuguese East Africa and South African Union." *The State* 1 (1909).
Phillips, L. *Transvaal Problems.* London: John Murray 1905.
Plaatje, S.T. *Native Life in South Africa.* London: P.S. King 1916.
Praagh, L.V., ed. *The Transvaal and Its Mines.* London and Johannesburg: Praagh and Lloyd 1906.
"South African Native Races Committee." *The Natives of South Africa: Their Economic and Social Condition.* London: John Murray 1901.
"South African Native Races Committee." *The South African Natives: Their Progress and Present Condition.* London: John Murray 1908.
The Statist's Mines of the Transvaal. London 1900–9. [Continued as] *The Statist's Mines of Africa.* London 1910–14.
Williams, B. *The Selborne Memorandum.* London: Humphrey Milford 1925.

SECONDARY SOURCES

Books

Adam, H. *Modernising Racial Domination: South Africa's Political Dynamics.* Berkeley and London: University of California Press 1971.

Arrighi, G. "Labour Supplies in Historical Perspective: A Study of the Proletarianization of the African Peasantry in Rhodesia." In *Essays on the Political Economy of Africa,* edited by G. Arrighi and J.S. Saul. New York and London: Monthly Review Press 1973.

Beinart, W., and Bundy, C. "State Intervention and Rural Resistance: the Transkei, 1900–1965." In *Peasants in Africa: Historical and Contemporary Perspectives,* edited by M.A. Klein. Beverly Hills and London: Sage Publications 1980.

Bozzoli, B. *The Political Nature of a Ruling Class: Capital and Ideology in South Africa, 1890–1933.* London: Routledge and Kegan Paul 1981.

Brookes, E.H. *The History of Native Policy in South Africa from 1830 to the Present Day.* Cape Town: Nasionale Pers, 1924.

Bundy, C. *The Rise and Fall of the South African Peasantry.* London: Heinemann Educational 1979.

Cartwright, A.P. *The Corner House.* Cape Town and Johannesburg: Purnell 1965.

- *Gold Paved the Way.* New York: St. Martin's Press; London: Macmillan 1967.

Davenport, T.R.H., and Hunt, K.S., eds. *The Right to the Land.* Cape Town: D. Philip 1974.

Davies, R.H. *Capital, State and White Labour in South Africa, 1900–1960.* Brighton: Harvester Press 1979.

Denoon, D.J.N. *A Grand Illusion.* Harlow: Longman 1973.

Doxey, G.V. *The Industrial Colour Bar in South Africa.* Cape Town: Oxford University Press 1961.

Duffy, J. *A Question of Slavery.* Oxford: Clarendon Press 1967.

Frankel, S.H. *Investment and the Return to Equity Capital in the South African Gold Mining Industry, 1887–1965.* Oxford: Basil Blackwell 1967.

Fredrickson, G.M. *White Supremacy.* New York: Oxford University Press 1981.

Gordon, C.T. *The Growth of Boer Opposition to Kruger, 1890–5.* Cape Town: Oxford University Press 1970.

- "Aspects of Colour Attitudes and Public Policy in Kruger's Republic." In *African Affairs* no. 3, edited by K. Kirkwood. St. Anthony's Papers no. 21. London: Oxford University Press 1969.

Greenberg, S.B. *Race and State in Capitalist Development.* New Haven and London: Yale University Press 1980.

Gregory, T.E.G. *Ernest Oppenheimer and the Economic Development of Southern Africa.* Cape Town: Oxford University Press 1962.

Gutkind, P.C.W. et al., eds. *African Labour History.* Beverly Hills: Sage 1978.

Hammond, R.J. *Portugal and Africa, 1815–1910: A Study in Uneconomic Imperialism.* Stanford, Calif.: Stanford University Press 1966.

Hammond-Tooke, W.D. *Command or Consensus: The Development of Transkeian Local Government.* Cape Town: D. Philip 1975.

Hancock, W.K. *Smuts.* 2 vols. Vol. 1: *The Sanguine Years, 1870–1919.* Cambridge: Cambridge University Press 1962. Vol. 2: *The Fields of Force, 1919–1950.* Cambridge: Cambridge University Press 1968.

313   Bibliography

Hellmann, E., ed. *Handbook on Race Relations in South Africa.* London: Oxford University Press 1949.

Horwitz, R. *The Political Economy of South Africa.* London: Weidenfeld and Nicolson 1967.

Houghton, D.H. "Migrant Labour." In *Africa in Transition,* edited by P. Smith. London: Max Reinhardt 1958.

Hunter, G., ed. *Industrialization and Race Relations.* London and New York: Oxford University Press 1965.

Isaacman, A.F. *The Tradition of Resistance in Mozambique.* London: Heinemann 1976.

Johnstone, F.A. *Class Race and Gold.* London: Routledge and Kegan Paul 1976.

Katzenellenbogen, S.E. *South Africa and Southern Mozambique: Labour, Railways and Trade in the Making of a Relationship.* Manchester: Manchester University Press 1982.

Koss, S.E., ed. *The Pro-Boers.* Chicago and London: University of Chicago Press 1973.

Kubicek, R.V. *Economic Imperialism in Theory and Practice: The Case of South African Gold Mining Finance, 1886–1914.* Durham: Duke University Press 1979.

Lacey, M. *Working for Boroko.* Johannesburg: Ravan Press 1981.

Laurence, P.M. *The Life of John Xavier Merriman.* London: Constable 1930.

Legassick, M. "South Africa: Forced Labour, Industrialisation and Racial Differentiation." In *The Political Economy of Africa,* edited by R. Harris. Cambridge, Mass.: Schenkman; New York and London: distributed by Wiley 1975.

Levy, N. *The Foundations of the South African Cheap Labour System.* London: Routledge and Kegan Paul 1982.

Lewsen, P. *John X. Merriman: Paradoxical South African Statesman.* New Haven and London: Yale University Press 1982.

McCracken, J.L. *Politics and Christianity in Malawi 1875–1940.* Cambridge: Cambridge University Press 1977.

Macmillan, W.M. *Complex South Africa: An Economic Footnote to History.* London: Faber and Faber 1930.

Marais, J.S. *The Fall of Kruger's Republic.* Oxford: Clarendon Press 1961.

Marks, S. *Reluctant Rebellion: The 1906–08 Disturbances in Natal.* Oxford: Clarendon Press 1970.

Newitt, M.D.D. *Portuguese Settlement on the Zambesi: Exploration, Land Tenure and Colonial Rule in East Africa.* London: Longman 1973.

Pachai, B., ed. *The Early History of Malawi.* London: Longman 1972.

Palmer, R., and Parsons, N., eds. *The Roots of Rural Poverty in Central and Southern Africa.* London: Heinemann Educational 1977.

Perrings, C. *Black Mineworkers in Central Africa.* London: Heinemann Educational 1979.

Phimister, I.R., ed. *Studies in the History of African Mine Labour in Colonial Zimbabwe.* Salisbury: Mambo Press 1978.

Ranger, T.O. "Revolt in Portuguese East Africa: The Makombe Rising of 1917." In *African Affairs* no. 2, edited by K. Kirkwood. St. Antony's Papers no. 15. London: Chatto and Windus 1963.

- *Revolt in Southern Rhodesia, 1896-97*. London: Heinemann 1967.

Richardson, P. *Chinese Mine Labour in the Transvaal*. London and Basingstoke: Macmillan 1982.

Robinson, R.E., and Gallagher, J., with Denny, A. *Africa and the Victorians. c.*1961. Reprint. Garden City, N.Y.: Doubleday 1968.

Simons, H.J. and R.E. *Class and Colour in South Africa, 1850-1950*. Harmondsworth: Penguin 1969.

Thompson, L.M. *The Unification of South Africa, 1902-1910*. Oxford: Clarendon Press 1960.

Vail, L., and White, L. *Capitalism and Colonialism in Mozambique*. London: Heinemann Educational 1980.

Van der Horst, S.T. *Native Labour in South Africa*. New impression. London: Frank Cass 1971.

Van der Poel, J. *The Jameson Raid*. Cape Town: Oxford University Press 1951.

- *Railway and Customs Policies in South Africa, 1885-1910*. Royal Empire Society Imperial Studies, no. 8. London 1933.

Van Onselen, C. *Chibaro: African Mine Labour in Southern Rhodesia, 1900-1933*. London: Pluto Press 1976.

- *Studies in the Social and Economic History of the Witwatersrand, 1886-1914*. 2 vols. Vol. 1: *New Babylon*. Vol. 2: *New Nineveh*. Johannesburg: Ravan Press 1982.

Warwick, P., ed. *The South African War: The Anglo-Boer War, 1899-1902*. London: Longman 1980.

Weinthal, L. *Memories, Mines and Millions: Being the Life of Sir Joseph B. Robinson*. London: Simpkin, Marshall 1929.

Wilson, F. *Labour in the South African Gold Mines, 1911-1969*. Cambridge: Cambridge University Press 1972.

Wilson, M., and Thompson, L.M. *The Oxford History of South Africa*. 2 vols. Oxford: Clarendon Press 1969, 1971.

Yudelman, D. *The Emergence of Modern South Africa: State, Capital and the Incorporation of Organized Labour on the South African Gold Fields, 1902-1939*. Westport, Conn.: Greenwood Press 1983.

Articles

Arrighi, G. "Labour Supplies in Historical Perspective: A Study of the Proletarianization of the African Peasantry in Rhodesia." *Journal of Development Studies* 6(1970): 197-234.

Beinart, W. "Joyini Inkomo: Cattle Advances and the Origins of Migrancy from Pondoland." *Journal of Southern African Studies* 5(1979): 199-219.

Bell, R.T. "Migrant Labour: Theory and Policy." *South African Journal of Economics* 40(1972): 337–60.

Berg, E.J. "Backward-sloping Labor Supply Functions in Dual Economies – An African Case." *Quarterly Journal of Economics* 75(1961): 468–92.

Bozzoli, B. "Capital and State in South Africa." *Review of African Political Economy* 11 (1979): 40–50.

Davies, R. "Mining Capital, The State and Unskilled White Workers in South Africa, 1901–1913." *Journal of Southern African Studies* 3(1976): 41–69.

Denoon, D.J.N. "Capital and Capitalists in the Transvaal in the 1890s and 1900s." *Historical Journal* 23(1980): 111–32.

– "The Transvaal Labour Crisis, 1901–6." *Journal of African History* 8(1967): 481–94.

Diamond, C.R. "The Native Grievances Inquiry, 1913–1914." *South African Journal of Economics,* 36(1968): 211–27.

Garson, N.G. "'Het Volk': The Botha–Smuts Party in the Transvaal, 1904–11," *Historical Journal* 9(1966): 101–132.

Harries, P. "Labour Migration from the Delagoa Bay Hinterland to South Africa, 1852–1895." University of London, Institute of Commonwealth Studies, *Collected Seminar Papers on the Societies of Southern Africa in the 19th and 20th Centuries* 7(1975–6): 61–76.

Jeeves, A.H. "The Control of Migratory Labour on the South African Gold Mines in the Era of Kruger and Milner." *Journal of Southern African Studies* 2(1975): 3–29.

Katz, E.N. "White Workers' Grievances and the Industrial Colour Bar, 1902–1913." *South African Journal of Economics* 42(1974): 127–56.

Kubicek, R.V. "The Randlords in 1895: A Reassessment." *Journal of British Studies* 11(1972): 84–103.

Legassick, M. "South Africa: Capital Accumulation and Violence." *Economy and Society* 3(1974): 253–91.

Lonsdale, J., and Berman, B. "Coping with the Contradictions: The Development of the Colonial State in Kenya, 1895–1914." *Journal of African History* 20(1979): 487–505.

Mackenzie, J.M. "African Labour in the Chartered Company Period." *Rhodesian History* 1(1970): 43–58.

– "Chartered Africans: Colonial Office, Settlers and B.S.A. Co., Rhodesia 1890–1923." University of London, Institute of Commonwealth Studies, *Collected Seminar Papers on the Societies of Southern Africa in the 19th and 20th Centuries* 4(1972–3): 77–86.

– "Sambo and Economic Determinism: A Comment on Charles Van Onselen's 'Black Workers in Central African Industry'." *Journal of Southern African Studies* 2(1975): 98–101.

Makambe, E.P. "The Nyasaland African Labour 'Ulendos' to Southern Rhodesia and the Problem of the African 'Highwaymen', 1903–23: A Study in the Limitations of Early Independent Labour Migration." *African Affairs* 79(1980): 548–66.

Marks, S., and Trapido, S. "Lord Milner and the South African State." *History Workshop* 8(1979): 50–80.

Mawby, A.A. "Capital, Government and Politics in the Transvaal 1900–1907, a Revision and a Reversion." *Historical Journal* 17(1974): 387–415.

Newitt, M. "Migrant Labour and the Development of Mozambique." University of London, Institute of Commonwealth Studies, *Collected Seminar Papers on the Societies of Southern Africa in the 19th and 20th Centuries* 4(1972–3): 67–76.

Ranger, T.O. "The People in African Resistance: A Review." *Journal of Southern African Studies* 4(1977): 125–46.

– "Reflections on Peasant Research in Central and Southern Africa." *Journal of Southern African Studies* 5(1978): 99–133.

Sanderson, F.E. "The Development of Labour Migration from Nyasaland, 1891–1914." *Journal of African History* 2(1961): 259–71.

Vail, L. "The Making of an Imperial Slum: Nyasaland and its Railways, 1895–1935." *Journal of African History* 16 (1975): 89–112.

Van Onselen, C. "Black Workers in Central African Industry: A Critical Essay on the Historiography and Sociology of Rhodesia." *Journal of Southern African Studies* 1 (1975): 228–46.

– "Worker Consciousness in Black Miners: Southern Rhodesia, 1900–20." *Journal of African History* 14(1973): 237–56.

Wolpe, H. "Capitalism and Cheap Labour Power in South Africa: From Segregation to Apartheid." *Economy and Society* 1(1972): 425–56.

Unpublished Material

Duminy, A.H. "The Political Career of Sir Percy FitzPatrick, 1985–1906." PHD thesis, University of Natal, Durban, 1973.

Ellsworth, R.E. "Economic Regionalism, Political Centralism and South African Union." Research essay, Queen's University at Kingston, 1981.

Grey, P.C. "The Development of the Gold Mining Industry of the Witwatersrand." D. Litt. et Phil. thesis, University of South Africa, Pretoria, 1969.

Ibokette, I. "Labour Strategies in the Transvaal Gold Mining Industry, 1890–1910." MA thesis, Queen's University at Kingston, 1983.

Mawby, A.A. "The Transvaal Mine Owners in Politics." Seminar paper, University of London, c. 1973.

Moroney, S. "Industrial Conflict in a Labour Repressive Economy: Black Labour on the Transvaal Gold Mines, 1901–1912," BA honours thesis, University of the Witwatersrand, 1976.

Richardson, P. "Coolies and Randlords: The Structure of Mining Capitalism and Chinese Labour, 1902–1910." Seminar paper, Oxford University, n.d.

Index

cattle advances, *see* advances

Central Mining and Investment Corporation, 62, 81, 132, 158-60, 169; *see also* H. Eckstein and Co., Wernher, Beit and Co.

Chamber of Mines: development of labour policy, 31-3, 69-73, 254-9; disunity in, 40-1, 210-11, 254-8; establishes Native Labour Department, 41-2; implicated in illegal recruiting, 89; and Modus Vivendi agreement, 44; negotiates deferred pay agreement with Mozambique, 214-20; and recruiting prospects in Nyasaland and East Africa, 221-5; relations with government, 11-15, 38-41, 46-8, 59, 71-2, 199-211; and Transvaal-Mozambique Convention of 1909, 15; viewed by historians, 6, 253; *see also* mining groups; mine owners; NRC; WNLA

Chamberlain, Joseph, 221-2

Chaplin, F.D.P., 245

chiefs and headmen: as recruiters, 4-5, 45, 94-5, 156-65

Chinese labour: arrival of, 47, 221, 256; crisis of, 1906-7, 62-3; and colour bar, 30, 69; repatriation of, 32, 57, 59, 80, 92, 199-200, 209

City Deep GMC, 174

collieries, Natal, 174-5

Colonial Office, 200-9, 221-6

colour bar, 30-4, 66-8

Coloured Labourers' Health Ordinance, 1905, 52, 224, 231

compounds, mining, 22,

50, 166-8, 170, 225, 231-2, 263; *see also* gold mines and mining

Consolidated Gold Fields, 40, 104, 123-4

contractors, labour, 13, 159-60; attack on WNLA in 1911, 212; in the Cape, 103, 109-12; effect on black mine wages, 126-7; origins of, 92, 96-9; political power of, 18, 113-18; in northern Transvaal, 243-7; relations with mining companies, 100; weakness after 1912, 259-60; *see also* recruiting; trader/recruiters

Cooke, H.S., 242-3, 249-50

Creswell, F.H.P., 14, 66-8, 199, 219, 233-5, 240

Crown Mines, 61, 158-9, 168-9, 174

Davies, Rob, 5, 30-1, 33, 70-3

desertion, from gold mines, 28, 48, 165-9, 171-7; *see also* black miners

director of native labour, 106, 112, 172, 213, 234, 242, 249-50

Dower, E., 79-81, 89, 95, 108, 112, 117, 161, 242

East Africa, 221-2

East Rand Proprietary Mines, 61, 124-32

Eckstein, F., 75, 207

Eckstein, H. and Co., 40, 60-5, 93, 98, 103-5, 205; *see also* Wernher, Beit and Co.

Elgin, Lord, 200-4

Eliot, Charles, 222

Engelenburg, F.V., 65

Erskine, David, 243, 245-6

Erskine, M. St. V., 101-2, 104-5

Evans, S., 63-4, 195

Far East Rand, 61

farming, *see* agriculture

Farrar, G., 63, 131-2, 207

FitzPatrick, J.P., 43, 63-5, 73

"Fokkies" and "Forage," 177-8

Frames, P. Ross, 213, 216, 219

Fricker, R.G., 94, 195

gangers, *see* white miners

General Mining Corp., 71

George Goch, GMC, 172

Glen Grey Act of 1894, 16, 107

Goerz group of mines, 40, 77

gold mines and mining: compound conditions and health, 22, 166-8, 170, 225, 229-35, 263; early expansion, 37-8; liquor traffic on, 170-1; mortality rates on, 227-8, 234; ore deposits, 6-9, 37-9, 130, 201, 254; profitability of, 37; reorganization of production, 60-2, 254; *see also* Chamber of Mines; mining groups

gold price, 7

Government Native Labour Bureau 20, 76-82, 159-64, 168

Gxowa, September, 163-4

Hadley, James, 166, 178, 180

Hamilton, J.G., 129

Harris, Lord, 60

Het Volk: election victory, 1907, 62-4; labour policy of, 68, 71-9, 106-19; and WNLA crisis, 1906-7, 200-11; and tropical recruiting, 228

High Commission Territories, 4, 159, 161, 168, 173

Holmes, G.G., 202-7